RUSSIAN ART

DMITRI V. SARABIANOV

RUSSIAN ART

From Neoclassicism to the Avant-Garde

PAINTING

SCULPTURE

ARCHITECTURE

With 354 illustrations, 81 in colour

THAMES AND HUDSON

FRONTISPIECE

Isaac Levitan *Autumn Day: Sokolniki* 1879

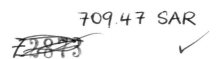
Typeset in Monophoto Caledonia
Printed and bound in Singapore

CONTENTS

PART III · 1895–1917

Foreword

Anyone familiar with Russian avantgarde painting, and with artists such as Mikhail Larionov, Natalia Goncharova, Marc Chagall, Vasily Kandinsky, Kazimir Malevich, Pavel Filonov and Vladimir Tatlin, may well ask the question: what were the antecedents of this movement? To put it another way, was the avantgarde the continuation of an essentially Russian tradition, or rather the response of Russian artists to Western European influences?

The history of Russian art can help us at least to clarify the question, even if it provides no clear-cut answer. Firstly, it illustrates the relationship between the Russian avantgarde and medieval culture, and specifically the painting of ancient Rus. Secondly, we shall see how Russian art of more recent times has generally tended to develop along universal lines, if somewhat spasmodically. In other words, the great achievements of various periods of Russian art cannot be ascribed to foreign influence alone.

Russian culture experienced its first great heyday a thousand years ago, not long after ancient Rus had embraced the Graeco-Byzantine variety of Christianity. It was interrupted by the Mongol and Tartar invasion. Although this tragic event in Russian history set back the country's cultural progress for many generations, it did have one most positive result: Europe was saved from the barbarians. Russia, however, took two hundred years to recover from the onslaught. Only after liberation from foreign domination was the nation able to regain its momentum. The fifteenth and sixteenth centuries witnessed a new flowering, above all in the art of Andrei Rublev and Dionysius, and in hipped-roof architecture. Thereafter, however, Russian civilization trod its own individual path. It was never to enjoy a Renaissance, and only threw off its medieval character to join the mainstream of European development towards the end of the seventeenth century.

The eighteenth century played a decisive part in the evolution of Russian art. These were the years when Russia finally joined the family of Europe and experienced her Age of Enlightenment. Her art successively developed the great European styles – first Baroque, and later Classicism. It was a tremendous turning-point in the life of the whole nation, and its impact was similar to that experienced by the Western European world at the time of the Renaissance. In Russia all these ideas and tendencies coincided in the eighteenth century, and it was this concentration which enabled her eventually to clear the barriers between the two worlds. The essential character of Russian culture began to manifest itself in its tendency to make up for lost time by initially making dramatic leaps forward, subsequently slowing the pace and finally almost coming to a halt. It proved its ability to perform simultaneously most of the tasks which other nations had been able to confront in a leisurely way over long periods of their historical development.

Russian art of the nineteenth century, and the beginning of the twentieth, fits into the same general pattern of stylistic change that characterizes all European art. The years covered by this book are traditionally divided into three distinct periods corresponding with the artistic and historical developments which were taking place in Russia as a whole. The first period covers the first half of the nineteenth century, whose art, though still a continuation of eighteenth-century concepts, nevertheless opened the way to new movements – Romanticism and the early and middle Realist schools. The second period stretches from the mid-fifties to the nineties, the years when Realism achieved its apogee and thereafter went into decline. The last of our three periods, which includes the end of the nineteenth century and the first two decades of the twentieth, comes to an end with the Revolution of October 1917. These years saw an explosion of ideas and rapid artistic renewal which found their finest expression in the Russian avantgarde.

But not only in the avantgarde. Russian art of the nineteenth century also had its heroes – Orest Kiprensky, Alexei Venetsianov, Alexander Ivanov, Pavel Fedotov, Ilya Repin, Vasily Surikov, Valentin Serov and Mikhail Vrubel – to all of whom the present author has paid special attention in this book, and for one particular reason. Both the Russian avantgarde and ancient Russian icon-painting are well known and highly appreciated in Europe and America; our nineteenth-century painters, however, are virtually unknown outside Russia, and yet they undoubtedly deserve a place in the annals of world art.

The artistic 'superpowers' long ago agreed upon a hierarchy of excellence, in which nineteenth-century Russian art appears to have no place. Let us hope that this injustice will be gradually remedied. If the present book contributes in some small way towards that end, the author will feel that his mission has been fulfilled.

Note: marginal references are to the colour plates

PART I · 1800–1860

1 The End of Russian Classicism

The first few decades of the nineteenth century saw the somewhat unusually harmonious development of a number of artistic movements in Russia. Classicism, already a fully mature and independent style, entered upon the new era with confidence just as the Romantic and early Realist schools were coming into existence.

As if by previous agreement, these movements gradually divided the various branches of the arts into spheres of influence. The newborn Romantic and Realist movements found their fullest expression in painting and drawing, but left little mark on architecture and sculpture, realms where classicism held almost total sway. Classical painters, it is true, dominated the official artistic hierarchy of the time, but with the benefit of hindsight we can see how very meagre their attainments really were.

Classicism lingered in Russia too long. It had made its first appearance in the 1760s, when its sheer simplicity overcame the grandiloquent style so typical of the Baroque period, but by the turn of the century it was already well past its heyday and seemed set – like Neoclassicism in most of the countries of Western Europe – to quit the stage. Certain facts of national life, however, combined to extend its longevity in Russia, where classicism was nourished by the patriotic emotions which prevailed in society before and during the war against Napoleon, and was further inspired by the ideal of unity between all sorts and conditions of men against the common enemy. It gained strength, too, from the triumphalism which followed military victories and temporarily damped down the internal contradictions of Russian life. All these elements were vital in stimulating and prolonging the fecundity of classicism right up to the 1830s.

Russian classicism – as opposed to the French variety – may indeed be termed simple 'classicism', without the prefix 'neo'. That is to say, Russia's first and only classical period occurred in the eighteenth century, when the rest of Europe was already experiencing it for the second time. Russian art in the seventeenth century – when

classicism was blossoming in Europe – was characterized by bright and colourful architecture with much superficial ornamentation, and by loquacious frescos attempting to overcome the medieval approach to painting. Russian culture in those years was much further from understanding and empathizing with classical antiquity than it had been in the fifteenth century, at the time of Andrei Rublev. The great Russian icon-painter apprehended antiquity as a living tradition, received directly or indirectly from Byzantine masters, rather than as an inheritance from the distant past. He had little or no knowledge of *ancient* culture. We have already stated that Russia had no Renaissance; and thus she never benefited from a familiarity with ancient Greek and Roman art. It was through foreigners, some working in the country and others teaching apprentices in Holland, Germany or France, that Russian practitioners of classicism first became acquainted with antiquity. They were eager to learn and avid for the European experience, which they absorbed with tremendous enthusiasm. But the Russian classical movement also had its own national role to fulfil.

ST PETERSBURG

By the beginning of the nineteenth century classicism had put its seal on the new Russian state founded by Peter the Great a hundred years earlier, and especially on St Petersburg, the true embodiment of his vision of the state. Founded at the dawn of the eighteenth century on a swamp at the very edge of the Russian empire, the city flowered like an exotic plant in an alien land. Turning its face to the West and its back on the boundless, somnolent Russian heartland, St Petersburg eventually became the perfect symbol of the Russian longing to catch up with Europe, in the process outdoing European cities in its order and symmetry. Late Russian classicism was the dominant influence on the completion of St Petersburg, in accordance with the plans for the city which had been drawn up in the eighteenth century.

One of the most important ideas now put into practice was the new emphasis on the role of town planning in

< **Adrian Zakharov**, Tower of the Admiralty, St Petersburg, 1806–23

Andrei Voronikhin, Cathedral of the Virgin of Kazan, St Petersburg, 1801–11

architecture. In the first three decades of the nineteenth century architects were to achieve perfect solutions to the problems of planning St Petersburg's squares and main thoroughfares, organizing space with what may be considered a characteristically Russian sense of proportion. This was the triumphal age of the architectural ensemble, when architects took a holistic view of their task. They transformed whole city areas by making individual buildings into the foci for integrated compositions and linked them together in an overall ensemble. A number of such ensembles combined to create a harmonious urban environment.

Most of St Petersburg's ensembles were built on sites which had already been partially developed in the eighteenth century. These sites generally lacked any central focus, however, and it was left to the architects of late Russian classicism to forge such unifying elements. Voronikhin, for example, while building the Cathedral of the Virgin of Kazan, simultaneously created a harmonious square on Nevsky Prospect; and his College of Mines, built near the mouth of the Neva on Vasily Island, eventually came to be seen as a gateway to the city. The completion of Thomas de Thomon's Stock Exchange created an ensemble at the other end of the island. Rossi put the finishing touches to the Palace Square ensemble

by erecting a monumental arch between the two wings of the General Staff Headquarters. Zakharov, with his new Admiralty building, imposed an overall sense of unity on several huge squares by opening them up to each other. All these projects were dominated by the deliberate use of the laws of geometry to master space, with the conscious aim of creating a majestic capital which would be a model for the new empire.

Let us now examine some of these works in more detail. Andrei Voronikhin (1759–1814), one of the foremost late classical architects, epitomizes the continuity between the architecture of the eighteenth and nineteenth centuries. (He was particularly active in the 1790s.) He was probably the illegitimate son of Count Stroganov, president of the Imperial Academy of Arts in St Petersburg, and it was his putative father who commissioned him to remodel the interior of the Stroganov palace, originally built by Rastrelli in Baroque style. He also built country houses for the nobility, but it was not until the dawn of the new century that he was presented with really challenging architectural projects. His career culminated in the construction of the Kazan Cathedral on Nevsky Prospect between 1801 and 1811.

The details of the commission were laid down by the Emperor Paul I himself. During his short rule he

Andrei Voronikhin, The College of Mines, St Petersburg, 1806–11

Thomas de Thomon, Stock Exchange, St Petersburg, 1805–10

destroyed many venerable Russian traditions, succeeding thereby in stirring up discontent not only among the common people but among the nobility as well. Paul decreed that the cathedral, with its curved colonnade, must evoke the architectural masterpiece of Rome – the basilica of St Peter. Voronikhin satisfied this demand in an ingenious and original manner, by building the cathedral in the form of a palace. Keeping the side aisles very narrow, he was able to create an extremely wide central nave under a spacious dome. He screened the main body of the church with a four-column colonnade (in order to conceal the asymmetry of the northern facade facing the Prospect) and – in contrast to Bernini in the Vatican – opened up the colonnade towards the city. Thoroughfares led from the semicircular 'plaza' thus created into side streets. He opposed the broad, colonnaded wings with a towering dome set on a drum and elevated base. By the beginning of the nineteenth century the distinctive profile of St Petersburg – vertical above horizontal – was already familiar. It was a continuation of the traditional design of the ancient monasteries, with their tall bell towers, and walls extending over a kilometre or more.

All the fundamental principles of the urban architecture of the day are contained in the Kazan Cathedral. All the same, in its style – the choice of Corinthian order, the proportions of the long, fluted columns, the unworked granite walls – the cathedral is an echo of the past. As we walk round the semicircular colonnade we enjoy everchanging vistas. We are struck by new perspectives on the square; and the complex interplay of the columns strikes a Baroque note. Reality seems illusory and illusion real.

Untypically for Russian late classical architecture, which is usually in yellow and white, the cathedral, built of local stone, is predominantly in natural shades of grey. There is a hint of knightly elegance and a sense of estrangement from its surroundings. We sense an intriguing contradiction here between the new ideas of urban architecture and the last faint echoes of the eighteenth century.

The College of Mines (1806–11) on Vasily Island displays no such contradiction. The mighty twelve-column Doric portico, with its impressive pediment, is set against a plain facade; broad steps, flanked by sculptures, link the College to the spacious embankment. Every element of the building, a good illustration of late classical style, is commensurate with its position at the approach (by river) to the city.

New ideas of town planning were accompanied by an increasingly monumental approach, and strict geometric forms began to prevail. Buildings were designed in the form of cubes, parallelepipeds, truncated pyramids, cylinders and half-cylinders. Walls were preferred undecorated and flat. The main features of the architecture of St Petersburg in the first two decades of the nineteenth century were simplicity, austerity, gigantic dimensions and grand scale. It is revealing that there was little, if any, interest in palace architecture in this period; the new style was mainly manifested in official and public buildings.

These new tendencies were of foreign origin. They were already in evidence at the end of the eighteenth century in France, where there was, however, a marked gap between theoretical architecture and actual building practice. Designs on the drawing board became ever more fantastic as the likelihood of their being realized diminished, but this did not lessen their appeal for architects themselves all over the civilized world. Russian architects also came under the spell of 'gigantomania', but they were able to entrust their thoughts and projects not only to paper but to the building site as well.

The new Admiralty building (1806–23) is the outstanding example of this 'gigantomania'. It is the work of one of Russia's greatest architects, Adrian Zakharov (1761–1811). Having completed his course at the Imperial Academy of Arts, he was given a bursary to continue his studies in France, working in Paris under the supervision of Chalgrin, the famous architect of the Arc de Triomphe. The lessons he learnt in Paris were not wasted. He became obsessed with the idea of transforming free space into architecturally regulated space. He also had to take account of Russian tradition as he wrestled with the real-life problems of the construction of the new Admiralty. It was as though the previous century had already prepared the groundwork necessary for the creation of Zakharov's masterpiece. The original Admiralty building determined and defined the site to be developed by the new architect. The spire (the only detail of the whole ensemble left unchanged by Zakharov) was already in place, the focal point of three great central thoroughfares. Three squares, one on each side of the Admiralty area, were waiting to be completed. One vital step was needed to transform the whole composition.

Zakharov was so successful in rearranging the interrelationship between the various parts of the ensemble that the Admiralty became the true centre of the city, a usurpation that even the neighbouring Winter Palace, the splendid Imperial residence built in the eighteenth century by Rastrelli, could not prevent. In fact, Zakharov's building had two advantages over Rastrelli's: it united disparate elements in a vast space, and became a dramatic symbol of the relationship, vital for St Petersburg, between city and river, city and sea.[1]

Zakharov chose the form of an open rectangle for the building itself – the traditional configuration for palaces and country estates. It opened towards the river. The courtyard, which in the case of a palace or country mansion had the function of a *cour d'honneur*, took on the character of a back yard. The main facade, over 400 metres long, overlooking Admiralty Square, simultaneously separates and unites the city and the river. At first glance it seems to be concealing the Neva like a huge screen, in which the central arch is no more than a narrow slit revealing the courtyard and embankment. The wings of the Admiralty, with their 150-metre-long facades, complete the two other main squares as they march towards the Neva. The tempo of their progress to the river seems all the more dramatic when we compare it with the impregnability of the main facade. The composition records the relationship between land and water, no mere coexistence, rather the dynamic symbol of Russia gaining access to the sea – a vision dear to Peter the Great.

Zakharov's design consisted of two buildings in the form of an open rectangle, separated by a canal which ran from the Neva. Ships entered and left the canal (long since filled in) under the arches of the two pavilions facing the river. The inner building – smaller and lower – was a

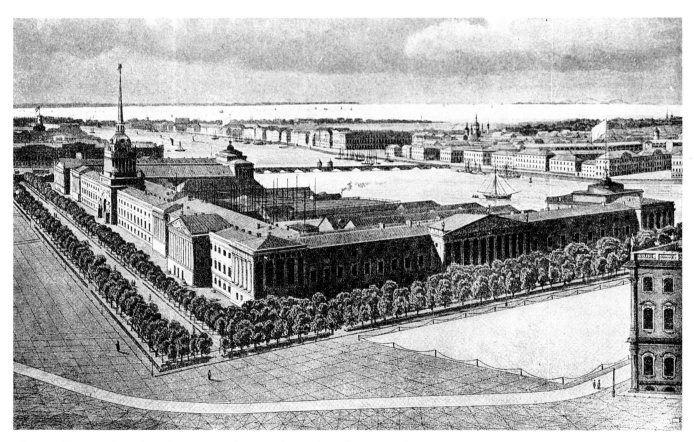

Adrian Zakharov, The Admiralty, St Petersburg (Lithograph, mid-nineteenth century)

shipbuilding and repair yard; the outer – larger and higher – housed the administrative offices. As we imagine the scratching of the clerks' pens on their official documents mingling with the din of hammers from the yards, the scene irresistibly recalls the figure of Peter the Great himself, the royal carpenter of the Amsterdam wharves.

The great length of the facades posed a particular problem. Zakharov devised a solution which maintained their dynamic character while avoiding dullness and repetition. A series of repeated designs, imaginatively linked, lends unity and variety to the composition. The famous spire rises above the three-tiered, central, cubical pavilion set into the main facade. Two arched side pavilions – also cubical – overlook the river; each is simply crowned by a low drum and flagpole. Each wing of the main facade is an identical three-part composition punctuated by six- and twelve-columned porticos, the latter projecting. The side facades, one looking onto Senate (now Decembrists') Square, the other overlooking the Winter Palace, repeat the composition with slight variations.

The outstanding feature of the Admiralty is the spire above the central pavilion. Zakharov expressed the theme of upward striving with great brilliance. The structure becomes lighter as tier succeeds tier. Space gradually envelops its higher levels, threatening an invasion which can only be withstood by the golden rapier, boldly thrusting towards the sky.

Zakharov attached great importance to mythological symbolism, which he expressed through sculpture, both freestanding and in relief. There are allusions to allegories of Russian rivers, the four elements, the four personified parts of the world, the four winds and the four seasons; the months of the year, personifications of glory, sea nymphs bearing the heavenly sphere, ancient heroes, warriors and gods; and Neptune presenting Peter the Great with a trident, the symbol of naval power.[2]

The Admiralty deserves such close attention because it expresses to the full the character of early nineteenth-century Russian architecture. In this unique building we see the perfect match of architectural genius and the aesthetic demands of the period. Contemporary with the Admiralty, the Kazan Cathedral and the College of Mines is the Stock Exchange (1805–10), the work of the French architect Thomas de Thomon (1760–1813), who worked in Russia for the last fifteen years of his life. Like several other foreign architects who came to Russia, Thomon found his second homeland there, and was able to apply his talent on a scale of which he could never have dreamt at home.

The Exchange was begun at the end of the eighteenth century by Giacomo Quarenghi. The Italian architect had

Thomas de Thomon, Mausoleum of Paul I, Pavlovsk, 1805–10

intended it as a continuation of the row of splendid public buildings already adorning the Vasily Island embankment, but by the time Thomas de Thomon came to the project this approach was no longer in keeping with the new spirit of town planning. The Exchange, set on the spit of Vasily Island, washed by the Greater Neva on one side and by the Little Neva on the other, was destined to become the focus of a great architectural ensemble at the very heart of the city.

Thomon shaped the ragged contour of the spit into a harmonious embankment with a semicircular promontory. He created a square in front of the Exchange, which was designed in the style of a classical Greek temple, with Tuscan order columns on all four sides. The building's effectiveness resides less in its size than in its immaculate proportions. Another square was laid down at the rear of the Exchange, in the shape of a horseshoe, overlooked by the Twelve Colleges (government ministries built by Trezzini during the reign of Peter the Great and later assigned to the University). Thomon also envisaged a customs house and warehouses in the classical style to the left and right of the Exchange; these were elegantly executed some twenty years after his death by Luchini and Zakharov.

By the beginning of the nineteenth century many styles had left their mark on St Petersburg in the hundred years of its history, but classicism still remained the dominant influence. Carlo Rossi (1775–1849) was its supreme practitioner. The son of a celebrated Italian ballerina who made her career in St Petersburg, he spent his life in the city and contributed more to its splendour than any other architect. At the height of his powers, between 1810 and 1830, he was the undisputed master of ensemble design. Commissioned to build a palace or theatre, he transformed the whole area involved, creating spacious new squares and completing the ensembles of others already in existence. It is to Zakharov and Rossi that St Petersburg owes its fame as a city of vast plazas. The concept of the square was of the utmost importance to Rossi. His work can only be fully appreciated from a distance and from many different angles. He shaped huge reservoirs of space into squares and streets, which he lined with houses, opening up surprising new perspectives. He made use of eighteenth-century conventions, especially in the field of palatial architecture, and liked to break the monotony of walls with pilasters and abundant sculptural decoration.

There is a bold and inventive quality to all Rossi's most important work, a good example of which is the Mikhail Palace (1818–25), built for Grand Duke Mikhail Pavlovich, youngest brother of Alexander I. It is now the State Russian Museum. Rossi created a square in front of the Palace; a new street leading to Nevsky Prospect provided a charming view of the ensemble.

The General Staff Headquarters (1819–29), another of Rossi's projects, brilliantly completed the semicircular Palace Square. He united the two wings of the building with a wide triumphal arch, crowned by a sculpture of the Chariot of Glory being pulled by six horses. A street running under the triumphal arch and a second arch – set at an angle to the first in order to accommodate a bend – connects the square to Nevsky Prospect. From under the triumphal arch there is a magnificent view of the Winter Palace. Rossi's classic simplicity is in striking contrast to the elaborate late Baroque of Rastrelli's facade. His design is an imaginative solution to the problem posed by the irregularity of the square and the need to create an impressive public building worthy of its place opposite the Imperial Residence.

Rossi was responsible for the completion of a series of four great interconnecting squares, Palace, Razvodnaya, Admiralty and Senate, which stretched for more than a kilometre. This panorama of St Petersburg stands as a symbol of reason and will taming the irrational wilderness of Russia's vast hinterland. The extended horizontal line of splendid public edifices is in deliberate contrast to the two vertical elements – the Admiralty spire and the Alexander column, erected in Palace Square by Montferrand in 1829. The spire and column appear to arrest the forward flow of the squares, drawing space around themselves and imposing order and relation on their surroundings.

One of Rossi's most elaborate and significant achievements, begun in 1828 and completed six years later, was the complex of buildings surrounding and including the Alexander Theatre. He designed the squares and streets (one of which today bears his name) around the main element of the ensemble – the theatre itself. It is of strictly geometrical construction, but each of the four facades displays an individual design, related to its own particular setting. The rear facade, like a piece of stage scenery with an architectural theme, seems to close off Theatre Street, lined on each side by a continuous row of houses with dynamic matched columns and arches. The long side facades feature projecting porticos. The main facade, facing the square and Nevsky Prospect, is the most impressive, with mighty pylons enclosing a spacious loggia with slender Corinthian columns.

By the time he retired in 1832 Rossi had made a major contribution to the appearance of nineteenth-century imperial St Petersburg, now renowned for its palaces, theatres, splendid pavilions, columns and ornamental railings. But there is another side to the city – that of barracks and military institutions. This aspect of St Petersburg is also impressive and boasts some distinguished architects, among them Rossi's contemporary, Vasily Stasov (1769–1848). Of course, Stasov did not only design barracks and 'regimental' churches (i.e. churches commissioned by regiments for their own use), victualling depots and imperial stables. He was also charged with creating palace interiors, a triumphal arch, belfries, orangeries and lighthouses, which are all imbued with his distinctive style – massive, solid and static. His monumental architecture has a grim and austere character. He greatly favoured cast iron, the material used in the construction of his famous Moscow Gate (the triumphal arch erected on the outskirts of St Petersburg to commemorate the military successes of Nicholas I).

By the 1830s this unique city was almost fully formed and already surrounded by a lively mythology.[3] Conceived as a fundamental challenge to Muscovy, it had stood for a century in stark contrast with Moscow and Russia in general. Now it became the symbol of the hoped-for transformation of Russia, even a kind of Utopia. For some it was exotic but desirable; for others, the abominable creation of an evil spirit. Classicism instilled both patriotic sentiment and strong faith in the inevitability of absolutism. At the time when classicism began to decline, the inner, secret, crude life of St Petersburg, its contemporary life, its realities and contradictions were still not as apparent as they were to become ten to fifteen years later; and this image of the city was not yet the object of artistic scrutiny. In the early years of the nineteenth century, ominous features, threatening signs of alienation, began to emerge, and they grew clearer as classicism – having lost touch with contemporary life – became outdated. The real nature of the city was to be most vividly expressed not in architecture, but in the writings of Gogol and Dostoevsky, the poetry of the Symbolists and the work of the World of Art group.

The evolution of the 'image' of St Petersburg is revealing. It began as a symbol of perfect order, a sort of heaven on earth, but the novels of Dostoevsky, who uncovered the cancers at the heart of the city, described a living hell.[4] This contrast is hardly surprising. From the moment of its inception the city harboured an inner contradiction: standing well away from the heart of Russia, metaphorically and literally, it was nevertheless the symbol of her ambitions. The contradiction is reflected in the architectural approach of Moscow and the provinces on one hand, and that of St Petersburg on the other. In the early nineteenth century the new capital exerted a strong influence on Moscow, which now also began to favour monumentalism and the new approach to town planning, i.e. the creation of ensembles – in fact all the characteristics of late classical style. At the same time Moscow's architecture never ceased to express the distinctive way of life of the former capital, preserving its independence by adopting the Petersburg/European experience for its own purposes.

MOSCOW

An intensive programme of building was initiated in Moscow after the war against Napoleon, which had inflicted dreadful damage on the city. The second decade of the nineteenth century saw the restoration and modernization of the centre. Osip Beauvais or Bove (1784–1834) was one of many who contributed to the transformation of three great squares: Red Square, Theatre Square and Manège Square. Painstaking and assiduous, he was Moscow's nearest equivalent to Rossi, who, however, was incomparably more talented. Bove was born in Moscow and spent nearly all his life there, studying neither in St Petersburg nor abroad. He learnt his architecture by practising it, continuing in the tradition of Kazakov, the well-known eighteenth-century Moscow architect. He cleared Red Square of its little shops and market, and constructed a new building, with a mighty Doric portico and a cupola, to house the new shopping arcades opposite the Kremlin. The cupola marked the square's main axis, which continued through the cupolas of Kazakov's Senate building looming behind the Kremlin wall. I.P. Martos's monument to Minin and Pozharsky (the heroes of the Russian resistance to the Polish invasion in 1611) was erected in front of the shopping arcades soon afterwards. (It now occupies a different spot in Red Square.)

Moscow's squares have a very different atmosphere from St Petersburg's, mainly because their designers frequently had to accommodate already existing medieval buildings, with their many historic associations and

Carlo Rossi, Arch of the General Staff Building looking towards Palace Square, St Petersburg, 1819–29

Carlo Rossi, Theatre Street (now Rossi Street), St Petersburg, 1828–34

vivid evocation of bygone days. The second half of the nineteenth century saw the emergence of a new attitude to the past. Architects turned enthusiastically to medieval forms and inevitably the central squares began to be reconstructed according to old Russian styles; many old buildings (including Bove's shopping arcades) were pulled down and new ones, with a medieval Russian look, put in their place.

Moscow squares are somewhat enclosed: they do not merge or flow into one another like those of St Petersburg. Theatre Square is a good example. Most of the houses round the perimeter of the square were built in the same style, with repeated arcades at ground level. They were a worthy accompaniment to the Bolshoi Theatre towering above the surrounding buildings. Narrow streets, radiating from the square, kept it rather isolated from and independent of its neighbours, even though its actual size was similar to many in St Petersburg.

Isolated single buildings and squares are another typical feature of Moscow. Privacy was prized more highly than the public display so popular in the new capital. Muscovites expected their houses to protect them

from intrusion. They favoured courtyards and often placed a long building at right angles to the street, with the main part of the house hidden in a courtyard, where people could pursue their daily lives well away from prying eyes.

Private houses of modest proportions were built in large numbers. The master of this genre was Afanasy Grigoriev (1782–1868) who designed houses for the Krushchev family (now the museum dedicated to the life and work of Alexander Pushkin) and the Lopukhin family (now the Leo Tolstoy museum) on Kropotkinskaya Street (formerly Prechistenka). Both are typically Muscovite. The Krushchev mansion (1815–17) is set in the corner of a small estate, its main facade facing the street, the second facing a little lane, and the third overlooking the garden. The three facades differ in their manner of decoration, a feature which adds to the attractiveness of the house.

Domenico Gigliardi (1788–1845) was another architect who made a brilliant contribution to Moscow's residential and public buildings, as well as to estates outside the city. Brought to Moscow when he was one year old, he received his early architectural training from

his father and later studied at the Academy in Milan. A perfect example of his work is the Lunin mansion (1818–23) on Nikitsky (now Sovorovsky) Boulevard. Its composition is as free and asymmetric as that of the Krushchev house. The right wing of the house is a two-storey building with a small colonnaded portico, rather old-fashioned but elegant; the left is a long, simple, undecorated, single-storey block. The architect's artistry and sense of proportion are displayed in the design of the central section, which is grander than the rest: a loggia, with elevated Corinthian columns and triple windows with decorative arches, distracts from the monotony of the wall. Typically Muscovite in its design, the mansion is set well back in a courtyard. Gigliardi made use of a similar design in his building for the Board of Guardians (Opekunsky Sovyet) on Solyanka Street. The side facade overlooks the street; the main body of the building is the central focus of a symmetrical composition. This is famous for its beautiful interior, in which pairs of Tuscan columns, bearing low arches, separate rooms of equal size – an inspired combination of elegance and mathematical precision.

(*Left*) **Osip Bove**, Shopping Arcade, Red Square, Moscow (watercolour) (*top*) **Afanasy Grigoriev**, Krushchev Family House, Moscow, 1815–17 (*above*) **Domenico Gigliardi**, Lunin Family House, Moscow, 1818–23

Gigliardi collaborated with Grigoriev on Moscow mansions and on two manor houses, for the Usachev estate on the river Yauza and the Kuzminky estate near Moscow. In the Usachev estate a traditional facade with an eight-columned portico, raised on an arched plinth, looks over the street. Behind the house is a large park with pavilions and gazebos; paths lead down to the river. A striking view of the side facade – a composition of two pilasters with a projecting entablature and an arch – may be seen from a ramp curving down to the garden from the ground floor.

The Kuzminky estate is interesting for its large stable complex, whose sober, down-to-earth character contrasts with a formal and monumental arched musical pavilion with a niche on the far wall. The niche is decorated with Gigliardi's favourite motif, paired columns bearing an entablature. Gigliardi gave Moscow architecture a

Domenico Gigliardi, Board of Guardians, Moscow. Operation Wing, 1823–26

slightly Italian flavour, in sharp contrast to the French influence so apparent in St Petersburg, but this should not be taken to mean that Russian architecture was simply divided into two opposing schools. They were more like two separate currents in one broad stream, each with its own structure, tone and preferences.

Individual houses were the commonest form of living accommodation in Moscow and most provincial towns and many such residential areas have survived intact to our day. But the provinces, in their turn, were influenced by contemporary ideas of town planning at the beginning of the nineteenth century. Central areas were systematically redesigned, new squares laid down and large shopping and trading centres created. The principal town of every 'gubernia' (province) was obliged to construct an administrative building. A preference for neoclassical style dominated country towns well into the middle of the nineteenth century, and the newly-awakened interest in the national heritage, so influential in Moscow during the 1830s, at first hardly touched provincial areas of Russia.

Russian urban architecture in the first decades of the nineteenth century therefore spans a wide spectrum of styles and approaches. At one extreme is the utopian ideal, the cult of regular proportions and monumental triumphalism epitomized by the architecture of St Petersburg; at the other, the Muscovite and provincial longing for comfort and intimacy, and for a family home where the charms of everyday life nestled snugly behind a classical portico.

In other words, at a time when painters were already beginning to express themselves in many different styles, architecture was still dominated by classicism, which was required to satisfy an ever-increasing variety of demands. It was as a result of this pressure on architects that the Romantic approach began to influence them, and especially the Romantic perception of space as limitless, exemplified in the vast squares of St Petersburg. The Biedermeier concept of residential building crept in, especially in the provinces, heralding the inevitable death of classicism.

SCULPTURE

The classical period in Russian sculpture coincides with that of architecture, but its style became outdated somewhat earlier and yielded more readily to Romantic innovation. The evolution of the work of Ivan Martos perfectly illustrates the birth, development and decline of classical sculpture; Shchedrin and Prokoviev were others who made a gradual transition from the eighteenth to the nineteenth centuries. Every stage in the development of classical architecture can be easily distinguished both by its particular qualities and by its most prominent practitioners; in sculpture, however, such divisions are almost impossible to discern.

Mikhail Kozlovsky, the finest of the eighteenth-century classical sculptors, died in 1802 at the very height of his powers. Other artists – especially Martos and Shchedrin – continued working alongside sculptors of the new generation, strengthening their authority and attaining the status of 'master'.

As the nineteenth century opened Ivan Martos (1753–1835) had already established his distinctive style and was poised to address himself to some complex artistic problems. His best early works are funerary monuments. In the 1880s he outgrew the urge to portray the mystical horror of death so characteristic of Baroque tombs, and evoked instead a feeling of resignation, imbuing his marble reliefs with tenderness, clarity and purity of rhythm. A good example of his mature style is the tomb of E.I. Gagarina (1803), which is not only a summation of twenty years of development in funeral sculpture, but also a work of transcending quality. Martos here broke free from allegorical personification and its complicated relationship to reality. Changes in the artist's style are very apparent in this monument. The soft folds of earlier sculptures, intended to evoke an elegiac mood, are replaced by strictly geometrical forms; the figure herself is columnar; her pose and gesture, pointing to the earth where the ashes are interred, are unambiguous and final. The complex array of emotions formerly inspired by the depiction of the grief-stricken mourner and the sorrowing messenger of Death gives way, in this monument, to a perception of Gagarina herself, portrayed as a classical beauty, symbolizing her own death and immortality.

The following year Martos was commissioned to design the monument to Minin and Pozharsky, who organized the defence of Russia against the Polish invasion of 1611. There was little distinguished eighteenth-century Russian sculpture and Martos had few predecessors to pit himself against. Carlo Bartolommeo Rastrelli (father of the famous architect) had created the equestrian monument to Peter the Great in the 1750s. Catherine the Great, on the advice of Diderot, later

Ivan Martos, Design for funerary statue of E.I. Gagarina, 1803

commissioned a statue on the same subject from the French sculptor Falconet. At the turn of the century Kozlovsky constructed the monument to Field Marshal Suvorov. Martos, however, faced a far more difficult challenge – that of combining two figures in one work. His first version was a stylized Greek 'Tyrannocide', but he subsequently found his own, more dramatic solution by deciding to depict the moment when Minin, a merchant, summons Prince Pozharsky to lead the Russian people against the invader. Pozharsky has not yet recovered from wounds and, sword and shield in hand, rises with great difficulty from his bed.

This concept did not occur spontaneously to Martos. It was vigorously discussed at the Society of Literature, Science and the Arts, a forum for enlightened ideas of which the sculptor was a member. The idea the monument should present, therefore, became a matter of national importance; not surprisingly, as the work itself was begun in 1804, shortly before the outbreak of the war against Napoleon, and completed in 1818, when Russia

Ivan Martos, Monument to Minin and Pozharsky, Moscow, 1804–18

was still basking in victory. Minin and Pozharsky's historic act of heroism was an indirect celebration of General Kutuzov and his army, the saviours of Russia in her struggle against the French dictator. Minin's determined gesture points at the Kremlin, demanding that it be defended. That sacred symbol of Russia was already secure by the time the monument, facing the Kremlin and with its back to Bove's building, was unveiled in Red Square.

The tenets of classicism constrained Martos from presenting the full drama of Minin's appeal to the Prince, and permitted him only to hint at his subjects' passionate love of the Fatherland. He also faced the problem of how to dress his heroes. At the end of the eighteenth century historical and contemporary figures were generally depicted in historically correct costume, as for example in Houdon's portrayals of George Washington and the seventeenth-century Admiral Turville. But Martos was separated from his heroes by two hundred years, during which time Russia had changed from a medieval to a modern nation; bound by the rules of classicism, he could hardly clothe them authentically. He found a brilliant

compromise: the figures are dressed in a blend of an antique tunic and the Old Russian long, belted shirt worn over the trousers. The whole composition is a timeless and profoundly significant monument to patriotism. Martos's classicism is neither refined nor naturalistic, but sober, heroic and majestic, qualities which distinguish him from certain other artists of the period.

Martos's finest achievement is the bas-relief on the left butt end of the Kazan Cathedral in St Petersburg. *Moses Striking Water in the Wilderness* (1804–07) was carved in local stone from the Pudozh area. There is not the slightest trace of Baroque in this work, which extends along the front of the attic storey. The action, against a neutral and unlandscaped background, moves from both sides towards the centre. The characters are gathered into rhythmically repeated, separate groups. This is the artist's most purely classical work.

Fyodosy Shchedrin (1751–1825), like Martos, made a successful transition from the old century to the new. Together with many of his contemporaries he studied at the St Petersburg Academy of Fine Arts under a French professor of sculpture, Nicolas-François Gillet. He spent several years in Italy and – unlike Martos – in France, where he studied with Allegrain, but his best work was done in Russia and includes the fountain sculptures of *Perseus* (1800), *Neva* (1804) and *Sirens* (1805) for Peterhof, the summer residence of the Tsars outside St Petersburg. He also sculpted individual figures and groups for the Admiralty, the best-known of which are the pairs of sea nymphs supporting heavenly spheres.

We have already mentioned the emphasis on mythology evident in the Admiralty. The same applies to Peterhof (now Petrodvorets), where Shchedrin's free-standing sculptures are part of the Great Cascade behind Kozlovsky's famous figure of Samson wrenching open the lion's mouth. The figures are treated naturalistically; the allegorical element is secondary. We may consider it, in fact, as a kind of natural mythology. The realistic, rather than idealized, bodies of the Sirens emerge from their fishtails, signifying a miraculous transformation only possible in the realm of myth. There is a wonderfully natural quality about the way they blow into their horns and spurt out water.

Neva stands nearby, at the very bottom of the Cascade. She sits on a dolphin, leaning to one side and supporting herself on a stone with a hand which holds a snake. We hardly perceive these allusions as allegorical because the meaning of *Neva* is embodied in her naturalness and the unashamed revelation of her nakedness. And yet Shchedrin here follows a conventional symbolism somehow akin to the natural elements (stone and water) shaped by the hand of Man in the pond of the Great Cascade. Myth and reality here approach each

Fyodosy Shchedrin *Sea Nymphs Supporting Heavenly Spheres* 1812

Vasily Demut-Malinovsky *Pluto's Rape of Proserpine* 1809

other very closely, but it is not detailed allusion which so convincingly animates the mythological figure. The sculpture seems actually to embody the River Neva, in all its noble tranquillity; she exists for herself alone and not for her admirers. Thus Shchedrin comes nearer to achieving the ideals of antiquity than some other masters of Russian classicism who concentrated merely on its external trappings.

Historians of Russian art are in general agreement that Shchedrin's greatest work is the pair of grouped figures flanking the Admiralty arch: *Sea Nymphs Supporting Heavenly Spheres*. They were carved in Pudozh stone in 1812. Two traditional motifs – the Three Graces and Atlantis – are combined in the *Sea Nymphs*, as D.E. Arkin accurately observed.[5] These motifs appear, at first sight, to contradict each other – the Graces, after all, were surely not intended to bear heavy weights. Shchedrin reinterpreted both motifs. The heavenly sphere, though huge, does not strike us as over-heavy; and the nymphs reveal their majestic grace, strength and beauty in the very manner in which they cope with their burden. The works of Shchedrin, like those of Martos, possess an air of

sublime severity and an uncompromising classicism; the contours of his figures are unsoftened by any hint of sfumato.

The Admiralty figures, as we have noted, mark an important phase in the development of the synthesis of architecture and sculpture. The building was, indeed, very richly decorated with reliefs, masks, individual and group sculptures, many of them conventionally set at the corners of pediments, on attic storeys and on the archivolt of the arch. But sculpture was gradually beginning to disengage from architecture. The *Sea Nymphs* stand on their own with, in the background, a wall on which two winged glories are depicted in relief. It is as though they themselves have chosen this place, for there is no purely architectural justification for their position. The physical link between sculpture and architecture gives way to the figurative. The *Sea Nymphs*, in particular, contain many of those sculptural qualities which Zakharov expressed in architectural terms, such as geometry, harmony of form and classical – i.e. formal – beauty.

This process, the separation of sculpture from architecture, seems only natural at a time when freestanding sculpture was growing increasingly fashionable, especially in the work of such European masters as Canova. But the significance of the Admiralty in this regard lies in the *quality* achieved in the synthesis of the two art forms, a synthesis which reached its apogee well before the long stagnation which set in as the century reached its halfway point.

The relationship between the architecture of the Admiralty and its sculpture is the finest flowering of that synthesis in late Russian classicism. As the synthesis developed the harmonious balance was lost, even though Voronikhin and Rossi collaborated closely with some of the new generation of talented sculptors such as Stepan Pimenov the elder (1774–1833) and Vasily Demut-Malinovsky (1779–1846). These two were the most distinguished among many who worked in the genre of the sculptural decoration of buildings, freestanding monuments and funerary groups. Their most important contributions were to Voronikhin's College of Mines and to three of Rossi's buildings: the General Staff Headquarters, and the Yelagin and Mikhail Palaces.

The sculptures in front of the College recall Shchedrin's *Sea Nymphs*. They stand at a certain distance from the wall, on specially built pedestals, flanking the broad flight of steps leading to the portico of the College. The themes treated – *Hercules and Antea* (Pimenov) and *Pluto's Rape of Proserpine* (Demut-Malinovsky) – are, of course, concerned with the earth and the underworld, but the figures' real relationship with the College of Mines is an aesthetic one. They express the tension and struggle of opposing forces, reflecting the mighty mass of the building itself; they act as a kind of tuning fork for the College and its massive pediment, supported by huge, fluted columns, its plain-hewn walls and the yawning spaces between the columns.

Another masterpiece by the two sculptors is the Winged Chariot of Glory which crowns the triumphal arch of the General Staff Headquarters opposite the Winter Palace. Sculptors frequently turned to the triumphal theme, but this Chariot is the finest example of its kind and perfectly complements the surrounding architecture. The rhythmical movement of the six horses, fanning out from the figure of Glory standing on the Chariot and flanked by warriors, seems to determine the sense of direction of the whole semicircular complex. The sculpture is constructed of copper sheets; the integrity of its striking silhouette is best appreciated from a distance.

Even the greatest sculptors occasionally betray their weaknesses, however, and some of the reliefs (especially on Rossi's buildings) strike us today as mere architectural detail. The monumentalist and heroic style of earlier classicism was becoming exhausted, but a new understanding and interpretation of antiquity was at hand.

Samuel Galberg *Portrait of A.A. Perovsky* 1829

Samuel Galberg (1787–1839) and Fyodor Tolstoy (1783–1873) were among those of the new generation who specialized in freestanding monumental sculpture, although less successfully than Demut-Malinovsky and Pimenov. Galberg found his metier in portrait sculpture. He chose the form known as 'herm', already popular with Houdon and other European sculptors. Galberg more or less standardized the presentation of his dozens of busts. They are usually of men; the sides are cut flat and the naked torso, set on a pedestal, forms the lower part of the portrait itself. None of his busts features clothes or headdress, and it must be said that there is a certain monotonous sameness about all his heads and faces. Thus I.A. Krylov, the fabulist and playwright, aging and stout (1830), bears a resemblance to the handsome young Romantic author, A.A. Perovsky (1829), and both display similarities with the noble and ascetic features of Martos as an old man (1839). All Galberg's busts, irrespective of age or personality, bear the stamp of heroic perfection, only partially modified by a certain individuality in the faces themselves, and the result is generally a nice balance between classical convention and naturalistic detail. This 'naturalistic physiognomism' fitted into the classical canon and heralded the approach of academic art.

Fyodor Tolstoy bequeathed a richer and more complex body of work to posterity. Of noble birth, he was intended for a military career, but his life changed drastically when he chose to become a professional artist. He briefly attended the St Petersburg Academy of Fine Arts, although he never fully enrolled. He became a passionate student of classical antiquity and eventually a curator at the Hermitage. He was elected a fellow of the Academy for his artistic achievements and, in 1828, its vice president. Much of his work has its roots in the traditions of amateur or dilettante art, which was very popular in aristocratic circles in the early nineteenth century. The nobility loved writing verses and drawing charming scenes for their family albums, playing the violin or flute and presenting plays or *tableaux vivants* at home. Fyodor Tolstoy liked to cut out black paper silhouettes of portraits, battle scenes and landscapes, which he then glued onto card. He also enjoyed inventing optical illusions, such as flowers in a transparent glass, berries scattered on a table, and flies or butterflies crawling over a book, *jeux d'esprit* which he was careful to ensure never overstepped the bounds of taste. His still-lifes blended poetic naturalism with a classical choice of subject; he also indulged in romantic scenes and pleasant domestic interiors.

The drawings illustrating *Dushenka* ('My Little Sweetheart', a frivolous and risqué poem by the eighteenth-century writer Bogdanovich) form an important part of Fyodor Tolstoy's *oeuvre*. The sketches appear to be drawn in one uninterrupted line, reminiscent of Flaxman, the famous English sculptor and draughtsman, in his illustrations of Homer. But Tolstoy added an individual touch to the technique. His drawings are full of a gently mocking irony, achieved by observing classical models through the prism of everyday life. Although he rather stripped antiquity of its heroic aura, Tolstoy expressed his love and admiration of it with romantic fervour.

His true forte, however, was sculpture, and especially relief sculpture, the genre in which he most clearly revealed his fresh interpretation of classical antiquity. His series of reliefs on the theme of Homer's *Odyssey* (1810–15) consists of four scenes: *The Feast of Penelope's Suitors; Telemachus at the Palace of Menelaus; Ulysses, Returning Home, Slaughters Penelope's Suitors*; and *Mercury Leading the Shades of Penelope's Suitors to Hell*. Relatively small and finely carved in wax on a graphite board, they show a large number of figures against a background of landscapes and interiors. The four scenes are interpreted spatially as well as pictorially, unlike most classical reliefs of the period, but lack any trace of Baroque. Tolstoy's treatment of the whole composition proves his subtle understanding of antique art. The figures, set at elaborate angles, are elegantly foreshortened, and the action moves smoothly from

Fyodor Tolstoy *Triple Entente* 1821

background to foreground. At the same time, the artist accentuates the plane by means of a strict linear rhythm.

Much of Tolstoy's work displays his knowledge of the various traditions and techniques of classical culture. He relished working on a small scale and raised the art of medal portraiture to new heights. Between 1814 and 1836 he created a series of twenty-one medals, commemorating the war of 1812, which were greatly admired by his contemporaries for the scrupulous care with which he attended to every detail. But technical virtuosity was not the only reason for the success of the medal series; equally important were the subject-matter, which gave voice to the patriotic mood of the Russian people, and the skill with which he contrived to make two or three figures embody the crucial events of the war. Even the most heroic subjects, as interpreted by Tolstoy, seem imbued with grace and an almost mannered elegance; but they are saved from any hint of preciosity by the artist's tact and exquisite sense of proportion. He admired classic art, and especially its aesthetic element, which he prized above all other characteristics, but he neither wished nor attempted to imitate it. Fyodor Tolstoy may be considered as the first aesthete in the history of Russian art, a harbinger of the trend towards 'Art for art's sake' which was initiated at the end of the nineteenth century by members of the World of Art group (*Mir iskusstva*). They were to revive the art of silhouettes, miniatures and genre painting – in other words, all those fields in which Fyodor Tolstoy excelled.

Tolstoy should not be thought of as a full-blown classicist. Perhaps 'Romantic classicist' is a better description for one of the first artists deliberately to use a mixture of styles in his work, a practice more characteristic of painting than of sculpture. Herein lies Tolstoy's uniqueness.

PAINTING

Painting, and especially history painting, was the most purely classical of the arts in nineteenth-century Russia, and in protecting that purity it early on condemned itself to creative sterility. The style is particularly associated with such 'distinguished' professors of the Academy as Andrei Ivanov (father of the famous Alexander Ivanov), Alexei Egorov and Vasily Shebuyev.

These three were at the very top of the Academic tree, and their kind of history painting, faithful to the traditions of eighteenth-century classicism, was considered the most important. It did include, admittedly, several new elements, in particular a willingness to address fresh themes and subjects from Russian history, ancient and modern, in addition to the traditional episodes borrowed from Homer and the Bible. In 1813, for example, the Academy commissioned from two students, M. Tikhonov and V. Sazonov, a history painting of a contemporary event, to wit, 'Russian citizens proving their faith in God and their loyalty to the Tsar in choosing death by firing squad rather than obeying Napoleon's orders, thus dying in piety and steadfastness of spirit'. For a brief moment it seemed that, as had happened in England, France, America and Spain, contemporary events had found a hold in Russian painting too, and that such events would receive the same attention as those from the distant past; but in fact the two young painters represented their subjects merely as actors playing out their roles according to the conventions of classical theatre, their gestures and poses recalling the heroes of ancient Rome. And indeed this was to be the one and only example of recent history breaching the stronghold of Russian history painting. Thereafter, only episodes from the distant past of Russian history were to be depicted. Some notable examples are the struggle of the independent republic of Novgorod the Great against the domination of Moscow in the fifteenth century; Prince Dmitri Donskoi on the field of Kulikovo (the battle which effectively marked the liberation of Russia from the Tartar and Mongol yoke); the people of Kiev fighting the tribal Petcheneg in the tenth century; Mstislav Udaloy (the Bold) in single combat with Prince Rededya; and Igolkin the merchant heroically killing a Swedish soldier who had insulted Peter the Great and being torn to pieces by the Swedish mob. Such themes

Alexei Egorov *Torture of the Saviour* 1814

enabled the past to be compared with the present and parallels to be drawn between them, but classical painting found it impossible to illuminate the mysteries of the past or treat historical men and women with insight and understanding. Unlike Russian classical sculpture, it substituted instead a pathos and emotional zeal that were simply false.

Clearly, command of the laws of composition and anatomy, together with a training firmly based on classical models, laid the way open for such works of art (perfect in the Academic sense) as Egorov's *Torture of the Saviour* (1814), a painting imitated and even copied by generations of students at the Academy. By such means Russian Academic art was established and developed; and it was to be particularly enriched by its contacts with the new movements of Romanticism and Realism.

All the painters mentioned above were fettered by their loyalty to classicism, and above all by the demands of history painting, the most conservative discipline of all. Egorov and Shebuyev felt liberated whenever they worked on other motifs, as though styles in painting and drawing must be for ever rigidly compartmentalized.

Russian Romanticism had its beginnings in landscape and portrait painting, where classicism had the least historical justification for its continued existence.

2 Early Romanticism

A cursory glance at Russian painting of the first thirty years of the nineteenth century reveals that it had not yet been invigorated by the Romantic spirit. Russia had no equivalent to the fantasies on the theme of Ossian which had swept Europe at the turn of the century, nor to Fuseli's paintings, which had shocked the public with spine-chilling scenes, nor yet to the drawings of Blake, who invited his admirers to explore unknown and mysterious worlds. Russian painting was even more remote from the world of Goya, who had known the extremes of intense creative energy and bottomless despair. The Romantic mood was present, nevertheless, hidden in the depths of human experience, avoiding loud ostentation and external expression. It became a vigorous element in landscape and portraiture, while remaining almost absent from history and genre. Its influence, therefore, was partial, but its achievements considerable, though incomplete.

There is a simple historical explanation for this lack of completeness. Russian social development in the first three decades of the century had not yet progressed to the stage of open conflict between individuals and society. In addition, disillusion with the previous century's enlightenment had not yet set in, nor was there any protest against the social regimentation which had characterized those years. Russia was ready to respond to the Romantic call, however, because her people, with the experience of Western Europe before them, were in a position to evaluate the consequences of the French Revolution and to foresee the future of their own country. Artistic thinking was at a roughly similar stage in many different countries, even those in which the social and political environment was less than welcoming, as was the case in Russia, where there were obvious and remarkable manifestations of Romanticism by the early nineteenth century.

Romanticism probably moved along a broader front in literature than in the plastic arts. Literary Sentimentalism, which had made its appearance at the end of the eighteenth century, led directly to Romanticism, even though the process of development was long and leisurely. It was not until 1810 or thereabouts that signs of a mature Romanticism could be detected, especially in the work of the poet V.A. Zhukovsky, who put into practice the principal postulates of German Romantic aesthetics, such as Schelling's theory of Man's intuitive grasp of the world through poetry and philosophy, and the belief in divine inspiration and in the individual Genius as the channel through which Mankind could realize its poetic potential. A couplet written in 1819, entitled 'Inexpressible', illustrates the impossibility of expressing in words the fullness of Nature and Life:

> *All we cannot grasp jostles in a single sigh;*
> *Only silence speaks clearly.*

These lines foreshadow the famous maxim of Feodor Tyutchev: 'A thought expressed becomes a lie', a maxim which pungently summed up the Romantic idea. It was also chosen, significantly, by the Russian Symbolists as their motto on the eve of the twentieth century.

Romanticism established its hold over painting in a rather different manner. It progressed spasmodically, and without any theoretical support. At the beginning of the century Russian painters had little access to German philosophy, but they breathed the air on which the bacilli of Romanticism were borne, absorbed the mood of the time and sensed the future. In addition, writers greatly influenced some painters, especially Kiprensky and Orlovsky, the two most consequential figures in Romantic painting in the first twenty years of the century.

Whereas in literature some poets occupied a midway position between Sentimentalism and Romanticism, there were no such transitional figures in the field of painting. The most distinguished portrait painter of the 1790s was Vladimir Borovikovsky, famous for his paintings of women in sentimental style. He abandoned the sentimental tradition in the course of the next ten years and turned to classical portraiture; many other artists followed the same pattern. Hardly any painters of significance in the 1790s joined the new Romantic movement, which had to wait for a new generation of younger artists, less inextricably bound to the old traditions.

This was the generation which created the general atmosphere marking the beginning of the Romantic movement and a new kind of portraiture. Its principal practitioners were Orlovsky, Varnek, Egorov, Shebuyev (the last two, we recall, were academicians whose main genre was history painting and who only worked in the Romantic manner in their spare moments) and Venetsianov, who, just before his heyday as a master of genre painting, unexpectedly blossomed as a Romantic portraitist. The outstanding figure among all these portrait painters, however, was Kiprensky, who was closely connected with literary circles and made use of the new poetic concepts in the creation of his own pictorial Romanticism.

Orest Kiprensky (1782–1826) was a typical Romantic. The story of his life is legendary[6]; his contemporaries considered his personality unbalanced and his behaviour sometimes odd. He was born the illegitimate son of a nobleman, whose steward – a serf – adopted him. The nobleman granted him his freedom, and acknowledged his talent at a very early age by sending him to the Academy at St Petersburg, where he studied history painting under Professor Ugryumov; among his fellow students were Andrei Ivanov, Egorov and Shebuyev. Even at the Academy his behaviour was challenging and unorthodox.

He spent most of his life in Italy, which Russian intellectual society of the day considered to be heaven on earth and a country created specially for painters. In spite of this apparently ideal environment he was unhappy there. He had a hostile relationship with the colony of Russian painters, among whom it was rumoured that Kiprensky had killed one of his models; word of the alleged crime even reached Russia. On his second visit to Italy he married an Italian girl, the daughter of one of his models, and was obliged to enter the Catholic faith, an act his contemporaries considered a shocking betrayal of Orthodoxy. After a stormy life he died in a state of depression and illness, far from his native land.

The Romantics glorified unhappiness and transformed it into a cult, whose adherents aspired thereby to an elevated spiritual existence. Artists actively sought out hardship and tragedy, apparently impoverishing themselves deliberately, suffering illness and dying far from home. They often ended up abandoned by society, locked away in lunatic asylums or in shabby garrets in provincial backwaters. For many years Kiprensky's fundamental tragedy was his separation from his homeland, but he contrived further destructive conflicts for himself. He was obsessed by the idea that his destiny lay in history painting – a result of his academic training – but in reality he only painted portraits, a contradiction he invented and imposed on himself.

Orest Kiprensky *Portrait of Adam Schvalbe* 1804

His professional career began at a time when Russian society was living in the hope and expectation of change. But these dreams of social improvement were doomed to bitter disillusion, and Kiprensky, who belonged to the disappointed generation, sought a distinctive artistic response. He found refuge in an ever more acute perception of the beauty of the world, which allowed him to lose himself in his dreams and sorrows and resolutely deny that there could be any obstacles to human happiness.

In the compromise between the real and the ideal which is the stuff of every portrait, Kiprensky tended to favour the ideal, though of course his work contains elements of both. The fact that every one of his sitters was unique did not conflict with his sense of the ideal: on the contrary, that very sense predetermined his portrayal of the sitter, because Kiprensky believed that behaviour and outward appearance could be made to reveal the unique character within. His sense of the ideal was born of his time and epoch, and derived from a new understanding of people's creative potential. He often lent his subjects aspects of his own personality: this was not poetic licence but a transcendingly truthful expression of human nature.

Kiprensky began his career with a striking and original work. The year before he completed his diploma-

Orest Kiprensky *Portrait of E.P. Rostopchina* 1809

Orest Kiprensky *Portrait of Chelishchev as a Boy* 1808–09

painting in 1805 (*Dmitri Donskoi at the Battle of Kulikovo*, which bore all the hallmarks of classical painting) he painted a portrait of his stepfather Adam Schvalbe. No other portrait of the time can rival this in its breadth of vision, boldness and evocation of the mood of the sitter. The artist ignores his subject's position in society; he concentrates on his stepfather's inner world, on his spiritual and intellectual qualities, above all his ability to feel and to express what he feels. Schvalbe is depicted in a state of high drama, close to an explosion of passion, his flashing eyes moving energetically and suddenly freezing. His body is compressed into the confines of the narrow board on which it is painted, as if striving to expand the frame. We seem to be witnessing an attempt at self-assertion and self-definition: the figure and the head are trying to emerge from infinite space in order to conquer their amorphousness and take concrete shape.

The next stage of Kiprensky's work was, paradoxically, a pause in his progress, while he reverted to traditional eighteenth-century techniques, but his artistic destiny had been determined by the portrait of Schvalbe, and some fifteen years after its completion he was to paint some of his very best portraits. They bear all the signs of great inspiration, profound thought and a perfect technical command of his art. Among them are two self-

portraits dating from the first decade of the century. In one, he poses with paint-brushes behind his ear, in the other he is wearing a pink kerchief.

Three other notable portraits are those of Chelishchev as a boy (1808–09), E.V. Davydov (1809) and E.P. Rostopchina (1809).These paintings, for all their separate individuality, share a common mood. In the course of his career Kiprensky fundamentally rethought the challenges involved in painting children, women and military heroes as well as self-portraits, made various innovations and rejected outmoded ideas in all these fields; in the Rostopchina portrait, however, the painter is still quite close to the eighteenth-century masters, especially Rokotov, one of the most lyrical of Russian portraitists.

Rostopchina must have been an ideal sitter for Kiprensky. A modest woman with a complex and reserved personality, she was seen by her contemporaries as a rather governessy figure, although she was, in fact, the hostess of a famous literary salon. Her restraint, however, is not an insuperable obstacle to Kiprensky, for he manages to evoke a confessional mood, albeit an involuntary one, in her expression. As in most of his early portraits, Kiprensky excludes hands from the painting. All the attention is concentrated on the face, and especially on the eyes. These sparkling eyes, gazing slightly upward, pierce the surrounding gloom; her figure, turned in the same direction as her head, is static, yet somehow soft. The sloping contour of the shoulders, the turned-up edge of the lace collar, the dark background into which Rostopchina herself is sunk, all serve somehow to restrict her freedom of movement. In contrast to the body, the eyes elevate and liberate her spiritual energy from its mortal cage. Her penetrating look is one of rejoicing and inspiration. The painting's colour scheme, based on a gentle contrast between light and shade, seems a fitting accompaniment to the eyes. Grey and brown tints, in some places shading into red and pale yellow, are carefully juxtaposed to create a mood of restrained harmony. This restraint contrasts all the more strongly with the shining eyes, which reveal the full and emotional nature of Rostopchina's soul.

The best of Kiprensky's early portraits possess a special pictorial and compositional expressiveness. It is interesting to compare the Rostopchina portrait with that of Chelishchev as a boy, where he fundamentally reinterprets the image of the child – i.e. in the spirit of Romanticism. In the eighteenth century the child had been seen merely as a small adult. Kiprensky rejects this perception and reveals the personality of the boy, showing particular interest in his psychology. Chelishchev is depicted as standing on the threshold of intellectual awakening. He is an observer, even a dreamer, about to discover a beautiful and complicated world. However, he remains very reserved in his relationship to the world, as if hesitating momentarily before finally facing it. A pensive reverie, convincingly conveyed, gradually discloses the boy's complex personality. Kiprensky does not direct the boy's energy outwards. The movement of body, head and eyes is dispersed in three directions, with a consequent dissipation of energy, rendering the location of the figure in its surrounding space uncertain and fluctuating. Kiprensky was generally more interested in his subjects' moods than in their characters. In the Chelishchev portrait he proposes a new way of using colour to heighten expressiveness. He applies the principle of 'colour accord', consisting in this case of three components: red, blue and white. A triangular piece of the boy's red waistcoat, edged by the blue of his jacket and his white collar, is the most striking flash of colour. The red is solid and consistent, except at the very bottom of the triangle, where dabs of dark blue from the jacket intrude onto it. Red and white are laid on thickly and remain unsmoothed, leaving clearly visible brushmarks. The blue has a different resonance: it emerges from the depths of the shaded areas, only occasionally gaining purity and clarity. The whole accord is a triad of liberated colour qualities, a metaphor in colour of the inner life of young Chelishchev. The unmixed colours of the accord are juxtaposed and compared, then merge together in other parts of the canvas or relate to each other in complex ways, particularly in the rendering of the face. Here, shades of pink echo the red of the waistcoat, the delicate blue of the boy's veins recalls the blue of the jacket, and flecks of white match the white of the collar. The colours which make up the accord account for most of the colour scheme of this part of the canvas, but other colours, mixed and less intensive, produce new colour qualities. Nevertheless, they retain all the ingredients of the colour metaphor mentioned above, and this is particularly crucial to the depiction of the face, which seems to radiate waves of some sort.

Kiprensky's self-portraits are undoubtedly the best of his early work. There was no consistent tradition of self-portraiture in eighteenth-century Russian painting and drawing, perhaps because the awakening self-awareness of the Russian people was far from complete, and a sense of self-worth was only just beginning to develop as the eighteenth century dawned. This was particularly true of artists, who, until this time, had generally been considered as mere craftsmen. It simply did not occur to most of them to paint portraits of themselves.

With the advent of the Romantic era the situation changed drastically, as is shown by the unprecedented number of early nineteenth-century self-portraits. Kiprensky's truest work in this genre includes the *Self-portrait with Brushes behind the Ear* and the *Self-portrait with Pink Kerchief*. The message of the former is determined by the theme itself – the painter at work in a moment of creative inspiration, the moment when Genius alights on the artist's soul. However, the creative impulse is depicted in a restrained manner. The painter is not presented here as an initiator of conflict or a conqueror, but as a fascinated, if confused, observer trying to accustom himself to the ways of the world . . . The eyes almost follow the angle of the head, yet glance slightly to one side, a device which the artist uses to indicate tension around the head and body, as if restraining the figure's impulse to move towards the observer. In the treatment of light and shade two contrasting elements may be discerned. In some places the figure stands out quite clearly from the dark background; in others it actually merges into the background so completely that it is impossible to make out where the figure ends and the background begins. This technique creates the impression that real life is unfolding before the observer and that the figure actually exists in the surrounding space.

Orest Kiprensky *Portrait of E.V. Davydov* 1809   >

Orest Kiprensky *Self-portrait with Pink Kerchief* 1806/09

Orest Kiprensky *Self-portrait with Brushes behind the Ear*
1806/09

Kiprensky, as depicted in this self-portrait, reveals a somewhat contemplative character. The work invites comparison with certain portraits by Runge, a German contemporary of Kiprensky's, whose philosophical and meditative qualities consistently express the specifically national character of German Romanticism. Although Kiprensky and Runge do have a certain amount in common, the Russian's work, unlike Runge's, contains no symbolic or allegorical subtext – Kiprensky has a much more immediate and spontaneous relationship with reality. He entrusts his subject – in this case himself – to the experience of real life, and for this reason portrays himself in a realistic context and a down-to-earth situation.

In his self-portraits Kiprensky reveals different aspects of himself. In the self-portrait with a pink kerchief, painted at the same time as the one with paintbrushes, he depicts himself in more traditional guise, not at a moment of creative impulse or self-confrontation in front of a mirror, but face to face with the observer, with whom his pose gives him the opportunity to establish a link, even some sort of spiritual contact. The link is a weak one, admittedly; interested though the subject is in the external world and the observer, a considerable distance still separates him from them. We sense that Kiprensky is admiring himself in this portrait, but not to the point of dissipating his energies; on the contrary, he jealously preserves his spiritual potential. The spiritual integrity, artistry and harmony evident in this self-portrait are especially attractive. The harmony, in particular, is revealed in the equilibrium of all the varied elements of the picture. Thus, the relationship of light and shade is one of calm and gentle transformation; the use of colour is extremely complex, with olive-green and gold tints juxtaposed, separated and mixed together. There is a liberal use of texture, with Kiprensky's broad brush-strokes easily visible; in some places the paint is laid on thickly, in others lightly and thinly. These blendings of colours and textures deliberately exclude the possibility of sharp contrast – hence the all-pervading sense of balance.

After the completion of this important painting Kiprensky began to devote all his attention to drawing. Some of his best graphic portraits date from the years between 1810 and 1820. The majority are in Italian pencil; occasionally he worked in pastel, chalk and watercolour. Among his sitters were friends and acquaintances, veterans of the Napoleonic campaigns in Europe, writers and poets. Some of the best of these portraits are those of A.R. Tomilov, E.I. Chaplitz, N.V. Kochubey (all 1813), N.M. Murabyov and K.N. Batyushkov (both 1815).

1 **Orest Kiprensky** *Portrait of the Poet Alexander Pushkin* 1827

2 **Silvester Shchedrin** *In the Environs of Sorrento near Castellammare* 1828

3 **Silvester Shchedrin** *New Rome* 1825

4   **Silvester Shchedrin** *Vine-covered Veranda* 1828

5 Alexei Venetsianov
Self-portrait 1811

6 Grigori Soroka
Portrait of Elizabeth Miliukova
Late 1840s

7 **Vasily Tropinin** *Portrait of the Artist's Son c.* 1818

8   **Alexei Venetsianov** *Spring Ploughing* 1820s

9   **Alexei Venetsianov** *Harvest Time: Summer* 1820s >

10   **Alexei Venetsianov** *The Morning of a Landowner's Wife* 1823

The graphic portraits are very different from the oils described earlier. Kiprensky successfully conveys the passing mood of his sitters, who are shown engaged in some activity and in a specific context. The drawings share a common graphic technique, characterized by a mix of thick, bold strokes and slim, elegant lines; a rich range of shades of black on white paper; and great freedom and variety in the treatment of detail. The portraits established drawing, which had been seen hitherto as a medium for sketches and preliminary drawings, as an independent branch of art.

Kiprensky never again reached the artistic pinnacles of his early years. It was not that his development as an artist ceased, but he only rarely achieved the profundity of his early portraits. The Romantic mood dominates his later work. In his portraits of Zhukovsky and Uvarov, both painted in 1816, before his departure from Russia, and in that of Golitsyn, painted in Italy in 1819, the sitters appear to have been assigned specific roles in advance, Zhukovsky as poet, Uvarov as a young man in high society, Golitsyn as aristocratic traveller and philosopher. Their poses, facial expressions, dress, surroundings and background all match their roles.

Many of Kiprensky's Romantically inspired paintings of the 1820s may be considered as masterpieces of Russian art, among them the portraits of E.S. Avdulina (1822) and Alexander Pushkin (1827). The Avdulina portrait is a fascinating blend of two contrasting tendencies: openly Italian influences (Italian classical art greatly impressed Kiprensky after his arrival in Rome) and the general Romantic idea, which itself contains elements of Biedermeier. This portrait has often been compared to Leonardo's *Gioconda*. It can indeed be seen as a kind of paraphrase of Leonardo's famous work, even though Avdulina is depicted as an archetypal woman of the Romantic era, who has lovingly cherished her inner world, a fragile and unstable world, as liable to sudden destruction as a flower whose petals fall from their stem onto a window-sill. Avdulina is immersed in her own emotions, whose complexity is hidden from the outsider's gaze. It is impossible to penetrate the secrets of her soul, but Kiprensky offers a kind of oblique access to it. We imagine Avdulina wavering between resignation to her duties and escape into her dreams, and we sympathize with her own recognition that she is beginning to fade.

1   The portrait of Alexander Pushkin was painted at a troubled period in the lives of both poet and artist. After the failure of the rebellion of December 1825, the soul of educated Russia was plunged into despair. The prospects for social harmony seemed to have vanished for ever. Pushkin deeply mourned the fate of the Decembrists, as the (mainly aristocratic) revolutionaries were known, for he had numbered many of them among his personal friends. Five of the plotters were executed and many others exiled to Siberia. Kiprensky, in his own way, was also acutely uncomfortable in the reactionary Russia of those days. He had returned from Italy, but felt himself a fugitive in his own country, and was on the verge of leaving for Europe yet again (as, in fact, he did, in 1828).

It was at this point that he met Pushkin and painted his richly evocative portrait. The poet is shown in typical Romantic stance, his arms folded on his breast, his gaze directed somewhere to the side. He seems to be frozen in mid-movement, as if attempting to restrain some impulse. There is an air of casual elegance and society chic about his pose. Draped in his 'Childe Harold' cape, he could almost be taken for any ordinary denizen of the literary salons. Indeed some of Pushkin's contemporaries disliked the portrait, maintaining that Kiprensky had turned him into a dandy, but behind this image a very different mood may be sensed, a melancholy rooted in the impossibility of solving the conundrums of existence. What we observe in this painting is society itself in the process of abandoning its careless egoism, beginning to gain insight, through Pushkin's eyes, into the fundamental problems of life. This is the message we should read in Pushkin's expression, a message which liberates the painting from its specific context and enables it to achieve a universal significance.

Perhaps the most important feature of this work is not the pictorial energy concentrated in the canvas (as in Kiprensky's early portraits) but a luminous quality radiating from the man himself, from his body and his accessories. It is at its most intense in his eyes, his face and the fingers of his right hand. Light shines from his clothes (a striped plaid, a bow and collar) and even from the background, illuminating the surrounding space. The delicate lines of his silhouette, of his clothes, his features and hair create an impression of transparency and fragility, lending a brittle quality to the poet and the objects around him, and imbuing all with a sublime spirituality.

Few of Kiprensky's later works are equal to the portraits of Avdulina and Pushkin. His artistic fate was no less cruel than the tragedy of his personal life. Naturally, he developed and improved his art; he was an active painter in intimate contact with those around him, and he refused to rest on his laurels or exploit the fruits of his early creative achievements. But his progress was constantly bedevilled by setbacks. Consider, for example, his small, semi-genre paintings of Italian boys and girls holding bunches of flowers or baskets of fruit. These pictures stand at the threshold of Russian salon art, which found its themes and motifs in Italy and flourished there during the 1830s and 1840s, supplying an undemanding and undiscriminating public with pictures of, for exam-

Orest Kiprensky *Portrait of E.I. Chaplitz* 1813

Orest Kiprensky *Portrait of E.S. Avdulina* 1822

ple, lovely girls playing the tambourine or drinking wine during the October festival. Kiprensky sometimes indulged this taste but equally often found the strength to resist the temptation. Probably no other great Russian painter was so vulnerable to extremes in his art. His various periods differ in significance, spells of success being followed by decline. Apart from his early years, his career is a story of superb works of art alternating with productions of undoubted mediocrity. This inconsistency is rooted in his unusual personality. He was an impulsive, impressionable man prone to sudden enthusiasms, prolonged passions and vanity. His works are so closely related to his personality that every aspect of the man may be found in one or other of them. Living for and in art, Kiprensky embodied the Romantic ideal and the historic inevitability of its appearance in Russia's cultural development. The history of art proves that the most significant art appears when the individual peculiarities of the artist cross the path of history. This was the case with Kiprensky.

No other portraitists of Kiprensky's stature emerged in Russia at the beginning of the nineteenth century, but one or two of his contemporaries deserve a mention. Varnek, for example, conscientiously learnt the lessons of the academic school as well as the techniques of Romantic portraiture and used them to produce a number of routine – even hack – works.

The work and personality of Alexander Orlovsky (1779–1832) were much more interesting and varied. He was Polish, and spent his youth in Poland, where he studied under the French painter Norblen. At the beginning of the nineteenth century he moved to St Petersburg, where he spent the rest of his life. Orlovsky brought to Russia some of the motifs and techniques of Western European Romanticism. On the other hand, strongly influenced by Russian art and culture, he gradually weaned himself from the old and accustomed himself to the new.

His usual subjects in the early St Petersburg years were equestrians, shipwrecks and military bivouacs. He originally based these paintings (in oil, watercolour or gouache) on real-life experiences and memories of his own, but as their popularity increased he began to produce them by rote to satisfy demand. He then turned to new subjects, mainly in drawings. Among his favourite themes were street scenes, with prisoners in transit begging passers-by for charity under the indifferent eye of their escorts; fops, dressed to kill, galloping by in horse-drawn cabs; carts, standing together near a market; horse-races on the icebound Neva; and coaching inns. Collectors particularly prized his single-figure compositions of a Bashkir or a Tartar in authentic national costume, on horseback or on foot, armed with a bow and a quiverful of arrows. The drawings contain more than a hint of the exotic, and reveal Orlovsky's irrepressible curiosity about different aspects of life. They recall those sketches by foreign artists who travelled in Russia and recorded with relish any titillating scenes they came across, such as a mountainous old woman in a bath-house, or methods of corporal punishment. The so-called 'costume genre', which flourished in the late eighteenth and early nineteenth centuries, spawning all sorts of albums, prints and lithographs, is in the same tradition. Orlovsky differed from his predecessors in his liberated approach and his refusal slavishly to obey the rules of any genre. His lively interest in the world around him was very much in tune with the times and prepared the ground for genre painting, whose preoccupation with everyday life did not, apparently, conflict with his Romantic aspirations.

Orlovsky was a very innovative caricaturist. Until he entered the field the chief influences on Russian caricature had been, first, the English tradition; and second, *lubki*, cheap prints illustrating themes from native myth and folklore. These were at the peak of their popularity during the war against Napoleon. The element of grotesque was only introduced into caricature with the advent of the Romantics. Orlovsky was always on the lookout for the new and the curious, emphasizing and exaggerating any unusual physical or psychological features he could find – or sometimes invent! – in his subjects. Many famous literary names among his acquaintances fell victim to his pen, as well as architects (Quarenghi, for example) and government officials. Orlovsky's free spirit and his independence of any official institutions – he never belonged to the Academy of Fine Arts – enabled him to exploit branches of art more closely associated with amateur art and dilettantism, than with the established schools.

Orlovsky's finest works, however, are indubitably his portrait drawings (mainly in Italian pencil), which almost reach the standard of excellence set by Kiprensky. Admittedly, Orlovsky's drawings tend to strive for effect, as, for instance, in his self-portrait of 1809, done in charcoal, sanguine and chalk. The artist appears to be in a state of some restlessness and agitation, perhaps even fury. His head is sharply angled to one side, the frowning face distorted with wilful tension. All these features reveal Orlovsky's own intensity of feeling. His emotional state is directed outwards, penetrating the surrounding space and destroying the harmonious relationship between man and his world.

Some of his other portraits, in which the 'Romantic idea' is less obvious than in the 1809 self-portrait, also succeed in recreating his subjects' personalities and conveying their hidden emotions and innermost impulses. All told, Orlovsky made a great contribution to

Alexander Orlovsky *Self-portrait* 1809

Russian portrait drawing of the early nineteenth century.

Neither Kiprensky nor Orlovsky nor Varnek was a professional landscape-painter and they hardly ever painted 'pure' landscape, but this genre was also much influenced by the Romantic movement and was second in importance only to portraiture in the 1830s. The harbinger of this development was Silvester Shchedrin (1791–1830), who, accurately speaking, belongs to the generation which followed Kiprensky's. It was he who initiated the 'Italian period' which, in the work of Mikhail Lebedev and later Alexander Ivanov, produced the best of Russian landscape-painting until the middle of the nineteenth century. This branch of art had flourished vigorously at the end of the eighteenth century in the elegant views (*veduti*) of the 'Palmyra of the North' (St Petersburg), in picturesque canvases by Silvester's uncle, Simeon Shchedrin, who celebrated the 'English parks' attached to the great residences round the capital, and in Mikhail Ivanov's accurate and matter-of-fact records of different regions of the country.

The turn of the century, however, saw the onset of a period of stagnation which only dramatic change could overcome. The first signs of such a change were in the air when Silvester Shchedrin was a student of the St Petersburg Academy. His early work was in the main-

stream of accepted tradition and gave little hint of the
originality to come. He was particularly adept, for
example, at exploiting 'coulisses' (the elements arranged
round the sides of a composition so as to direct the eye to a
central point) in his paintings, and at organizing fore-,
middle- and background perspective. Other classical
techniques included the combination of browns, greens
and blues, and the use of 'staffage' (the small figures used
to animate a landscape) to bring out the background.

His style began to change when, after the award of a
bursary by the Academy in 1819, he went to Italy, never
to return. That country had already swallowed up
Kiprensky, who arrived in Rome three years before
Shchedrin; Ivanov would be devoured not long after. In
those days Italy was the dream of Russian painters, and
for a number of reasons. First, the St Petersburg
Academy of Fine Arts worshipped at the shrine of
Raphael; second, a sojourn in Italy was an indispensable
part of the study of genuine Roman antiquity; third, a
painter could test his skills against masterpieces which
had gained universal approval; and, most important of
all, Italy seemed to be the very embodiment of beauty,
where Man could live in perfect harmony with a bright
and colourful Nature. Artists of every kind shared this
view of Italy as the ideal country; Pushkin, too, dreamt of
Italy, though he never succeeded in going abroad, and
Gogol felt it to be his natural home.

Shchedrin's life there was a happy, creative and
productive one. His paintings were much sought-after,
and he spent his earnings generously, perhaps too
generously, on all the pleasures that life had to offer. It
may have been this self-indulgence, rather than the fever
unsuccessfully treated by his Italian doctors, which led to
his early death, but he used his potential to the full, and
his death symbolizes the demise of early Romanticism in
Russian painting. Shchedrin's correspondence, a marvellous source for anyone wishing to gain insight into the life
of the Russian painters in Italy, describes a zestful life
over which premature death never managed to cast a
shadow. He was a dutiful son who wrote regularly to his
family (his father, Fyodor, was a celebrated sculptor). In
his letters, always centred round some amusing event, he
regaled them with a detailed and vivid account of his life
in Rome and Naples. He was delighted by carnival, loved
the theatre and never tired of the openness and spontaneity of Italian life.

In the 1820s, when Shchedrin was already a mature
artist, most of the European schools were experiencing a
rebirth of landscape painting. In England, Constable was
the first European painter actually to paint in the open
air. In Italy, there was a whole school, under Posilippo,
whose members concentrated their attention on a careful
and consistent study of their natural surroundings. The

Silvester Shchedrin *Coliseum* 1819

young Corot, too, was travelling round Italy in the 1820s,
and may well have worked alongside Shchedrin. German
Romantic landscape artists, especially Caspar David
Friedrich, were preoccupied with artistic challenges far
removed from *plein air* painting, although one painter of
the following generation, Blechen, did restore Germany's
lost mastery of chiaroscuro. Shchedrin is part of this
general pattern, and by no means inferior to his Italian,
German and French contemporaries. He numbered
German and Italian, as well as Russian art-lovers among
his clientele, whose enthusiastic support enabled him to
concentrate on, and perfect, a subtle use of colour and
perspective, and thus to keep pace with the general
development of European painting.

Shchedrin's very first work in Rome was significant in
itself. As he wrote in one of his letters home: 'The
Coliseum has commissioned me to paint its portrait!' To
fulfil this 'commission' he set up his studio in the attic of a
house opposite the Coliseum and painted a free composition at close quarters, unfettered by any a priori
requirements. It is a detailed and accurate account of the
romantic ruin, and especially of the play of light pouring
through the arches.

In the early twenties he found a subject which he was
to exploit for some time on account of its popularity with

the public. This was the waterfalls at Tivoli outside Rome. Several variations reveal the painter's aims and intentions. He does not sink into the elegiac fantasy usually indulged in by poets contemplating the cascades, nor is it the drama of the scenery which excites his painterly eye. He prefers to express his joyful admiration of nature's beauty and harmony, rather than to abase himself before the mighty power of the falls. The sharp drop of the cliff, with its covering of bushes and grass, the varying surfaces of stone and the foam on the water – these are the aspects of Tivoli that fascinate him, not as specific examples of natural phenomena, but as evidence of the unity and freedom of nature. Nevertheless, there is a somewhat parochial quality about the Tivoli paintings. He is still working in the conventional range of browns; the masters whose work he had copied in museums seem to be breathing over his shoulder.

In the mid 1820s his work changed drastically, with a painting entitled *New Rome*, of which about ten versions remain extant. He paints Rome 'from the inside', as a living city rather than a museum piece. The painting does feature St Peter's basilica and the medieval Castel Sant'Angelo, but they are not the focus of attention. The basilica seems to hover above the city, where life runs its normal course. Fishermen are catching fish in the Tiber from the quay, as well as from rowing boats and a long wooden barge. A cart has arrived from somewhere. Men and women scurry about, and these figures are not 'staffage', merely animating the landscape. The presence of a genre element does not mean that it is a genre painting (though Shchedrin's human figures, by occupying a dominant position in the pictorial space, sometimes do betoken the transformation from landscape to genre). What is significant in *New Rome* is the attention Shchedrin pays to the living aspects in the scene, natural as well as human. It is the relationship between light and air that he attempts to convey. In one of his letters he describes his desire to dispense with brown museum tints, and to master the range of 'cool' colours. After long observation and concentrated on-site study, Shchedrin did succeed in creating the complex interplay of grey and silvery tints which dominate the picture. These colours reproduce the subtle movement of the waves of the Tiber and evoke the shimmering humidity which envelops and blurs both people and objects. It is difficult to say with certainty whether Shchedrin achieves the full *plein air* effect in *New Rome*. Much depends on one's definition of this quality, which became so crucial during the nineteenth century. Shchedrin offers us his own definition, based on a deep understanding of the way colour is determined by light and air.

He spent the last fifteen years of his life mainly in Naples. He painted embankments, bays (for example

Silvester Shchedrin *Aqueduct at Tivoli* 1822

Sorrento), and vine-covered verandas with the sea stretching into the distance beyond. His landscapes always feature a strip of land or water in the foreground, as if to enable the observer to relish life in this paradise on earth. The intoxicating and languorous beauty of Italy became Shchedrin's main inspiration. There are no vast spaces to arouse the soul and transport us into other worlds. Solitude here leads not to despair, but to a sense of oneness with the universe. His Naples paintings may lack the formal attributes of Romanticism, but they surely reveal the Romantic mentality which alone could so truly reveal nature to man. Nature serves not simply as a background to human life and history: men and nature are destined for each other and remain forever entwined.

Shchedrin was the first Russian landscape painter to grasp the true essence of nature. The 'sweet and charming' themes of his later work led to yet more changes in his technique. He returned to warm, even hot tints, and his palette became brighter and more intensive. He often made use of contrast, for example drawing the dark outline of a figure or a rock in the Bay of Naples against a background of evening sky lit up by a dramatic sunset. The compositions of his paintings also reveal his predilection for contrast and dynamic action. They are frequently based on a diagonal, as in several versions of

Silvester Shchedrin *Moonlit Night in Naples* 1828

4 the *Vine-covered Veranda* (1828), where the motif of movement towards the background is emphasized, first by the diagonal positioning of the veranda from left to right, second by the alternating strips of sun and shade on the ground, and finally by the unbounded space stretching into the distance. Warm colours and tones dominate the 'Veranda' paintings. Shchedrin particularly likes to direct the eye to a splash of red of some sort (more often than not, a hat or a fragment of clothing on a traveller resting under the shade of a tree), but the range of colours used throughout the painting prepares us for that red splash. Yellows, oranges and pinks seem to be gathered from the four corners of the canvas as if intending to meet at the small area of red, the focus of all the colours in the painting. The return to warm colours did not mean that the *plein air* quality of Shchedrin's mid-1820s paintings was lost. On the contrary, his later works give an especially convincing account of light and air themselves, and of aerial perspective.

Shchedrin became more interested in dramatic and striking settings towards the end of his career. The last motif to preoccupy him was *Moonlit Night in Naples*, of which he painted a number of versions. This subject introduced a new element, i.e. a spectacular contrast between two sources of light: the moon, and the campfire on the shore. This type of contrast was to become a hallmark of the new Romantic movement, especially as expressed in Maxim Vorobiev's innumerable paintings of moonlit nights, storms and lightning. Shchedrin stopped at the threshold of late Romanticism. Three years after his death Karl Briullov's painting *The Last Day of Pompeii* crossed that threshold. It is the archetypal late Romantic work. Shchedrin's *oeuvre* at the end of the 1820s contains little internal conflict or confusion. He was still bound by a certain Romantic contemplativeness, but we may consider that his death saved him from having to make a difficult choice, namely: whether to ally himself with the new tendency within the Romantic movement, or to become gradually an anachronism, remaining faithful to the original ideas of that hidden Romanticism which spurned rebellion, conflict and the destruction of the harmony between Man and the Universe.

3 Early Realism

There was no outright conflict between the various movements in Russian painting in the first half of the nineteenth century. Kiprensky did not denounce classicism; on the contrary, he had come under its influence, as his diploma-painting for the Academy shows. Orlovsky, who did oppose the Academy, had no argument with its 'style' but simply needed his artistic freedom. Shchedrin disliked the Russian classical landscape painter Matveev, whom he visited shortly after his arrival in Rome, but he expressed his antipathy only in a letter to his parents. Each of the three painters mentioned above had to free himself from the shackles of classicism with a greater or lesser degree of continuity, depending on the kind of artistic challenge each man set himself.

Early Realism, which may be described as the Russian version of Biedermeier, came upon the artistic scene in the 1820s in an equally peaceful manner. Its formation was inseparable from the establishment of 'genre' in Russian painting and drawing. Genre began to be explored at the very beginning of the nineteenth century, insinuating itself into a number of other styles before establishing itself in its own right. Thus, it is to be found in Shchedrin's landscapes and Kiprensky's portraits of Italian boys. The genre drawings of Orlovsky, the Romantic, were the result of his observations of everyday life. Even Kiprensky, early in his career, sometimes painted peasant scenes, as witness his study of a barge-hauling gang (*burlaki*) on the river, a theme which was to become very widespread throughout Russian art. Tropinin mixed genre with portrait-painting. It was rather as though genre were poised for an independent role in Russian painting. The final and decisive steps in this direction were taken by Venetsianov in the 1820s, and later by his many followers. Tropinin, Venetsianov and his students generally make up that group of nineteenth-century Russian painters associated with early Realism, which coexisted without conflict with other styles. There are, for example, elements of classicism to be found in Venetsianov. He himself wished to become an Academician at the St Petersburg Academy of Fine Arts, that stronghold of classicism, where he hoped to put his own system of teaching into effect. Tropinin borrowed generously from Sentimentalism, and some of his portraits display Romantic features.

Early Realism began to come into its own in the early 1820s, the decade which saw Tropinin's and Venetsianov's work mature. They were already past their first youth and into their forties when their hour finally struck. Vasily Tropinin (1776–1857) had a particularly hard life. He was a serf until the age of 45. Soon after beginning his studies at the St Petersburg Academy of Fine Arts he was recalled by his owner, who kept him on his estate for many years, during which time his talent developed very slowly. He paid occasional visits to St Petersburg, where he availed himself of the opportunity to copy classical paintings and drawings; otherwise he painted purely from life. When he was living in serfdom he was obliged to fulfil the duties not only of a painter, but also of a gardener and valet. Those of his early paintings – originals and copies – which have survived bear the mark of the Sentimentalist tradition. While still at the Academy he painted a picture of a boy weeping at the death of his bird. Early in the new century he painted *A Young Girl from Podol* (a town in central Russia), a moving portrayal of beauty and piety. He also proved himself faithful to the eighteenth-century traditions in his studies for a group portrait of his master's family, and for a double portrait of the Morkov brothers and Natalya Morkova, both dating from the year 1813.

By the 1820s Tropinin had evolved his own creative principles. In general he remained a portraitist, but his portraits were enriched by elements of genre. He also painted a number of genre paintings which were semi-portraits in character. This blend of genre and portraiture became his hallmark, but it should be emphasized that Tropinin painted hardly any purely genre paintings. His mature portraits from the 1820s and 1830s are associated with his life in Moscow, where he enjoyed wide acclaim and popularity. Tropinin suited Moscow perfectly: its inhabitants, especially the middle-ranking nobility, might have been born to be painted by him. In a sense he was the antithesis of Kiprensky; Tropinin was interested first and foremost in the character of his sitters, and only secondarily in their mood and state of mind. His Moscow

(*far left*) **Vasily Tropinin**
*Portrait of
K.G. Ravich* 1825

(*left*) **Vasily Tropinin**
*Portrait of
Natalya Morkova* 1813

Vasily Tropinin *Portrait of Bulakhov 1823*

portraits are always simple, almost homely. His subjects reveal little sense of inner turmoil and appear to experience no spiritual excitement, totally unconcerned, apparently, with any of the profound questions confronting the rest of mankind. They are so solidly ensconced in their chairs or armchairs that we sense they must have been leading the same comfortable lives for many years; they are positively bathed in peace and quiet. These portraits are not only an accurate depiction of real people but a faithful rendering of the entire milieu in which the sitters exist and have their being. It matters little that there are few telling details to be found in these paintings – the characters themselves reveal everything we need to know about them. We can almost follow Tropinin's thoughts simply by scrutinizing their clothes and head-gear, as well as the books, guitars or other articles that surround them.

Among Tropinin's best works are the portraits of his son (*c.* 1818), Bulakhov (1823), Ravich (1825), Pushkin (1827) and Zubova (1834). The portrait of his son is remarkable for its expressive power and pictorial quality. The boy is shown from the chest up, sharply turned to one side, as if the painter had caught him in the very act of turning. The right side of the head and shoulders are brightly lit by sunlight, which introduces an element of casual liveliness. The boy's uncombed and dishevelled hair sparkles in the warm rays of the sun. The various

7

parts of the composition are defined by a sumptuous use of light and shade.

Tropinin generally painted his subjects *en déshabille*. Bulakhov, for example, wears a soft blue dressing gown trimmed with fur. He sits at an angle, looking at us in a friendly sort of way. The good humour of the man, as well as a certain placid thriftiness, are conveyed by his genial expression. Tropinin concentrates his attention on the ordinary flow of real time in which the life of his subject is unfolding. There he sits, having closed the book he is holding in his hand; he turns his head to us and fixes us with his gaze, but there is no indication that this movement is the culmination of some crucial action.

The portrait of Ravich is a rare example of Tropinin's emphasis on the sense of time. Ravich clearly expresses his fascination with the life around him. He seems to be engaged in a lively conversation with us; his eyes sparkle in his mobile and expressive face.

Even when the model (or the painter's self-imposed artistic challenge) demands a Romantic interpretation, that interpretation is modified by Tropinin's characteristic inclusion of everyday detail. This applies particularly to the portrait of Alexander Pushkin, done at the same time as Kiprensky's portrait of the poet. Like all Tropinin's models, Pushkin is shown wearing a dressing gown, though he is, admittedly, in a moment of inspiration. The concentration in his face, and the sharp turn of his head, are in some contrast to the relaxed, domestic setting. His poetic soul seems totally at variance with the homely dressing gown.

Tropinin's interest in the atmosphere and physical conditions in which people lead their lives culminated in the development of a particular style which combined portrait with genre. In his varied range of paintings of guitar players, and of girls making lace or doing gold embroidery, the portrait is usually rather generalized and lacking in individual features. However, he always depicts some action – however unambiguous and simple. These works show particularly clearly how close he was to the Sentimentalist tradition of the earlier, eighteenth-century generation, although in Tropinin's case the tendency towards genre is more marked.

Tropinin's best-known version of *Lacemaker* (1823) shows how little now separated genre from portraiture. To judge from a surviving preliminary study for this work, he began with a rather realistic drawing of the young woman whom he was to idealize in the finished painting. He erased her blemishes, making her face more attractive and her figure more rounded and feminine, but it is still a recognizable portrait of the girl in the preliminary drawing. The genre theme is also given a slightly novel twist. Tropinin describes every detail of her method of working the lace; the result is almost as realistic as a still-

Vasily Tropinin *Lacemaker* 1823

life. But there is no conflict in the painting, no message of any sort; indeed, had Tropinin attempted to convey such a 'subtext', he would have destroyed the portrait character of the picture and transformed it into a genre work.

Such a mix of styles – in this case portrait, genre and still-life – is typical of the early Realistic period in Russian painting. Works of this sort frequently included an element of landscape as well, never fully exploited, just hinted at in a somewhat schematic way. A similar syncretism is to be found in the work of Venetsianov and his students. It is typical of 'Russian Biedermeier', which was based on a mixture of different styles and genres.

Tropinin continued working until the 1850s. His *oeuvre* played an important part in the establishment of the Moscow-based tradition of painting. Many aspects of the Moscow approach to teaching painting were developed under his influence. The Moscow School of Painting, Sculpture and Architecture was founded around the middle of the last century. In many ways the antithesis of the St Petersburg Academy of Fine Arts, it was renowned for its democratic ethos and strong sympathy with Realism, and its forward-looking character owes much to Tropinin.

All the same he was no more than a transitional figure along the road to Realism, whose main champion was Alexei Venetsianov (1780–1847). Venetsianov was an ordinary civil servant, a land surveyor and draughtsman, who originally took up painting as a hobby when he was in his twenties. He moved from Moscow to St Petersburg (probably studying under the painter Borovikovsky) where he quickly filled some large gaps in his artistic education. He was appointed to the Academy, and, following his self-portrait and a portrait of Golovachevsky (an elderly professor at the Academy) he himself became an Academician at the age of thirty. He produced no works of particular interest to the history of Russian art during the first twenty years of the century. During this time Venetsianov lived and worked as if in anticipation of future success. He became interested in Romantic portraiture and in caricature, a field in which some people discern pointers to his future development, especially as it was in caricature that he had his first artistic confrontations with reality. He even attempted history painting, a genre quite alien to his talents.

In all these fields of endeavour, however, he was working against the grain of his true artistic nature. The Romantic mood was not to his taste, caricature divided him from his own poetic approach to the interpretation of reality and, although he never lost his interest in history painting, it too was alien to him. He was born to be a genre painter, and genre painting was waiting for its hour to strike. The first traces were already discernible in the eighteenth century. An illustration of this tentative beginning is a single painting by I. Firsov, entitled *The Young Artist*, which took contemporary French genre painting as its model. Other examples of this 'pre-genre' are two works by M. Shibanov, *Arranging a Marriage* and *The Peasant's Midday Meal*, both painted in the historical manner. There were also drawings by I. Ermenev, remarkable for their sharp critique of society, and various accurate records and descriptions of street life by a number of foreign artists. These isolated works do not add up to a movement, and for this reason we cannot describe genre as having established itself in the eighteenth century. That would have been impossible in the rigid, conservative Russia of the time. The nation was not yet prepared to change the conventional and ceremonious character of Russian life. Its view of the world was still encumbered by old ways of thinking, which obstructed understanding of the simple verities of human existence. Not until Russia had suffered the tragedy of a great war and was already past the first flush of victory would she permit the themes of everyday life to become a fit subject for art.

Although, as we have said, genre painting had been waiting too long to come into its own, it was now in a position to benefit from some of the styles which had overtaken it. Portrait, landscape and still-life painting were all part of the 'memory' of genre, as we mentioned

above in our analysis of the work of Tropinin, and this is even more true of Venetsianov and his pupils.

This seemingly endless period of waiting suffered by painters is a phenomenon typical of nineteenth-century Russian painting. Russian art, unlike its Western European counterparts, was utterly dominated by the 'law of the generations', which imposed its own timetable on all artistic development and cruelly suppressed any such development deemed superfluous by the establishment. The 'law' was the inevitable outcome of the synthesizing character of Russian culture, which encouraged painting and literature to keep in close touch with each other as well as with everyday life, and to reflect the spiritual self-awareness of the nation as a whole. This principle held sway over painting as over other areas of Russian life.

The particular circumstances in which a branch of art develops may influence but not dictate the quality of that art. The artist will eventually make use of his talents within the styles and conventions accepted by the age he lives in. This was certainly the case with Venetsianov, whose experience, reflecting the rich and complex entanglement of classicism, Sentimentalism, Romanticism and early Realism, paved the way for genre painting. It was as though Venetsianov, like so many of his predecessors in the history of nineteenth-century Russian art, consciously exploited the peaceful co-existence of different movements, enabling himself to combine the classical concept of stability of life with a free and unencumbered understanding of its beauty.

Venetsianov's life and personality were in accord with his artistic development. Sometime after 1810 he bought a small estate in the province of Tver, where, except for wintering in St Petersburg, he spent the rest of his life. He busied himself with the daily life of his village world, a life which sometimes threatened to absorb him to the exclusion of all else. The more he immersed himself in it, the harder he strove to discern a general principle in the simplicity of rural life, namely the cycles of nature and man's eternal unity with nature.

Once settled in the country, Venetsianov began to paint subjects from peasant life. His best work dates from the 1820s and includes *The Threshing Floor* (1822–23); *The Morning of a Landowner's Wife* (1823); *Young Shepherd Sleeping* (1824); *Spring Ploughing*, and *Harvest Time: Summer*, also from this period; as well as many posed studies of individual peasants. Venetsianov himself attributed this new phase to the great impression that one particular work by the French artist François-Marius Granet had made on him. In fact, Granet's painting, of the interior of a church in a Capucine monastery in Rome, only gave a fresh stimulus to Venetsianov's quest for a satisfactory artistic idiom. His response to Granet's painting was *The Threshing Floor*

Alexei Venetsianov *The Threshing Floor* 1822–23

for which he prepared in a rather peculiar way. He had the back wall of one of his wooden barns removed, and then placed some of his serfs – for he was now a serf-owner – round the opening thus created; others were positioned at the back of the barn, near a horse. Finally, he painstakingly set about reproducing the light streaming into the interior from several directions. In *The Morning of a Landowner's Wife* he turned to the interior of his own house, portraying a lady giving her serf-girls their orders for the day. *Young Shepherd Sleeping* is a *plein air* work, depicting the early morning landscape, with nature awakening and a young shepherd still asleep by a birch tree. Subsequent paintings dealt with the themes of peasants at their seasonal labours. All his work, in other words, was derived from the life around him, and from subjects close at hand.

Not since the great icon painters had there been anything comparable to Venetsianov's contemplative and lyrical understanding of life. What was it that enabled him to achieve such harmony of form and content? Not the 'prettification' of reality indulged in by some classical painters; nor the agonizing process of conflict later to be undergone, for example, by Alexander Ivanov; nor yet the concept of catharsis following tragedy espoused by the Romantics. No, it was purely his poetic observation of truth, of beauty and of the laws of human and natural life. In Venetsianov's view there was a satisfying logic and consistency to the business of everyday life, whose various activities and phenomena could be grouped together into certain permanent categories. Venetsianov chose the most important (in his opinion) as suitable subjects for his painting. Among them were nature in its primal manifestations of earth and sky; animals and people working the land; the plants and stones covering the surface of that land; clouds; the mother and her child, a unifying symbol of the continuation of the human race;

and finally the homes of men and women. His imagination transformed his village world into a little prototype of the universe, and Man into a spokesman for the human race. Venetsianov's ambition was to describe the essence of life, and in his village he found everything he needed for the fulfilment of this task. The unique quality of his art was rooted in this desire, which determined his techniques of composition, his treatment of light and colour, and influenced his choice of subject – including his human subjects, and the way they behaved, moved, gesticulated. His motifs express the simplest elements of human activity: his people work, rest and sleep; mothers suckle their babies; young girls feed animals; children are absorbed in their play. Some, but not all, of his subjects posed, enabling him to reveal their characters in a simple and natural way.

Venetsianov tended to avoid subjects containing internal conflict or any sense of development through time, although he occasionally hinted at the possibility of a temporal approach. In one painting, entitled *Summer*, some older children, who have probably brought the baby to its mother, are standing next to her as she breastfeeds it; but Venetsianov appears to ignore this activity, presumably a thematic excuse – which could well have been dispensed with – for the main subject. He is interested not in the process of development, but in that which has already gained full embodiment and stability, as if he is thinking only in terms of complete and immutable phenomena. In *Spring*, a woman leading a horse by its bridle gives the impression of having discovered her relationship with the space around her long before the 'moment' of the painting. She steps lightly, barefoot, over the ploughed earth, occasionally glancing at her toddler sitting nearby at the edge of the field, but this episode neither detracts from nor destroys the stylized setting. There are a number of such settings in Venetsianov's work: a peasant woman holding a sickle, scythe or rake; a peasant (male or female) putting on *lapti* (bast shoes made of woven bark); an adolescent with an axe; a woman holding her baby in her arms, or breastfeeding. Venetsianov's students, whom he taught to think in similar categories, gradually extended the variety and range of acceptable settings.

There is nothing unusual in this approach. In seventeenth-century Dutch and Flemish painting, too, we find 'set' scenes, such as a Dutch courtyard, card games, fighting in the inn, music-making, or a visit from the doctor. Such Dutch and Flemish scenes, which had only recently sprung from various mythological, allegorical or theatrical sources, varied richly within each category, whereas in the case of Venetsianov and his pupils the tendency is to concentrate on their basic essence.

He (and his pupils) applied a similar concentration to their subjects' movements and gestures, which are graphic and unambiguous. He preferred to depict the body or turn of the head at a fixed angle. His models' legs and feet are always comfortably positioned for sitting, walking or standing, with special attention being paid to the way they bend or turn. Some sit with one leg folded under the other, others with legs crossed. The rhythmic element is deliberately stressed. His peasants' arms and hands always move with purpose, spread out wide, each hand holding a horse by its bridle, or else firmly grasping a sickle, axe or earthenware pitcher. Sometimes they proffer the observer a thick slice of bread, or proudly display a basket of freshly-gathered mushrooms. Even in his painting of the young sleeping shepherd – where movement of the hands is precluded by the theme itself – the boy's palm is turned outwards in a questioning gesture, as if Venetsianov is perturbed by the casual purposelessness of the hand.

When Venetsianov used Granet's *Interior of the Capucine Monastery in Rome* as a model for painting from life, he in fact gave this approach an entirely new and individual interpretation and meaning which differed fundamentally from Granet's. For Granet, pictorial space was all-important, drawing the observer into the depths of the interior and rendering the human figures subordinate. Venetsianov, however, required that his figures dominate the space and become the focus of the composition, or at least that there be equilibrium between figures and space. Only in his very first painting *à la* Granet (*The Threshing Floor*) is the balance weighted slightly in favour of space.

Sometimes, especially in the work of his later years, we do find a wide expanse of space. The composition of *Summer*, for example, is such that the lines of perspective – the shadows thrown by the barn, and a strip of unharvested rye – direct the eye deliberately into the depths of the painting. But the eye soon digresses horizontally to either side, in spite of the vertical format of the canvas. The horizontal of the raised wooden platform on which the woman sits initiates this digression, which is continued by lines drawn parallel to the terrace. They are wave-like, variously darker or lighter, now concentrated, now diffuse, and eventually lead to the line defining earth and sky. In these 'waves' space itself becomes a topic of the painting and transforms the horizontal even more convincingly into a distinctively Russian way of perceiving space.

We touch here on one of the most important aspects of Venetsianov's work. He was the first Russian painter to discover and appreciate nature in its free and pristine state. His understanding of nature was the result of a scrupulous study of the heavens and the earth. He paid great attention to the foregrounds of many of his

Alexei Venetsianov
Young Shepherd Sleeping
1824

paintings, filling them with painstakingly depicted ploughed land, grass, stones and leaves. We vividly sense the presence of the soil under its grassy cover; the soil seems to stretch endlessly into the distance, eventually breaching the bounds of the picture, because there are no 'coulisses' to hinder them. The painter comprehends this infinitude of earth, and of the space above it, not as some sort of philosophical category (as did his younger contemporary, Alexander Ivanov) but as an actual fact, indeed as the place where man lives out his life and fulfils his potential. The earth, which is man's home, also aspires to the grandeur of the universe. In Venetsianov's work these extremes merge and unite.

He never specifically painted pure landscape, being unable to conceive of nature as separate from man, and his depiction of nature cannot be considered as lyrical. His concept of the beauty of nature is fundamentally ontological, that is to say, it simply exists, independent of any concept man may have of it; it must be discovered and understood. To attribute a soul to it would be a work of supererogation, for it is animated from the very first moment of its existence. Every blade of grass, every branch of every tree and every bush possesses this spirit. There is no reason to measure nature against the state of the human mind, or to expect a response from nature to the moods of man. Here we again touch on the idea, mentioned above, of the artist achieving a profound understanding of the law of existence and then of carefully stepping back from it. Venetsianov chooses the most perfect manifestation of nature, and the one which

most purely expresses its beauty. He seeks no complex transformation of nature. He loves summer, daytime, sun and clear skies; he ignores sunsets, wind and storm. He is content when nature is silent, and indeed, nearly all his paintings are taciturn. The beauty of nature is best disclosed in silence because there should be no element of chance in nature: it should appear before us revealing only its finest qualities. Thus nature is interpreted by Venetsianov as though it were human, in a somewhat canonical manner.

His approach to interiors is closely bound up with his view of the relationship between man and nature. It was in his interiors that Venetsianov first adopted the painting from life approach. His paintings dating from the early 1820s – *The Threshing Floor*, *The Morning of a Landowner's Wife*, *Morning in the Country: the Family Drinking Tea* (which survives only as a lithograph) – also concentrate mainly on the problems surrounding this relationship and open the way to the future development of genre painting, which was to become so popular in the years between 1820 and 1850. These works were followed by some noteworthy interiors by his pupils Zelentsov, Alexeev, Tyranov, Krendovsky, Slaviansky and Soroka; and by Fyodor Tolstoy, who was independent of Venetsianov's group. Venetsianov transformed the painting of interiors, or more precisely, actually established it as a genre, by giving it a totally new meaning from that which it had in the eighteenth and early nineteenth centuries. At that time, interior painting had many of the features of architectural composition, and

Evgraf Krendovsky *Provincial Town Square* (detail) 1840s(?)

the subjects treated were palatial halls, art galleries, ceremonial staircases, large interiors of great churches and cathedrals, and all, of course, decked out in splendour. They had none of the atmosphere of a home, and were not treated by their painters as places where people actually lived. Venetsianov enriched interior painting by introducing to it the idea of private life, and democratized the genre by bringing it closer to everyday life and reducing it to simple human proportions.

The Morning of a Landowner's Wife most fully represents Venetsianov's concept of the interior genre. Here he achieved complete unity between nature, people and the objects surrounding them. Looking at this picture, we are immediately struck by the remarkable yet simple perfection of his depiction of the light streaming through the window, illuminating the figures and objects nearby. Some of the light steals into dark corners, silvering the half-shadows and lighting up the polished surface of the table which reflects the objects like a mirror. These reflections, patches of light and reflections in a mirror (so often employed by Venetsianov's pupils) convey no sense of uncertainty or transience, nor yet any lurking doubt as to the reality of the scene. For Venetsianov all these many aspects of the play of light are part of the real world, filled with a permanent and stable beauty. Light itself possesses immutable qualities. It always features in Venetsianov's paintings, spreading across a field of rye in *Summer* or rising to the sky in *Spring* or, in the *Young Shepherd Sleeping*, filling every blade of grass with a yellowish-green. But Venetsianov could not, and would not, exaggerate the effect of light to the point where it threatened to destroy the unity of the component parts of the world depicted in the painting.

For him, light was just one of the elements of nature; that is to say, it alone could not transform the world, but in conjunction with other elements gave expression to it.

Light, in an interior, penetrating through windows or open doors, unites man with nature. Venetsianov was the first painter to reproduce the effect of simply gazing through a window into a room or through the open doors of a threshing barn. A small section of landscape, seen within the frame of the door or windows, creates a kind of bridge between the interior and the exterior worlds, a bridge that contains no mystery and hides no secret.

There is another typically Russian characteristic in the composition of Venetsianov's interior scenes. His *The Threshing Floor* stretches deep into the background, parallel to the surface of the earth. In his *The Morning of a Landowner's Wife* the window, set into the back wall of the room, also increases the horizontal expanse of visible space. Venetsianov's pupils would later enthusiastically exploit the motif of a suite of rooms *en enfilade* to achieve the same end. Here we once again come across the leitmotif of extended length which we met in Venetsianov's compositions based on horizontals, and even earlier in the horizontal spread of the architecture of St Petersburg. It is worth noting that the interior theme was treated rather differently in German painting, where, as a rule, the interior of the room is enclosed and there is no access to other rooms, or to the open air and the landscape outside. Clearly, therefore, various features of Venetsianov's work embodied aspects of national artistic thinking.

It was precisely this quality that eventually brought him recognition and renown. His work was bought by collectors and patrons of the arts, he began to attract followers and was soon surrounded by pupils. The school of art associated with his name became an important factor in Russian artistic life between 1820 and 1850. He taught his students in two different locations: in St Petersburg, of course, and in Safonkovo, his estate in the country, where he gathered around him many talented peasant lads from nearby villages.

His method of teaching favoured painting from life, and only allowed for the copying of models in the studio in the final stages of the course. He made his pupils draw and paint simple objects in oils, and assigned great importance to perspective, which he took to be one of the most important elements in an artist's education, and even something of a science. All kinds of painting – genre, portraiture, landscape, interiors and still-life – were of equal importance and interest to him, the only exception being history painting. In this he differed from the policy of the St Petersburg Academy of Fine Arts, which placed history painting above all other genres.

The genre paintings of Venetsianov's pupils were neither more nor less advanced than the master's own work. They, too, avoided any hint of conflict and never depicted figures united by some common activity. The paintings were still eventless; in other words they were based on the poetic portrayal of a situation, rather than on the narration of an incident.

The work of Venetsianov's circle recalls similar developments in Western European movements, especially the German and Austrian Biedermeier schools. But the 'Venetsianovites' were a rather distinctive group. The artistic community they formed had something of the character of the medieval artisan guilds, relying more on a set of rules and principles agreed in advance than on individual manifestations of originality. As in the case of medieval art, practically every more or less competent work issuing from Venetsianov's circle possesses several good qualities. It must be stressed that this was rather unusual in nineteenth-century Russian art, where there was nearly always a yawning gap between the highest levels of achievement and the rest of the field. The value of these works derives not from the special qualities of their individual creators but from the whole tradition in which they were steeped, and from previously elaborated creative concepts. This is not, of course, to imply that there was a dearth of bright and original talent among members of the circle – it was the talented ones who achieved the marvellous simplicity and clarity of the group's most moving paintings.

Probably the most versatile member of the circle was Alexei Tyranov, who painted landscapes, portraits, interior and genre scenes as well as still-lifes. In *Studio of the Chernetsov Brothers* (1828) he combined all these genres within one canvas. There is an obvious element of portraiture in the realistic depiction of the brothers, and

Grigori Soroka *Study in Ostrovki* 1844

Alexei Tyranov *Studio of the Chernetsov Brothers* 1828

the genre element is represented by a hint of activity – one of the brothers is playing the guitar. The objects, especially the artists' palettes lying on a chair, are painted with all the detail one might expect in a still-life. Finally, as a touch of landscape, a view of the city is visible through the window, and the whole scene is imbued with a sense of tranquil lyricism.

Grigori Soroka *Fishermen: View of Lake Moldino* Late 1840s

A painting by Evgraf Krendovsky entitled *Provincial Town Square* is a typical work of the Venetsianov school. Against an unmoving background of typically Russian provincial classical architecture, a busy street scene unfolds at a slow and tranquil pace. Families, decorous couples and women carrying buckets of water stroll through the town, while hansom cabs race past with their passengers. Bullocks slowly drag wagons laden with barrels. These various groups, scattered round the square (which recalls a waste land), are all separate entities, in the sense that no common activity appears to unite them. Krendovsky scrupulously but affectionately paints in every detail of his figures, wonderfully evoking the character of this provincial crowd.

Grigori Soroka (1823–64) may justifiably be considered the most talented of Venetsianov's pupils. His life was tragic. A serf who was never granted his freedom by his master, he was only freed after the abolition of serfdom in 1861. But even then he came into bitter conflict with his landowner, over the question of the conditions under which he might buy the land he lived on. As a result he was arrested and eventually committed suicide in order to escape the humiliation of corporal punishment.

Soroka's best work was done in the 1840s, when he was still a student. He painted some marvellous canvases full of optimistic lyricism and calm expressiveness. These works include *Study in Ostrovki* (1844) and *Fishermen: View of Lake Moldino* (some time after 1845). In *Ostrovki* the objects on the table, the plain timbered floors and walls and the figure of the boy all seem to have been caressed by the painter's brush. In *Fishermen*, the surrounding area and, so to speak, the entire universe are filled to overflowing with peace and tranquillity. It took a serf, so closely linked to his homeland and so familiar with the perfect simplicity of its natural beauty, to immortalize the Russian countryside with such moving affection.

Some members of the circle broadened the boundaries of genre painting, touching on fresh and different aspects of life, depicting not only peasants but artisans and craftsmen, minor civil servants, representatives of various professions, scenes of city life, the streets of St Petersburg and provincial towns, carriers, pedlars and hawkers. By the 1840s the movement already had many adherents. Nevertheless, history painting took the leading role in Russian art in the 1830s and 1840s, and the St Petersburg Academy, the stronghold of classicism, enjoyed a new heyday. The champions of early Realism had, however, strengthened their position; in their work genre painting approached close to that turning-point which Pavel Fedotov was actually to reach in the 1840s.

6

4   The Fate of Romantic Academic Art

The third decade of the nineteenth century saw Russian history painting cast off the traditional conventions of orthodox classicism and open up new vistas to the future. Karl Briullov (1799–1852), who won renown as one of the greatest painters of his day, breathed new life into history painting. He was well known in Europe, particularly Italy, and became the first painter to earn fame for Russian art beyond the country's borders. This fame was somewhat excessive, overshadowing the very real achievements of such early nineteenth-century Russian masters as Kiprensky, Venetsianov and Shchedrin, not only abroad but in the minds of their fellow countrymen as well. Nikolai Gogol, for example, claimed that Russian painting owed its regeneration to Briullov, and considered him the *fons et origo* of its real history. Briullov's successes seem less impressive in the context of the achievements of the century as a whole, especially as his work contains elements of Russian academic and even salon art, but he undoubtedly deserves his prominent position in nineteenth-century Russian cultural life.

He was born in the same year, 1799, as Pushkin. His personality was fully in tune with the mood of independent thinking and inner liberation of the creative mind characteristic of the 'Pushkin era', as it is sometimes known. Briullov was an artist to the very marrow of his being, and his contemporaries considered him to be the true embodiment of the artistic spirit. He did everything possible to strengthen this image. He liked to lose himself in bouts of artistic inspiration, occasionally behaved somewhat capriciously, staged creative flights and indulged in fits of melancholy. His behaviour was partly genuine and partly staged. Sometimes he conducted himself in a manner which would have been incomprehensible to painters of an earlier age. He refused, for example, to paint the portrait of Nicholas I when the Emperor arrived late for his first sitting. This act was a colossal leap for Russian consciousness, a leap from the previous state of artistic subjugation into creative freedom. His personal freedom, however, was only relative, limited both by the artistic traditions then current as well as by certain pressures which official circles exerted upon

him. Nevertheless we may confidently assert that with Briullov, the social standing of painters underwent a transformation from a state of semi-servitude to the occupation of a place in the 'beau monde'.

His creative development was relatively straightforward. Everything seemed to come easily to him. The son of a master engraver, a professor at the St Petersburg Academy, he rapidly distinguished himself from his fellow students, astounding his teachers with a superb talent for drawing and an aptitude for composition. After graduating from the Academy he was sent to Italy on a scholarship, funded by the recently established Society for the Support and Encouragement of Artists (*Obshchestvo pooshchreniya khudozhnikov*). Instead of staying just a short time in Italy, however, he spent the next fifteen years there, and in the 1830s gained a reputation in that country with which he returned home. The 1820s, his Italian period, saw the first blossoming of his gifts. He was not yet weighed down by the monumental commissions or great projects which were to come his way in the future, but he was already aware of his potential as an innovator. He spent these years searching for a way to paint in a spirit of idyllic and contemplative lyricism. In this respect he very much resembles Shchedrin and Venetsianov, though in some ways he was inferior to both of them. Shchedrin, for example, was a finer painter of air and light effects. When Briullov was obliged to include such effects he used superficial techniques to solve the problem, for example keeping to the use of 'local colours' (see p. 105). As for Venetsianov, the natural and ingenuous lyricism of his paintings could never be matched by Briullov.

And yet some of Briullov's paintings from this period do have considerable merit. Take, for example, his *Italian Midday* (1827), which shows the upper body of a young woman in the act of picking grapes; or the genre scene depicting pilgrims who have entered a church and are just about to kneel. These pictures contain neither action nor conflict; indeed, in this period he rarely devoted much time or space to the narration of a simple story for the entertainment of the observer. Briullov's main aim was to celebrate the brilliance and beauty of Italian life.

A similarly idyllic mood characterizes many other of his works, inspired by various themes from Greek and Roman mythology and classical poetry. In an unfinished painting entitled *Hermione with Shepherds* (1824), an episode illustrating Torquato Tasso's poem 'Jerusalem Liberated' is treated as a pastoral scene. The family of shepherds, made up of several generations, exist in perfect accord with nature, as if in the Golden Age. Even such action-packed and dynamic subjects as *Diana and Actaeon* (1823–27) and *Gilas Lured into the Water by Nymphs*, which betoken a sad end for the participants, are interpreted by Briullov as idyllic scenes portraying various metamorphoses of the natural order.

In the 1820s Briullov was reinterpreting classicism in the Romantic idiom, and by the end of the decade he had come to the end of his youthful period, characterized by a rather simplistic and optimistic *Weltanschauung*. The first and most important indication of a new outlook on life was his masterpiece, *The Last Day of Pompeii* (1830–33), the painting which was to make him famous.

The dramatic scene is set on a huge canvas: the inhabitants of Pompeii, whom the eruption of Vesuvius has taken completely unawares, are desperately fleeing for their lives. Chariots lie overturned, their terrified horses blinded by lightning. Riders gallop away. Houses

Karl Briullov *Italian Midday* 1827

are collapsing. Two sons are trying to carry their old father to safety. A mother shelters her daughter with her body. A young woman, already dead, lies on the street, her arms outstretched, her little child still alive by her side. All men are equal in the face of approaching death. Pagans and Christians, inspired artists and common craftsmen, young and old, all become the victims of nature's fury, nevertheless preserving their human dignity before a destiny which is about to snatch their lives from them. The whole scene, recalling a sumptuous and carefully staged theatrical production, is illuminated by lightning and reflected flames. In spite of the horror there is an air of solemnity about the catastrophe.

Two contradictory concepts are combined in *The Last Day of Pompeii*. On the one hand the whole picture conveys the idea of global catastrophe, a concept which could be easily abstracted from the concrete historical event in an ancient Italian town of the first century AD and applied to all of mankind, independent of time and place. We are probably justified in assuming that the idea of catastrophe was in some sense intended to reflect the events of 1825 and the whole atmosphere of severe reaction which followed the abortive attempt to overthrow the autocracy. Indeed, Alexander Herzen – one of the most profound nineteenth-century Russian thinkers – interpreted Briullov's painting precisely along these lines. Gogol, on the other hand (in an article devoted to Briullov's masterpiece), praised the artist's loyal adherence to the ancient ideal of man as a dignified being. In fact the painting proves both Herzen's and Gogol's interpretations correct. Moreover, surviving studies of the picture reveal how the two concepts were continually competing for supremacy in the artist's mind. The sense of catastrophe prevails in some of these preliminary sketches, which are notable for their particularly dynamic quality. People's movements resemble a sort of avalanche. Themes of violent death, the inevitability of a tragic end to life, and submission to fate are dominant. The Romantic perception of space, from whose depths the crowd is being ceaselessly ejected, is the main medium through which these themes are expressed. The composition of some of the other studies, based on a pyramidal figure, is more classical and static. The victims are divided into groups which complement each other and convey a sense of rhythmical order. In the studies, Briullov consciously or unconsciously explores these contrasting approaches, and both are discernible in the finished version, which neatly avoids either extreme and presents us with a perfect compromise between the two.

In the final analysis this compromise is between classicism and Romanticism, and is an excellent illustration of the whole development of Russian history

Karl Briullov *The Last Day of Pompeii* 1830–33

painting between the 1830s and the 1860s, at the time of the emergence and establishment of Academicism. Briullov, as an innovator, was bound to make both 'good' and 'bad' discoveries. The eclectic nature of his art paved the way for major academic canvases on universal themes, as well as for a type of painting aimed at 'creating an effect', and at immersing the observer in *la dolce vita* of Italy. Nevertheless, *The Last Day of Pompeii* contained several novel elements which significantly influenced the course of Russian history painting. Briullov initiated a new interest in the portrayal of large groups. Unlike the history painting of the previous generation, *Pompeii* contains no single protagonist. Drastic social change, the historic events of the early nineteenth century and the submission of individuals to the spirit of the times all brought improvements to history painting.

Another of Briullov's innovations was his attention to documentary accuracy. Just when he was considering the idea of this great canvas, Italian archaeologists – with many of whom he was on friendly terms – were engaged in the excavation of Pompeii itself. Here, before the gaze of the astonished Europeans, was emerging an ancient city, with its architecture and remains of everyday life, all

hitherto completely unknown to scientists, writers and artists. Briullov selected a specific part of the town, in other words an actual historical location, as a background for his portrayal of the disaster. In addition he drew upon an account by Pliny the Younger of people fleeing the town. Pliny, in a letter to Tacitus, vividly and in great detail described many episodes later incorporated by Briullov into the painting. Well before Briullov, of course, painters had made attempts at historical accuracy, but their results had been rather approximate. From now on, the study of documentary sources and the search for archaeological authenticity were to become the rule in history painting.

Many other interesting features may be discerned in the painting. In spite of the rather theatrical poses and gestures of his subjects, Briullov succeeded in depicting their actions in a lively and convincing way. He copes brilliantly with the problem of showing bodies at various complicated angles, emphasizing their contrasting movements and achieving thereby a perfect balance. Nearly all his figures, incidentally, were inspired by masterpieces of Greek and Roman sculpture, or by sixteenth- and seventeenth-century Italian Academic paintings.

Briullov treated colour and light according to the strict Academic canon. His colours are lightened or darkened in order to delineate figures, clothing and objects. The contrasting effect of warm red tints, which take up a considerable portion of the canvas, and cool, light tints of yellow and grey (concentrated at the centre of the painting) derives more from an arbitrary whim of the artist than from a true relationship between light and colour. A cold, golden-hued light gives the figures the appearance of statues with shimmering marble surfaces. The sky, a mixture of red and black criss-crossed by lightning, is a borrowing from Romanticism, reinterpreted in Academic style. The Romantic approach is revealed above all in the subject itself (the patterns of movement), but as the painter gives them substance they begin to achieve a classical form which was already out of date by the 1850s. This indeterminate quality probably contributed to the success of the painting. The grandiose spectacle offered by Briullov was expressed in a language at once dramatic and familiar, a language which the educated public, very eager to participate in discussion of some of the great events and questions in the history of mankind, relished and understood.

The Last Day of Pompeii brought Briullov success and fame which were never to be repeated by his later history paintings, such as *The Death of Inez de Castro* (1834), *Genserich's Invasion of Rome* (1835) and *The Siege of Pskov by the Polish King Stephan Batori*, an episode from Russian history painted after his return from Italy. He made no aesthetic or artistic progress, attempted no new techniques of style or form, and sought no new challenges of an historical or philosophical nature. His history paintings after *Pompeii* were swamped by the flood of Academic works in the same genre which, ironically, owed their inspiration to Briullov's masterpiece.

A new tendency began to manifest itself in Briullov's work, however, in the field of portraiture. The period between 1820 and 1850 saw a certain change in the kinds of people being painted, and in methods of portraiture. Before this time portraits had been generally ceremonial and formal, differing very little from the official portraits typical of the previous century. Now, however, a certain narrative element began to be included, usually an allusion to some noble moment or special event in the life of the sitter. A typical example is Briullov's *Horsewoman* (1832). The young girl depicted was the ward of Countess Yulia Samoilova, a well known patroness of music and the arts, and a close friend of the artist himself, who painted many portraits of the Countess. The girl is posed as an Amazon, seated calmly and proudly on a rearing horse. Her blue-white dress is shot through with silver. She gazes at the observer with some condescension and disdain. A lapdog and a little girl look on from the balcony

of a villa set in the midst of greenery, and their admiring gaze serves to intensify the splendour of the scene and the dignity of the young noblewoman. This large canvas, painted in accordance with the strict rules of classical composition, but with an added ingredient of Romantic tension, would have graced the interior of any great palace. Its decorative quality is particularly well judged: the contrast between the silvery dress of the rider and the dark brown coat of the horse acts as a kind of tuning fork for this decorative quality.

In the 1820s and 1830s Briullov painted a considerable number of similarly formal portraits. The best include *Countess Yulia Samoilova Returning from a Ball* (1834) and *Countess Yulia Samoilova with her Ward, Leaving a Masquerade* (1839), in which the Countess is portrayed as a splendid, proud personality with a heightened sense of her own dignity. After about 1835, however, this formal mood in portraiture began to give way to the atmosphere of the salon, strongly influenced by the Romantic approach. Take for example the portrait of Nikolai Kukolnik (1836), a well-known writer, poet and translator. He is portrayed sitting in an isolated spot, with the ruins of a wall behind him. Also visible in the background is a strip of sea, with a patch of cloudy sky above. He leans on a cane, top hat in hand. His pose of a contemplative dreamer is rather at odds with his gaze, directed straight at the observer, and with the almost imperceptible smile playing around his thin lips. This divergence between the intended Romantic image and the actual message implied by the portrait to some extent sharpens the impact of the painting and lends it an unexpected pungency. Kukolnik gives the impression of being somehow 'above' the Romantic approach, which seems to have been imposed on him; it is as though he has agreed, for a little while, to abide by the rules of the Romantic game.

In contrast with the Kukolnik portrait Briullov's study of another writer, A.N. Strugovshchikov (1841), combines the subject's role in life with his pose and mood in a much more harmonious and integrated way. Strugovshchikov is in relaxed pose, his hands casually resting on the arms of his chair, but his gaze is troubled – evidence of some inner discord and spiritual conflict. Strugovshchikov comes over as a representative of a lost generation, unsure how and to what to apply his energies, talents and intelligence. Briullov here offers us his diagnosis of the sickness of educated Russian society: that surfeit of enforced, or voluntary, idleness which had produced a multitude of so-called 'superfluous' people.[7] The mood of the sitter, as depicted by Briullov, reflects the feelings of the painter

Karl Briullov *Horsewoman* 1832   >

Karl Briullov *Portrait of A.N. Strugovshchikov* 1841

Karl Briullov *Portrait of I.A. Krylov* 1840

12 himself, who was to evoke the very same atmosphere in his self-portrait some years later (in 1848).

This self-portrait was to become a model of the genre in the late Romantic period. Briullov portrays himself as tired, disillusioned and weary of life, sick and helpless in the face of failure. According to the memoirs of one of his students, the picture was painted under somewhat unusual circumstances. Briullov was seriously ill and grew a beard during a long spell on his sickbed. Frustrated by this unwonted inactivity, he eventually asked his pupil to stretch a canvas on the frame for him. He then rose from his bed and painted the self-portrait within a short space of time. Even in his illness he was not averse to a little play-acting, and in this self-portrait he could not resist indulging in an ostentatiously artistic gesture. The role he assumes goes well with his features, accurately reflecting his state of mind as well as the general state of Russian society towards the end of the reactionary and repressive reign of Nicholas I.

The Strugovshchikov portrait, together with the self-portrait, signified profound changes in Briullov's artistic evolution. In rejecting the formal or ceremonial setting, he also abandoned the reliance on 'local colour' favoured by the Academic school, using instead a unified range of colours. In both paintings he builds up a colour-composition based on red and red-brown tones, and gives the

smallest of hints as to the texture of the paint and his technique of achieving it by leaving rather noticeable brush marks on the canvas and marking the colour reflexes.

Briullov's late portraits contain elements of Realism along with the more familiar Romantic features. They become more 'businesslike', firmly set in a context of time and place, which are likewise interpreted in a precise and mundane manner. Character and personality are more faithfully depicted. The portraits of Vasily Zhukovsky (1837) and Ivan Krylov (1840) typify these developments, which culminated in yet another of Briullov's masterpieces, the portrait of his old friend, the Italian archaeologist Michelangelo Lanchi (1851). It was completed after Briullov, sensing his impending death, had left Russia to end his days in Italy. He depicts Lanchi, momentarily disturbed at his work, turning his head towards the observer. The old scholar exudes an air of almost grim austerity. Although Briullov retains, at least to some extent, the Romantic, elevated concept of man, the archaeologist is shown in a realistic and rather ordinary context. Period details and the description of the surroundings provide plenty of clues about when and where the portrait was painted, and even permit us to speculate as to what may have preceded the 'moment' of the portrait and what may follow. Lanchi's psychological state is in full communion with his physical being – body and soul existing together in a single dimension.

Briullov's later portraits are part of his artistic bequest to painters of the second half of the nineteenth and the early twentieth centuries. He devised, and imaginatively elaborated, a rich variety of compositions, containing a number of set elements and preordained poses, which were to retain their usefulness and importance for many years to come. His achievements in portraiture contributed to the Realist tradition rather in the same way that he enriched the development of history painting. The generation following Briullov's, especially Alexander Ivanov and Surikov, benefited greatly both from his theoretical approach and his actual working methods, which, thanks above all to his eclectic facility, helped to establish Academicism as the dominant style in Russian painting.

Round about 1850 history painting was being strongly influenced by the Academic style championed by, among others, Fyodor Bruni (1799–1875), a contemporary of Briullov's and his rival, both for fame and for recognition by the St Petersburg Academy of Fine Arts. As early as 1824, when Briullov was indulging in fantasies of the Golden Age, Bruni was also in Italy as the recipient of a scholarship from the Academy. Here he painted *The Death of Camilla, Horatio's Sister*, a work fully in accord with classical doctrine and of which Camuccini (a leader of Italian classicism to whom Russian painters as well as many others paid homage) could have been proud. *Camilla* retained a purity of style which was already becoming obsolete, adhering even more strongly to pure classicism than many historical works painted a quarter of a century earlier. The very subject – Horatio's strangely heroic act in killing his sister, who had fallen in love with an enemy of the Horatians – the bas-relief principle of the main composition and 'coulisses', and the idealized treatment of space and its background in a manner reminiscent of stage scenery, all bear witness to the classical purity of the painting.

Bruni's favourite painting, however, was his large canvas entitled *The Brazen Serpent*. This work, on which he was engaged for fifteen years (between 1826 and 1841) is considered to be his masterpiece and a major work of Russian Academic art. The subject is an episode from the Old Testament: God's visitation of a plague of poisonous snakes upon the Jews, as punishment for their rebellious

Fyodor Bruni *The Death of Camilla, Horatio's sister* 1824

Fyodor Bruni *The Brazen Serpent* 1826–41

spirit during their wanderings in the desert after the flight from Egypt. Bruni presents a dreadful scene of human suffering, horror and death. Some of the victims writhe in pain, others try desperately to escape; finally, all resign themselves to their fate. *The Brazen Serpent* is shot through with pessimism, grim foreboding and terror. The artist presses classical, romantic and naturalistic techniques into service in order to convey his meaning as vividly as possible and to render a pseudo-historical event more plausible while preserving the grandeur of the historical genre. Thus, the composition is treated classically, while the austere landscape of the chasm, in which the event is taking place, is imbued with the romantic spirit, and the physiological details of human suffering are reproduced with impassive and naturalistic realism. To heighten the desired dramatic effect Bruni uses light as if on a stage, to illuminate the separate groups of figures standing out from the gloom. This eclecticism is the main indication that the painting is a work of the Academic school. The same mix of styles is to be found in the works of other painters of the day, such as P.V. Bassin, A.T. Markov and F.A. Moller. In Moller's *The Apostle John Preaching on the Island of Patmos* (1856) eclecticism is

ubiquitous, not only in the way the composition is built up, but in its subject, motifs and in the objects chosen for inclusion. Moller was attracted by the idea of confronting Christian with antique, pagan characters, each provided with their conventional attributes and traditional iconography. Thus religious eclecticism is here apparently being pressed into support for artistic eclecticism.

The Academic style of painting consolidated its hold on the historical genre for a long time, dominating it until the 1860s, and eventually becoming an obstacle against which the coming generation would be obliged to rebel. Another academic stronghold – or refuge – was the Italian version of genre painting, in which both historical and contemporary subjects were seen through the prism of antiquity as interpreted by the Academics. The Italian beauties of the day, raising their wine-filled goblets, dancing and making music, recalled the Venuses, Amours and Bacchantes of antiquity, and the Italian October festival of the grape harvest also provided many suitable subjects. Painters liked to clothe their girls in white dresses and adorn them with colourful kerchiefs, under which the satiny sheen of their skin could be seen as they raised their gilded beakers, glittering in the sun. These

Maxim Vorobiev *Jerusalem at Night* 1830s

details are typical of the prettification obligatory in salon art, that forerunner of modern mass culture. A kind of 'luxury for the poor', associated in our day with an excessive Italianization, was the main target aimed at by the artists who contributed most to the blossoming of the Italian genre in Russian painting. This genre is the first example of a branch of Russian salon art growing away from the main stem, a branch which was to enjoy a long and productive history.

Landscape painting, which had managed to accommodate two such different styles as classicism and Romanticism, also joined the growing eclectic-academic fold. This blending of styles is especially noticeable in the work of Maxim Vorobiev (1787–1855). He was at the height of his powers in the 1830s, following in the footsteps of Silvester Shchedrin, who had flourished ten years earlier. Together with Briullov in his *Last Day of Pompeii*, Vorobiev initiated the final stage of Romanticism when he turned to themes demanding dramatic composition and the effective treatment of light. His favourite subject was the moonlit nights of St Petersburg, a theme to which he devoted a number of paintings. He was not the man, however, to restrict himself to St

Petersburg, any more than he could have settled in France or Italy after being sent there on a scholarship. Vorobiev was a travelling painter. As a Romantic, he was attracted by the Orient, which inspired *Jerusalem at Night* in the 1830s. In Italy he was fascinated by the motif of the storm, a notable example of which is to be found in *An Oak Tree Split by Lightning* (1842), and by the bright and colourful Italian sunsets, seen for instance in a painting entitled *Sunset in Rome* (1851). His method of composition consisted in combining a classical landscape with romantic effects of light and colour. In addition, he exploited the romantic liking for limitless space and for aerial perspective in support of linear perspective.

Vorobiev taught landscape painting at the St Petersburg Academy; nearly all the major landscape painters from the period between 1830 and 1860 studied under him. Among them was the well-known and extremely productive painter of seascapes, Ivan Aivazovsky (1817–1900), whose work spans almost the entire century. His favourite subjects were raging seas and scenes of shipwreck. *The Ninth Wave* (1850), one of his most famous works, refers to the belief among Russian seamen that the ninth wave is the most powerful and destructive.

Ivan Aivazovsky *The Ninth Wave* 1850

Aivazovsky's paintings are immediately effective, and very colourful, even if they do sometimes tend to deliberate overstatement.

11 Three other pupils of Vorobiev, the brothers G. and N. Chernetsov and Mikhail Lebedev, had little in common either with their teacher or with Aivazovsky. The Chernetsovs depicted modest landscapes in various parts of the Russian Empire – the mountains of the Caucasus, the banks of the Volga River and a number of provincial towns; they are also known for their paintings of military parades in St Petersburg. Their work is not obviously Romantic and is actually more akin to Biedermeier, its simplicity and spontaneity placing the brothers nearer to the Venetsianov circle.

Lebedev (1811–37) was a very talented landscape painter whose death at the age of 26 cut his career tragically short. He studied under Vorobiev at the Academy and went to Italy on a scholarship in the 1830s, where he continued in the tradition of Shchedrin's Italian landscapes, rather than joining the trend towards late Romanticism. In the short period he spent in Italy he rapidly acquired the techniques of *plein air* painting, thereby freeing himself from the limitations of the old, stylized treatment of colour and light, and exploring with

growing confidence the relationship between an object and its surroundings. He showed almost no interest in distant views or limitless space (unlike Alexander Ivanov), preferring to focus his attention on the foreground and often composing a sort of interior within his landscape.

This approach is illustrated by such paintings as *Path in Albano* (1836) and *In Guigi Park* (1837), among others. The perspective provided by a road or alley, together with the interplay of light and shade combined with aerial perspective, create a sense of movement into the background. Lebedev also immersed himself in the real world of objects, which he placed directly in front of the observer, as if with the intention of bringing man into closer contact with his environment. Lebedev's general artistic approach shows a distinct tendency towards Realism, but his early death robbed him of the opportunity to complete many of his projects. Academicism, therefore, did not extend its sway over all landscape painters in the period between 1830 and 1860. As we shall see in the next chapter, the same was true of history painting, which was to be dominated by the mighty figure of Alexander Ivanov. A similar situation arose in respect of genre painting, where the tradition of early Realism led to critical Realism, initiated by the work of Pavel Fedotov.

Mikhail Lebedev
Path in Albano
1836

Mikhail Lebedev
In Guigi Park 1837

5 Alexander Ivanov

The figure of Alexander Ivanov (1806–58) is central to Russian painting in the years between 1830 and 1850. Eventually he was to eclipse the other artists of the day; he created a 'continent' for himself. Although he had much in common with his contemporaries, he was cast in a very different mould. He became a recluse, never knew success during his lifetime and was considered a failure, a judgment apparently borne out by the long list of his uncompleted works. His *magnum opus*, on which he was engaged for twenty years, was left unfinished; his cycle of biblical studies, intended as preliminary work for a mural, were never transferred to walls or ceilings and remained as watercolours; and even the product of his youthful dreams and fantasies, *Apollo, Hyacinth and Zephyr*, was never quite completed.

He spent nearly all his adult life in Italy, leaving Russia in 1830, at the age of 24, not to return until a month and a half before his death. His life in Italy was neither as stormy as Kiprensky's nor as comfortable and enjoyable as Shchedrin's. He was never on intimate terms with his fellow artists in the Russian colony in Rome; as he grew older, he shut himself up more and more within the four walls of his studio, becoming increasingly mistrustful of, and estranged from, the outside world. This isolation was relieved only by the warmth of his friendship with a few other expatriates living in Rome, among them three Russians, Rozhalin, Chizhov and Gogol, and a German, Overbeck, who was a well-known leader of the Nazarene group of artists. With these companions he was able to indulge in sophisticated discussions, which taught him much about philosophy, history, religion and art and influenced his personality to a considerable degree. It was only later in life, therefore, that Ivanov became an artist-philosopher; in his younger days he had lacked the opportunity to acquire much knowledge or to develop his intellect because his father, a professor of painting at the St Petersburg Academy, cared little or nothing for such matters and knew no more than he was obliged to as an Academician. Alexander Ivanov never sought the easy approach in his work or thought, feeling the need, perhaps more than any other Russian painter, to understand contemporary philosophy and critical theology.

With the help of Rozhalin and Overbeck he read Schelling. With Gogol he discussed ethical problems, studied Strauss and considered the ideas of the Slavophiles. He met Alexander Herzen, the distinguished Russian philosopher in exile, and spoke with Chernyshevsky shortly before the latter's death, desiring to know their opinions about the proper aims of artistic creativity.

Nevertheless, he was his own man. He read his Bible, making notes as he read and writing a commentary for his own use, as well as copying out passages which particularly struck him. He personally conceived the idea of the artist as prophet and throughout his life searched for a single theme which would enable him to incorporate simultaneously all the most critical questions facing mankind. As a mature artist he inclined ever more strongly to the principle of what may be termed 'ethical Romanticism'; to put it another way, he emphasized the moral, rather than the aesthetic, element of Romanticism. This ethical principle obliged the artist to observe the world through the prism not of beauty but of virtue and truth.

Ivanov began his career as a thoroughgoing classicist. In his first painting, *Priam Begging Achilles for Hector's Body*, which dates from 1824, he satisfied all the strict requirements of the classical canon. The picture lacks the conspicuous mastery which distinguished even the early works of Briullov, but the composition is harmonious and the subtle interplay of contours sounds a ceaseless melody. These qualities, together with a pleasing combination of red, yellow and orange tints, express an elevated and Homeric mood in a modest but dignified way. However, there is more than this to the painting. The subject itself presented a challenge to Ivanov, who had to convey to the observer the following complex situation: old Priam, having penetrated the enemy's camp in order to beg Achilles, his son Hector's murderer, to return his body, comes upon Achilles at the very moment when he is mourning the death of his friend, Patrocles, killed by Hector. Ivanov rose to the challenge without having recourse to any of the theatrical effects so characteristic of classicism. The body-language, movement and posture of the figures are the sole means by which the external drama and the inner tension of the episode are expressed.

As Ivanov continued on his artistic pilgrimage the worlds of the Old and New Testaments began to open before him. In 1827 he finished a work entitled *Joseph in Prison, Interpreting the Dreams of Pharaoh's Butler and Baker*, commissioned by the Society for the Support and Encouragement of Artists. Ivanov used the story – Joseph, while in prison with the servants of the Pharaoh, foretells salvation and happiness for the butler, and execution for the baker – to explore various interesting artistic possibilities. By using one model for both dreamers (thus depicting them as twins, equal in every sense) he abandons them, as it were, to the hand of fate[8], which then ordains death for one and safety for the other. Some kind of external power begins to rule their lives. It seems to lurk in the dark shadow in which their separate figures are picked out by the light. This deadly game of fate, which paralyses their will and ability to act, went well beyond the classical approach to the interpretation of real events. Ivanov here stretched to the limit the traditional classical technique of forming figures by means of chiaroscuro. The young painter was clearly searching for a new artistic language, but he realized that this 'classicalized Caravaggism' was a sterile experiment, and he never repeated it.

In 1830 Ivanov found himself in Italy, where he began to search out his true essence and artistic destiny. Overwhelmed by all he saw there, he could not but turn to the themes of antiquity. For several years (between 1831 and 1834) he worked on *Apollo, Hyacinth and Zephyr*. Briullov was painting *The Last Day of Pompeii* (also in Italy) at the same time, but Ivanov was evidently in no hurry to turn to a subject of such universal significance; he was still fascinated by the idyllic vision of antiquity common in the 1820s, which perhaps found its most perfect expression in this work.

Apollo, Hyacinth and Zephyr is Ivanov's subtle and profound portrayal of the Golden Age of mankind. The composition, consisting of three figures, seems to be the very embodiment of music and harmony. Ivanov's account is free of superfluous detail. Clues to the elucidation of the episode, such as the dead deer and the discus (the instrument of Hyacinth's imminent death) leaning against a stone, are hard to discern. Nothing must be allowed to distract from the all-absorbing music lesson being given by Apollo, who sits on the stone in a royal pose befitting the Lord of the Muses. Peace and concord hold sway between the three figures representing the three Ages of Man – childhood, youth and maturity. The heroic quality of the god is modified by this union of three souls in harmony. *Apollo, Hyacinth and Zephyr* bears witness to that happy period of Ivanov's life in Italy when

Alexander Ivanov *Priam Begging Achilles for Hector's Body* 1824

Alexander Ivanov *Joseph in Prison Interpreting the Dreams of Pharaoh's Butler and Baker* 1827

Alexander Ivanov *Apollo, Hyacinth and Zephyr* 1831–34

he was intoxicated with nature and antiquity. He was confident that the Golden Age was not yet over, and that the painter, as well as the subjects of his painting, was still living in that paradise. The message of the picture is not 'I, too, have been in Arcadia', but 'I am in Arcadia now'. As he began to realize that Arcadia no longer existed he was impelled to abandon the work, which was never to be completed. *Apollo* was Ivanov's first attempt to interpret an historical subject not as some sort of episode in the past, but as a contemporary event continuously unfolding before us – even though we know that it belongs to history.

In the 1830s Ivanov switched from antique to biblical themes, as he had ten years previously. Many and various projects were maturing in his mind. Inspired by the Nazarenes, who often explored the theme of Joseph, Ivanov returned to his favourite Old Testament character, this time treating two episodes in his life: the first was *Joseph and Potiphar's Wife*, the second, *Joseph's Brothers Find a Goblet in Benjamin's Sack*. But these two stories did not allow him to address certain vital questions concerned with human existence. For this he turned to the Gospels, where he soon selected the subject of Christ's appearance before the people at the time of John the Baptist's prophecy of the coming of the Messiah. But before beginning on this work he decided to paint his *Christ Appearing before Mary Magdalene* (1834–36), which was to become a sort of dress rehearsal for the main work.

Ivanov worked on the actual composition of *The Appearance of Christ to the People* in the mid-1830s. Study followed study, and a general plan for the painting gradually emerged. In 1837 he began to work on the huge canvas proper; it was to remain on the easel of his Rome studio for nearly twenty years, until it was taken to St Petersburg by the artist when he returned there shortly before his death. The selection of the subject and the manner of its realization were important steps along the path to the creation of this masterpiece. He had long been obsessed by the subject, which embraced, in his opinion, all the central events and questions of human existence in the past, present and future. It was completely in tune with the artist's passionate preoccupation with the idea of man's moral transformation and spiritual enlightenment. All the religious, historical and moral problems with which Ivanov was grappling are here combined in one event. There is no single episode to be found in the Gospels which totally coincides with the scene depicted on his canvas, for he merged a number of separate events from the Gospel story: John's prophetic sermon and his baptism of the people; the presence of the Apostles Andrew, John and (?) Peter; and the appearance of Christ, a solitary figure, approaching the crowd from the

distance. Equally, there is no direct analogue to the scene in traditional Russian Orthodox iconography. This combination of a number of episodes was a bold experiment and a happy discovery. The gathering together, at one place and one time, of a number of people who must accept or reject the new faith, enabled him to reveal the complex process of inner change within a number of human souls. At the same time the artist wanted to portray the whole scene in a lively and convincing manner, free from any traditional classical stylization. The grandeur of this moment, so vital to the fate of mankind, had to be evoked realistically enough to inspire in the observer the sense of being actually present at an event taking place before his eyes. Ivanov's search for the ideal composition was to be dominated by the question of how to express this union of apparently incompatible elements.

It took him some considerable time to arrive at a satisfactory solution to the compositional dilemma. With each succeeding study the figure of Christ was gradually moved further into the background; the number of other figures was increased, and Christ's appearance was transformed from a 'mere' miracle into an historical event. In the earliest sketches, Christ seems to appear from beneath the ground, while the reactions of the other characters reveal their utter astonishment. As the studies proceed, astonishment yields to expectation, and the emphasis is transferred from the miracle of the appearance itself onto the emotional reactions of the people, gathered round the Baptist, to the unique event. Towards the end of the 1830s Ivanov formulated the main elements of the composition and realized them on the canvas. At the same time as he was working on the main painting, he kept a working copy. (This version, from the Soldatenkov Collection, is now on display at the Russian Museum in Leningrad.) This smaller, working copy shows all the changes and corrections which the main work underwent in the course of time. In 1839, after a trip to Venice, he did another version in Venetian colours, with the specific aim of working out his colour scheme. After 1837, when the large canvas received its first colour base and the composition was already fundamentally in place, he began work on studies of individual figures and on the background landscape.

If we were to assemble all Ivanov's studies of heads and figures for this painting we would understand how great were the demands he made of himself in his search for perfect solutions. He required not only that the gestures be expressive of emotion; each individual figure had to be assigned a specific pose or gesture unique to him or her. Each character went through a lengthy evolution in this individuating process. Ivanov carried out life-studies and copied antique busts and Byzantine frescos. Women often posed for male characters. By interweaving

Alexander Ivanov *The Appearance of Christ to the People* 1837–58

such varied sources he eventually achieved his aim – not simply by combining various heads and bodies, but by consistently exposing those hidden, inner qualities implicit in each of the studies.

At the same time he was forming groups, and groups within groups, each independently significant but also contributing to the composition as a whole. Examples of such groups are: the slave with his master (his back to the observer); the naked, shivering man with a boy; the young man leaving the water and the old man with a staff; and St Andrew with St John the Evangelist. Nathaniel is engaged in some kind of dialogue with (?) St Peter, as is John the Apostle with a red-haired youth. Every nuance of the body-language is determined by the message Ivanov wishes to convey. He presents his vision of the complex and graduated relationship between these people, gathered at the bank of the River Jordan, as they react in their different ways to the Baptist's sermon and the appearance of the Saviour. One of Ivanov's greatest problems was how to integrate the various groups (and the individuals that make them up) into a harmonious composition. Needing to forge a unified entity from this monumental canvas, he turned to the principle of

symmetry. He grouped his figures in such a way that the centre of the painting remains open, reserved for the figure of Christ. Figures to one side of the centre are virtually repeated on the opposite side. Movement is directed towards the centre from both left and right. The 'coulisses' of the composition are complete in themselves. To the left, that part of the canvas containing figures (the old man and the boy leaving the water) gives the impression of *descending movement*; to the right, the corresponding part of the canvas seems to ascend, as though left and right are rhyming opposites. The sense of *ascending movement* is created by the group of descending Pharisees and riders. In spite of these distractions, the principle of bas-relief dominates the composition; in addition, there is a tiered element, the lower tier being occupied by John the Baptist and the people, while the upper tier is reserved for the figure of Christ.

Although Ivanov succeeded in conveying the impression that a real event is being played out before the observer, the overall plan has a rather prearranged, a priori character. The whole composition is dominated by and subject to the central figure of Christ, and reflects the artistic experiments of the 1830s, when a classical component was obligatory in the fusion of classicism with Romanticism. But as Ivanov, while working on the landscape section, mastered the depiction of space and devised his own *plein air* techniques, his new approach and methods came into conflict with this fusion, which had been his starting-point in the 1830s. It was for this very reason that the painting was never completed. A good illustration of the conflict is afforded by comparing some of Ivanov's multi-figure compositions on biblical themes with *The Appearance of Christ*, and, likewise, by comparing some of his *plein air* landscapes, or studies of boys (dating from his later years), with corresponding parts of *The Appearance*. Ivanov himself perfectly well understood the impossibility of his ever completing *The Appearance of Christ* and in the 1850s he hardly touched the painting. In spite of all the contradictions discussed above, and although it was never finished, this work became one of the most remarkable monuments in Russian culture to spiritual profundity and to the unremitting search for perfection – a true inspiration to future generations of artists.

At the end of the 1830s and into the 1840s, Ivanov concentrated his energies on the landscape for *The Appearance* even though he did not attach much importance to the landscape genre as such and totally subordinated it to the main tasks presented by the painting. Nevertheless, his landscape studies outgrew their function of mere preparatory work, and, judged purely from an artistic point of view, may be considered to excel the main painting itself. Admittedly, the representations of Nature are to some extent inspired by the elevated content of the main work. Nature had to be shown in all its rich variety and in a splendour appropriate to the significance of the event. Ivanov strove to reveal Nature in its objective reality, to comprehend its laws and to penetrate the secrets of its primary elements: water, earth, vegetation, the sky and space. He used *plein air* techniques to depict great areas of space, while preserving strength and intensity of colour. He also struck a happy balance between volume and space.

In his approach to these two aspects of reality he significantly prefigured some of the important achievements of the final decade of the nineteenth century. It is already accepted practice among Soviet art historians to compare Ivanov with the Impressionists, as well as with Cézanne. Even though these latter have little in common, there is an element of truth in the comparison. Examination of Ivanov's study of a naked boy posed against white drapery, dating from the 1850s, illustrates great skill in *plein air* techniques: the interrelated red, white and blue hangings cast their reflections on the white sheet, and shade it with pale blue and pink tints, which also mingle on the boy's skin. Clearly, Ivanov was very far from being an Impressionist, even in his well-known painting entitled *The Branch*, dating from the end of the 1840s and the beginning of the 1850s. Here the background, rendered in a mix of blue, green and yellow, creates an illusion of infinite depth without the aid of any additional linear perspective. But Impressionism demands a more systematic breaking down of the palette, as well as more open texture. Ivanov's work does contain elements which might have led him to develop into an Impressionist, but the fact is that he himself put obstacles in the way of such a process. He was a synthesizer rather than an analyst in his perception of Nature, an approach which excluded that lyrical element which inevitably transforms Nature's objective qualities into a kind of analogue (expressed in terms of Nature) of the inner world of a particular individual.

Rejecting the principle of lyricism, Ivanov deviated, as it were, from the mainstream of European landscape painting, which had been greatly influenced by Corot and the Barbizon school. This new trend in European landscape was concerned with all that was specific, particular and unique in Nature; Ivanov, on the other hand, was something of a generalist. He wished to discern a microcosm of the universe in each and every phenomenon of Nature. For Ivanov, a single branch or stone might stand for the whole world. This attitude may recall the creative philosophy of Cézanne, although we must again bear in mind the tentative nature of such comparisons. Cézanne represents a later generation of painters; and painting in the intervening period underwent its own significant evolution. Cézanne returned a sense of wholeness and unity to a world which had been dismantled by the Impressionists, whereas Ivanov's tendency to unify disparate elements of Nature manifested itself well before Russian landscape painting developed the realistic lyricism which was to continue for the next fifty years.

A number of the artistic questions to which Ivanov addressed himself were, in a sense, ahead of their time, but they remained questions in embryo. For this reason we can discern elements in his work that could have led either to Impressionism or to Cézanne. Some of Ivanov's motifs and compositional techniques are close to Cézanne's. Both frequently painted coves and bays from elevated angles; both favoured painting the ground in close-up. Ivanov, like Cézanne, was fascinated by every stage of the growth of a tree, from its invisible roots to its topmost twigs. Neither painter included human figures in his landscapes, with the occasional exception of nudes (Cézanne's *Baigneuses* and Ivanov's studies of boys). More important than these external similarities, however, was the desire, common to both painters, to comprehend the basic laws of Nature.

11 **Mikhail Lebedev** *In the Park* Early 1830s

12   **Karl Briullov** *Self-portrait* 1848

13   **Karl Briullov** *Portrait of Nikolai Kukolnik* 1836 >

14   **Alexander Ivanov** *The Branch* Late 1840s or early 1850s

15   **Alexander Ivanov** *The Olive in the Ariccia Valley* 1842 >

18   **Alexander Ivanov** *Jesus Walking on the Water* 1850s

< **16**   **Alexander Ivanov** *The Appian Way* 1845

< **17**   **Alexander Ivanov** *On the Shore of the Bay of Naples* 1850s

19   **Pavel Fedotov** *A Poor Aristocrat's Breakfast* 1849

20   **Pavel Fedotov** *Encore, again Encore!* 1851–52

Ivanov's landscapes may also be considered as preparatory work for various aspects of the scene of the Messiah's appearance. Their motifs include some of the most significant of natural phenomena: earth, stones, water; broad marshes, hazy with mist; trees, set against a mountain range in the distant background; a huge stratum of air moving over these mountains and directing our eyes towards infinity. He began his preliminary work with studies of trees and marshes. He painted tall groves, and forests which had overgrown various old, neglected parks outside Rome, such as Guigi and Ariccia; later he concentrated more and more on a single tree. His wide landscapes, filled with forests, marshes and distant prospects, reveal spacious panoramas, skilfully and harmoniously blended with backgrounds, rendered by a complex range of dark blues mixed with pale blue, greenish and yellow tints. These shades mark out space, as it were, into separate layers. Ivanov himself called this favourite technique of his 'an overflow of blues'.

16 Two spacious landscapes, *The Bay of Naples at Castellammare* (1846) and *The Appian Way* (1845), though originally intended as studies for the main canvas of *The Appearance*, became well-known works in their own right. *The Bay of Naples* is markedly horizontal. A strip of land lies in front of a stretch of sea. In the background a mountain, with a village perched on its spur, encloses the bay. The painter selects a low viewpoint, enabling him to 'fill up' the narrow confines of the canvas with a sense of depth. No view of the open sea unfolds before the observer: the canvas is limited to the bay enclosed by the mountain range. But how different is this bay from Shchedrin's tranquil coves! Ivanov's whole landscape breathes with the idea of infinity. His space soars over every obstacle set in its path. Mountains, shore and houses are all part of this motion, which distracts the observer's mind from the everyday world and offers it global, even cosmic perspectives. Unsurprisingly, man is absent from this landscape as from so many others of Ivanov's, for his presence would have caused conflict between the general and the particular. Whereas the German Romantic painter Caspar David Friedrich chose deliberately to sharpen this conflict, Ivanov consciously avoided it. He devoted himself totally to a different idea, that of Nature in all its grandeur, not competing with the human race but living according to its own laws.

The Appian Way has an even stronger claim to be considered as a landscape with a philosophical and historical message. It depicts the Roman *campagna* at sunset. The obligatory dome of St Peter's dominates the panorama of Rome, visible in the distance. Foreground and middleground are given over to some of the simplest elements of Nature, brown earth (with some scanty grass and a few bushes pushing through), stones, ruins, as well

as to the Appian Way itself, almost completely eroded from the face of this eternal land. The idea of Nature as a unique and independent entity seeks direct expression. The simplicity of the composition is striking; one half is given over to the earth, the other half to the sky, while the dominant diagonal of the road, penetrating the background, stops at the horizon. The diagonal begins, not at the corner of the canvas, but beyond the frame, and putatively continues beyond the bounds of the picture. This technique serves, in a sense, to expand the boundaries of the space depicted, and avoids the impression of fragmentation by ensuring that form and content in the structure of the painting are in balance.

Ivanov's studies of stones deserve special attention. If Constable may be credited with discovering the sky for landscape, then Ivanov is the true discoverer of stone. The Earth itself is embodied in Ivanov's stones. They are, so to speak, small copies of mountains. We may perceive the mountain in *The Bay of Naples at Castellammare* as a huge stone, with folds and hollows in its almost crystalline structure. The mountain, in its turn, is a model of the Earth. We can follow the process of descent from Earth to stone, or conversely, the ascent from stone to Earth, each stage in one process corresponding to a similar stage in the other.

Ivanov's best landscapes must be numbered among his masterpieces, but he also excelled in other genres. Especially noteworthy are his studies of boys in the open 17 air, a still-life with hangings (painted specifically with the central section of *The Appearance* in mind) and the portrait of Vittoria Marini (also probably a study) which is remarkable for its sense of inner harmony.

The best of his studies of biblical themes are also outstanding. These studies, to which Ivanov devoted almost all his later years, deserve special comment. They were projected as murals, to be housed in a special building, but this dream was never fulfilled: they remain as watercolours on paper, numbering many dozens, with several subjects repeated in different versions. Some are merely sketched in, others are in varying degrees of completion. Many are finished works of art in their own right.

Ivanov returned to the Old and New Testaments throughout his life. As well as writing his own private commentary on the Bible he was also interested in the new critical theology popular at the time. A work dating from the 1830s, by the German theologian D.F. Strauss, *The Life of Jesus*, was of particular importance in the genesis of this series of biblical scenes. Following Strauss, Ivanov became interested in contrasting and comparing motifs which had features in common, even though they derived from widely differing mythologies, and this approach stimulated his interest in very varied artistic traditions. Just as, earlier in his career, Ivanov had defied the academic canons by turning not only to Leonardo and Raphael, but to Giotto and the sixteenth-century Venetians, so now he became absorbed in the art of ancient Egypt, Assyria and Babylon. He copied reliefs and murals from reproductions, fascinated equally by their clothing, headgear and hairstyles, by the way their figures twisted, posed and gestured, by their linear rhythm and by the range of colours they displayed.

Ivanov himself never organized his biblical studies into separate categories, but we may tentatively assign them to basic thematic and compositional groups. He frequently painted crowd scenes, usually with Christ preaching or simply surrounded by vast numbers of people walking by his side or standing before him, listening and observing. Ivanov indicated heads and figures with casual dabs and strokes of his brush. These swaying crowds, silent though they are, appear to be on the verge of some tremendous headlong movement, and we are left with an irresistible sense of history in the making.

Ivanov suddenly switched from these crowded compositions, grandiose in concept and monumental in form, to small-scale biblical scenes of everyday life. One of these quasi-genre studies portrays the Apostle obeying Christ's order to unloose a she-ass and bring her to the Master. A study entitled *Three Strangers Prophesying to Abraham the Birth of a Son* (dating from the 1850s) has a distinctly genre feel to it, even though its ancestor is the Trinity theme so ubiquitous in Russian icon painting. The three travellers are comfortably settled on the ground around a dish of lamb. One of them, a young man, is stretched out on the grass, with only his feet and ankles protruding from under his tunic. Another of the travellers, the old man, is sharply turned to one side; all his attention is fixed on the figure of Sarah, and although his face is not visible we sense that he is consumed by curiosity. These two characters recall Ivanov's numerous studies of young boys, but in this particular study there is a transition from the genre level to a more elevated, historical perception of the world. The gesture of the bearded stranger, pointing to Sarah and symbolizing the prophecy itself, is heavy with meaning. It is emphasized not only by the freezing of the gesture but by the main linear thrust of the work, passing over the reclining body of the young man and ending at the figure of Sarah. The principles of composition employed in this study are quite different from those in *The Appearance of Christ*. The study lacks any kind of preselected compositional 'figures' (in the geometrical sense of the word). Ivanov allows himself to be guided by the event itself, whose logic dictates the position of the figures and objects in space, and hence on the paper.

Alexander Ivanov *The Bay of Naples at Castellammare* 1846

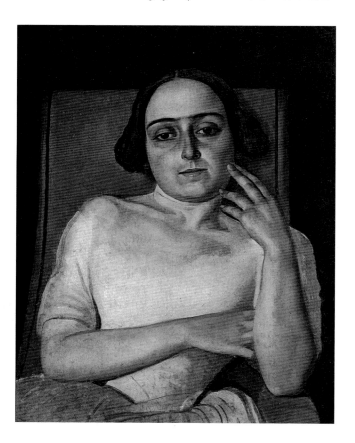

(*above*) **Alexander Ivanov** *Portrait of Vittoria Marini* Late 1840s

(*right*) **Alexander Ivanov** *Naked Boy* c. 1850

A separate group of studies consists of theomachist themes, usually in two-figure compositions, such as *The Archangel Gabriel Strikes Zacharias Dumb, Jacob Wrestling with God* (both from the 1850s), and others. The human protagonists of these drawings are on an almost equal footing with God or with the angels sent by him. They struggle with the angels, their palms turned upwards questioningly, defiant in their unbelief. Human and divine are set on the same level, although in this context the divine must inevitably triumph.

One of the most perfect studies, *The Virgin with Disciples and Friends of Jesus Observing the Crucifixion* (1850s), illustrates some of Ivanov's later artistic discoveries. It belongs to what we may term the 'historical' group. Here Ivanov is concerned neither with interpreting myth or miracle, nor with comparing his chosen subject with any mythological parallel. As with *The Appearance of Christ* we are shown a real historical event – even the composition recalls *The Appearance*. Through the open gates of a fence we see space stretching into the background; in the foreground, figures move from both sides towards the opening to gaze at Christ in the distance – not, in this case, approaching the crowd, but hanging on the Cross at the place of execution. For the arrangement of the figures Ivanov again employs a bas-relief technique, which enables him to reveal their linear structure with particular clarity, his specific source of inspiration being a famous Egyptian relief depicting women mourners. But for all their similarities, *The Appearance* and *Virgin with Disciples* are organized on very different principles. In the latter, the bas-relief principle does not diminish the sense of space or depth in the background, which is treated conventionally. All the forms are arranged on the paper so as to create a system of lines and spots on a single plane. However, the line which, in *The Appearance of Christ*, was no more than a defining edge between volume and space, here attains a special richness, now rising sharply, now descending weakly or wavering in nervous hesitation.

Those studies dealing with a different kind of miraculous phenomenon may be considered as yet another separate group. In *The Appearance of Christ* Ivanov progressed beyond the depiction of a miraculous event and portrayed an actual historical episode. In the studies, however, he depicted fantastic or improbable situations and provided them with mythological explanations and justifications. In one study, *The Appearance of the Angel Announcing the Birth of Christ to the Shepherds* (1850s) the Angel hovers like a pillar of light over the terrified rustics. Some of their poses recall figures in Briullov's *Last Day of Pompeii*, but with the difference that in Ivanov's painting the gestures are not inserted simply for effect: every one of these gestures is justified by the meaning of

the event. The miracle catches shepherds and even sheep by surprise, and their shock is vividly portrayed. Landscape, too, is very important in this study – a sleepy, practically deserted town, a long curved aqueduct, a high tower partly obscured by the Angel's wing. As usual in Ivanov's studies the architectural detail is historically accurate, but this authenticity is a means rather than an end in itself, and its function is to convey the majestic and historic quality of the event.

One of the finest of all the biblical studies is *Jesus Walking on the Water* (1850s). It is pictorially and graphically perfect, and discloses a rare freedom and a powerful imagination. Christ moves very rapidly upon the surface of the water, stretching his hand towards St Peter. High on the crest of a wave, a boat with oarsmen is visible in the background. The figures are drawn in simple outline. The dabs of colour representing them rarely coincide with the silhouettes for which they are intended; for example, blue, brown and grey dashes of colour relate to Peter's outline but also go well beyond it. The boat and oarsmen are indicated only by the device of leaving a patch of the brown paper unpainted. It would be difficult to find in the art of the 1850s (not only in Russia, but in the whole of Europe) a bolder, more innovative or more forward-looking piece of work.

Alexander Ivanov's later works assured him of a special place in the history of Russian art. He encompassed the grandeur of scale typical of the period spanning the eighteenth and nineteenth centuries; equally, he was one of the first to work in the style of the new Realism. The version of Realism he himself explored was less akin to that which burgeoned in the second half of the nineteenth century; rather it prefigured developments at the beginning of the twentieth. In the course of his development as an artist he skilfully combined the old with the new and exploited the advantages of both. It was these characteristics which condemned him to artistic isolation. Although he had no pupils or immediate imitators, his achievements initiated an internal tradition which later followers partly developed, although none of them would succeed in recreating the totality of Ivanov's experience.

18

(*opposite above*) **Alexander Ivanov** *The Appearance of the Angel Announcing the Birth of Christ to the Shepherds* 1850s

(*opposite*) **Alexander Ivanov** *The Archangel Gabriel Strikes Zacharias Dumb* 1850s

6 The Beginnings of Critical Realism

Pavel Fedotov's professional career as an artist was very short. He was an amateur and student of art until his thirties and was dead by the age of 37. Nevertheless, this sensitive and gifted man had a great impact on Russian culture. His significance lies in his ability to convey, in an inspired and elevated artistic language, the joys and despair of the human predicament as well as the extremes of nobility and degradation of which the human soul is capable.

He was born and brought up in Moscow. After graduation from the Cadet Corps he went to St Petersburg, where he served in the Corps de Garde. Like many of his fellow officers he wrote poetry, painted and played the flute, but it never occurred to him to become a professional artist. He quickly made a name for himself, however, with his portraits and drawings, his superiors encouraged him further, and before long he was invited to attend special classes for budding painters of 'battle pieces' at the St Petersburg Academy of Fine Arts. Admittedly these somewhat unsystematic studies contributed little to Fedotov's development: he was essentially a self-taught man. His success was due to his talents, his lively intellectual curiosity and his thirst for knowledge. He was well-read, completely familiar with the history of art and a constant visitor to the Hermitage Museum. Fedotov followed a number of artistic traditions, among them genre painting. Influential among his artistic antecedents were Venetsianov's circle, especially for their choice of locations and their interest in authentic domestic interiors. Another important element in his development was the Russian tradition of book illustration, which in the 1840s received a strong qualitative and quantitative boost from the democratization of Russian culture. A new sort of book was beginning to appear for a new class of reader. It was not just that a different type of literature was being produced; the actual books themselves were changing from expensive luxuries for the rich to popular objects accessible to all. Illustrations were reproduced by the new method of transferring a drawing onto a woodcut and printing the result in large editions, sometimes using metal castings or polytypes. Woodcuts themselves also underwent con-

siderable changes: they were now carved on the butt end of the wooden board, which simplified the process and enabled artists to vary their techniques. For example, they could now explore the use of staining and the shaping of figures by means of chiaroscuro effects. These new techniques were much better suited to the depiction of complex scenes with psychological overtones, featuring extensive detail and personalities in conflict.

Distinguished illustrators of the 1840s included V. Timm, G. Gagarin and especially Alexander Agin. The latter won fame for his illustrations to Gogol's *Dead Souls*, which were published in an album independent of the text. Fedotov, too, illustrated some contemporary Russian writers, in particular the young Dostoevsky. Book illustration never became one of his principal interests, although it remained a major source of creative inspiration to him on account of its critical approach, its tendency to portray conflict and its narrative element.

In addition to the national tradition, European painting also exercised a great influence on Fedotov, in particular Dutch and Flemish genre painters of the seventeenth and eighteenth centuries. Fedotov was the last major Russian artist to work in the European tradition of 'small-scale' genre. As for more contemporary influences, the most significant were two Englishmen – David Wilkie and the great Hogarth. Fedotov was very interested in Hogarth and wrote about him at length, striving not only to learn from but to surpass the English master. We have already discussed the role of amateurism – or dilettantism – in Russian culture during the first half of the nineteenth century. Fedotov was swept to fame on the crest of the dilettantist wave. It was thanks to this pursuit of culture in the home (which flourished at many different levels of society) that Fedotov managed to avoid the perils and pitfalls of academicism in his art. He was attracted by *lubki* (the cheap popular prints already described) and wrote verses in the same spirit to accompany his paintings. He even read his doggerel aloud at exhibitions. He often used proverbs as titles for his work. There is a strongly folkloristic element in his narrative approach, his emphasis on detail and his interpretation of dialogue and conflict in the event itself.

Pavel Fedotov *Fido's Illness* 1844

Fedotov's early work is of little general interest. Some of it is unoriginal, the rest is lacking in skill; the true Fedotov was still maturing in the 1830s. Early in the 1840s he was faced by the dilemma of whether to resign his commission in the army, risking almost certain poverty as a professional artist, or to continue his military career while remaining a dilettante. It became the crucial question of his life and he received conflicting advice from various sources. Karl Briullov, for example, to whom Fedotov showed his drawings, recommended him not to change his way of life, expressing his opinion that a professional artistic career needed to be pursued from a very early age. But Fedotov rejected the great man's authoritative pronouncement, did indeed leave the army in 1844 and devoted himself passionately and exclusively to painting. In this year, the turning point in his life and art, he completed a series of sepia drawings which became his artistic manifesto.

In this series Fedotov abandoned his earlier, lyrical view of the world about him, and substituted a satirical and critical approach, giving events from everyday life a grotesque interpretation. Two of the drawings depict the death of a dog, which causes its capricious mistress to be ill and turns the household upsidedown. Another drawing has a young husband who has been cuckolded. Yet another shows the scene in a fashion house, where elderly husbands are obliged to spend a fortune on their young wives' outfits. Some of his scenes hint at a tragic tale: for example, an old painter with his indigent family. Fedotov's world, riddled with the ills caused by the contradictions and defects of society, is populated by characters typical of the St Petersburg of the 1840s. People of every class – civil servants, tailors, pedlars, merchants, undertakers, aristocrats and paupers – parade through these urban interiors previously unknown to Russian art, though very familiar to readers of Gogol and Dostoevsky, whose characters often lived huddled together in screened-off corners of rented rooms or shabby boarding-houses.

The very atmosphere of urban life of the 1850s was loaded with contradiction and conflict. Fedotov developed this embryonic social critique as his interest in moral edification and the exposure of hypocrisy sharpened. But he was still too heavy-handed and his message was laborious and verbose. His compositions generally contain a number of episodes unfolding in parallel; the

(*left*) **Pavel Fedotov** *The Newly-decorated Civil Servant* 1846
(*above*) **Pavel Fedotov** *The Fastidious Bride* 1847

normal sequence of time is suspended, with several events taking place simultaneously, connected not in time but by a common theme. Editing out some of this activity would have resulted in less crowded, cleaner and clearer compositions. All his objects and characters have, first and foremost, an informative function – to tell us what is going on. The idiom of the drawings is that of caricature, grotesque and exaggeration. Fedotov's aim is to make us laugh. His conversion to the critical approach, with its determination to unmask every form of social injustice, obliged him to renounce the search for beauty in favour of portraying all the wickedness and cruelty which distorted humanity and natural harmony. Indeed the beauty of the world was a closed book to him until he deflected the scourge of his criticism from evil individuals onto the social conditions which made them what they were. The sepia drawings, therefore, are a staging-post in his career, rather than an end in themselves.

Fedotov's next phase began with a switch to oils and the abandonment of techniques of caricature. He endeavoured to understand more fully the true meaning of the events he portrayed, and to express that understanding not in satirical but in tragic terms. In the few short years between 1846 and 1852 he was to undergo a profound and intense artistic evolution.

His very first oil painting, *The Newly-decorated Civil Servant* (1846), has a strongly denunciatory tone. The bureaucrat, who has just received his first honour, is portrayed as the very embodiment of vice. Unlike the

sermonizing of the sepia drawings, however, the message is simple and clear. What interests Fedotov is the opportunity for irony which presents itself. He creates an almost theatrical scene: the newly-decorated official, in the pose of a Roman orator, proudly displays his medal, pinned on his dressing gown, to his cook. In response, this lady – who is also his mistress – pushes a worn-out boot under his nose. The situation, the objects and characters, are all absurd: the objects, for example, are inappropriately placed, and the self-importance of the civil servant clashes with the mockery of his cook. The Russian title of the painting contains a pun: *Svezhiy kavalyer* means, literally, the 'fresh cavalier'. The irony of the painting resides in the title: the 'cavalier' is not at all 'fresh' after the previous evening's drinking-bout.

The painting has a number of other features which distinguish it clearly from 'classic Fedotov'. Its manner is unsure, its execution too tentative. Fedotov does not attempt complicated feats of colour; the objects displayed, devoid of harmony, are not there to be admired – they simply tell the story. The work is important less for its qualities than for the fact that it helped him to acquire the technique of painting in oils.

His next painting, *The Fastidious Bride* (1847), was a significant step forward. Fedotov took the subject from one of the moral fables of I.A. Krylov, which tells of an elderly bride, who refused all her suitors in her youth and who is now obliged to marry a hunchback. In the painting, however, the moral of the tale is of only superficial importance. Fedotov's aim is not to convey Krylov's moral but to reflect the artist's – and the observer's – thoughts about the way life is. Fedotov attaches no guilt to any of the actors and thus has no need to exaggerate and distort in order to humiliate his characters for our amusement. His criticism is no longer particular and specific but general and philosophical. The world in general may be bad, but individual aspects of it can reveal their beauty. The objects depicted in the painting still fulfil their informative function, but they also exist independently of the story. Fedotov's brush follows the convoluted twists of the torchère and the round table, and traces the fine work of the parrot's cage, the decorative picture-frames and so on. Any article fashioned by the skilful hand of man interests him, however strongly it may attest to the bad taste of its owner. Some of the objects are chosen for descriptive purposes, others for their innate beauty. In this particular painting he rather favours the descriptive mood, as evidenced by his use of red and gold tones to evoke the essential vulgarity of the scene.

The composition of the painting is itself something of an achievement. What we are actually shown is the culmination of a series of actions. Whereas in *The Newly-decorated Civil Servant* the characters are obviously posing, in this painting their concentration is directed not outwards but inwards, upon their own actions unfolding independently of both observer and artist. Fedotov contains the action in his mind and gathers all the visible clues together into a single moment of time. This treatment of time is characteristic of mature genre thinking, which is revealed particularly clearly in Fedotov's next painting.

The Major's Courtship (1848) displays, as clearly as if it were being enacted on the stage, the ridiculous but (for some of the participants) humiliating scene of the impoverished and prodigal aristocrat asking for the hand of the merchant's daughter. Fedotov recreates the situation with some humour, inviting us to laugh while at the same time admiring the brilliantly rendered objects which make up the world of the picture. And yet there is

Pavel Fedotov *The Major's Courtship* 1848

something shocking lurking behind the humour, for this is a world ruled by lies and pretence, where everyone dissimulates and marriage, in particular, is reduced to the status of a dirty deal. As in the previous painting, however, Fedotov leaves us to draw our own conclusions about the distortion and corruption of man in a world dominated by evil. His characters are quite ordinary people who hardly deviate from the norms laid down by society. Inasmuch as they are human archetypes they may even be said to be perfect. Fedotov here recalls Gogol. The heroes of both are 'pearls of creation' and 'crowns of perfection'. Life itself, and the painter's eye, have moulded them with such accuracy that they actually attain the status of models. The painter's search for perfection leaves its mark not only on the characters, but on every object, on the composition, on the colours – on the painting as a whole.

The figures of the two women in light-coloured dresses stand out from the dark background. Various shades of brownish red and greenish brown, softened by shadow in the middle ground, echo the main colour motif, which is the iridescence of these dresses. The 'porcelain' surface of the canvas and the scrupulous attention to detail are some indication of the work which went into achieving a perfect and complete result. The composition serves the same aim. First of all it reveals the logic of the event, which uncoils like a spring and comes to a climax in the central figures of the women. Nowhere does the actual action slow down, rather it dies away at the end, which is depicted in the middle ground to the left of the painting. The merchant's daughter is poised to rush through the door into the next room. One function of the composition of the painting is to tell the story by developing the action; but there is another function, namely, to create balance, an architectonic quality and perfect harmony of the forms. The composition is run through by two invisible lines, which intersect and balance each other, in fact two diagonals; one is the 'line of light' through the three rooms and the other is the central axis.

By the end of the 1840s Fedotov had fully mastered his art and achieved a name for himself. Apart from genre paintings he completed many small, intimate and subtle portraits, as well as a large number of drawings and sketches. His work, at an academic exhibition in St Petersburg and later in Moscow, received wide acclaim and found many buyers. It seemed that he had won his duel with fate, and that the risky decision he had taken five years earlier had been vindicated. It was at this very moment that his troubles really began. The echoes of the European revolutions of the late 1840s were beginning to be heard in Russia. In particular, a group of revolutionaries led by Petrashevsky was being tried in St Petersburg.

Many of them, including the young Dostoevsky, were sentenced to death. The execution was to be carried out in one of the central squares of the capital, and it was only at the very last moment that the terrified victims heard that the Tsar had substituted long periods of hard labour and exile for their death sentences. Among the prisoners was a close friend and colleague of Fedotov's, the engraver Bernardsky, with whom he had intended to publish an album. The trial put an end to this venture, and as a result, Fedotov began to lose his clientele. He was harassed by the censor and was soon unable to support himself. He could not, after all, escape his fate, which now proceeded to deprive him of all he had won. The many abuses and contradictions of the 1840s, the very source of his art, brought about his downfall. The last two or three years of his life were a period of spiritual anguish, despair and eventually mental illness. His last months were spent in a lunatic asylum, where he died at the age of thirty-seven.

Fedotov's unhappiness, disillusion and pessimism between 1850 and 1852 produced, however, his very finest paintings, among them three versions of *The Young Widow*, *Encore, again Encore!* (both 1851 to 1852) and *The Gamblers*, together with a series of preliminary drawings. *The Young Widow* introduces us to late Fedotov, though the painting has much in common with his earlier work. One new quality is particularly striking, namely, the total absence of any satirical element. The mood of the painting is entirely tragic. There is no direct moralizing on the part of the painter, rather an attempt to express his sympathy and compassion; the result is an interpretation very different from any encountered in his earlier work. There is no open conflict or action in the painting: we see only the consequences of an event in the past. Comparison of the three versions of this work reveals Fedotov's developing attitude to his subjects. In the first version (1851), the widow herself is an organic part of the total situation, her face bearing the signs of suffering and her swelling stomach betraying her pregnancy. In the second version (1851 to 1852), Fedotov frees her from excessive signs of her condition; her figure is more slender and her face more beautiful. However the figure is still lost in, and suppressed by, a pictorial space which is too large, dominating and overcrowded. In the final version (also 1851 to 1852), the widow occupies the centre of a more compact composition, which is constructed upwards, so to speak, and into the background. The vertical rhythms of the interior emphasize the dominant position of the figure. The placing of her hands, the folds and hem of her dress, the gentle line of her arms, her soft satin skin – all these features make up the image of an almost unearthly being. The woman stands above that earthly dimension which can promise only pain and

Pavel Fedotov *The Young Widow* 1851–52

death. Irrationally, hopelessly, romantically – dare we say it? – she resists and challenges an evil world. The picture marks the advent, in Fedotov's artistic philosophy, of a new romantic element with much potential for development.

The Russian title of his next painting, *Encore, again Encore!* contains the sole element of humour in the work, and one difficult to convey in English. The 'encores' are of course in French, the 'again' is in Russian. The subject is of the utmost simplicity and triviality, but Fedotov transforms it into a vehicle for a highly expressive message of great significance. He converts a small, unimportant event into a symbol of inactivity, which itself becomes a metaphor for the tragedy of uselessness and stagnation. An officer is playing with his dog while his servant looks on. The poodle jumps in response to his master's monotonous commands (referred to in the title) rather as a pendulum marks out the flow of wasted time disappearing into a futile infinity. The painting is a memorial, as it were, to wasted time. Every detail of the characters and their surroundings is imbued with a sense of the meaninglessness of the officer's existence. The scene is a symbol of suffocation, depression, hopelessness and spiritual languor. The profound message of this work is the product of a colossal intellectual and emotional tension within Fedotov himself, who had deep personal experience of the pathetic tragedy being played out within the four walls of the officer's room.

It was this personal experience of Fedotov's which determined the pictorial and compositional techniques employed. Still-life elements are treated in a novel way; for example, the objects scattered on the table make up the centre of the composition between the main lines of perspective, organizing the movement of figures and space around themselves. The two human figures loiter round the objects frozen on the table, long ago abandoned by their owner. But it is they – the objects – which possess real life, which emerges not from the physical surface of the earthenware pitcher, the mug or the candle, but from within, from their 'souls'. His treatment of still-life from now on has the aim of animating objects rather than exciting our admiration of them. The composition of the painting contains an internal contrast. It is symmetrical and seems, at first glance, to be finite and closed; within the composition, however, dynamic movement dominates and leads to a culmination. This movement is realized on the surface of the painting. The main compositional lines lead the eye towards the centre, a tiny window in which light and colour are contrasted. The brightest, warmest tones of red, blazing in the candlelight, are applied round the window, through which the cool, pale blues of the moonlit snow are visible on the roof of a log cabin in the distance. The warm tones of the interior seem to come up abruptly against the winter cold, scorch the snowy landscape and then recoil. This is the culmination of the idea of the struggle between colours which dominates the canvas. The greatest achievement of this painting was its ability to express the immensely complex substance of life. Generalized truth here combines with the artist's living voice, resonant with passion and a tragic sense of inescapable futility.

The Gamblers (1852) is dominated by the image of an evil and crippled world, becoming distorted and split, losing its clear outlines and degenerating into a place of shadows and delusions. It is a world which defies rational analysis and leaves us rejected and alone. Even as the artist tries to withstand it he finds himself in its power.

The preliminary drawings – both sketches and studies – for *The Gamblers* are particularly expressive. They are done in Italian pencil and 'belila' (paint mixed with egg white) on grey or blue paper. This became Fedotov's favourite technique in his last two years, giving his work a touch of the picturesque. There is a special sharpness about one of the drawings on blue paper. The gamblers are incorporeal and ephemeral, shadows rather than bodies, shakily rocking in some sort of unstable and ill-defined space. By some miracle the tables and chairs are – or appear to be – supported on thin poles. Twisted lines become curves. Some parts of the bodies have disappeared, as if eaten away by space. The shadows thrown by the figures and objects are also shaky and indeterminate. These shadows fall in different directions; this was Fedotov's first attempt to convey the play of several sources of light, an effect he exploited to the full in the final version. Thus we observe pictorial and graphic techniques being used to achieve the effect of a mystical 'semi-existence'.

In his studies of individual figures, he concentrated on poses, heads twisting, movements of the arms, hands and legs, and shadows. He was fascinated by the absurdity of certain of these poses and movements. In one of the drawings a folded leg looks like a stump. In other studies, one part of the leg – from the knee to the foot – disappears completely. All the preliminary drawings for *The Gamblers* are remarkably creative and bold; they are unrivalled by the graphic or pictorial work of any other Russian artist of the time. Like *Encore* they reveal a certain 'super-realism', a quality which also distinguishes the writing of Dostoevsky, who similarly considered the concept of super-realism a more appropriate description of his work than mere realism. Fedotov, like Dostoevsky, presents life in concentrated form and his interpretation of the world differs from our normal perception of reality.

The Gamblers retains many of the features explored in the studies. The finished version may seem somewhat more realistic than the studies, but it displays the same

Pavel Fedotov *The Gamblers* 1852

qualities of condensation and concentration. Unlike them, however, its compositional pictorial and plastic structure reveals a certain contrast between the objective and defined on the one hand, and the diffuse and unstable on the other. An indistinct world of dark corners, corridors and general spatial uncertainty is created around the figures at the heart of the composition. Specific objects and characters appear to be deliberately focused, and preserve that physical and spiritual deformity so clearly depicted in the studies. The characters are comparable with their ill-defined surroundings. These two contrasting elements are set close together, preserving their separate identities but seemingly connected by direct lines. The figures move, yet a sense of paralysis dominates the canvas. Movement is frozen; every gesture is fixed. This paralysis is akin to that concentrated atmosphere which surrounds the characters and emphasizes their general state of torpidity.

Fedotov's last works, though interesting in their own right, contributed little to Russian painting as a whole and for a long time their fate was oblivion. Fedotov's legacy to the second half of the century was his powerful emotional critique, and it fully justifies his right to be considered as one of the fathers of mature Realism in the middle and later years of the nineteenth century. It is no accident that this stage of Realism was given the appellation 'critical': it was imbued with the spirit of protest against the world around it and devoted to the task of analysing and unmasking the contradictions inherent in society. Fedotov's brand of critical Realism, with its lyrical touch, differs from that which flourished in the 1860s. Thus we may say that his work defined the first – poetic – stage in the development of critical Realism in Russian painting. As for the achievements of his later years, they were to be truly discovered and fully appreciated only in the twentieth century.

7   Sculpture and Architecture

In the 1830s painting indubitably occupied the key position among the plastic arts, with 'drawing' contributing to the maintenance of this position as and when it could. Sculpture and especially architecture, therefore, had to be content with secondary roles. As classicism declined, these two branches of art experienced a crisis, adapting only with great difficulty to the new directions in which Russian art and culture were developing in the second half of the nineteenth century. Romanticism and early Realism could not take root in sculpture, whose only products of any interest and value were those which interpreted their subjects along classical lines. Those innovations which did derive from Romanticism or Realism were merely superficial additions to the underlying classical vision.

This situation is well illustrated by the work of Boris Orlovsky (1792–1838), one of the most remarkable Russian sculptors of the 1830s. Born a serf, he trained as a marble-cutter and craftsman, and his remarkable talents quickly attracted the attention of many famous sculptors of the time, including Martos. He was granted his freedom and, after a short period of study at the St Petersburg Academy of Fine Arts, was sent to Rome with a bursary to study under Thorwaldsen, who soon expressed himself delighted with his Russian pupil. In Italy he produced a number of statues of individuals and groups during the 1820s, such as *Paris*, *Satyr Playing on a Pipe* and *Satyr and Bacchante*, which resembled the work of his teacher in their choice of motif and treatment of marble. Orlovsky had a forthright talent, moderated by a certain idyllic pensiveness, and he interpreted the themes of antiquity in an original and Romantic, rather than heroic style; but this line of development was soon interrupted by his recall to Russia. Back home, he was entrusted with major projects, including the monuments to two heroes of the recent Napoleonic war – Kutuzov and Barclay de Tolly. One of the strict conditions of the commission (originally the subject of a competition) was that the heroes be depicted in modern dress, with no reference to the 'antique' conventions. The only Russian sculptor of the day who was equal to this challenging task was Orlovsky. He shows the two great generals as if

Boris Orlovsky
Satyr and Bacchante 1837

standing on the field of battle, trampling on the enemy's flags. Their poses are pregnant with meaning – Kutuzov is decisive, while Barclay reveals a certain diffidence and reserve. Their obligatory generals' uniforms and over-coats did not prevent Orlovsky from exploiting the tradition of classical drapery to convey an air of dignity and majesty. The determined gesture of Kutuzov's outstretched hand allows the drapery simultaneously to fall away from and to tighten revealingly round the rather stout figure of the field marshal. The folds of his clothing seem to arrest his movement and confer on him a sense of grandeur, whereas the treatment of Barclay's dress liberates the figure, whose pose expresses doubt and inward concentration. Both figures are columnar and thus in perfect accord with the portico and colonnade of the Kazan Cathedral where they were to stand.

The statues, especially that of Barclay de Tolly, display remarkable psychological insight as well as historical authenticity, both derived more from the new realistic approach than from classicism. Nevertheless, the generally classical treatment of the characters' portrayal is quite unmistakable. Orlovsky treads a fine line between classicism and realism and his work brings to a close the long history of monumental Russian classical sculpture, which had begun in the eighteenth century with Rastrelli the Elder's equestrian statue of Peter the Great and continued with Falconet's masterpiece of the *Bronze Horseman*, Kozlovsky's *Suvorov* and Martos's *Minin and Pozharsky*.

Whereas Orlovsky's sculpture signified the last stage in the development of Russian classical monuments erected in honour of historical figures, his near-contemporary, Baron Pyotr Karlovich Klodt (1805–67), played a similar role in the history of monumental decorative sculpture. He produced the very last work in the genre to enjoy great success, namely the group of four *Horse-tamers* on the Anichkov Bridge in St Petersburg (1833–46). Each group consists of a naked youth struggling to control a rearing horse; each illustrates in different ways the relationship between Man and Nature untamed. The four compositions – different versions of the same duo – present a clear and classical image of dramatic combat. The boy's pose varies from the graceful gait of a victor to the semi-prone position of the defeated. The basically classical character of the work is to some extent enlivened by the Romantic impulse, and by the interesting and unusual treatment of the theme of confrontation between human intellect and elemental animal strength. However, just as elements of realism in Orlovsky's work do not dilute the essentially classical nature of his monuments, so the romantic aspects in Klodt coexist with his classical treatment of forms: clear silhouettes, stylized plasticity and idealized modelling.

Boris Orlovsky, Monument to M.I. Kutuzov, St Petersburg, 1829–32

Boris Orlovsky, Monument to M.B. Barclay de Tolly, St Petersburg, 1829–36

In Klodt's memorial statues it is the monumental element which is the weakest. In the equestrian statue of the Emperor Nicholas I, on which he worked between 1850 and 1859, Klodt proved his mastery of detail and his perfect calculation of the centre of gravity, but the statue nevertheless lacks the 'weightiness' indispensable to a memorial work. The statue, the main element of the Emperor's monument planned as the central point of Montferrand's remodelled St Isaac's Square, became nothing more than an absurdly overgrown statuette.

Klodt's memorial statue (1848–55) of the fable writer Krylov does not attempt to create a monumental effect. It is set in a secluded corner of the Summer Garden, screened all around by trees. No vast piazzas or wide perspectives open up behind the figure of Krylov, who is sitting comfortably on a chair, absorbed in his book. Klodt gives the great writer a relaxed and everyday look, fully consistent with the popular impression of him as a slow-moving, even lazy fellow by no means cast in the heroic mould.

Klodt's observant eye and close attention to detail were put to excellent effect in the field of small decorative sculpture intended for viewing at close quarters. His group entitled *Mare and Foal* (1840s) is a typical example of this sort of 'cabinet' sculpture which covered the tables, *étagères* and whatnots in countless homes, from the mansions of the highest in the land to the humble dwellings of the lowliest clerks. *Mare and Foal* is a direct antecedent of the work of the early twentieth-century sculptor Pavel Trubetskoi.

Another St Petersburg sculptor working in the field of cabinet sculpture was Nikolai Pimenov (1812–64), also known as Pimenov the younger. His very expressive *Portrait of a Young Man* (1844) is a plaster figure of a youth sitting on a sort of stone slab, perhaps enjoying the surrounding countryside. Pimenov's other works are of little interest. In 1836 he attempted the promising theme of a *Young Boy Playing 'Babki'*, a children's game akin to knucklebones. This was part of a programme, initiated by the Academy of Fine Arts, and dedicated to the depiction of genuine Russian customs. Two of the other participants were Alexander Loganovsky (*Boy Playing 'Saika'* – another game) and Anton Ivanov (*Boy Playing 'Gorodki'* – similar to skittles). Despite the efforts of these artists and of the leadership of the Academy to establish this new movement in sculpture (analogous to those which had arisen in the work of Venetsianov and his pupils) early Realism never really caught on in sculpture. The Academic traditions appeared to be invincible; those academically perfect bodies of naked boys could hardly convey the reality or the poetry of Russian national customs. Russian sculpture made no further progress for many years and naked models in the pose of sowers and scythers were still appearing as late as the 1860s.

We have already mentioned a number of artists more or less closely connected with the Academy of Fine Arts. Moscow, the former capital, produced only one significant sculptor, Ivan Vitali (1794–1855). Italian by birth, the son of a modeller, he was a talented marble cutter who set up his own studio in Moscow and eventually

(above) **Pyotr Klodt** *Horse-tamer* 1833

(opposite left) **Pyotr Klodt**, Monument to I.A. Krylov, St Petersburg, 1848–55

(centre) **Ivan Vitali** *Saint Isaac the Dalmatian Blesses Emperor Theodos* 1841–44

(left) **Nikolai Pimenov** *Young Boy Playing 'Babki'* 1836

transformed himself from a master craftsman into a true artist. He worked in several genres, producing portraits and statues, fountains for Moscow squares, a victory chariot for a triumphal arch, and finally a sculpture to adorn the pediment of St Isaac's Cathedral in St Petersburg. A number of neo-Baroque features are noticeable in his work; not the mere reminiscences of Baroque found in the work of certain eighteenth and early nineteenth-century artists, but a deliberate return to Baroque techniques and forms. On one of Vitali's fountains the interwoven figures of boys surround a column supporting the bowl; they make up a complex composition of forms flowing into each other. Great importance is attached to the play of light and shadow, the latter hiding in the depths between the volumes. Vitali's chosen motif of playful wrestling itself invites such a Baroque, dynamic treatment of the figures, their poses and their gestures. The figures decorating the pediment of St Isaac's are even more Baroque in character. Parts of the figures hang down from the cornice, breaking up what should, classically speaking, be the plane separating sculptural space from that of the observer.

Vitali's last significant work is a marble *Venus* (1852–53). The beautiful goddess raises her slender left knee in a graceful movement in order to fasten her sandal. This statue, with its gentle marble sfumato, seems to stand on, but by some miracle not to cross, the threshold of salon-academic art of the middle years of the nineteenth century.

Russian sculpture of the 1850s, having exhausted all the potential of classicism, found itself in a state of crisis. The crisis was to last for several decades and was only relieved at the end of the century by the advent of a new movement linked with Impressionism, Symbolism and Art Nouveau.

The fate of Russian architecture was similar to that of sculpture. The dominance of classicism was beginning to weaken even here, where its sway had been strongest. Those few architects who kept the faith between the 1830s and the 1850s were considered old-fashioned. E.D.

< **Auguste Montferrand**, St Isaac's Cathedral, St Petersburg, 1818–58

Andrei Shtakenshneider, Mariinsky Palace, St Petersburg, 1839–44

Tyurin, for example, worked in Moscow, where he completed the ensemble of Manège Square with the erection of the University church of St Tatiana, at the corner of the square and Nikitskaya Street. The church, with its soft, rounded contours and harmonious colonnade running along the half-rotunda, is in happy accord both with the classical style of the Manège and with the stately yet decorative portico of the University. Even Tyurin adulterated the strict classical principles with eclectic elements towards the end of his career.

P.C. Pavlov continued the traditions of the classicism which had flourished in St Petersburg between 1810 and 1830; his splendid staircase for the Board of Guardians building (1834–39) is an echo of former glories. But the superb classical training he received at the Academy of Fine Arts was too narrow to encourage the exploration of new directions in architecture. 'Pure', undiluted classicism was becoming a rarity. Its rules were being increasingly infringed and its principles modified. Forms lost their former harmony, became heavier and more complicated and absorbed elements of other styles such

as Renaissance. A good example of this development is the remarkable St Isaac's Cathedral (1818–58), designed by the French architect Auguste Montferrand (1786–1858). The cathedral is an extraordinary blend of a basilical groundplan and a central cupola, conceived in grandiose dimensions and worked out in the smallest detail. The resulting mixture is disappointing: the cathedral seems cumbersome and unbalanced; it lacks purity of silhouette, evoking a sense of grim alienation instead of the required stateliness.

Three architects working in St Petersburg as well as Moscow, A.P. Briullov (1798–1877), A.I. Shtakenshneider (1802–65) and K.A. Ton (1794–1881), were more creative in their use of eclectic elements and the application of the new historical method. Some of Briullov's work completes existing ensembles. His Guards' headquarters (1840), for example, enclosing Palace Square on one side, is a tactful and intelligent architectural solution to a complex problem. The Guards' building, with its modest Ionic colonnade running along the facade, is not intended as a challenge to the Winter

Palace or the General Headquarters; it gives the impression of having respectfully taken a pace backwards so as not to interrupt the dialogue of the two 'giants'. At the same time Briullov's traditional, rather impersonal classicism, enlivened by one minor innovation (a motif derived from Pompeii, decorating the piers between the first floor windows), does its best to complement the ensemble envisaged by Rossi and Rastrelli. Briullov was adept at selecting decorative and compositional techniques appropriate to the task in hand. In Pargolovo (a village outside St Petersburg), for example, he built a church in Gothic style. In the centre of St Petersburg he designed the Lutheran church of St Peter along the lines of a twin-towered Romanesque, or Gothic, basilica. His Pulkovo Observatory building is a mixture of classical and Renaissance styles.

Andrei Shtakenshneider is renowned for the palaces he designed in differing styles. The classical Mariinsky Palace, on St Isaac's Square, was built in 1841 for the Grand Duchess Maria, eldest daughter of Nicholas I. The Nikolaevsky Palace (1853–61), the residence of Grand Duke Nicholas, the Emperor's son, is in Renaissance style, while the Novy (New) Mikhailovsky Palace, built for another of the Emperor's sons, Grand Duke Mikhail, is Baroque. They do, however, have certain features in common. The rather boring and repetitive facades are in sharp contrast to the impressive and spacious interiors. Space flows from one room to the next and up and down steep flights of stairs. Shtakenshneider preserved total symmetry for the facades while rejecting every principle of balance and restraint in the design of the interiors, where everything is calculated to surprise, an effect to which the very contrast between the interiors and the exteriors contributes.

The approach of Konstantin Ton, the architect of the Great Palace in the Moscow Kremlin, was similar to that of Shtakenshneider. Its unimpressive facade, consisting of repeated elements of Renaissance and old Russian architecture, seems deliberately designed to conceal a number of splendid and richly ornamented halls, whose decor and colour scheme correspond with the ribbons of the five principal orders of the Russian Empire – the orders of Sts George, Catherine, Vladimir, Alexander and Andrew. The main facade is so faceless that it does not even include the entrance, which is set at the side of the palace, deep in the courtyard. An arch, leading to the entrance, is decorative rather than formal.

Ton's most important building was the Cathedral of Christ the Saviour (1839–83). It stood not far from the Kremlin, whose architectural forms it echoed. The proportions and general harmony of form of the exterior were unremarkable. The disproportion between the huge central dome and its four much smaller companions at the corners, together with the mix of elements of Byzantine and old Russian style borrowed from various architectural periods, combined to produce a ponderous, clumsy and static building. The interior, by contrast, possessed a quality of grandeur and splendour, achieved by enlarging the space under the cupola and concealing the supporting pillars behind the wall of the gallery running round the inside of the Cathedral. Wishing to incorporate significant old Russian and Byzantine traditions into the design of the Cathedral, Ton devoted many years of study and experiment in the field of Orthodox Church architecture to the project, which became the starting-point for further development in church architecture. Ton himself was responsible for the plans, realized and unrealized, of churches all over Russia, and his basic design determined the character of new Orthodox churches throughout the Empire and beyond its borders.

One stream of Russian architecture between 1830 and 1860 maintained strong links with the Romantic movement. The Romantic architects turned to the pseudo-Gothic style already widespread since the eighteenth century. One of the most remarkable examples of this trend is the Marfino estate (1837–39) for which the architect M.D. Bukovsky (1801–85) built or rebuilt the Palace, two extra wings, a church, a bridge over the lake and a number of domestic buildings. The Palace facade is divided by a number of pilasters which project so sharply that they are virtually buttresses and incidentally reveal the structure of the building.

In the design of the Palace a certain rationalism tempers the recreation of the Gothic style, but the marvellously poetic bridge is in perfect harmony with its natural surroundings. The pseudo-Gothic style of Marfino is by no means a superficial veneer covering conventional buildings which could as well have become classical if they had been dressed in columns. Bukovsky succeeded, more than any of his contemporaries, in using the renewed idiom of pseudo-Gothic to express the Romantic concept.

To conclude this short review of Russian architecture between 1830 and 1850 let us return to our starting point. The single style which had previously united all architecture, of whatever genre, was now shattered. What had only recently been a mighty torrent was now divided into separate streams, all of which lacked power, consistency and singlemindedness. But the conscious absence of style (or, to express it another way, a multitude of styles) is itself a style of sorts. This very condition would ensure the further development and renewal of Russian architecture.

PART II · 1860–1895

1 The Realists of the 1860s

In the second half of the nineteenth century Russian art, in all its variety, was ranged between two opposite poles – the Realist and the Academic. This polarization was quite clearly marked; apart from the Romantic tradition, which was itself almost exhausted, there were virtually no other movements. Realism and Academicism, admittedly, often approached each other and interacted, as painters were attracted now to one extreme, now the other. The pole of Realism, however, exercised the stronger pull.

Russian Realism was typical of its time and yet in many ways unique. Nearly all the European schools passed through this very important phase of historical and artistic development, which perhaps manifested itself most brilliantly in French painting during the middle years of the nineteenth century. Realism brought with it new principles and established a new style.[1] In the age of positivism, the energetic development of the exact sciences and the birth of new scientific concepts drastically changed man's view of the world, and art stood shoulder to shoulder with science in the vital process of enriching man's insight into that world. The artistic process acquired some of the features of scientific experimentation, concentrating on the understanding and interpretation of concrete facts and transforming the resulting artistic image into broad generalizations based on those facts. Realist art hitched its star to contemporary life, usually turning to themes and characters taken from real life and attaching particular importance to the signs and symbols of the present day. When historical subjects *were* treated, even those from the distant past, they were interpreted in a modern idiom. Relying for its subject-matter on the true facts of the contemporary world, Realism was bound to become socially partisan, addressing social problems and provoking its public to consider the many contradictions in society. Sometimes it even offered its own solutions. These changes in the very structure of the artistic process, almost revolutionary in their impact, vividly expressed the spirit of the times.

This was the case in France, as elsewhere, but Russian Realism owes its peculiar character to the evolution and influence of its own special traditions. It grew and established itself at a time when the ulcers on the body of Russian society were becoming all too visible. The process of reform, whose delay had resulted in ever sharper social divisions, was now of the utmost urgency. Aesthetic and political ideas and activities were interwoven as never before in the history of Russia. There is no better example of this phenomenon than the author, revolutionary, philosopher and aesthete, Nikolai Chernyshevsky, who was imprisoned for his democratic opinions for many years. His thesis, 'The Aesthetic Relationship between Art and Reality', submitted in 1855, sounded a clarion call to progressive writers, dramatists, artists and musicians. It should not be forgotten, either, that serfdom was abolished in Russia only in 1861, and even then its after-effects lingered on for many years, due to the halfheartedness and incompleteness of the peasant reforms. The struggle against serfdom and its continuing consequences was waged in an atmosphere of unremitting reaction which excluded any possibility of open political opposition (let alone revolution) and slowed the nation's social progress almost to a halt. Nevertheless, the Russian people were ready for social change. The philosopher and author Alexander Herzen described the 1830s and 1840s as 'an incredible period when a state of slavery coexisted with inner liberation'.[2] But real liberation did not follow; indeed, the normal political processes in the struggle for such liberation were almost totally banned. Under these conditions it was hardly surprising that the only outlet for the expression of democratic ideas was through literature and art. Never before had Russia produced men of the calibre of Herzen, who was not only a revolutionary, but a philosopher, author, theoretician of art, literary critic, economist and sociologist. Only in eighteenth-century France was a similar combination of gifts to be found – among the great Encyclopaedists. But there was a specific reason why a man like Herzen should appear in Russia at precisely the time he did. Herzen himself explained the unique circumstances of Russia as follows: 'For a people deprived of its social freedoms, literature is the only platform from which it can make the cries of its conscience and indignation heard.'[3] In this situation,

Vasily Perov *Easter Procession* 1861

literature and art must inevitably become directly embroiled in social questions, nearly always defending the interests of the most oppressed sections of society. They embodied the critical mood of the age, touching its rawest nerve, ruthlessly exposing its inner conflicts and subjecting every artistic image to rigorous ethical evaluation.

The festering sores of social life were so glaring that they simply cried out to be depicted on canvas or described in the pages of novels. In Russia, more than in any other country, the essential prerequisite of the Realists' approach was the direct confrontation of social problems. At the same time, the complex web of mutually dependent relationships of people vis-à-vis each other and society demanded profound psychological analysis. It was these two tendencies – the social and the psychological – which crucially shaped the specific creative impulses of Russian writers, dramatists and artists.

In the nineteenth-century context, of course, it was literature which had the greatest potential for fulfilling

the obligations the period imposed on the arts. The nineteenth century was predominantly 'literary' the whole world over, but especially in Russia, where literature acquired tremendous social influence. From the 1850s onwards such writers as Turgenev, Herzen, Tolstoy, Dostoevsky, Nekrasov, Chernyshevsky, Goncharov and Saltykov-Shchedrin confronted the most intractable questions of the day, illuminating them and raising them to the level of universal significance. These writers brought the most profound insight to bear upon the character, behaviour and condition of Man in society. They were inspired by a high sense of morality and taught that the supreme aim of art was to serve humanity.

According to Georgi Gachev, literature came into existence before philosophy and subsequently took upon itself the function of philosophy. 'In the nineteenth century intellectual and artistic activity would inevitably become the central focus of Russian national life.'[4] This activity was literature, and even though the moral critique and evaluation of the social circumstances and

Vasily Perov *A Village Sermon* 1861

actions of literary characters became all-important, such morality did not exclude the need for beauty and truth. As Leo Tolstoy expressed it: 'Real talent has, as it were, two shoulders. One is ethics, the other aesthetics. If ethics is too high, then aesthetics is too low, and talent becomes lopsided.'[5] Tolstoy himself, like Dostoevsky, was able to achieve a perfect balance between these two forces. Others were less successful.

Painting, which could not aspire to compete with literature, made more modest progress along the route which literature was so energetically pioneering.

In 1862 Vasily Perov, a Moscow painter, bewildered the public as well as the authorities in St Petersburg when his canvas entitled *Easter Procession*, painted a year earlier, was exhibited. 'Although the picture was rapidly removed', wrote an eye-witness (in a letter to the well-known collector Pavel Tretyakov), 'it still raised quite a storm of protest. Let us hope that Perov will not end up in the Solovetsky monastery rather than in Italy.'[6] This was an unambiguous reference to a notorious place of exile in the remote north of the empire. Never before had the threat of such punishment loomed over any Russian painter. On this occasion, admittedly, the pessimism of Tretyakov's correspondent was misjudged, as Perov left for Paris after being awarded a scholarship from the Imperial Academy of Arts, but the very idea of such a threat was evidence of the new role painting was beginning to play in Russian society.

In the second half of the nineteenth century Russian Realism became known as 'Critical Realism'. Its origin lay largely in the situation in the 1860s – the decade in which Russian art was most preoccupied with criticizing and exposing the ills of society. During the years of reform, when the whole of society was in turmoil, Russian painters were inspired by the struggle against social evils, as well as by the hope that they would be able to pursue their ambitions independent of the dictates of the Imperial Academy. The changes taking place in Russian artistic life were evidence of the new 'social status' of artists. 1863 saw the famous 'revolt of the 14' – the ostentatious resignation from the Academy of fourteen students in their final year, who refused to paint the obligatory diploma-paintings on traditional mythological themes. These rebels formed their own 'Artists' Cooperative Society' in St Petersburg, a kind of artistic commune which provided them with an independent status. In the first half of the nineteenth century, of course, there had also been artists who opposed and even defied the Academy, but these were isolated and individual cases. Now for the first time, however, an organization had appeared – a whole collective of followers of the new 'artistic religion'.

Moscow's response to the new social situation manifested itself in actual works of art rather than in artistic gestures and 'happenings'. Graduates of the Moscow School of Painting, Sculpture and Architecture were less fettered by academic doctrines, and ordinary Muscovites led more natural and less artificial lives than their fellows in St Petersburg, which was dominated by the demands of the Imperial Court. It was Moscow which gave birth to the famous Maly Theatre and inspired the plays of Ostrovsky. The ancient former capital was the ideal soil to nurture those early shoots of genre art which were later to acquire such social significance.

Vasily Perov (1834–82) was the main exponent of these new tendencies. He was the virtual leader of the painters in the 'Men and Women of the 1860s' (*shestidesyatniki*) movement, giving them a sense of direction and proportion, influencing their development and embodying all their conflicts and contradictions. His insight into his fellow men and women was even greater than his talent as a painter. He espoused various causes with great passion, staged protests and publicly proclaimed his sympathies. He was the very leader the new Realists needed in the 1860s, when the struggle against all that was old, decrepit and decayed in Russian social life was all-important.

Perov's time as a student was a period of measured development. He adopted the semi-academic, semi-naturalistic style typical of the day, and his apprentice-ship concluded with an attempt to compare himself with

Fedotov, whose fame as a genre painter was then at its height. This comparison, together with his studies, led Perov to an understanding of the necessity to engage art directly in the social struggle.

At the beginning of the 1860s, after graduation from art school and a year's work at the Academy, Perov painted three works which expressed his fundamental philosophy: *A Village Sermon* (1861), *Easter Procession* (1861) mentioned above, and *Drinking Tea in Mytishchi* (1862). The first of these paintings was awarded the Academy's gold medal, which carried with it a grant to work abroad. This was the last occasion on which the Academy felt able to approve of the new direction art was taking, and in the following year it abandoned the practice of allowing its students to paint subjects of their own choosing. It was this decision which led to the 'revolt of the 14'. Indeed, the Academy did not understand the implications of awarding Perov its gold medal.

His pictures of the early 1860s are remarkable for their mood of protest against the existing order, and against the squalor and ignorance in which the poor were obliged to live. All three paintings have an anticlerical slant, but their message goes well beyond the limits of their nominal subjects. They denounced the rich and powerful who were still depriving the people of their rights and keeping them in darkness and poverty, and highlighted the scandalous contrasts and inequalities between the classes which were the abiding curse of contemporary Russian society. The principal task Perov set for himself was to present this situation before the observer in all its raw and glaring horror. He depicts his scenes with total objectivity; they unfold in their own space, a space quite independent of the observer's. This quality is most obvious in *Easter Procession*. The procession, which includes a drunken priest, a woman gaping mindlessly with an icon in her hand, an old man holding an icon upside down, and similar characters, passes before the observer almost parallel to the plane of the picture. At the centre of the canvas the procession curves towards the observer and then moves away. Perov shows his characters one after the other, together with all the ills of village life which the characters are intended to personify. This is the world against which Perov pits himself, his committed position giving him the right, as it were, to shape the action to his will. In this painting the participants are deprived of their free will, permitted by the painter only to act out their prescribed roles. Their faces and figures lack independent existence and only interest Perov insofar as they can be made to fulfil these roles.

Perov's brand of rationalism, apparently so opposed to the emotional explosion which inspired these three denunciatory pictures, is also expressed in the way the painter relates the figures to the landscapes and interiors. Whether it be the cold, soulless church interior or the grim landscape against which the ugly scene of the drunken Easter procession is set, he uses the surroundings to ram home his angry message.

This stage in his career saw the emergence of an interesting relationship between form, which was simply a means for Perov, and content. He used a kind of ready-made form, inherited from his teachers, the product of the mixture of styles which occurred in the middle years of the century. To some extent he adapted this form to his own purposes, although at first the adaptation was somewhat superficial. He produced these three works, expressing his underlying philosophy, at an extraordinarily early age (when he was still a student), and his search for content – his message – was far more advanced than his technical grasp. His paintings dating from the early 1860s are generally characterized by a certain crudeness of line, and by the use of 'local colours' (i.e. the colours of objects as seen in daylight against a white background, irrespective of surrounding influences such as shadows and reflections), although the colours are juxtaposed and united by chiaroscuro. A few years later, Perov would transform these adopted forms by integrating their pictorial and compositional logic with the powerful content of his convictions. In the early 1860s, however, he still had a long way to go.

Perov's works from the early 1860s constituted a real revolution in Russian painting. He was followed by dozens of other artists, similarly striving to expose social evils and to unmask those responsible, generally ascribing guilt to those in authority. Perov himself received a travelling scholarship, went abroad and did indeed spend about two years in Paris; but, yearning for the Russia which was his true inspiration, he ended his studies prematurely. Even this short period in France, however, was a time of progress which brought about a fundamental change in the conception of genre painting. The passion for exposure was succeeded by the impulse towards sympathy and understanding. His Paris sketches, studies and single-figure compositions are devoted to very simple folk – itinerant musicians and circus artistes, children and old people – rendered somewhat sentimentally. There is no trace of the earlier frank demonstrativeness or straightforward story-telling. Perov continued to develop this approach, first adopted during the Parisian period, until the end of the 1860s.

Perov's genre painting blossomed after his return to Russia, in the middle and late 1860s. These were the years of his best work in this field: *A Village Funeral* (1865), *The Drowned Girl* (1867) and *The Last Inn by the Town Gate* (1868). These paintings depict various aspects of social life and address many problems of the day, such

Vasily Perov
A Village Funeral
1865

Vasily Perov
The Drowned Girl 1867 >

as the living conditions of the peasants, urban poverty and the appalling position of women, but they are united by a single theme – the expression of grief. It is significant that Perov's main genre paintings can be grouped according to the relationship of the artist to his subject rather than according to the subjects themselves. We may trace his evolution from hatred (*Easter Procession*) to sympathy (*The Last Inn*). To express the former he makes use of a demonstrative quality; to achieve the latter he heightens the emotions and increases pictorial and compositional concentration. The earlier work merely describes an event which does not destroy the static nature of the composition and colour; the later painting surmounts the event itself with its own compositional and pictorial dynamic.

A Village Funeral, pregnant with the poetry of grief, ushered in a new kind of genre painting. Pictorial and compositional techniques were subordinated to the need to convey this emotion to the observer and to make him a participant in the unfolding tragedy. The movement of the sledges along the snowbound road is directed into the background, drawing the observer into the space of the painting. The landscape, melancholy and bereft of hope, is in tune with the mood of the grieving burial party. The rhythm of the rounded outlines – the contour of the horse

and its shaft-bow, the bent back of the peasant widow-woman – contribute to the mournful atmosphere. The treatment of colour supports these rhythmical elements. Browns, yellows and greys, crowded together as closely as possible, create a sense of almost melodious unity and strengthen the feeling of depression. The motif of the moving sledges, so typical of the Russian rural landscape, is significant in itself. This theme of endless movement through unlimited space has many layers of meaning (here it stands as a metaphor for ceaseless suffering on this earth) and permits Perov to interpret time in a new way. Time is no longer given concrete expression, as in earlier paintings; in *A Village Funeral* it is in some way infinite, as if drowned in silence and waiting.

The Drowned Girl illustrates the next phase in Perov's career as a mature artist. We see the corpse of a woman who has ended her earthly sojourn by suicide and the frozen figure of the policeman, waiting for dawn. The outlines of the Moscow Kremlin are barely visible through the fog, the mighty citadel which is so far removed from all the misfortunes and unhappiness which plague the people of the city. All these elements evoke the mood of tragic hopelessness of the suicide itself as well as the senselessness of existence in general.

The same theme of passive waiting, with no prospect

23

of release from the burdens of daily life, provides the basis for Perov's best painting – *The Last Inn by the Town Gate*. The canvas is devoid of action and sparse in detail. Horse-drawn sledges at the entrance to the inn, and a woman, waiting perhaps for some drunks to emerge, comprise all the story the artist wishes to tell. Only one 'explanatory' detail strikes the eye: the coat of arms (the Imperial double eagle) on the pillars, which locates the action at the city boundary. Other details are included for their emotional and psychological impact. Smoke rises from the chimney, only to be blown low again by the wind, which has already piled snow on the windowsills and porches of the houses; crows and jackdaws, doubtless screeching their senseless caws, fly across the light sky; a tree branch has been caught up and then discarded on the roadside by some passing sledge. All these details increase the atmosphere of numbness and depression. This 'Russian melancholy' was a frequent theme in so many pain-ridden works of poetry, prose and music of the time. In painting, it was most brilliantly realized in this work by Perov, who expressed it by means of two contrasting motifs – static waiting, and the road running into the distant background. The meaninglessness of the waiting and the endlessness of the road are somehow similar. Perov gives a tremendous sense of completeness

to the composition by placing, in the foreground, a classical triangle made up of the two sledges set at an angle to each other and, opposed to it, the diagonal of the street, where faint light alternates with deep shadow and the shrill radiance of the sunset sky. The energetic brushwork of the whole painting, and especially of the snow-covered ground, conforms to this dynamic. The brushwork not only follows the forms, but also lies on the surface of the canvas, acquiring its own rhythmical expressiveness and validity. The contrast of the fading brown-red and grey tones with the pure, clear light of the sky creates an effect of depth of space, obviating the need to measure or mark out this space naturalistically by means of landmarks of any kind. Perov exploits all his compositional and pictorial techniques to heighten the drama of the situation. His genre paintings were to be dominated, until the end of the 1860s, by the emotions of the artist himself, who seems to figure in them as the main character.

By the beginning of the 1870s the enthusiasm for paintings which were denunciatory and/or sympathetic in tone, Perov's inspiration for fully ten years, was a thing of the past. A new generation of painters, who wished to affirm certain social values rather than to deny them, appeared on the scene. We shall discuss these new

tendencies in more detail below. As for Perov, his main
genre paintings in the 1870s depicted hunters, fishermen,
wildfowlers and pigeon-fanciers, going about their business, absorbed in their relationship with nature, and
expressing neither the fury nor the sorrow of the artist.

Perov also tried his skill at other, less socially
committed genres. He turned to historical themes and
conceived the idea of a triptych dedicated to Pugachev,
the famous leader of a popular rebellion in the eighteenth
century; these experiments, however, met with little
success. In the early 1870s he founded, together with
Kramskoi, Ge and other masters, a new kind of portrait
genre with a complete programme of its own and a
specific plan to create a series of portraits of prominent
contemporary fellow countrymen, including progressive
figures in the arts – writers, composers, artists and actors.
Perov's best contributions to this project were his
portraits of the celebrated playwright Alexander
Ostrovsky and the great writer Fyodor Dostoevsky
(1872).

It is the everyday aspect of life which is remarkable in
the Ostrovsky portrait. The playwright, a Muscovite, is
depicted in his dressing gown, facing the observer as if
ready and willing to converse with him. Perov's aim in
this work is to describe the specific behaviour of his
subject at a particular moment in time. The momentari-
ness of Ostrovsky's state is conveyed by his gaze and by
his actual and potential movement. In Perov's portraits
the traditional triad – model, artist, image – is weighted in
favour of the model, who largely dictates the character of
the image, although the painter's role is also very
important. Perov wishes to penetrate to Ostrovsky's very
essence and to understand him fully (an understanding of
which he was perfectly capable). He presents his model
as a man isolated from his environment, but also
perceives elements of his everyday life. It is not simply
that Ostrovsky is painted in his dressing gown, rather that
we can vividly imagine his unshown physical environment. This characteristic derives from Tropinin's
approach to portrait painting.

In contrast to the Ostrovsky painting, Dostoevsky is
portrayed as deeply immersed in thought. He exists in a
world of complex feelings. The overriding aim of this
work is to understand that state rather than Dostoevsky's
character. This state is realized in time, flowing one-
dimensionally; Perov does not select a single moment in
that time, however, but the whole of time unfolding.
Dostoevsky's is an enclosed and private world, one which
appears all the more impressive to the observer, who sees
it as at once comprehensible and somehow incomprehensible in all its complex multidimensionality. The self-
sufficiency of the writer's spiritual existence is strengthened by the composition of the portrait. The circle

Vasily Perov *Portrait of Fyodor Dostoevsky* 1872

formed by his coupled hands assists in the separation of
the space in which the figure is set. The painting's gentle
tones, based on the relationship between various shades
of brown, create an equivalent to the fullness and
complexity of the life of the great writer.

Perov's highly successful portrait period is related to
the next stage (that is, post 1860s) in the development of
Russian painting. Returning to the 1860s themselves, we
should mention some other genre painters whose work is
partly encompassed by this decade. Nearly all of them
were followers of Perov; most were Muscovites. N.V.
Nevrev, with his *Scene from Everyday Life under
Serfdom. From the Recent Past* (1866) betrayed an
unmistakable reliance on the tradition of realistic theatre
dealing with themes from everyday life. V.V. Pukirev,
who caused a sensation with his painting *The Unequal
Marriage* in 1863, showed that it was possible to graft the
techniques of academic painting onto the denunciatory
genre. Illarion Pryanishnikov, like Perov (his older fellow
student at the Moscow School of Art) evolved from
moralizing subjects, in such paintings as *Jokers at the
Bazaar* (1865), to the emotional scene of his landscape
Empty Wagons (1871–72). A.L. Yushanov, in *Seeing off
the Chief* (1864), showed himself a follower of Fedotov as
well as of Perov, describing with marvellous humour and
observation the hosts and guests at a house party saying
goodbye to a departing general.

Leonid Solomatkin *Carol Singers* 1872

Illarion Pryanishnikov *Jokers at the Bazaar* 1865

Leonid Solomatkin *The Wedding* 1872

Only one important artist stood apart from this group of genre painters who so passionately preached and protested, mocked the wicked and took the side of the oppressed. This was Leonid Solomatkin (1837–83), who began his studies at the Moscow School of Art and continued them at the St Petersburg Academy of Fine Arts, though without completing the course. While Solomatkin's themes were similar to those treated by other artists in the 1860s, his choice of subjects was determined less by his denunciatory attitude than by the realities of contemporary life. Such themes and subjects, already tackled by writers, seemed to lie on the very surface of daily life. Naturally, painting itself had to make an effort to come into contact with this surface, but after Perov's heroic endeavours all these themes became popular and accessible to all, although the manner in which they were interpreted was, of course, another matter. Solomatkin remained independent of the social commitment of the *shestidesyatniki* (see p. 104). He did not preach or teach, nor was he particularly distressed by the social vices he saw all around him. He happily, and with great interest, observed these phenomena; he found them amusing. Solomatkin consciously strove to imitate folk idioms and popular prints (*lubki*), and made copious use of grotesque, exaggeration and distortion of reality in order to draw out the typical features and characteristics of his subjects. The presence together of *lubki* and grotesque elements in his work is not surprising, for grotesque is an essential part of the popular way of artistic thinking. For Solomatkin this thinking was not so much a model as a point of convergence, for he suffered from acute alcoholism for many years. He sank deeper and

deeper into the social underworld, growing ever closer to the wretched inhabitants of that world and acquiring that simple-hearted, even naive outlook on life which so often conceals a certain penetrating sharpness of eye. The characters he depicted are unique – policemen invited to a party at the house of a merchant; beggars keening for alms; a pitiful musician with his daughter, playing upon a pipe in a pub before a guest sprawled on a chair; and peasants gathering in crowds in front of a pub or inn.

Ugliness and beauty were sometimes ruthlessly polarized by Solomatkin. His painting *The Wedding* (1872) is completely dominated by sharply grotesque forms. In the stuffy atmosphere of a drawing room, seen through a gloomy, yellowish haze which makes the figures seem like shadows and the faces like masks, family and friends offer their congratulations to the bride and groom. Distorted by the semi-darkness, the unlovely newly-weds are surrounded by hideous faces, the gaping mouths cackling and roaring with laughter as glasses are raised for the toast. By contrast, in *On the Tightrope* (1866) the slim and delicate figure of the girl in her white and pale blue dress moves lightly and elegantly, high above the crowd of spectators. She represents the 'pole of purity'. Many of Solomatkin's characters – aged invalids going to collect their pensions, an ancient museum watchman busily darning, a lamp-lighter on his ladder, homeless tramps in rags and tatters – elicit our spontaneous sympathy.

Solomatkin is an exceptional figure in the history of Russian art. There is a surprisingly strong link between him and the Moscow Primitive painters who were inspired by his art in the first decade or so of the twentieth century.

2 The Society for Travelling Art Exhibitions ('The Wanderers')

As the 1860s drew to a close the Russian Realists and the enlightened public came to the conclusion that the democratic tendencies now so evident among painters required some kind of systematic organization. The framework of the Artists' Cooperative Society (described in the last chapter) was too narrow; the Society, in any case, was beginning to disintegrate. It was at this point that the idea of a Society for Travelling Art Exhibitions (*Tovarishchestvo peredvizhnykh khudozhestvennykh vystavok*) was mooted; it was formed in 1870. The moving spirits behind the new collective were G.G. Myasoyedov, recently returned from a stay abroad, I.N. Kramskoi, who had already demonstrated his organizational talents at the time of the 'artistic rebellion' in 1863, V.G. Perov and N.N. Ge.

The new Society included nearly all the best painters in the country, and its activities were based on more flexible economic principles than its predecessor's had been. It was no longer a commune, where work and profits were shared equally, but an association of free painters, each able to exhibit and sell his paintings as he wished, and to take his full share of the profits deriving from exhibitions. Private initiative was encouraged, but self-interest was not the main aim of the organization. The members of the Society, who became known as *peredvizhniki* (travellers or wanderers), took upon themselves new obligations, namely, to take exhibitions to various cities and towns of the empire in order to introduce a wider public to the latest artistic achievements and developments; to educate the population at large; and to struggle for social reform. They amounted to a sort of social crusade into the provinces and coincided with the *narodniki* (Populist) movement's better-known 'crusade among the people'.

The Society agreed on certain rules and regulations to be followed but felt it unnecessary to publish a specific programme, although such a programme did exist in the minds of its members, who were united in their intentions. Pride of place went to the principle of serving the democratic ideal and the interests of society. Those interests could be defined only by the people, to whom all the efforts of the artist must be directed: he was

dependent on, and subordinate to, the will of the people. As I.N. Kramskoi put it: 'The artist should learn profound obedience to, and accept his dependence on . . . the instincts and needs of his own people. He must find a way to harmonize his inner feelings and personal impulses with those of society.'[7] The *peredvizhniki* understood the need not only to depict villagers, peasants and other ordinary folk, but to express their sense of hope, their faith in the future. A show of sympathy by itself was not enough: they must reveal the strength, the moral worth and the natural intelligence of the people they painted.

These new challenges strongly influenced the way the artists approached their work. Being immersed in real life, continually analysing and understanding it, they were inevitably driven towards the Realistic method. It was no coincidence that Realism was one of the Society's founding principles and one to which its members wholeheartedly subscribed.

Realism and populism predetermined the third component of the Society's famous triad – national consciousness. Indeed, a true picture of life does demand a recognition of the national basis of that life and the use of specifically national artistic idioms. These artists believed, further, that such national features were themselves a consequence of this true picture. However, they were not yet particularly preoccupied with the idea of the national spirit, nor did they specially admire the national style of life; they did not, therefore, seek support in the traditions of medieval or folk art. Such questions were only to arise at the turn of the century.

Realism, populism and national character, the watchwords of the Society for Travelling Art Exhibitions, united its members and guaranteed their success among that section of the thinking public who were deeply interested in such matters.

The members adhered to their artistic credo so faithfully that some of their individuality was bound to be sacrificed to its demands. The brightest stars among the membership occasionally found themselves in conflict with the Society. The landscape painter Kuindzhi, for example, who remained somewhat apart from other landscape painters, was unable to reconcile himself to the

Ivan Kramskoi *Self-portrait* 1867

Society. N.N. Ge, during the period of his membership, had to force himself to reject his recent work (that is, all he had hitherto produced independently) and it was not until the end of the *peredvizhniki* period that his originality was free to blossom anew. At the same time, the strongest personalities among the membership (Repin, for example), who embodied the strict spirit of the movement, became the 'legitimate' leaders of the Society. It was this subordination to the common cause which enabled the Society to remain strong for many years and to express the general artistic mood of the time.

The question of how artists should be organized was an acute and painful one in the nineteenth century. By that time the disintegration of earlier societies and collectives was complete. The medieval guilds, dominant for centuries but under threat since the Renaissance period, had almost totally disappeared from the artistic scene. This disintegration coincided with changes occurring in the very nature of art, which reflected ever more strongly the individuality of the artists themselves. Artists, having freed themselves from their former constraints, were drawn to the more liberal organizations gathered around rich patrons and continued, within these groups, to hand down the secrets of their profession from generation to generation. In the seventeenth and eighteenth centuries artists had formed organizations centred on Church and Court, but in the nineteenth these institutions had outlived their usefulness and no longer answered the needs of the social structures which were coming into being. Academies, which had played an important role in artistic education and the establishment of an orderly relationship between art and the state during the seventeenth and eighteenth centuries, were gradually revealing their innate conservativism.

Right from the beginning of the nineteenth century artists felt an urgent need for different forms of cooperative grouping which would be founded on the new and emerging social and artistic principles. The first half of the century was marked by attempts to revive artistic societies based on religion, as for example the Brotherhood of St Luke, otherwise known as the Nazarenes. The very form of such a brotherhood awakened historical analogies and was noticeably backward-looking in tone. Romantic utopianism imbued the approach of the Pre-Raphaelite Brotherhood, which was preoccupied with spiritual questions in contrast to the materialistic ambience of the nineteenth century.

Simultaneously, a new form of Salon exhibition arose as a consequence of developments in painting together with new techniques and methods of artistic production. Exhibitors were not, as a rule, required to subscribe to any particular set of ideas, a situation which allowed them to fulfil one of the main functions of nineteenth-century art, namely the organizing of exhibitions and museums. The Salon played a considerable role in the artistic life of Europe and became the arena where various movements struggled for primacy and outdated principles could often be defeated. It was not surprising, however, that this new academic art turned into 'Salon art', which rapidly transformed the word 'Salon' into a term of opprobrium. Just as national or world exhibitions replaced Church and Court, so the Salon replaced the guild, studio or brotherhood. Whereas works of art had previously been permanently on display in churches or at court, they were brought to the Salon, a showplace, for only a limited period.

As a phenomenon of artistic life the Society for Travelling Art Exhibitions was the meeting point of two traditions: that of the artistic community on the one hand, and that of individuals and bodies organizing exhibitions on the other. Their successors were, respectively, the resurrected Brotherhood and the Salon. The Brotherhood had its own aims and aesthetic programme. The Salon served as a place where art and the interested public could come together. These two traditions, once merged, might produce a new type of artistic community, but only if the aesthetic and social anachronism of the Brotherhood, and the Salon's general indifference to ideas, could be overcome.

21   **Ivan Kramskoi** *Portrait of A.D. Litovchenko* 1878

22 **Vasily Maximov** *The Arrival of the Sorcerer at a Peasant Wedding* 1875

23 **Vasily Perov** *The Last Inn by the Town Gate* 1868

24 **Ivan Kramskoi** *Inconsolable Grief* 1884 >

25 Ilya Repin *Easter Procession in Kursk* 1880–83

27 **Ilya Repin** *Bargehaulers on the Volga* 1870–73

28 **Konstantin Savitsky** *Repairing the Railway* 1874

< **26** **Nikolai Yaroshenko** *Life is Everywhere* 1888

29 **Vasily Surikov** *The Morning of the Streltsi Execution* 1881

30 **Vasily Surikov** *Menshikov in Berezovo* 1883

The nineteenth century had long been ready to give birth to the type of artistic activity which finally came to fruition in the Society. We recall the Salon des Refusés and Nadar's Impressionist exhibitions. Although they also belong to the 1860s and 1870s, they already reflect a new stage in the development of European painting. No such communities arose during the heyday of French Realism, when Courbet was at his most active. The 'pavilion of Realism' never grew into a community. The young Dutch and Belgian artists who cut their links to the Academy and declared themselves followers of Courbet created neither a community nor a society for themselves. The Russian Society of *peredvizhniki*, therefore, can undoubtedly be seen as a unique and progressive phenomenon in the history of European artistic groups.

It was quite logical that the Society should arise in Russia precisely in the early 1870s, at the dawn of a new period in the development of social and political awareness. Russian society was undergoing profound change. When, in the 1860s, the principal social forces were concentrating on the struggle against serfdom and its after-effects, it was the nihilistic and critical mood which was dominant; in the 1870s, on the other hand, the supreme questions were: how was Russia going to develop and who would become the main force for progress? The arts – and specifically painting – immediately responded to the new social situation. One burning issue concerned the concept of the 'positive' hero. The denunciatory/sympathetic approach, which accounted for the special features of the art of the 1860s, yielded to a new concern, namely the need to discover an affirmative element and cultivate a positive outlook. The practice of healthy criticism must not, of course, be sacrificed. Most important of all, the faithful portrayal of facts, the principle already established as the new basis of art from the earliest days of Russian Realism, must be maintained. At a stroke this new, affirmative requirement transformed the relative importance of the various genres in painting. In the 1860s 'genre', a sort of megaphone for the denunciatory movement, had dominated the scene. In the 1870s it was joined by history, landscape and portrait painting, none of which had been able to flourish in the previous, more critical decade. This direct dependence of artistic change on social and historical change is further evidence of the fact that the relationship between artistic and political activity in the second half of the nineteenth century was stronger than ever before.

Of the four major figures named above as the effective founders of the Society for Travelling Art Exhibitions, one – Vasily Perov – belongs primarily to the 1860s, and another, Grigori Myasoyedov, whose achievements we shall examine briefly in the next chapter, was not particularly gifted. Kramskoi and Ge, however, occupy a very significant place in the history of Russian art, and it is essential to include them in our survey of the evolution of Russian painting in the 1870s, for it was their work which virtually initiated the *peredvizhniki* movement. Indeed, both painters were far ahead of many of their colleagues in their ceaseless struggle to remain faithful to elevated artistic ideals and great traditions.

Ivan Kramskoi (1837-87) might well have emerged as an important painter and pioneer of new ideas in the 1860s, when he headed the movement of protest against the artistic rigidity of the day. In fact, his hour – inevitably – struck in the 1870s. It is quite impossible to imagine Kramskoi, who hardly turned his hand to genre, in the same company as Perov and the denunciatory genre painters. His dream was to create a history painting of the same quality as Alexander Ivanov's *Appearance of Christ to the People*, and he considered his work as a portraitist to be no more than a regrettable necessity. There was a considerable degree of self-deception in this ambition, for a truly monumental historical canvas was quite beyond his abilities, while his portraits assured him of a permanent place in the history of Russian painting.

Kramskoi was not a talented artist, but he was a profound thinker, even if he retained a certain provincial air because his education never filled the gaps in his philosophical knowledge. He was born in a small provincial town, Ostrogozhsk, near Voronezh. His father was a petty civil servant. Young Ivan spent several years as a skilled retoucher in a photographer's studio, before moving to St Petersburg and enrolling as a student at the Academy of Fine Arts in the late 1850s. To begin with he displayed little originality, obediently fulfilling all the requirements of the traditional Academy against which he was later to rebel. Among his achievements in the 1860s is a series of several dozen portraits, executed in the 'wet sauce' technique with minute attention to detail (the hand of the experienced retoucher is very evident). Although these portraits brought Kramskoi closer to the new hero of the 1870s they still lacked the power to express psychological or artistic truth.

The only work to foreshadow Kramskoi's promising future was his self-portrait of 1867. This painting, together with Ge's portrait of Herzen and the works of Perov discussed above, marked a new stage in the development of the portrait. This genre now acquired a fresh character associated specifically with the *peredvizhniki*. It abandoned its earlier role, that of commemorating private individuals, and became instead a socially committed and public genre. Kramskoi, in his self-portrait, was the first to express this commitment – and he expressed it 'through himself'. Nearly every stage in the development of Russian portraiture was marked by the appearance of a new hero, whom the artist was obliged to

Ivan Kramskoi
Christ in the Wilderness
1872

find, reveal and understand, and Kramskoi's portrait handsomely fulfilled this obligation. The half-length figure is set in an oval, giving the composition a deliberately casual character. At first glance the oval frame and the painter's fixed stare, directed straight at the observer, return us to the romantic self-portraits of the early nineteenth century. The Kramskoi portrait, however, does not display the features of a great artist endowed with divine genius; the image is rather that of a judge and a harsh critic. His gaze, which is stern, captious and demanding, bespeaks his agitation, his social awareness and a guarded readiness to do battle. His outward appearance is simple – the clothes informal but very neat, the pale face adorned with a rather thin beard and moustache. The face, highlighted by means of a light-coloured patch, is unaccented by the use of colour. The sitter, far from being embellished, is shown as somewhat more humble than he really is, but this impression applies only to the outer appearance. As we look at the portrait, which emphasizes the artist's moral values, we realize that the man presented for our inspection is clever, honest and ever thoughtful. He will tolerate no lies and entertain no selfish ambitions; on the contrary, all his thoughts are dedicated to the common good and to the concepts of social justice.

Kramskoi's self-portrait opened a direct route into the 1870s. Soon afterwards he painted *Christ in the Wilderness* (1872), one of his greatest works and one of the more important landmarks in Russian art during the second half of the nineteenth century. Having chosen the gospel story of Jesus's temptation in the desert, he depicted Christ seated on a stone, sunk deep in thought as if in the process of deciding the most difficult and complex question of his life. Kramskoi himself explained the meaning of this work to the writer Garshin as follows: '... There is one moment in the life of every human being ... when he is totally absorbed by the question of whether to turn to the left or to the right, whether to take a rouble in God's name or, on the other hand, to resist evil.'[8] Kramskoi described the painting as possessing a 'hieroglyphic language', meaning that the contemporary implications of the subject interested him as much as the biblical story. For Kramskoi, Christ stood as a metaphor for contemporary man, for Kramskoi himself, a man on the verge of deciding his fate, ready to sacrifice himself in the great cause of truth and justice, yet horrified by the immensity of the task he has taken upon himself.

Just as Kramskoi trod in Ivanov's footsteps, many later painters would, in turn, become followers of Kramskoi. Biblical themes were to have a place in Russian realistic painting for many years, nearly always touching a contemporary nerve; the figure of Christ became a hero-figure, comparable to the contemporary activist, thinker and fighter. For Russian painting this work was a significant step in the transition from the 1860s to the 1870s. Since the contemporary hero could not, in his natural guise, make an immediate appearance in genre and history painting, his place had to be taken, for the time being at least, by his historical counterparts.

Kramskoi did not entirely fulfil his stated idea. He successfully created the figure of a pensive Christ, his eyes fixed, his hands clasped; he vividly conveyed, too, the agony of the thinking process itself, exploiting the experience which psychological portraiture had already begun to accumulate. Nevertheless he failed pictorially: the painting lacks integration, all the details of the landscape on this big canvas are too drily depicted, and the stones and earth recall plaster casts.

At the end of the 1870s Kramskoi began work on the 'second act' of the gospel story with a painting entitled *Loud Mockery. Rejoice, King of the Jews*, but he never managed to complete the painting. The turn of the decade was probably the least appropriate period for his 'hieroglyphic language', because it was just at this time that the contemporary hero-figure began to take pride of place.

Kramskoi was particularly active as a portrait-painter during the 1870s, when he painted Russian scholars, writers and fellow painters. Many of these portraits were commissioned by P. M. Tretyakov (1832-98), the famous Moscow collector and patron of the arts. These were the years when the collection of portraits of prominent figures in Russian culture and national life was being formed. Perhaps the most brilliant manifestation of Kramskoi's understanding of human nature was his portrait of Leo Tolstoy (1873), one of the finest of the many portraits of the great writer painted between 1870 and the early 1900s. Kramskoi painted Tolstoy on the latter's estate at Yasnaya Polyana. He was working on his novel *Anna Karenina* at the time, and his conversations with Kramskoi helped him in creating the character of the painter Mikhailov, who expressed, in the novel, Kramskoi's own views on art. Tolstoy paid considerable attention to Kramskoi, and this contributed largely to the painter's success.

Kramskoi reveals the writer's personality in all its profundity, portraying him as a great analyst of the human condition grappling with the problems of our earthly existence. His perfectly depicted gaze expresses not only the workings of the analytic mind, but also anxiety and watchfulness, even suspicion. We sense that Tolstoy is familiar with all the ills besetting humanity, those ills which preoccupy him now and which are,

Ivan Kramskoi *Portrait of Leo Tolstoy* 1873

Ivan Kramskoi *Portrait of P.M. Tretyakov* 1876

indeed, the cause of his agitation. Kramskoi sees him as a perfect example of a man endowed with an elevated moral sense, a profound mind and intellect, above all with a sense of responsibility for the fate of mankind. Kramskoi ascribed this ideal spiritual profile to nearly all his models, seeking and finding in them not only their individual characters but the general types he wished them to represent. In the Tolstoy portrait, individuality and type are combined in perfect union.

A similarly programmatic element is particularly marked in the portrait of another famous writer, M.E. Saltykov-Shchedrin (1879). His figure is stretched upwards; the head and shining brow, painted from a low angle, loom over the observer, so that Saltykov-Shchedrin looks down at us rather condescendingly. An atmosphere of isolation surrounds the writer, enclosed in his timeless thoughts which have been tested in the hard school of long experience. The portrait reveals the whole biography of the man.

From a purely artistic point of view one of Kramskoi's finest portraits is that of the history painter A.D.
21   Litovchenko (1878). The two artists were old friends. The painting catches a specific moment in time, Litovchenko standing with one hand behind his back while the other holds a cigarette; a glove dangles from the pocket of his overcoat. The figure's contour, rather more important here than hitherto, is well 'inserted' into the light background. The pictorial freedom of the work is apparent in the openness of the texture and whole manner of execution, an openness Kramskoi had never achieved before and which he unfortunately never really developed.

Kramskoi's later years as a portraitist were characterized by a tendency towards the picturesque on one hand and stiff formality on the other. His models were more frequently drawn from the ranks of high society, even including grand duchesses. His colleagues and other contemporaries began to detect and criticize elements of 'Salonism' in his work. In spite of some interesting portraits dating from the 1880s, therefore, it is the previous decade which must be seen as the acme of his artistic achievement.

In the 1870s positive developments were taking place within two distinct social groups – the intelligentsia and the peasantry. Kramskoi, like Perov, painted portraits of peasants, which were intended to embody particular types of person and idea. In his *Forester* (1874) he created the image of a rebel – sharp-eyed, decisive, caught in a moment of active movement, a bullet-holed hat on his head. *The Observer*, in contrast, is dreamy, gentle and totally absorbed in his contemplation of nature. *Peasant with a Bridle* (1883) is an idealized vision of the peasant, intelligent, gentle and radiating kindness. In Kramskoi's

oeuvre these peasant portraits take the place of genre, to which he rarely had recourse, and then only in a manner very different from that of his fellow *peredvizhniki*. He was not attracted to the idea of detailed subjects, narrative paintings, everyday settings or scenes with conflict implicit in them, and such conflict is absent from his few genre paintings of the 1870s. In an unfinished work entitled *Inspecting the Old Manor House* (1873), mood is substituted for action. The setting is an interior, occupied by two figures – the caretaker, opening doors, and the landowner, absent from his property for a long time and suddenly seized with old memories. Kramskoi here exploited a situation (typical of the time) which enabled him to introduce a psychological element into his genre painting.

He continued to avoid narrative genre into the 1880s. During this period his pictures were increasingly marked by a mere superficial prettiness, which was rewarded with a conspicuous lack of success, not surprising at a time when other artists were discovering beauty in the ordinary and simple rather than in the extraordinary and unusual things of life. Kramskoi preferred the unusual, a predilection exemplified by two paintings dating from 1880. *Moonlit Night* portrays a young woman in a white dress, seated by a pond in the moonlight. *The Unknown Woman* provoked much speculation at the time as to the identity of its subject; indeed, this very conundrum and the general air of mystery attending the 'beautiful stranger' were all part of Kramskoi's intention. Some of his contemporaries interpreted the painting, and the figure itself, as bearing a critical message. This reading seems highly improbable, given the general context of Russian painting of the 1870s and 1880s and in particular the artistic orientation of Kramskoi himself, whose search for beauty brought him close to the borders of Salon art.

It was only in his last major painting, *Inconsolable   24
Grief* (1884), that he managed to escape the flavour of the Salon and to overcome the contradiction between Truth and Beauty – in the main, probably, because the subject was directly concerned with a personal tragedy of Kramskoi and his wife, namely the death of their son. The face of the grieving woman, who stands by flowers prepared for the funeral, is turned towards us. She holds a handkerchief to her lips; she is numb in the silence surrounding her. The situation presents Kramskoi with another opportunity for psychological interpretation. The absence of activity and of any narrative element causes the figure to become the centre of the static composition, which is very carefully calculated. There is nothing incidental about the interior setting, the objects portrayed or the manner of their portrayal. Although Kramskoi reproduces the beauty of the individual objects, the flowers and the hangings with especial care,

Ivan Kramskoi *Forester* 1874

this beauty is understated and remains subordinate to the psychological theme of the work. As a result the work expresses a true nobility, which is further enhanced by the stricken woman's restraint and the wisdom her agony has taught her.

Inconsolable Grief stands out among Kramskoi's *oeuvre* of the 1880s. Having reached, and passed, his artistic prime in the 1870s, he gradually dissipated his former energy and vision and lost his position as the spokesman of the artistic avantgarde.

The path of Kramskoi's life and career coincided with that of Nikolai Ge (1831–94) only in the early 1870s, when they were among the founders of the Society for Travelling Art Exhibitions and simultaneously exploring new ways of painting historical subjects. Before and after this time, however, the two artists always found themselves at some distance from each other. Ge graduated from the Academy of Fine Arts in 1858, well before the 'artistic revolt of the 14'. He was a pupil of Bassin, a follower of Karl Briullov. Ge himself worshipped at the shrine of the 'great Karl', preserved the romantic tradition and was very much part of the legacy of the first half of the nineteenth century. He outlived Kramskoi, and his last years were, artistically, some of his best. In his late works he discovered a new expressionism and provided a foretaste of twentieth-century art. In the course of his career he experienced many creative triumphs and setbacks, together with alternating fits of enthusiasm and despair.

After graduating, Ge spent several years in Italy in an extremely difficult and dramatic search for his own identity. Themes from contemporary life had no appeal for him, for he was unable to discover any embodiment of the ideal in the character of contemporary man. He also turned his hand to a number of historical subjects, without managing to identify a hero of his own. Only the drama of the gospel story provided him with inspiration, and his work on *The Last Supper* was an important stage in his development as an artist.

Ge deviated from the traditional approach to his subject by placing Christ and the Apostles at the table not at the moment of the Saviour's prophecy of his imminent betrayal but a short while later, as Judas is leaving the room. His figure conceals a candle, so that he resembles a grim shadow, come from another world and about to return thither. Ge interprets the whole episode, not as a trivial betrayal, rather as a collision of spiritual and material worlds, the insoluble conflict of two contradictory ideas.

The Last Supper combines realistic, academic and romantic features. In his method of working on the individual figures, and in the peculiar process by which he reached his final version, Ge followed in the footsteps of

Alexander Ivanov. The treatment of the objects portrayed, the modelling of the figures and their unusual poses all recall academic techniques. The romantic tradition is echoed in his treatment of light and the use of sharp contrasts: huge shadows fall from the figures onto the floor and the walls, creating an impression of unearthliness.

The painting created a sensation when it arrived in St Petersburg from Italy. Exhibited in 1863, it was one of the sparks which lit the 'revolt of the 14'. Many critics disliked the realism of the work and objected that it reduced the Gospel story to the level of banal argument. Saltykov-Shchedrin was ecstatic; Dostoevsky disapproved. All in all, *The Last Supper* played as important a role in the development of Russian art in the second half of the nineteenth century as Perov's genre paintings. For each of the movements of the early 1860s the academic approach was either a starting point or an obstacle to be overcome. Even Perov, the most radical of the genrists, was bound by the academic programme for many years, even if, superficially, he appeared to be opposed to the Academy. Ge, on the other hand, renewed the academic tradition from within, as it were; rather than breaking away completely, he gnawed away at its foundations. It is for this reason that *The Last Supper* exercised such a tremendous influence on the development of Russian art.

Ge's work in the middle and late 1860s, however, was not marked by any particularly fruitful advances. His drawings were good but he seemed to falter when faced with a large canvas. His yearning for pictorial freedom and the 'living form' (see below) remained unsatisfied at a time when historical paintings were expected to be shown in a finished, polished state. The beginning of the *peredvizhniki* movement coincided with a phase of contradictoriness and uncertainty in Ge's work, and the new philosophy of the *peredvizhniki* suddenly and drastically diverted his work from the path he had been following with such difficulty in the 1860s.

The purest expression of his new convictions was a work entitled *Peter I Interrogating the Tsarevich Alexei* (1871), which was shown at the first exhibition to be staged by the *peredvizhniki*. Many artists of the day were turning to the theme of the great reforming Tsar, after a period in history painting dominated by the figure of the despotic Tsar (in effect, Ivan the Terrible) and the opportunities this theme provided for paintings denouncing despotism. Ge's choice of Peter the Great was part of

(*opposite above*) **Nikolai Ge** *The Last Supper* 1863

(*below*) **Nikolai Ge** *Peter I Interrogating the Tsarevich Alexei* 1871

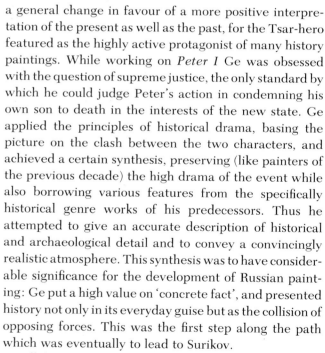

(*above*) **Nikolai Ge** *Portrait of Alexander Herzen* 1867
(*right*) **Nikolai Ge** *Portrait of M.E. Saltykov-Shchedrin* 1872

a general change in favour of a more positive interpretation of the present as well as the past, for the Tsar-hero featured as the highly active protagonist of many history paintings. While working on *Peter I* Ge was obsessed with the question of supreme justice, the only standard by which he could judge Peter's action in condemning his own son to death in the interests of the new state. Ge applied the principles of historical drama, basing the picture on the clash between the two characters, and achieved a certain synthesis, preserving (like painters of the previous decade) the high drama of the event while also borrowing various features from the specifically historical genre works of his predecessors. Thus he attempted to give an accurate description of historical and archaeological detail and to convey a convincingly realistic atmosphere. This synthesis was to have considerable significance for the development of Russian painting: Ge put a high value on 'concrete fact', and presented history not only in its everyday guise but as the collision of opposing forces. This was the first step along the path which was eventually to lead to Surikov.

All these aspects of the work, which made so positive a contribution to Russian history painting, had, however, a deleterious influence on Ge himself and his career. Having all but merged with the mainstream *peredvizhniki*, he found himself on the verge of betraying his own

artistic identity and the romantic basis of his work. His next paintings, also on themes from Russian history, were evidence of his crisis, of a collapse of morale and of an increasing shallowness: he had lost sight of his hero and his ideal. Bitterly aware of the hopelessness of his situation, he gave up his career as a painter in 1876, moved to a little farm in the Ukrainian province of Chernigov, and settled into country life.

It should be said, however, that Ge did not experience crisis in all the genres he undertook. In particular, some of his portraits, dating from the end of the 1860s and into the 1870s, are pictorially and psychologically excellent. Some, for example those of Herzen (1867), Shiff (1867) and Domanger (1868), were painted while he was still in Italy; others, such as Kostomarov (1870), Saltykov-Shchedrin (1872) and Nekrasov (1872), after his return to Russia. They all enriched the portrait gallery of distinguished Russians discussed above in relation to Perov and Kramskoi. Ge, though, painted in his own individual style, revealing in his subjects' faces their inner dramas, a kind of fever of their souls and a certain estrangement from the world. Alexandre Benois truly remarked of these portraits: 'It is not their outward appearances but, as in some old Italian portraits, their secret natures, mysterious, tortured and frightened, which stand revealed to the world.'[9]

Even these portraits, however, were not enough to save Ge from the destruction of his illusions and from prolonged crisis, which ended only in the 1880s when he experienced a fresh awakening of his powers and a renewed desire to work. This rebirth was closely connected with Leo Tolstoy, whose passionate advocacy of his beliefs captivated the languishing painter. He was particularly moved by one of Tolstoy's articles, lost no time in introducing himself to the great man and remained a devoted friend for the rest of his life, a devotion Tolstoy repaid with equal love and respect.

One tangible result of the friendship was Ge's portrait of Tolstoy, painted in 1884 in the writer's study at home in Khamovniki (Moscow). We see Tolstoy at work. He is writing, bent over his manuscript, his eyes full of concentration and his forehead gleaming as if radiating waves of light. Tolstoy is serious, wholly absorbed in his work, which requires the total dedication of all his inner resources.

Other portraits by Ge in the 1880s and 1890s spanned a considerable range. He comes close to Impressionism in his portrait of N. Petrunkevich (1893), a young woman reading a book with an open window in the background, which conveys a sense of peace and joy. A lightning sketch of an old woman, M.P. Svyet (1891), was done very quickly, literally in the space of an hour shortly before she died. Her exhausted old face, the head sunk weakly to one side, is depicted sharply and decisively: the generalized and simplified rendering of physical suffering and the expectation of surcease remind us of an icon.

The culmination of Ge's portrait career was his *Self-portrait*, begun in 1892 and finished in the following year, not long before his death. He portrays himself in old age, his beard unkempt, his searching gaze turned to the world with an unspoken question. A ray of light picks out the head from the darkness and gloom which otherwise dominate the scene. Now almost at the end of his life, the old gentleman has still not resigned himself to his surroundings or his impending death. He will protest, appeal and demand to be heard to his last breath. The self-portrait stands as a magnificent epigraph to all Ge's late work.

Starting from the end of the 1880s this work developed with unusual decisiveness and rapidity. He painted several large canvases in quick succession: *Christ and Nicodemus* (1889), *Leaving the Last Supper* (1889), *What is Truth?* (1890), *Conscience* (1891), *The Court of Sanhedrin* (1892), the unfinished *Golgotha* (1893) and several versions of *The Crucifixion* (1892–94). His vigour and the explosion of talent of these late years are truly remarkable. The younger genrists among the *peredvizhniki*, who had had their heyday in the 1870s, were already exhausted and evidently unsure which way to turn

Nikolai Ge *Self-portrait* 1892–93

artistically; yet here was Ge, an old man who had undergone all the turmoil of a crisis of creativity, persecution by the censor and problems in his personal life, suddenly flourishing again. He flared briefly, and burnt himself out. This was the blossoming not of Ge the artist, one who has finally found a means of expression for his skills, but the burning passion of Ge the human being, embodying all the moral potential of a lifetime in his work. His love for his fellow man, his acceptance of the ills of others as his own, his powerful desire to inspire mankind to virtue, these are the feelings with which all Ge's last work is imbued. This late *oeuvre* addresses questions of the highest moral significance. The subjects of his paintings are metaphors for those very situations with which Ge himself was confronted – suffering, doubt, yearning and death. His state of mind partly resembled that of the thief on the Cross, one moment full of hope, the next maddened by the threat of losing that hope. He was, too, like the suffering Christ, pressed to the wall, spat on and profaned by the members of the Sanhedrin, but steadfast in spirit and faithful to his beliefs. And he was like Judas, in that there is a traitor in each one of us, tormented by his conscience and fully aware of the wickedness of his actions. Ge himself lives in these paintings. This is the most organic form of existential

Nikolai Ge *Golgotha* 1893

Nikolai Ge *What is Truth?* 1890

creativity, whereby the moral qualities of the artist himself largely define the significance of his art.

Christ and Nicodemus, a stark depiction of two opposed figures, is pervaded by the strength of Ge's convictions. The head and body of Christ are dark against the light background; only the outline of the extended right arm and index finger, his eye and the little strip of colour above his eyebrows, gleam with specks of red and white. The figure of Nicodemus, on the other hand, is lit up by bright shafts of light which pick out his red face, a green patch of his clothing and his white turban from the surrounding gloom. Christ's finger all but touches Nicodemus's face, which is full of agitation and stubbornness. In this work, based like many others on the direct dialogue form, Ge creates a new image of Christ – an emaciated, half-starved creature, weak in body but strong in spirit, steadfast and faithful in his convictions.

This image was directly transferred to his next picture, *What is Truth?*, though in a different context. Ge chooses the moment when Pontius Pilate, unconvinced by Christ, poses the question of the title, less to Christ than to himself, and supplies his own answer, one of cynical indifference to the great problems of human existence. Although Christ plays a passive role in this scene, the now familiar idea of confrontation (cf. *Peter I*) is still present, perhaps more powerfully than before. Truth is on the side of the tortured, ragged Saviour, who progresses along his earthly path through suffering to painful death.

Ge's last works were the unfinished *Golgotha* and various versions of the *Crucifixion*. They are all means to an end which the artist expressed as follows: 'I will shake their minds with Christ's agony. I want them, not to sigh gently, but to howl to the heavens! After seeing my painting they will forget their petty troubles for a long, long time!'[10]

In *Golgotha* Ge followed up this intention by concentrating his attention exclusively on Christ's suffering. The Saviour is shown during the last moments before his death. He has already sensed his abandonment by his heavenly Father and the agony of loneliness in the face of death. As if in protest against the unlawful execution about to take place, an arm is stretched out from the edge of the painting, pointing at the Cross and at Christ. This is Ge making his own outspoken and straightforward comment, and prepared to use any means to make his case. His expressionistic frankness is a foretaste of the new artistic thinking of the twentieth century, a prospect strengthened by Ge's 'artistic language'. Christ's pose, the compact nature of the group of condemned men placed at the centre of the painting, a peculiar petrification symbolizing the momentary pause before their deaths, all this renders the composition static; but this static quality is in contrast to the painting's inner dynamic

Nikolai Ge *The Crucifixion* 1892

Nikolai Ge *Christ and the Thief* 1893

– contained in the expressiveness of the brushwork, the openness of colour, the density of the shadows falling as blue patches on the yellow earth and in the treatment (most unusual for a nineteenth-century painter) of line and colour.

These qualities are even more apparent in several versions of his *Crucifixion* – especially in one study now on display in the Kiev Museum of Russian Art. Ge made use, in two large canvases dating from 1892 and 1894, of some elements of naturalism and physiologism, which he needed for a more vivid portrayal of the sufferings of the dying Christ. In the Kiev study, however, it is the emotions of the painter himself which are all-important, his *own* suffering, protest and pain; his *own* passion, about to separate itself from the subject of the painting and acquire an independent existence. Ge boldly marks the heads and half-figures of the two principal characters – Christ and the thief who repented – with light outlines. Light strokes and patches are deliberately mixed with dark, straight lines with curved; the total effect is one of conflict and tension.

While both the technique and the composition of *Christ and the Thief* express Ge's inner feelings, the work is undoubtedly a clear forerunner of expressionism. It is the fullest realization of the concept of 'living form'. This idea requires that form correspond with the content and meaning of the subject treated; form is thus enabled to reflect the artist's every inner, spiritual impulse. It should be stressed, however, that the spontaneous, unformed and ecstatic elements so typical of expressionism are mostly to be found in Ge's sketches, studies and unfinished works. In his work, as in that of every other Russian painter of the second half of the nineteenth century, there remains a contradiction between the degree of completeness required of a painting and the freedom inherent in drafts, sketches and studies. This contradiction should warn us to apply the concept of expressionism to Ge's late works with circumspection, and only in a relative sense.

Be that as it may, Nikolai Ge trod a long and arduous road which came to an end only at the very threshold of the new artistic movements of the twentieth century.

3   Genre Painting and Ilya Repin

Although Kramskoi and Ge were two of the outstanding personalities among the *peredvizhniki*, they nevertheless stood somewhat apart from their colleagues in the movement because of their very individual approach to their art. Artists such as Repin, Maximov, Myasoyedov, Savitsky, Yaroshenko and Vladimir Makovsky concentrated on genre painting in particular, and became rather more representative figures of the movement. Although genre had lost the dominant position it had enjoyed in the 1860s, it still accounted for the vast majority of realistic paintings in the following two decades, and it continued to occupy the attention of painters and public alike. The success of genre ensured the prominence in realist art of pictures with an elaborate narrative element, sometimes including conflict. As Vladimir Stasov, the famous *peredvizhniki* critic put it, it was as though these painters were members of a mass choir. Genre, history and battle painting formed a kind of union, its basic principles clearly distinguished from those of landscape, portrait and still-life.

All the *peredvizhniki* genrists had much in common and their type of genre was stable and unchanging, which makes it all the easier to define those new features common to genre painting of the 1870s and 1880s. Although the genrists continued to fulfil a critical role, they now not only denounced social evils but sought new heroes and set out to approve positive aspects of the life around them. Their rejection of the unalloyed criticism of evil led, in turn, to a new treatment of reality, which was now allowed to speak for itself instead of remaining a mere vehicle for the expression of the artist's opinions. The whole thematic structure of painting, as well as the principles of thematic classification, were changed to accord with this general idea, summed up in a phrase of Repin's: 'matter as such'. Whereas in the 1860s thematic classification had depended less on the subject depicted than on the painter's relationship to his subject, now the emphasis was transferred to the subject itself. Peasant themes comprised one whole group, urban life another. Some artists turned to episodes from the revolutionary movement. Each of these groups was limited by its own themes, but together they made up the 'thematic code' of

the *peredvizhniki*. This concentration on reality transformed the artistic challenges facing them. The specific event in time, the precise definition of time coordinates, the seizing of an actual moment and its aftermath – these were the tasks of genre: to approach reality more closely than ever before, and to aim for the reproduction, almost the imitation, of real-life events. The danger of this situation was that reality might emerge trivialized and untransformed. Works of high quality were produced only by those artists who were able to transcend the real and concrete and to discover the logic and true meaning of an event.

A certain consistency is evident in the evolution of genre over the course of these two decades. It tended more and more towards the merely picturesque and to some aspects of monumentalism. Not all its practitioners succeeded in acquiring these qualities, and when they did it was sometimes at the cost of losing that element of the concrete and specific which was then the *sine qua non* of realism. Some examples of genre reveal frustration, contradiction and failure, but Repin, the supreme master, made up for the deficiencies of all the rest.

Of the painters working in genre in the 1870s and 1880s, Myasoyedov, Maximov, Savitsky, Yaroshenko and Makovsky are most worthy of our attention. Grigori Myasoyedov (1834–1911) began his career as early as the 1850s, graduated from the St Petersburg Academy well before the 'revolt of the 14' and spent many years working abroad. His best work was done in the 1870s; his major painting of the decade appeared in 1872: *The Zemstvo at Dinner*. (The *zemstvo* was an elected district council in Russia from 1864 until 1917.) Preserving, to some extent, the spirit of the 1860s, Myasoyedov exposed the inequality between the aristocratic and peasant members of the *zemstvo*. The two groups dine rather differently: the nobility are unseen, evidently sitting at table in the house, and only a servant (polishing a plate) is visible. The peasant members sit together near the house, eating bread and onions. It was not Myasoyedov's intention to extract any denunciatory message from this contrast; he was primarily interested in the faces and poses of the peasants themselves. In some of them he

Konstantin Savitsky *Greeting the Icon* 1878

Grigori Myasoyedov *The Zemstvo at Dinner* 1872

found not only self-respect and dignity, but also intelligence and spirituality. He used no artificial tricks in the arrangement of the composition, and details introduced into the picture (the chickens by the porch, a branch on the ground, a random ray of sunlight on one of the figures) are not essential to the narrative. Whereas in the 1860s such details were eloquent and explanatory, for Myasoyedov they were somewhat incidental, emphasizing the natural and uncontrived nature of the whole scene.

Vasily Maximov (1844–1911) was one of the most lyrical of the *peredvizhniki* genrists. Himself of peasant stock, he had deep insight into the peasant life with which he was so familiar. He favoured domestic settings and country rituals with their roots deep in the past. The fullest expression of his love of the poetry of peasant life was *The Arrival of the Sorcerer at a Peasant Wedding* (1875). Its characters are ordinary peasants, not dissatisfied with their daily lives and with no great intellectual pretensions. They are busy with a traditional activity, i.e. the celebration of a marriage taking place inside a candle-lit *izba* (the peasant log-cabin), now specially decorated with traditional gaily-coloured cloths and packed with wedding-guests. The unexpected appearance of the snow-covered old sorcerer introduces no real narrative element into this calm and lyrical scene. The composition as a whole, based on a tranquil line of heads and rhythmically alternating light and dark figures, creates an impression of harmony.

Unlike Maximov, Konstantin Savitsky (1844–1905) explored the social side of peasant life. Immediately after graduation from the Academy he drew attention to himself with a painting entitled *Repairing the Railway* (1874) which, while not losing sight of the critical element, laid special stress on the positive aspects of the characters. Two labourers with wheelbarrows are portrayed in a way which emphasizes their strength and dogged determination. Although the figures are deliberately placed at the centre of the composition this does not detract from its spontaneous character. The framework of the composition can be made out, even though it is somewhat obscured by a screen of realistic detail, i.e. the general hubbub of the building-site. Thus the people and objects make up intersecting diagonals, and the line of the horizon is deliberately lowered at the middle of the canvas. The actual centre of the painting is pointed up by the figure of one of the labourers, who is moving straight towards the observer. All these features, however, are natural elements of the composition. The treatment of colour, also very natural, achieves tonal unity; although greys, yellows and browns dominate the picture, the canvas is deliberately decolourized. This total unity anticipates the eventual development of *plein air* techniques by other artists.

Savitsky's most important work was probably *Greeting the Icon* (1878). Its main aim was to portray the various personalities of the group of people gathered round a wagon carrying a holy icon. We see old men and women, younger men and women with children. Some pray passionately, others are more restrained, yet others do not pray at all. The faith, hope and protest felt by various members of the crowd are revealed in their poses, gestures and facial expressions.

Like other painters involved with peasant themes, Savitsky, who was at his best in the 1870s, turned to fresh challenges in the following decade. He set about creating a new type of painting, large in size, monumental in concept and altogether heroic in style. He worked for many years on a large canvas entitled *Going to the War* (1888), in which he made use of various techniques to express the melodramatic and heroic qualities associated with a new kind of protagonist. For example, he divided the crowd into separate groups in order to reveal the structure of the composition rather than, as in earlier paintings, attempting to imitate real life. This 'monumentalism' was artificial and inappropriate to genre as practised by the *peredvizhniki*.

The paintings of those genrists who preferred urban themes reveal many of the characteristics of the short story or anecdote. Vladimir Makovsky (1846–1920) was the outstanding practitioner here. He was intrigued by comical situations. In one of his paintings (*In the Doctor's Waiting-room*, 1870) patients, waiting their turn to see the doctor, give each other 'medical' advice. In another (*The Nightingale's Admirers*, 1873) elderly folk are listening to the nightingale's song. A third (*The Bank Failure*, 1881), shows how various people react to the failure of the bank to which they have entrusted their pitiable savings. Amusing detail abounds in these scenes, all of it vividly conveyed.

The best of Makovsky's huge output are generally two-figure compositions with a narrative theme. An example is *The Visit* (1883): a peasant-woman is visiting her little son who has been 'put out to work'. The boy greedily eats the loaf his mother has given him as she looks sadly on. Makovsky simply and with sympathy describes human sorrow and the cruelty of harsh conditions. While his work cannot be seen as particularly progressive when compared with that of other painters of the 1880s he was able to take note of, and use, the achievements of his contemporaries. *The Visit* is dominated by grey tints, with reds and dark blues showing through. The colours are muted and the brushwork rather broad and bold.

Makovsky was a typical 'poet of everyday life'. Nikolai Yaroshenko (1846–98) represented a different tendency, and was known as the 'conscience of the *peredvizhniki*',

Vladimir Makovsky *The Visit* 1883

Nikolai Yaroshenko *The Stoker* 1878

especially after the death of Kramskoi. Yaroshenko, always socially committed, appealed to the conscience of the public, whom he continually reproached for their apathy and tirelessly attempted to arouse. Such reproach is evident, for example, in *The Stoker* (1878), a portrait of a labourer crippled by heavy work and driven almost insane by the monotony of his movements and the relentless heat of the furnace. The stoker is posed full-figure, his 'means of production' in his hand. We can recognize all the signs of an official portrait, but *The Stoker*, of course, conveys a very different message: no parody, this, but a powerful denunciation of particular working conditions.

In the 1880s, after a series of paintings devoted to the theme of revolutionary youth, Yaroshenko, like some other *peredvizhniki*, turned to subjects of more general, even symbolic significance. Impressed by Tolstoy's story 'What do people live for?' he painted a large picture entitled *Life is Everywhere* (1888). Tolstoy's question particularly interested Yaroshenko and he selected his material accordingly. He depicts convicts feeding pigeons through the window of a prison-wagon. His choice of characters is deliberate: a woman with her child, a young man and another, much older – rather archetypal images. Yaroshenko's realistic, almost naturalistic idiom, however, is at odds with the abstract quality of the characters' portrayal, an inconsistency which was a common feature of *peredvizhniki* genre at the end of the 1880s. Like other painters of his generation, Yaroshenko was unable to overcome the general crisis which struck all the *peredvizhniki*, with one exception – Repin.

Ilya Repin was born in the tiny provincial town of Chuguyev in the province of Kharkov. His father was a common soldier in a military settlement and Ilya's childhood was marked by poverty and hardship. He received some training in drawing and icon-painting in his home town, then went to St Petersburg and before long enrolled at the Academy. During the 1880s he was influenced by, and learnt from, two 'academies': the Imperial Academy of Fine Arts, and the 'academy of Kramskoi', i.e. the Society for Travelling Art Exhibitions, with which the young painter became very closely associated. He painted large canvases on biblical themes as well as genre works on subjects from everyday life; he also did drawings from nature. These separate activities gradually merged in the early part of Repin's career, enriching each other and laying the groundwork for major artistic achievements yet to come. In his work the academic discipline was reinvigorated by elements of realism and fresh psychological insights, while the genre and portrait traditions attained a new seriousness and depth. The clearest examples of this mutual enrichment are the two large canvases which concluded Repin's

26

Vladimir Makovsky *The Bank Failure* 1881

Ilya Repin *The Raising of the Daughter of Jairus* 1872

27 academic period: *The Raising of the Daughter of Jairus* (1872) and *Bargehaulers on the Volga* (1870–73).

The Raising of the Daughter of Jairus, for which Repin received the Academy's major gold medal, is one of his finest works. He was fascinated by this episode from the Gospels and succeeded in conveying two aspects of it in particular: the solemnity of the moment and the mystery of death. His treatment is dominated by the confrontation between the forces of light and darkness. This confrontation determined the dramatic nature of the work and placed it firmly in the Rembrandt tradition, which was always close to Repin's heart. He worked prodigiously at achieving the majesty of the pose of Christ, emerging from the darkness. The linear flow of the composition balances the painting's dramatic character, which is mainly expressed in the colour-scheme – a confrontation of light tones with dark. The unique appeal of *The Raising of the Daughter of Jairus* lies in the way historical significance and dramatic tension are interwoven.

The first version of *Bargehaulers*, on which he worked while still engaged on *The Raising of the Daughter of Jairus*, was exhibited in 1871 and later underwent several changes. It was to play a major role in the development of Russian genre painting in the 1870s. The concept of the work was five years in gestation, during which time Repin ceased to be a *shestidesyatnik* (man of the sixties – see above) and entered the spirit of the new decade. The idea for *Bargehaulers* came to him in 1868. He was walking with Savitsky along the banks of the Neva when he noticed a gang of such bargehaulers toiling past a group of young people out on a picnic. In the first studies the haulers look more like exploited animals than human beings, but in 1870, after a trip to the Volga in order to study their way of life, he began to see them as real people rather than personifications of an idea, discovering their virtues – strength, intellect and beauty. During the trip he also worked on the composition of the painting, grouping the gang in various ways before eventually finding the best solution, which was to place the men in a position almost parallel to the plane, frieze-like, in accord with the horizontal format. He divided the gang into separate groups gathered round figures taller than the rest. In his coordination of the main lines of the composition – i.e. the horizontal and diagonal lines – Repin harmonized the dynamic and static aspects of the whole. The impression of movement given by the gang serves to underline the brutal truth contained in the picture. In addition, Repin fixed this movement in time by painting the men from a low angle against the river and the far distance, thus sustaining the monumental effect of the whole scene.

Repin's determination to create a picture of general rather than merely local significance is reflected in his cast of characters. All eleven are metaphors for Russia itself; no two of them are alike. The gang is led by Kanin, an unfrocked priest with whom Repin became very friendly during his stay on the Volga; Kanin stands for the wisdom of the people. Next to him is a prize-fighting type (known locally as a *nizhegorodsky boyets*) who symbolizes physical strength, simplicity, naivety. The last of the leading trio is Ilka, a sailor, who stares out at us angrily. They are followed by men of various ages and nationalities: a tall fellow with a pipe, a sick old man and a young boy, Larka by name, who appears to be trying to throw off the towing-strap. Behind them are an ex-soldier, a Kalmik (member of a Siberian tribe) and a Greek. Different estates, ages and nationalities, therefore, go to make up Repin's 'population of the Empire'.

The significance of the work was described by Kramskoi as follows: 'Four years ago, Perov was ahead of us all', he wrote, 'only four years, but after Repin's *Bargehaulers* he is a thing of the past . . .'[11] Repin himself considered the painting as his final graduation work. He had already been awarded a scholarship for foreign travel but did not leave Russia until the picture had been completed.

He eventually went abroad in 1873, staying for a short while in Vienna and Paris before settling in Paris for the remainder of his three year tour. His letters to Stasov, Kramskoi and other artist-friends give a vivid picture of his interests at the time. Of the old masters, Rembrandt and Velasquez were his favourites. Among the moderns he was most intrigued by the Impressionists, but his attitude towards them swung between two extremes: one moment he was breathless with admiration, the next practically accusing them of shallowness and futility. Eventually the positive view prevailed, and the Impressionists were to exercise considerable influence on his work. Repin was at his best when his style was close to Edouard Manet's and his circle; henceforth, all his attempts at 'traditional' Russian painting, whether historical or mythological, were to fail, whereas his studies of contemporary Paris – for example *Paris Café* (1875) – were rather successful.

The most interesting products of this period, however, were his various studies of people and landscapes, done either as preliminaries to paintings or for their own sake. The best landscapes were of Paris and the Normandy coast, where Repin worked *en plein air* with Polenov, a fellow graduate, under the guidance of Bogolyubov, whose job it was to supervise scholars from the St Petersburg Academy in France on scholarships. Repin worked at perfecting a flowing brush which would suggest a figure or object with a single stroke; at this time he also developed a general silveriness of tone.

In 1876, immediately after his return to Chuguyev, he painted *On the Turf Bench*, which summed up every-

Ilya Repin *On the Turf Bench* 1876

thing he had learnt in Paris. This *plein air* group portrait, done in a free style, is full of light. Repin concentrates on the surface of the *picture* rather than on the surfaces of the *objects*, which are all very similarly treated. Poses and movements are depicted with rapid brushstrokes; the characters – all of them relatives of the painter – are treated to swift insight into their personalities rather than profound psychological analysis.

Of course, the lessons he learnt in Paris about *plein air* (which enabled him to emulate the early Impressionists) played an important role in his later career, lightening his palette and sharpening his eye. He never became an Impressionist, however, for the challenges awaiting him in Russia could not be met by an Impressionist response. He turned back, instead, to ideas which had been maturing in his mind since the early 1870s. This was no retreat: he needed not only to learn how to use all his Parisian experiences, but to get to grips with the psychology of modern man and the way his inner life could be reflected externally. His portraits were to play an invaluable role in this process.

Repin painted a large number of portraits in the late 1870s and during the following decade. Anyone, a Chuguyev peasant with the 'evil eye', a soldier returning from the wars, a distinguished composer, could attract his interest. He was intrigued by human qualities rather than by reputation or status in life, always searching for the individual element in his subjects, the way they thought, held their fingers or threw back their heads. He managed to reveal those things which normally remained hidden and never imposed a stereotyped image on his sitters.

A perfect example of his psychological insight is the portrait of Modest Mussorgsky (1881), painted in hospital shortly before the great composer's death. Mussorgsky is depicted in all the complexity of his emotions and mortal suffering. Looking into his soul we seem to be peering into an abyss swirling with the thoughts and feelings of the aged genius. The ungainly body, on the threshold of death, only emphasizes the expression in Mussorgsky's eyes, an expression combining suffering and hope, pain and faith, sadness and love. Beauty pierces the agony, disorder and sickness to illuminate his face and eyes. Repin 'divides' his subject in such a way that he comes to symbolize not only the fate of one man but all the burdens of contemporary life, as well as the final triumph of life over death. We can confidently speak here of the sitter's 'dialectic of the soul', and of the complexity and the dialectic quality of the portrait as a whole.

Ilya Repin *Portrait of Modest Mussorgsky* 1881

Ilya Repin *Portrait of P.A. Strepetova* 1882

Repin painted many first-class portraits at this time, among them those of the surgeon N.I. Pirogov (1881), the actress P.A. Strepetova (1882), A.I. Delvig, a senior civil servant (1882), the critic V.V. Stasov (1883) and the writer Garshin (1884). They are strikingly varied in composition and colouration; each subject is arranged in a different pose and seated at a different angle. Comparison shows that Repin used no fixed pattern in their compositions (which are also consistently 'anti-iconographic'), but relied on the individuality of his sitters to evoke his or her unique form.

Armed with this new psychological acuity, Repin was ready to take up the complex challenges which awaited him on his return to Russia in the early 1880s, when he began to work on his first genre paintings.

Even in the late 1870s two themes had emerged in his genre painting, sometimes juxtaposed, sometimes separately. Both – peasant life and the revolutionary movement – made their first appearance simultaneously, in 1877. He found plenty of material for peasant themes in Chuguyev and later in Moscow. He kept a kind of pictorial diary describing village scenes, such as an argument between two peasants, one poor and the other prosperous, lessons in the village school, a peasant celebration, the recruitment of a new soldier. There were also sketches of various characters, such as *The Sly Peasant* or *The Archdeacon*, which were later incorporated into paintings.

Repin was gradually working towards a major work, entitled *Easter Procession in Kursk*, which appeared in 1883. He experimented with various versions of the composition, each of which could have served as the basis of a separate painting. The final version shows a large crowd, with clear social divisions, moving along a dusty road. This crowd, Repin's symbol of contemporary provincial Russia, is intended to reveal the structure of Russian society, although the artist's own attitudes to it are hard to discern. The procession speaks for itself; the observer is at once a witness and a participant. The painting contains some localized conflicts, the main one being the clash between a village policeman and a hunchback, the latter being one of the few characters inspired by true faith and hope. The hunchback is sharply contrasted with other figures: the dull-witted peasants carrying an empty lantern, the choristers, privileged members of the procession, above all the gendarmes and village policemen. Although all the characters are given specific personalities, the painting remains natural and unified. Its message lies not only in the individual characters but in the image of the crowd as a whole. It

25

moves along the road like an avalanche, pushing from the back and sides and conveying the impression of a sea of noisy humanity. The painting is composed in such a way that the observer is included within the pictorial space; the true-to-life effect is a crucial part of Repin's intention. The composition itself enables him fully to reveal the internal logic of the event, as well as movement in all its forms. Movement, of course, is implicit in the procession; in addition, however, each character moves of his own will, independently of the procession, which appears to roll down the road and embrace the observer from all sides. We can almost touch and feel the characters around us, and this immediacy reduces the importance of harmony and balance. Repin's use of colour only increases the convincing quality of the painting, dominated by yellow-brown tints which absorb the rest – reds and greens. The intensity of the colour is gradually reduced towards the background. The complex colour-system recalls the experiences of his Paris and post-Paris years. It is basically a *plein air* work which stops short of Impressionism. Its concentration on character and psychology defines Repin as a realist profoundly preoccupied with analytical questions, which surely earns him a special place even among European realists. His critical impulse, in the guise of objectivity, obliges him to study 'human material', comparing the natures and special features of his characters and gathering them all together into a complex organic whole.

Easter Procession in Kursk marked the high point in Repin's development of the peasant theme. Simultaneously with that development he was working on the subject of revolutionary heroism. By the mid-1880s this was dominating his output in the form of a number of studies and paintings, one of the most important of which was the famous *They Did Not Expect Him* (1884–88). From now on his principal characters were to be revolutionaries and Populists – contemporaries in whom he could find the heroic qualities he sought. He also wished, however, to portray the tragic failure to which they were inevitably doomed. Most of these paintings, not surprisingly, are concerned with the death or arrest of the protagonist, as for example *The Propagandist's Arrest*, begun in 1878 but only completed in 1892. Its history is interesting. In the first version the agitator is seen among peasants, who react to him variously with sympathy, hostility or suspicion. The second version is totally different: he is quite alienated from his surroundings and in a state of clear confrontation with the other characters. Seized by a policeman, he casts an angry glance at the men by the window – among whom is the traitor. He is surrounded not by people but by emptiness. The sense of alienation is increased by the treatment of colour: his figure, combining warm red tones (auburn

Ilya Repin *The Archdeacon* 1877

hair and a red shirt), is contrasted with the cold, silvery light pouring through the window.

Repin did most of his work on the revolutionary theme in the mid-1880s, after leaving Moscow for St Petersburg (in 1882), although many of the ideas date from the turn of the decade. Take, for example, *Refusal of Confession before Execution* (1879–85). The composition is based on two figures, a priest and a convict, picked out from the darkness by a ray of light. The frozen 'instant' of the painting, which actually takes account of a long period of time, is a kind of summing-up of past events. This instant is not oriented towards the future – for there is no future: only execution awaits the prisoner. The past has left its imprint on his face; the traces of sleepless nights, torture, searching meditation and final victory over self-doubt are all too plain to see. It is this moral triumph, expressed in his pose and face, which is the conceptual centre of the work. This aspect of the treatment differs from that of the majority of Repin's paintings, which generally require the description of some action at a specific moment in time. By thus 'stretching' time, the artist intends the emotional impact of the painting to compensate for the absence of action. The colour range is limited to grey-browns and grey-blues, emphasizing the contrast between the dark, deep tones of the shadows and the silvery light which

Ilya Repin *The Propagandist's Arrest* 1880–92

Ilya Repin *Refusal of Confession before Execution* 1879–85

Ilya Repin *They Did Not Expect Him* 1884–88 >

pours from the window into the cell and illuminates the head and body of the condemned man as well as the priest's profile and his cross. The spareness of the composition is as emotionally concentrated and purposeful as the situation itself.

The theme of revolution, suffocated by the limitation of its settings to clandestine apartments and prison cells, needed to be taken out and exposed to everyday life. This was the context in which Repin conceived *They Did Not Expect Him*. Once again, as with *Easter Procession in Kursk*, the original concept underwent many changes in the course of time. The very first stages were worked out

in studies and sketches; the composition evolved while he was actually at work on the painting itself, when he found himself remodelling the principal characters. The painting depicts the dramatic and unexpected return from exile of a revolutionary. Repin builds the action like a drama – albeit one without a denouement. The children have not quite grasped who it is that has stepped into the room. Most important of all, the characters in the painting look as if uncertain of the righteousness of the revolutionary's deed, a deed which has inflicted so much trouble on his family and friends. Now, however, the moment of meeting and recognition is at hand: the

precise fixing of this moment within the general flow of the event enables the observer, watching the scene almost as a participant, easily to imagine the future course of events. Repin draws us into his own thoughts and feelings, allowing us to view the episode objectively, uninfluenced by any emotional impact, solely in terms of its own reality.

Repin builds his composition in such a way that the observer is almost within the space of the picture, or at least in a space identical to that depicted. Repin admits him, so to speak, under the crossfire of the main themes of his story. The positioning of the characters serves to convey the logic of the event. The main links between the principal character and the rest of the cast are strengthened in a dynamic and mobile way by various objects, i.e. the furniture, the direction in which the floorboards run, the open door. In the next instant a new situation will arise, but Repin selects the arrangement most appropriate to the situation at this particular moment. The picture is full of light and air, beautiful in its mixture of weightless grey-blues, yellows and transparent colours, but this beauty, like the colour scheme itself, bears no specific message, and the colours have no functional content.

Both *They Did Not Expect Him* and *Easter Procession* are supreme examples of genre in the 1880s. In these works, genre closely approached history painting in several ways: the significance of the ideas expressed in them, the universality of the message and the truth of a great event. This was a route to history painting from within genre, whose main source of inspiration – a real event in contemporary life – remained the basis of the artistic image.

True history painting, nevertheless, evaded Repin. In his best years – the end of the seventies and then the eighties – he painted three major historical works: *Tsarevna* [Princess, i.e. daughter of the Tsar] *Sophia* (1879), *Ivan the Terrible and his Son Ivan* (1885) and *Zaporozh Cossacks writing a reply to the Turkish Sultan* (1891). Although they all enjoyed great success and even fame in Russia, they cannot compare in importance with *Easter Procession* or *They Did Not Expect Him*. Repin was not of a particularly historical cast of mind. He could achieve an almost physiological authenticity in his depiction of the dying Tsarevich Ivan and the insane Tsar who could kill his own son; he could compose, in *Cossacks*, a veritable 'symphony of laughter' (as the art historian and critic Igor Grabar put it), but history painting was not his forte. He just could not envisage what life was like two or three hundred years earlier, and historical subjects appealed to him only if they had some kind of reference to contemporary events.

Like all the other *peredvizhniki* realists of his generation, Repin was at his best in the 1870s and 1880s. At the end of this time, it will be recalled, the *peredvizhniki* suffered a major artistic crisis. Unlike his fellows, however, Repin managed to overcome it and cross the fateful line dividing the 1880s from the 1890s, entering his late period with new ideas about composition similar to those of painters of the new generation, such as Serov. Repin's portrait-drawings and portraits make up his most interesting late work. Free of the earlier search for deep psychological understanding, their main aim is sharpness of characterization and purely pictorial artistry.

A particularly clear example of this new interest is the officially commissioned group portrait *Ceremonial Meeting of the State Council* (1901–03) and its preliminary studies. He was assisted on this project by two of his pupils, Kustodiev and Kulikov. It is a huge, horizontally-extended canvas portraying approximately one hundred

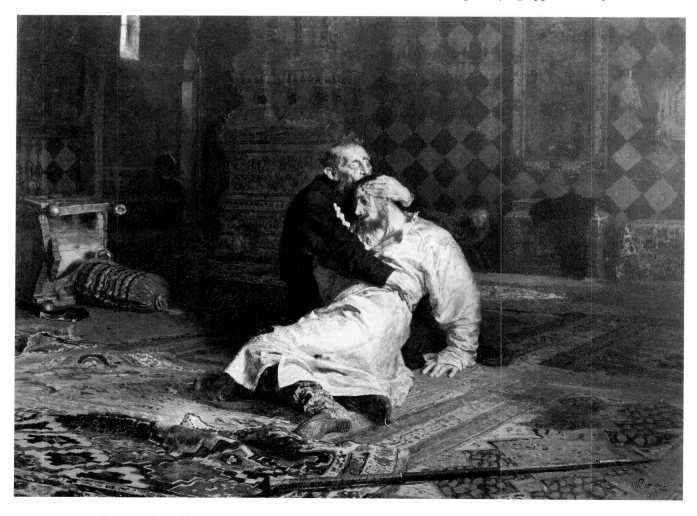

Ilya Repin *Ivan the Terrible and his Son Ivan* 1885

Ilya Repin *Gerard and Goremikin* 1903

Ilya Repin *A.P. Ignatiev* 1903

members of the Council, presided over by the Emperor during a special session to celebrate its anniversary. Repin accepted the commission on condition that he be allowed to draw a life-study of each of the members. These studies, which took one or two sittings, are among his best late works. They are done in a broad, free and impressionistic style, based on the laconic but expressive relationship between a few colours – gold, red and dark blue. Repin used a new, bold brush technique to create a form which did away with three-dimensional modelling and slavish realism, and highlighted or exaggerated, instead, one or two important features of his sitters' personalities. This method is well exemplified in his studies of A.P. Ignatiev (1903), I.G. Goremikin with N.N. Gerard (1903) and K.P. Pobedonostsev (1903).

Repin bravely joined his younger contemporaries in yet another field, namely that of graphic portraits. Up till now, his drawing had developed in parallel with his painting, gradually overcoming a certain dry constraint and acquiring a pictorial quality. Many of his numerous drawings successfully capture the essence of his models, immerse the object or figure in its surroundings and make

vivid use of aerial perspective. His quick sketches rival the output of that most tireless of nineteenth-century graphic artists, Menzel. However, his graphic technique was radically renewed at the beginning of the 1890s. A large portrait of the actress Eleanora Duse – in charcoal on canvas – appeared in 1891, followed by a series of other portraits in the same technique: M.K. Tenisheva (1898), V.A. Serov (1901) and I.S. Ostroukhov (1913). They are remarkable not only for their original technique (which Repin's pupil, Serov, also used) but for their fresh approach to the treatment of the creative personality. In the portraits of Mussorgsky or the actress Strepetova Repin was primarily interested in inner conflict and the relationship between an individual and society, but Duse's portrait brings out and exposes the artistic element. A refined graphic style, combining a harmonious correlation of the charcoal flecks with a softness of outline and a rhythmical arrangement of lines on the plane, matches the artistry of Duse's own soul.

In his late works, therefore, Repin prefigured the complex artistic problems facing the new era, revealing to the last the acuity, versatility and breadth of his talent.

4 History Painting

It was even harder for Russian history painting than for genre to free itself of its academic shackles. Even so politically minded an artist as K.D. Flavitsky, whose painting *Princess Tarakanova*, a condemnation of despotism, caused a sensation in 1864, could not escape the techniques of academicism and the influence of Briullov's melodramatic effects and brilliant palette. Only one history painter staked out an original position in the 1860s. This was V. Shwartz (1838–69) who, by applying the achievements of genre to his own field, did manage to make the break. This process, however, weakened

history painting's heroic idiom, which it was left to the artists of the 1880s to rediscover. Shwartz was a typical product of the 1860s, bringing the insights of contemporary historians (such as Kostomarov and Zabelin) and writers (Alexei Tolstoy, for example) to bear on his work. Historians of the day were particularly interested in the everyday life of the past, and Shwartz's originality lay in the way he combined a strict adherence to historical authenticity with a critical/denunciatory approach borrowed from genre. Both these aspects are evident in a painting Shwartz completed in 1864 and entitled *Ivan the*

Viacheslav Shwartz *The Tsaritsa's Spring Pilgrimage during the Reign of Tsar Alexei Mikhailovich* 1868

Terrible by the Body of his Dead Son. The choice of subject was itself extremely typical of the decade, for Ivan the Terrible symbolized *par excellence* the idea of the 'evil Tsar'. Shwartz achieved a truly dramatic effect in the way he conveyed the emotional and mental state of the despot as he spasmodically squeezes the shroud covering the Tsarevich's body.

As painters began to master the application of genre techniques to historical subjects, so they progressed from sixteenth- to seventeenth-century scenes. This was natural enough, because the seventeenth century, for all its dramas, seemed very much an everyday world, familiar, exhaustively studied and with many aspects of it still present in the nineteenth century. Shwartz explored a number of seventeenth-century genre themes, crowning his career with a lyrical work entitled *The Tsaritsa's Spring Pilgrimage during the Reign of Tsar Alexei Mikhailovich* (1868). Just as the simple Russian village, unchanged for centuries, calmly receives the solemn procession, so the grey tones of the Russian landscape absorb the bright yellows and pinks of the magnificent coaches. Shwartz's treatment of the landscape was so brilliant that for many art historians it is *the* source and inspiration of landscape painting in the 1870s.

The most interesting history paintings of the 1870s were the work of artists not specializing exclusively in the history genre. One example is *Peter I Interrogating the Tsarevich Alexei* by Ge, who enriched the archaeological approach of the 1860s with his new concept of historical drama and the struggle between opposing historical forces. Some genrists chose subjects combining historical and battle scenes. The battle pieces of Vasily Vereshchagin (1842–1904) make up a distinctive branch of genre and history painting in the 1860s and 1870s. Probably the most famous Russian painter in the world during his lifetime, Vereshchagin denounced war and exposed its horrors. His critical pathos, nourished in the soil of the 1860s, never flagged. He was very familiar with warfare, having fought in the Turkestan and Balkan campaigns. He died tragically during the Russo-Japanese war, in the company of Admiral Makarov on board the battleship Petropavlovsk when it exploded. Vereshchagin was a kind of war correspondent, moving from one theatre of war to the next, only occasionally renting a studio in Munich or Paris for a couple of years in order to escape the reproaches of Russian generals who accused him of distorting events. There he painted pictures using sketches and studies done in situ or, more often, from memory. Subsequently he organized his famous exhibitions, consisting of whole series of paintings depicting war in authentic detail. He developed an original and almost photographic technique perfectly appropriate to his needs.

The beginning and end of Vereshchagin's career were

Vasily Vereshchagin *Apotheosis of War* 1871–72

taken up with historical themes, particularly in his last great series, devoted to the 1812 campaign against Napoleon. He wrote an interesting article for the catalogue of his exhibition, describing his view of the war, its driving forces and the reasons for the Russian victory. As for his early career, during the campaign in Turkestan he was fascinated by ethnography and assembled a huge collection of antique clothes, weapons and other objects of the everyday life of the local population. He also produced a large number of studies and paintings, ethnographic in character and reminiscent of the archaeological and historical tendencies of the 1860s. In the 1880s he painted a largely historical cycle illustrating various methods of execution. However, his two most important series – on the campaigns in Turkestan and the Balkans – concentrated principally on the depiction of modern warfare.

The first series is a perfect example of Vereshchagin's narrative method. He composes complete stories through a sequence of paintings which together describe an episode of the war in Turkestan. They remind us of illustrations in a book. The first shows the Emir of Bukhara's spies surveying a Russian encampment. This is followed by an attack on the camp. The Russian soldiers rush from their tents, shooting wildly. Vainly attempting to resist the enemy charge, they die. The scene then changes to the residence of the Emir, to whom the trophies of war – the heads of Russian soldiers – are being displayed. The following picture shows a victory celebration on the square in front of the mosque, where the crowd gazes at these heads, now impaled on high poles. The series concludes with an edifying epilogue, entitled *Apotheosis of War* (1871–72). The observer is presented with a field of skulls making up a huge pyramid against the background of a lifeless desert and the abandoned remains of a town. It is a quasi-historical scene, recalling great battles and spoils of war in Turkestan in times past. In addition, it is devoted, according to the artist's own

Vasily Vereshchagin *Shipka-Sheinovo: General Skobelev at Shipka* 1878–79

Vasily Vereshchagin *Mortally Wounded* 1873

inscription, to 'all the great conquerors of the past, present and future'. Vereshchagin's near-photographic technique is ill-suited to the intended universal symbolism of the work. We may sum up this cycle, entitled *Barbarians*, by thinking of it as an unusual montage of actions taking place in various locations, at different moments of time and from different points of view.

Vereshchagin's subjects, always striking and dramatic, illustrate the most extreme situations and bloodiest episodes, and bear eloquent witness to the horrors of war and the barbarism of the victors. He indulges in little psychological analysis of his characters, concentrating instead on peculiarities in the figures and poses, which are, in some sense, a substitute for psychologically revealing facial expressions. These figures and poses are fixed with a photographic precision. A good example is *Mortally Wounded* (1873), a close-up view of a soldier who has thrown his rifle to the ground and presses his hands to his breast pierced by an enemy bullet. He is running, perhaps taking his last steps before collapse and death. This dying, mechanical run and the gesture of his hands are captured accurately and convincingly.

The same quality is to be found in *Shipka-Sheinovo: General Skobelev at Shipka* (1878–1879), one of the principal canvases of his Balkan cycle. The background depicts a formal military parade celebrating victory, with soldiers throwing their caps in the air as they greet the general riding past on his white horse. In the foreground are the dead, painted with Vereshchagin's characteristic cruel precision. There is a terrible realism about the way the corpses are strewn about, bent and twisted with their arms raised to heaven.

Vereshchagin's battle pieces – although based on contemporary material – describe real historical events and are, therefore, formally related to history painting. In fact, however, they are as far removed from the latter as many of the purely historical paintings of the 1870s' *peredvizhniki*, who reduced history to genre.

The antecedents of the true history painters, then, are Shwartz, whose approach was superficially historical; Ge, whose *Peter I Interrogating the Tsarevich Alexei* edged the painting of historical subjects towards social drama; and Repin, whose *Princess Sophia* added psychological insight to the genre. They are all pointers to the art of Surikov, the first 'pure' history painter, whose talent, maturing in the 1880s, was acknowledged as unique on the appearance of his first major work, *The Morning of the Streltsi Execution*. Surikov's originality lies first and foremost in his interpretation of the past and present as a movement of the popular masses. His true hero was the people itself, whose tragedy he fully understood. His art reveals the complex interrelationship between historical events and contemporary life. He did not intend his historical subjects as comments on contemporary matters, but his version of history was closely connected with his view of the present. Indeed, any true history painting is the product of several interacting factors: 1) the period selected by the painter, 2) the time in which he himself lives, 3) the actual historical subject, and 4) the position of the painter, who interprets his chosen topic according to his own view of the world, his ethical standards and his knowledge of history.

Surikov's own time was very similar to that portrayed in his work, that is the end of the seventeenth and beginning of the eighteenth centuries, a period of great change, when Russia was trying to cast off its medieval character. Many intellectuals of the time were constantly comparing contemporary Russia with her own recent history as well as with Western Europe, and Surikov was no exception. In the 1880s Tolstoy formulated his theory concerning the contradiction between the interests of the people on one side and those of society and social progress on the other, a theory based principally on his analysis of the era of Peter the Great. To others, the conflict between society and the individual seemed even sharper. This was a result of the increased importance being ascribed to the individual, who was now perceived not only as a hero, a doer of deeds and a sufferer, but as a fit subject for social and philosophical analysis. The individual and society were like two poles defining an axis round which various social interests revolved, a locus for the solution of many social conflicts as well as for clues to the future development of the nation.

Dostoevsky explored the question of individuality with unprecedented passion and profundity. He saw each human being as utterly unique and beyond rational comprehension, possessing vast potential and with certain inalienable rights. The emotional impact of this 'ethical individualism' is exploited to the full in his works. For Dostoevsky the individual was an end in himself rather than a means to the achievement of higher aims. His philosophy forbade the sacrifice of even one individual for the common good. Suffering and sacrifice, if freely undertaken, however, were instruments of redemption; the sufferer was no longer a passive victim but a creator, whose suffering was thereby transformed into joy. Dostoevsky even believed that such redemptive suffering was an authentic expression, indeed a necessity, of the Russian national character.

Similar ideas were symbolized by Surikov's Streltsi, who became the victims of social progress, and by the heroic pride of his Morozova. This woman, a Boyar and fanatical Old Believer, was prepared to accept death, the cross and the stake as the price of her own redemption – of her own will and for the sake of her beliefs.

Another acute question of the time was the future development of Russia. Surikov, who was neither a Slavophile nor a 'Westerner', wished to recreate the 'archetypes' of Russian history and to reveal through them the essence of the national character. He sought to detect the antecedents of the present in the past and the echoes of the past in the present. He was aided in this exploration of the logic of history by his talents as a prophet and a visionary.

Vasily Surikov (1848–1916) was born to an old Cossack family in Krasnoyarsk in Siberia, where he received his early artistic education before going on to the Academy of Fine Arts in St Petersburg. He showed no particular promise in the 1870s and hardly distinguished himself from his fellow students. The subjects set by the Academy did not appeal to him; St Petersburg provided no outlet for his historical flair. His only works of any interest from this period are a few drawings of Peter the Great, a city landscape featuring Falconet's equestrian monument of Peter and a painting, *The Prince's Court of Law* (1874), a somewhat inaccurate picture of medieval Russia.

It was not until the end of the 1870s, when he went to Moscow to work on the interior decor of the church of Christ the Saviour, that he truly 'discovered' Russian history. One day, according to Surikov himself, he had a vision of the execution of the Streltsi in Red Square. At this time he conceived the ideas for many of his later masterpieces, among them *The Morning of the Streltsi Execution* (1881), *Menshikov in Berezovo* (1883) and *Boyarina Morozova* (1887). All three works are thematically closely connected, the episodes described being

29
30

milestones in the transformation of Russia from a medieval to a modern state, when social progress was inevitably accompanied by tragedy and conflict. *The Morning of the Streltsi Execution* aroused his interest in the period of social stagnation which followed the death of Peter the Great and which was caused to some extent by the cruel policies of the late Emperor himself. *Menshikov* was the fruit of this interest. *Morozova* turned Surikov's mind to an even earlier period of Russian history; he saw in the Boyarina and her supporters the forerunners of the Streltsi. The three paintings are not only thematically connected: they are also a kind of historico-psychological trilogy, in which the masses as well as individuals participate, and where the relationships between protagonist and people, and protagonist and history, are defined anew in the attempt of each painting to find its own way of describing a tragic event. *Morning of the Execution* was the first stage in this search.

In sixteenth- and seventeenth-century Muscovite Russia, the Streltsi were members of a military corps instituted by Ivan the Terrible and enjoying certain privileges. In Surikov's painting, they have been brought to the place of execution in open carts by soldiers of Peter's Preobrazhensky regiment, which had remained loyal to the Emperor during the Streltsi uprising of 1698. Each of the condemned men holds a burning candle, the symbol of approaching death; each yields to his last emotions, either raging against, or passively accepting, his fate. Some give a farewell bow to families and onlookers, others have already withdrawn from further contact with the world. The final preparations are complete and the first victim is being led to the scaffold. The scene takes place against the majestic silhouette of St Basil's cathedral, witness to so many momentous occasions. In the confusion and turmoil Peter, mounted on his steed, appears as a merciless idol overcome by a terrible fury, the brutal 'Tsar-antichrist' who has offended against the true orthodox faith. Nevertheless, the tortures and hangings he has ordained are not for his own gratification, but for the sake of Russia and her future. Two irreconcilable forces are here in collision; both are convinced of the righteousness of their deeds. Tragedy is unavoidable.

The scene daringly combines in one action various events, details of which Surikov learnt as he studied the memoirs and diaries of the time as well as eye-witness accounts of the execution. He deliberately sacrificed historical verisimilitude in order to increase the dramatic impact of the work. Thus, his crowd is so dense that the central figures can hardly make headway through it; the spaciousness of Red Square is reduced in order to augment the atmosphere of tension; finally, the Streltsi's

poses, too elaborate and various to be natural in real life, are for that very reason all the more convincing and significant in the painting. Surikov deliberately decided on a 'psychological composition' with two central focuses: one is Peter, whose burning gaze pierces the Streltsi, the other (at the opposite side of the picture) a red-bearded Strelets, even now eager to enter into combat with the Tsar although his hands are bound and his legs are in stocks. This duel dominates the whole canvas. The line of tension, stretching from the red-bearded Strelets and some of his companions, descends gradually until, quite weakened, it meets a new outburst of emotion in the face and figure of the Tsar.

The flow and colour of the composition match the psychological clash. Surikov dramatizes not only the faces but the forms, swirling and coiling in the crowd of Streltsi. The contrast between the disorganized mass of Streltsi, horses and carts on the one hand, and the onlookers and the disciplined ranks of the Imperial guard on the other, culminates in a kind of psychological drama of its own. The texture of the painting, somewhat coarse and heavy, itself evokes its central idea, a drama of the masses imbued with the pathos of power and a kind of monumental realism.

Menshikov in Berezovo is a continuation of this approach. The historical and psychological aspects of the scene are prominent and the message Surikov wishes to convey determines the pictorial form. Menshikov, Peter the Great's imperial chancellor and favourite, had become the de facto ruler of Russia for about three years after the Emperor's death. Surikov, however, portrays Menshikov shortly before his death in 1729, in the Siberian exile to which he had been sentenced in 1727. He is confined to the tiny log cabin built with his own hands. There is a tranquil rhythm about the way the characters are placed around the table: the younger daughter reads her Bible, while the disgraced prince himself, his son and elder daughter sit silently immersed in their thoughts in the cold, dark room. The actual moment depicted is not in itself important, merely providing a background to the characters' inner world, which is revealed by Surikov with all his skill as a master of drama, composition and colour. Every aspect of the composition, every turn of a figure, every brushstroke is loaded with narrative significance. It is no coincidence that the figures are seated round a table, for the motif of the circle implies the unity of a family bound together by a single tragic fate. This unity, however, does not preclude the diversity and individuality of its members, expressed primarily in the plastic treatment of the figures. Thus, Menshikov's profile is stern and well-defined, the volume of his figure neatly and clearly inserted into the space of the cramped log cabin. This volume dominates the space, as if to signify the displaced ruler's power and will. His son and daughters are treated in a quite different pictorial manner. Maria, the elder, is ill, doomed and apparently broken on the wheel of fate; her tragedy is revealed by the fragility of the figure and in the contrast of her pale face with her black fur coat. Around the head of the younger daughter is an aureole of light; her dress, though colourful, does not disturb the general tone of the picture. The son conveys a mood of absent-minded reverie, expressed in the relaxed rhythm and rather flowing contour of his head, as well as in the immersion of his figure in the apparently fluctuating space. All the characters vividly express their own moods; they are no mere allegories, but live their own, independent and real lives within that special dimension created by the very form of the picture.

This form has its own laws. Surikov exaggerates the figures' sizes in order to emphasize the significance and even majesty of an essentially eventless scene. Colours are harmonized within a unified range dominated by greys and browns, through which gems of dark red and blue, gold and jet-black dimly glitter. The impression that these colours are somehow fettered, that their contained energy dare not burst out, gives the painting a tension matched by the texture of the canvas; thus the colours melt into one single flowing, energetic layer, pregnant with movement.

While Surikov was completing *Menshikov in Bere-zovo* he was also beginning his studies for *Morozova*, but this new work was interrupted by a spell of foreign travel. Within the space of six months he visited many cities in Germany, France and Italy, where he was most impressed by the sixteenth-century Venetian artists Veronese, Titian and Tintoretto. In Veronese's treatment of colour he found an authentic account of Venetian Nature and of the light and colours of that fabulous city and the Adriatic Sea. He was struck by the power of Michelangelo and the realism of Velasquez. He was also attracted by French Impressionism; one still-life of Monet's particularly astonished him. All these experiences were echoed in his later work.

Boyarina Morozova is central to Surikov's *oeuvre* in the 1880s. In this picture, as in *Streltsi*, he chose to depict characters prepared to suffer for their creed although in historical terms they are on the losing side and their beliefs are mistaken. These men and women are no mere footnotes to history; they are evidence of the tragedies which result from the clash of the best intentions of honest people and from the laws of history, whose workings are so difficult for us to fathom. Surikov blames no one for these broken lives; he simply depicts life as it was, or might have been, or is, in all its complexity, heroism and majesty.

Morozova was preceded by more preliminary sketches and studies than any other of Surikov's paintings. Like Alexander Ivanov fifty years earlier, he tried many variations of every figure and object, slowly evolving an image for each character. Sharp psychological insight was combined with plastic expressiveness, while pictorial and colour techniques were used to emphasize a particular facial expression, the purposefulness of an individual gesture or the penetrating quality of a gaze. Gradually an image emerged for each character, e.g. the withdrawn young Boyar girl, the 'God's fool' (*yurodiviy*), possessed by his faith, and Morozova herself in ecstasy. The combination of dark blue and gold stood for resignation and humility, that of white and black for the passionate call to resistance. Dozens of preliminary studies for the composition itself preceded the final version, in which Surikov attempted to achieve, as he himself put it, 'the mathematics of painting'.

The characters are arranged on the canvas so as to create the illusion of a narrow, crowded street in seventeenth-century Moscow. The dense crowd appears to sway. Every detail reinforces the momentary quality of the scene, even though the moment is frozen for ever. Time, presented to the observer as real and specific, becomes a part of history before our eyes. This stopping of time is justified by virtue of the fact that most of the characters are seen not in some passing mood but in their most typical and symbolic states, whether of strong emotions, fierce concentration or deep self-absorption. Each of the characters is some kind of model. The frenzy of the holy fool's parting blessing to Morozova, the wise restraint of a religious pilgrim, the meek piety of a young Boyar girl, the deep emotion of a nun, the doleful weeping of a keening pilgrim woman – all are part of the drama of the scene but symbolize, in addition, various unchanging conditions of humanity. They combine the specific and the typical, the temporary and the permanent. An everyday setting will not do for these characters; they demand an environment of concentrated, distilled reality. In real life, of course, the street in the painting could not accommodate such a large number of people, any more than Morozova's sledge could force its way through the crowd, but Surikov's concentrated reality is more lifelike than any literally accurate picture. This 'deceit' in the cause of truthfulness is typical of Surikov.

Although at first glance the composition seems fortuitous, there is actually a firmly logical basis to it. The characters actively in sympathy with Morozova are ranged along one diagonal, extending from the holy fool to the condemned Old Believer herself, who makes the sign of the Cross with two fingers in a final, symbolic defiance of the church reform (which prescribed signing

Vasily Surikov *Boyarina Morozova* 1887

with three). Morozova – and particularly this sign – is the
culminating point of the scene, and the bearer of the
painting's fundamental message. Another line – made up
of a row of heads on one level – leads to her raised hand.
The psychological tension is gradually decreasing at this
point, as if in preparation for a spurt of energy on
Morozova's part. The main compositional structures
meet at her head and hand. Together they create a single,
firm structure in which movement is halted forever. Like
a keystone, her head and hand hold this complex
compositional arch, which is made up of various, but not
dissimilar, squares (the heads) and oblongs (the figures).

The logic of the composition is evident not only in the
'psychological aspect' of the painting. The picture
conveys the impression of a sturdily constructed building,
erected by skilful hands according to immutable architectural laws. The canvas is divided into three zones. The
lower (the snow) and the upper (houses and sky) frame
the middle zone, which is crammed with activity, three-
dimensional forms and patches of colour. This division,
together with the balanced distribution of forms around
the centre, gives the composition its quality of completeness. By superimposing one zone on another, and thus
conveying the sense of movement into the background,
the artist avoids disturbing the plane and so preserves its
pristine integrity.

Surikov's use of colour is also significant. At first glance

it seems that he covers large areas of the canvas with one
colour; in fact, each incorporates a rich variety of shades
and tones. He employs colour to achieve a realistic effect,
to organize the canvas according to the laws of pictorial
form and to show Old Russian costume, architecture,
crafts and everyday life in all its beauty. In addition, the
colours work like musical sounds to create a particular
atmosphere. The dramatic quality of *Morozova* is largely
conveyed by means of colour. Most of the colour
combinations, which are informative and rich in psychological insight, tend towards blacks, whites and reds or
dark blues and golds.

Morozova completed Surikov's 'tragic' period, which
was followed by an 'heroic' phase. In the 1890s and 1900s
he painted another three major works, *Yermak's Conquest of Siberia* (1895), *Suvorov Crossing the Alps* (1899)
and *Stepan Razin* (1905–10). Although only the first
achieved the standard his work had reached in the 1880s,
all three have in common the motif of popular daring,
unity and cohesion round the figure of a Cossack chieftain
(Yermak, Razin) or military leader (Suvorov).

Yermak's Conquest of Siberia is a truly monumental
and dramatic interpretation of an historical episode.
Surikov superbly conveys the grandeur and glory of
Yermak's battle against the Siberian Tartars and other
tribes, vassals of the Tartars. The tragic element is absent
from this painting (although death found many victims in

Vasily Surikov *Stepan Razin* 1905–10

the war). For the Cossacks following their *ataman* (chieftain) Yermak into this long and dangerous campaign, the war is more like an adventurous game. Unlike the characters in *Morozova*, who are all carefully defined by their mood, character, social status and personal fate, those of *Yermak* are all very much alike – without in any way losing their individuality. Indeed, a kind of kinship of individuality is created. The idea Surikov wished to express in this work was the spirit of unity which can bind a group of people together, and he used both pictorial and compositional techniques to convey it. The Cossacks round Yermak form a solid band of supporters, a kind of mass, laden with energy about to explode, which creates an active rhythm, the rhythm of the battle itself, of lines spreading all over the canvas. The vast river is choppy, waves swell, the smoke of gunfire swirls, huge numbers of Tartars form a kind of snake in the background. The colour scheme, too, is dynamic and full of energy: browns and reds of various shades, greys and muffled blues are mixed together and integrated into a whole. Unlike *Morozova*, this painting contains no obvious decorative combinations. Surikov's purpose here is rather different: just as the contrasting personalities of *Morozova* gave way, in *Yermak*, to the unified group, so, in the treatment of colour, it is the general tone of the picture which dominates the individual colours. There is a certain nobility about the colouration of *Yermak's*

Conquest of Siberia, and it is not surprising that some critics compared this work to an antique brocade, somewhat tarnished by time but still imbued with an everlasting beauty.

In *Suvorov Crossing the Alps* the artist selected a celebrated episode of the Swiss campaign against Napoleon, when Russian soldiers under Suvorov's command achieved the almost unbelievable feat of crossing the Alps and thus saving the allied armies from destruction. The work scores a number of successes, as witness, for example, the fascinating faces of the simple soldiers, the frail figure of the Generalissimo himself buoying up their spirits with a joke, and the figures sliding rapidly down the snow-covered slopes. In *Suvorov*, Surikov encountered several problems quite new to him. He was dealing not with the Streltsi, or Peter the Great's Preobrazhensky regiment or Yermak's Cossacks, but with the soldiers of Suvorov's regular army, different men with different clothes in a different era, in which it was much harder for Surikov to detect the specifically national and traditional features which were of particular interest to him, and which he was now obliged to portray in European guise. The heart of the episode, Suvorov sharing a joke with his men, somewhat mutes the heroic atmosphere – as, indeed, does the very concept of the composition. Surikov concentrates on a specific moment and rejects his earlier 'historical stretching' of time. The composition, ill-suited

(top) **Vasily Surikov** *Yermak's Conquest of Siberia* 1895

(above) **Vasily Surikov** *Suvorov Crossing the Alps* 1899

to the dimensions of the picture, is reminiscent of a film still.

The internal relationship which united Surikov's earlier tragic trilogy is no longer present. Admittedly, *Yermak* and *Suvorov* address similar themes, but the third of the later works, *Stepan Razin*, cannot be said to fulfil that synthesizing role which *Morozova* played in the 1880s. Nevertheless, the work deserves our attention. Unlike *Suvorov*, *Razin* lacks any external dynamic element. Stepan Razin was the leader of an anti-government uprising of peasants, Cossacks and others, which ended with his execution in 1671. He is portrayed seated in the middle of a large boat sailing along the Volga. Razin is motionless, deeply immersed in his thoughts; his accomplices, too, are subdued. The rowers' movements are in equilibrium, their oars raised high above the water like the wings of a bird about to lift the boat into the sky. This 'flight', together with Razin's pose and the fact that the whole episode is based on a popular folk song, places the work into a new category, that of the *bylina* – the Russian traditional heroic poem – with added elements of the fairy tale.

In later years Surikov moved away from historical subjects and painted a number of landscapes and portraits, mostly of women. In his portraits he was primarily interested in national, even local types; as a result, their titles frequently contain, in addition to the names of the sitters, descriptions such as 'Siberian beauty', 'City girl' and 'Cossack girl'. He sought a timeless element in his models, never tying their mood to

a specific moment of time or submitting them to psychological analysis. He saw them, rather, as pure forms in space to which he could then attribute human characteristics. This approach distinguishes Surikov's portraits from the more established portraiture of the second half of the nineteenth century.

His later male portraits, including a number of self-portraits, are remarkable for their skill and expressive power, and reveal new artistic interests. He became close to members of *Bubnoviy Valet* (Knave of Diamonds), the first Russian avantgarde group, partly as a result of family ties – his daughter, Natalya, married Pyotr Konchalovsky, one of the leaders of the group. These last activities of Surikov's are further evidence of the fact that his art could never be contained within the rigid limits of traditional realism.

Surikov's greatness was not unreservedly acclaimed, and his exceptional qualities were only universally acknowledged with the passage of time, when it became clear that in the 1880s, when his powers were at their height, he was head and shoulders above his contemporaries. At one of the Travelling Exhibitions, for example, *Morozova* was shown next to *Christ and a Sinner* (1888), a work by Vasily Polenov (1844–1927). Many of the critics compared these two large canvases; by no means all preferred Surikov's. Polenov's approach, which diverged considerably from the tradition embodied by Ivanov, Kramskoi and Ge, reintroduced the genre element into history painting. He was primarily concerned to preserve the historical accuracy and authentic detail of ordinary

(*top*) **Vasily Polenov** *Christ and a Sinner* 1888
(*above*) **Vasily Surikov** *Townswoman* 1902

Genrikh Semiradsky *Frina at a Celebration of Poseidon, the King of the Sea, at Eleusis* 1889

life, and a good deal less interested in the image of Christ as Reformer or Martyr. Polenov seemed to be saying, in essence: 'This is how it was.' His guiding light was Ernest Renan's book *The Life of Jesus*, which also crucially influenced his late cycle of paintings on New Testament themes. Polenov's style effortlessly combined naturalism with some features of academic painting.

Pure academic painting of the 1880s concentrated on the history genre, producing a skilled painter in Genrikh Semiradsky (1843–1902), who enjoyed great popularity among the Russian public. He tackled various themes, among them events from Russian history and biblical episodes; he also contributed to the internal decor of the Cathedral of Christ the Saviour in Moscow. Most successful of all were his paintings on themes from ancient Greece and Rome. One of his most striking historical works is *The Torchbearers of Christianity*. It depicts the burning alive of early Christian martyrs on the order of the Emperor Nero, who turned this elaborate execution into a lighthearted entertainment. Semiradsky creates a dramatic scene which, while in no way concealing pain and suffering, elevates the feeling of horror to a kind of grandeur. Nevertheless, such bloody scenes, so eagerly exploited by academic painters, were not Semiradsky's staple fare. He favoured celebrations of all kinds, preferably with bacchanalia or naked beauties dancing solo and bewitching the public with their exquisite charms. His most characteristic works of this type are two large canvases, *Sword-dance* (1881) and

Frina at a Celebration of Poseidon, the King of the Sea, at Eleusis (1889). These scenes take place in sumptuous natural settings which display all the obligatory elements of the fabulous south – sea, green trees, hills surrounding a bay, bright sunlight and a fantastical play of shadows on the ground. Add to these a complete still-life made up of expensive items and objects of antique luxury. Semiradsky did not select the most graceful of models to express his concept of female beauty: his ideal has the figure of an antique statue enriched by sensuality.

Semiradsky's style is a perfect example of mature academic art. He aimed at what may be described as the 'illusion of reality' in these two multi-figure compositions. All the figures' movements and gestures were checked beforehand in studies from life, with the result that, placed together, the characters make up a crowd; the realism of their movements, however, is distorted, for the figures and groups, all in their specially reserved places, seem to be displaying themselves before us. Beneath their apparently casual and realistic surfaces, the compositions are decidedly traditional, with clearly-defined centres and well-balanced sides. At first glance they seem to be *plein air* works, on account of their treatment of natural light, but the *plein air* veneer is merely laid over an academic pictorial base. Semiradsky, like his fellow academic painters, sought a false, rather than true, realism.

Semiradsky's style and approach differed radically from that of Surikov; indeed, the two are at opposite poles

Viktor Vasnetsov *After Prince Igor's Battle with the Polovtsy* 1880

of the general development of the history genre. There was only one other artist of the 1880s who used some of the traditional academic techniques and whose achievements may be compared to Surikov's. This was Viktor Vasnetsov (1848–1926); like Surikov, he 'discovered' himself in the early 1880s.

He was born in one of the remote provinces of the Empire, educated at the seminary of Vyatka (now Kirov) in the north of Russia, and later moved to St Petersburg, where he became a student at the Imperial Academy of Fine Arts. In the 1870s he was occupied with traditional genre painting which, after continuously developing since the 1840s, was now beginning to run out of steam. In these years he was maturing quietly; he reappeared in the 1880s as a new man. At this time he was influenced by the famous Mamontov circle, a group of some of the best artists of the time who worked at Abramtsevo, the country estate near Moscow of Mamontov, a rich industrialist and patron of the arts. He commissioned Vasnetsov to paint some huge panels illustrating themes from history, fable and folklore.

The most brilliant example of Vasnetsov's new talent was his huge canvas *After Prince Igor's Battle with the Polovtsy* (1880). Its subject, taken from the famous twelfth-century epic *The History of Igor's Campaign* (*Slovo o polku Igoryevye*), is the battlefield strewn with corpses after the clash between Russian troops and warriors of the Polovtsi tribe. Vasnetsov borrowed from this literary masterpiece not only the bare facts it related

but its heroic spirit, approach to reality and lyrical atmosphere. Its influence is apparent in the composition, the colour scheme and the epic treatment of figures. The monumental character of the painting is evident both from its size, unusual for the time, and from the manner in which the scene is universalized. Vasnetsov, unlike Surikov, deliberately distances himself from specific fact, whether real or imagined as real. He sees fact itself as epic: objects, aspects of the landscape and figures all serve as particular poetic symbols and, accordingly, differ in appearance from their real-life counterparts. The flowers, grass and tussocks are there not simply to cover the earth but to represent the beauty of the Russian steppe. Every detail exists as an independent image; each blade of grass in the foreground rises, bends and droops separately; the camomile unfolds its petals and spreads among the green grass in strict symmetry. Grass and flowers, together with the reddish moon rising above the horizon (so straight it might have been drawn with a ruler), create a lyrical image of the homeland soaked with the blood of its defenders (the picturesque arrangement of whose corpses was a particular cause of confusion among contemporary critics). Characters and landscape are described in epic clichés: the girls are the very picture of beauty, the slain warriors radiate a herculean strength, the steppe is wide, the moon blood-red. The composition receives similar treatment; each object and figure, as if afraid of being distorted by its neighbours and their reflected colours, strives to achieve an isolated, indepen-

Viktor Vasnetsov *Alenushka* 1881

dent existence and to occupy a position on the canvas in which it may exhibit itself to the best advantage. Hence the strict definition of the outlines, the sculptural clarity of the forms and the rejection of *plein air* techniques. The symbolic language sought by Vasnetsov is borrowed from academic art rather than folklore, and attempts to imitate folklore in the use of local colour for objects (especially clothes) and in the somewhat naive refusal to depict aerial perspective.

Three other paintings by Vasnetsov employ similar techniques to illustrate themes from folklore and fable during this period: *The Magic Carpet, Alenushka* and *Three Princesses of the Underground Kingdom.* They differ from each other only in the extent to which they are more or less naturalistic or fantastical. The most realistic is *Alenushka* (1881), which was actually based on *plein air* studies and sketches. The scene (selected from a fairy tale) provided little opportunity for the creation of a non-real or fantastical scene, for it simply showed the little girl

of the title sitting, lonely and forlorn, on a stone by a pond. Although the setting obliged Vasnetsov to portray figures and landscape naturalistically, he did attempt to animate the various elements of the latter (the stones, reeds, birches and the leaves blown onto the water by the wind). This animation of nature is a distinct innovation in Russian painting, one which eventually led to Nesterov's background landscapes and Vrubel's poeticization of nature.

The central work in Vasnetsov's fairy tale and epic cycle is the large canvas entitled *Bogatyrs* (1898), the idea for which was conceived in the 1870s. He worked intermittently on the painting for twenty-five years. The bogatyrs (herculean heroes of Russian folklore) are portrayed, as described in a Russian *bylina*, on the frontier of the homeland, keeping careful surveillance on the enemy. In accordance with the *bylina*, Ilya Murometz is wise, calm and majestic; Dobinya Nikitich is impulsive, furious and fiery; Alyosha Popovich is cunning and dexterous, though rather simple in appearance. Even their respective horses agree with their *bylina* descriptions, blowing through their flaring nostrils, obstinately lowering their necks and bowing their heads. Vasnetsov's style here places him somewhere between Academicism and Art Nouveau. The idea of a totally balanced picture, of a static composition built on the three riders arranged into a kind of pyramid, derives from the Academic tradition. Among the Art Nouveau elements are the emphasis on linear expression at the expense of *plein air* effects; the new role given to patches of colour; and the transition from easel painting to the more abstract and architectural decorative panels.

Vasnetsov also attempted to revive a lay historical, and later a religious, version of monumental painting. In the 1880s he painted a large frieze, *The Stone Age*, for one of the halls of the History Museum in Moscow, and later spent many years working on the internal decor of St Vladimir's Church in Kiev. These murals are examples of an eclectic mixture of the medieval and academic traditions together with aspects of naturalism and Art Nouveau. They are a curious footnote to the history of Russian art.

Vasnetsov was also a prominent collector and student of folk art, which until that time had been completely cut off from established and professional art. He became one of the main exponents of the so-called neo-Russian style which was beginning to emerge from within Russian Art Nouveau. He was the first to use this neo-Russian style in theatre design, where he revived the tradition of a truly creative and original approach. His achievements in all these fields ensure him a special niche in the history of Russian culture as one of the godfathers of Russian Art Nouveau.

Viktor Vasnetsov *Bogatyrs* 1898

Viktor Vasnetsov *Three Princesses of the Underground Kingdom* 1884

5 Landscape Painting

Landscape painting experienced two peak periods during the latter half of the nineteenth century – in the 1870s and the 1890s. The first, which included painters of different generations, such as Savrasov (who had been waiting for two decades for landscape painting to come into its own) and Vasiliev, some twenty years younger than Savrasov, was soon exhausted. Savrasov was a lesser painter at the end of his career than at its outset; Vasiliev was dead by the age of 23; Kuindzhi had his last exhibition in 1882; Shishkin, though productive into the 1880s and 1890s, added nothing of artistic value to his earlier work. The vacuum of the 1880s was filled by artists of a new generation, headed by Levitan, which flourished during the 1890s but later receded in importance. Thus landscape developed quite differently from genre, portrait or history painting.

There were several interesting aspects to this development. All the great landscape painters were of a similar quality, which was not the case in genre and portrait, where there was a clear hierarchy of talent. Each made his own significant contribution to the genre, though they all had much in common. This situation changed in the 1890s with the appearance of Levitan as a clear-cut leader in whose reflected glory a number of his contemporaries were able to flourish.

All these landscape painters were narrow specialists who never tried their skill at other genres. Indeed, the young Levitan, unable to paint a woman's figure for his *Autumn Day: Sokolniki*, was obliged to ask Nikolai Chekhov (brother of the famous author) for help, and Savitsky had to paint the bears for Shishkin's *Morning in the Pine Forest*. From the 1860s onwards, and particularly in the 1870s, painters working in other genres could not do without landscapes, which were becoming an integral part of genre and history paintings. Many of the events depicted by Savitsky, Myasoyedov and Repin required natural settings; indeed, their figures and objects, dominated by the space around them, did not so much organize the space around themselves as actually dwell in it. In this situation genrists and history painters could not ignore the *plein air* developments of the 1870s. In fact it was Savitsky, Repin and Polenov, rather than the specialists, who became the first masters of *plein air* painting.

Ivan Shishkin *Morning in the Pine Forest* 1889

Portrait and landscape competed for a dominant role in genre and history painting. We recall the importance of portrait in Repin's genre works of the 1880s and the significant portrait element in Surikov. When, as in the 1880s, painters set themselves primarily psychological goals, portrait abandoned landscape. The 1890s saw the renaissance of landscape in all genres, particularly in the work of the younger generation, men such as Konstantin Korovin, Valentin Serov, Abram Arkhipov and Sergei Ivanov (the last two genrists).

Although the landscape painters of the second half of the nineteenth century limited their work strictly to their chosen genre, landscape enjoyed a complex and mutually rewarding relationship with the other genres. It could be richly narrative, although its practitioners did not incorporate genre elements in their work but preferred to tell their story through the landscapes themselves. The influence of genre was also evident in the landscape painters' preoccupation with simple natural phenomena and the Russian countryside, a fascination explained by the slow growth of urbanization (compared with Western Europe) and by the abiding – and very Russian – attraction the idea of peasant life had for the intelligentsia. On the very rare occasions when the *peredvizhniki* did paint townscapes they presented them as villages.

Man, with all his needs and troubles, was at the centre

Alexei Savrasov *Elk Island in Sokolniki* 1869

of *peredvizhniki* landscape. The approach to landscape initiated by Alexander Ivanov, who was interested not only in nature but in the Earth itself, had become exhausted, although the academic and romantic tradition was continued by such painters as I.K. Aivazovsky, L.F. Lagorio and A.P. Bogolyubov all through the second half of the nineteenth century. Aivazovsky's marine paintings attempted to create some kind of image of elemental forces, while Bogolyubov's townscapes hark back to the early part of the century, but these two had few followers. Moreover, those painters working within the old traditions were producing tired romantic clichés. Savrasov himself, one of the founders of *peredvizhniki* landscape, was prone to this weakness, which he only overcame with some difficulty.

Alexei Savrasov (1830–97) was educated at the Moscow Art College, where he also taught from the late 1850s. He only began truly to realize his talents in the late 1860s, which saw the appearance of a number of important works such as *Elk Island in Sokolniki* (1869), *Moonlit Night: Swamp* (1870) and *The Monastery of Pechora near Nizhny Novgorod* (1871). These were followed by such masterpieces as *The Rooks Have*

Arrived (1871), *Cart Track* (1873) and *Rainbow* (1875).

The Rooks Have Arrived is a perfect example of lyrical landscape, the most prominent variety of realistic landscape painting. The work was preceded by several studies of a Volga village which were not directly transferred onto the canvas but adapted to provide a more generalized picture and greater narrative power. In the foreground is the noisy bustle of the rooks and the twigs dropped from their nests lying in the trampled, melting snow. Village life pursues its normal daily round behind the fence which separates the foreground from the middleground, while distant views link this little local corner to the vast territories and splendour of Mother Russia. Although the subject is modest the painting conveys the sense of beauty through its evocation of a universal spring awakening, the promise of warmth and natural renewal, the serene life of a remote Russian village, the soft earth and its harmony with human nature. We may truly call this painting of Savrasov's a 'landscape of mood', a term more usually applied to the work of his outstanding pupil, Levitan. Savrasov, like Levitan, here adds a lyrical element to his simple subject by ascribing his own emotions to nature.

31

Alexei Savrasov *Rainbow* 1875

The Rooks Have Arrived is remarkable for its gentle manner. It conveys the spring light shyly pouring from the sky; greys, light blues and browns are in fine balance; light and dark, and light and shade, work together in harmony. The 'evenness' of the picture further strengthens the impression of clarity, calm and purity.

33   The subject of *Cart Track* is also very simple – just the track itself and windblown, weatherbeaten white willows to one side of it. The sky is more striking than the earth; strips of racing cloud obscure the sun, which still manages to light up the high sky and a little meadow in the distance. These effects of light are, perhaps, the real subject of the painting, rather than the puddle-filled, rutted little road. *Cart Track* is unusual in Savrasov's work in its rather direct illustration of a changing season. Such themes were more typical of Vasiliev than Savrasov, who usually favoured the slow transformation of one state into another, such as long drawn-out sunsets, or early spring with its promise of future blossom. His preferred themes inevitably led him to explore *plein air* techniques, though without sacrificing more traditional principles. In *Cart Track*, for example, the green is too local, i.e. it is hardly mixed with its neighbours and contains no reflections of other colours. His *plein air* studies at the end of the 1870s, which helped to liberate him from such received ideas, were Levitan's earliest inspiration.

Another celebrated landscape painter of Savrasov's generation was Ivan Shishkin (1832–98), whose approach to nature was far from lyrical. He preferred to emphasize nature's permanence rather than its states of change. His pictures have an epic character; his style is clear and tends towards naturalism. He studied first at the Moscow Art College and later at the St Petersburg Academy, with whose traditions he was actually more at ease. His career followed a pattern similar to Savrasov's, the early years being used to gain experience and lay the groundwork for his best work in the 1870s. Two themes dominate his paintings: forests (usually of tall pines) and fields. An example of the latter is *Midday: Countryside near Moscow* (1869), which marks the onset of his mature 35 period. It conveys the vast expanses of Russian fields; Shishkin interprets the theme of the road very differently from Perov in *The Last Inn by the Town Gate* described in an earlier chapter. There is neither melancholy nor despair about Shishkin's road, which is accompanied by high skies, ripe cornfields and bright sunshine. The style, unusually for Shishkin, is rather soft and gentle.

The next milestone in his creative development was *Pine Forest* (1872). For all the naturalness of the composition (particularly the brook lined with stones in the foreground) it still strikes us as rather calculated. Shishkin seems to be setting the stage for a display of the main object of attention, which is placed somewhat in the background – the pine forest itself with its mighty trunks and soaring crowns. The lighting contributes to the staginess; thus, the sunlit foreground is set against a shady background, and the central portion of the middleground – the treetrunks – is picked out by light, marking it out as the centre of the whole composition. This most typical of Shishkin's paintings bears within it the basic contradiction, inherent in his work, between his search for a generalized image, i.e. 'pine forests', and his attention to petty detail (executed with a rather dry technique) which obscures that image. Shishkin only rarely succeeded in reconciling these conflicting impulses.

One of his best paintings is *Field of Rye* (1878), which combines two themes explored in earlier works – a large field with a track winding through it; and the endless steppe and mighty pines, symbolizing the power of the Russian forest. Shishkin synthesized these motifs into a rather concise composition based on his favourite concept of 'natural balance': the horizontals are arranged in judicious harmony with the verticals, with the tall pines towering above the rye and flanking the long road like huge pylons. For Shishkin the weightiness and grand scale of nature are self-evident. A dried-out trunk is deliberately placed between the living trees as proof that nature is being neither idealized nor distorted.

In the 1880s and 1890s Shishkin produced further landscapes in the same spirit of 'monumental naturalism'. Problems of lighting were resolved, as before, by external means, as for example in his study of *Sunlit Pines* (1886). Here he chose a scene which emphasized light and deepened the shadows falling on the ground and trees. The drawing is very clear, and the bark, soil and grass are

Ivan Shishkin *Field of Rye* 1878

depicted in the same minute detail as before. The texture of each object is preserved intact and not sacrificed to the overall texture, as is the case with *plein air* works and particularly Impressionism, with which Shishkin had nothing in common.

The most talented landscape artist of the 1870s was Fyodor Vasiliev (1850–73), whose early death at the age of 23 prevented him from becoming a major figure in Russian art. His sparse artistic education consisted of a drawing course organized by the Society for Encouragement of Artists; he also received generous advice from Shishkin. His true spiritual mentor was Kramskoi, who befriended the 'young genius', as he called him, helped him in many ways and encouraged him to experiment. It took Vasiliev six or seven years to develop from a green young dilettante into a skilful painter with an individual style, unrivalled among his Russian colleagues in his use and understanding of colour. He spent the last two years of his life far from home, in the Crimea, in a vain attempt to cure the galloping consumption he had contracted in St Petersburg.

There is no direct link between the work of Vasiliev and Savrasov or Shishkin, although Vasiliev's artistic method is somewhat reminiscent of Savrasov's. Vasiliev worked in the open air, rearranging the landscapes recorded in his studies when he came to compose the final picture. His temperament, however, was quite unlike Savrasov's. He was fascinated by strong emotions and by those moments in nature most imbued with tension and expressiveness. He saw things with a 'different eye' which enabled him to perceive nuances and shades of colour as independent colours with qualities of their own. This sensitivity to the energies of colour earned Vasiliev a special place in Russian art at the end of the 1860s and the beginning of the 1870s. It is particularly evident in his early works (before 1871), which are more like studies than finished paintings. A good example is the small picture entitled *After the Rain* (1869) – a typical Vasiliev theme, for he liked nature in a state of change. The main impact of this painting, which depicts two men on a cart piled high with hay and pulled by two horses, derives from the relationship between the colours. They evoke a melody heard in the clear air after a thunderstorm against the background of a yellow evening sky. The canvas betrays Vasiliev's familiarity with the Barbizon School (and especially with Corot), to whose works in the Kusheliev Gallery in St Petersburg he devoted much study. Many of his other paintings dating from this time reveal the same free and picturesque qualities.

His last three years were devoted to what he and his patrons considered more serious goals, namely pictures which were both larger and more finished. The first was *The Thaw*, painted in 1871 before he left for the Crimea. The broad, panoramic composition conveys a slow, sad and pensive mood, which overcomes the observer as he contemplates this abandoned and impoverished corner of

Fyodor Vasiliev *The Thaw* 1871

Russia and the two tramps wandering along the slushy track. The depressing theme of the picture (so uncharacteristic of Vasiliev) may have its origins in various genre paintings of the 1860s, especially those of Perov.

Water Meadow (1872), which reflects a different mood, was painted in the Crimea from memory and preliminary studies. It, too, captures a moment of change in nature, though a rather less dramatic one. Signs of a passing storm have been moved into the background, while grass-covered earth washed by rain occupies the foreground. At the centre of the canvas is a pond, whose glittering surface reflects the light of the sky. A border between light and dark runs through sky and water and through the centre of the canvas from one side to the other. In the middleground a low hill on the left is finely balanced by bushes on the right. The tightly constructed composition contains the tension of the storm, but in spite of this contrast between the careful pictorial arrangement and the explosion of nature it describes, the total effect is one of harmony and wholeness.

Vasiliev spent his last few months working on a large canvas entitled *In the Crimean Mountains* (1873), after discovering that mountains could possess a profound spiritual significance. He wrote in a letter to Kramskoi: 'I am certain that a painting consisting simply of this blue air and these mountains, without a single cloud, would expose and then dissolve any wicked thoughts of those who looked upon such a scene so imbued with grace, infinite glory and natural purity.'[12] These words do not refer directly to *In the Crimean Mountains*, whose sky is

obscured by mist so that no blue is visible, but the point stands, for the mountains were the key to a new, moral interpretation of landscape; there is indeed something elevated and majestic about this picture. Vasiliev maintained a common tonal effect by harmonizing the browns, grey-blues and greens, deliberately restraining himself from highlighting individual colours for fear of destroying their overall unity. This fear was evidence of the still unresolved contradiction between his personal vision, so fully realized in studies, and the rather different creative process involved in bringing a painting to completion. There are two masterpieces from his Crimean period which, though unfinished, further illustrate this contradiction: *An Abandoned Mill* and *Marshland in the Forest* (both 1871–73).

The composition of *Marshland* is based primarily on colour. The subordination of its structure to effects of colour is seen in the gradual gathering of warm red tones towards the centre. This tension reaches its highest point in the two trees. As the eye moves sideways from the centre the intensity of colour gradually weakens. The bright colours are dulled and acquire new and complex qualities, i.e. they are whitened with grey, shaded by pale blue, or given extra weight by dark blue and brown. Vasiliev treats the marsh theme, which was very popular in the 1860s and 1870s, in a most unusual, exultant way, finding in it unlimited potential for the exploration of colour.

Vasiliev died at what would have been a turning-point in his career. But for his tragic loss Russian landscape painting might well have developed quite differently, for he was embarking on a new phase which transferred the spontaneity of his sketches to finished works of art. These developments were not related to the *plein air* movement as represented in the mid-1870s by Savrasov, Polenov and Repin; they were, rather, the first manifestations of decorativism in landscape.

In the second half of the 1870s it was Arkhip Kuindzhi who took up the torch of innovation in landscape painting. Greek by nationality, he was born in the south of Russia. He was largely self-taught, idolized Aivazovsky in his youth and made an unsuccessful attempt to enrol at the St Petersburg Academy, which many years later, however, awarded him all the appropriate academic titles in appreciation of his services to art. He started exhibiting in the late 1860s and in the 1870s became a member of the *peredvizhniki* group. His painting *The Forgotten Village* became a focus of attention at the third exhibition of the Society in 1874. This work, like so many others of the time, evokes a sense of sadness, despair and futility.

All the same, Kuindzhi was not really the type to shed such civic tears. As early as 1876 he exhibited a lyrical work entitled *Ukrainain Night*, in which he discovered the magical effect of moonlight on lush landscape, and which marked a new and successful stage in his career.

Fyodor Vasiliev *In the Crimean Mountains* 1873

Fyodor Vasiliev *Water Meadow* 1872

Arkhip Kuindzhi *The Dnieper in the Morning* 1881

Arkhip Kuindzhi *Moonlight on the Dnieper* 1880

37   Two paintings dating from 1879, *After the Storm* and
36   *Birch Grove*, exemplify his mature period. Choosing
unusual effects of sun or moonlight he captured special
and particularly beautiful moments in the natural cycle.
He increased these effects by all possible means, almost
to the point of distorting aesthetic norms: one more
brushstroke, we feel, and the whole thing would degener-
ate into chocolate-box prettiness. Kuindzhi never quite
overstepped the mark, however; his paintings always
impress, never repel. Nature appears not only at its best,
but in a state of purity, for Kuindzhi did not indulge in an
over-abundance of detail. His very method of working
helped him to select only the essential elements of
nature: he composed his paintings from memory without
recourse to studies or sketches he might have made
beforehand. There was no need, therefore, to edit out any
superfluous detail because he himself had constructed
the entire composition from scratch.

As a rule, Kuindzhi used simple compositional lines;
he liked horizontals and diagonals and interpreted
objects in a very general way, often neglecting detailed
dimensional modelling. Sometimes he boldly compared
objects placed at some distance from each other, superimposing figures onto the background in a manner reminiscent of oleographic techniques. This approach is particularly striking in *Birch Grove*, which is based on the
traditional schema of a romantic landscape. With extraordinary audacity and directness he confronted the three
'grounds': the foreground shaded, the middleground
brightly lit, the background shaded again but more
clearly visible against the light sky. The contrasts
between them are deliberately emphasized. Kuindzhi
multiplied the potential colour relationships within
nature without concealing the fact that the landscape was
a product of his own imagination.

In 1880 he completed and exhibited a single picture
entitled *Moonlight on the Dnieper*. This was in itself
unprecedented, because exhibitions of individual artists
were very rare and exhibitions of individual paintings
virtually unknown. The event greatly impressed the
public. Kuindzhi achieved his fullest effect by selecting a
point of view above his subject and from afar, excluding
foreground and lowering the line of the horizon, thus
giving over more than two thirds of the canvas to the sky.
All the beauty of nature seems to unfold from below –
indeed, from under the feet of the painter himself, who
appears to rule and create it. The picture presents a kind
of symbolic world, whose depicted space we cannot enter
because it has been transformed into a kind of theatre.
Nevertheless the landscape conveys a majestic and
elevated impression of the measured, quiet flow of the
profound river.

Kuindzhi's last exhibited painting, *The Dnieper in the*

Vasily Polenov *Grandmother's Garden* 1878

Morning (1881), differs slightly from previous works. The
foreground, with its flowering thistles raised to the
horizon, is emphasized. A soft mist covers the blossoming
steppe. The striking view is presented in an unexpectedly
gentle manner very unlike his previous works.

Perhaps sensing that he was to make no new creative
progress in his art, he ceased to exhibit but continued to
work, with the result that the paintings of his last three
decades were seen by the public only in a special
posthumous exhibition. His work as a professor at the
Academy, which he was invited to join after its reform,
bore rich fruit in such graduates from his studio as
Roerich, Rylov and Bogayevsky.

After Kuindzhi, the next most important figure in
Russian landscape painting of the late 1870s was Vasily
Polenov, who worked in several genres but whose true
vocation was landscape. The end of the 1870s saw the
appearance of *Moscow Courtyard* (1878), *Grand-*   38
mother's Garden (1878) and *Overgrown Pond* (1879).
The first became a kind of model for the painters of the
next generation. The composition unfolds horizontally to
describe the daily life of a typical Moscow courtyard in
every detail. This 'narrative' includes several episodes – a
woman carrying buckets of water, a horse in harness, a
little boy at play – and thus enables Polenov to juxtapose
landscape and genre as closely as possible. In the late
1860s Perov had already attempted to merge the two, but
at that time genre was still dominant. With Polenov the
two achieved equality in a single painting, which led to
the appearance of genre-landscapes in the work of his
pupils at the Moscow Art College, such as Arkhipov,
Ivanov and Stepanov. *Moscow Courtyard* also revealed

Polenov's mastery of *plein air*. He had recently returned from his studies with Repin in Normandy and in this painting he applied the techniques he had learnt there of rendering shadow by means of colour, using fine nuances of tone and generally displaying the dependence of colour on light. The further the object from the foreground, the less the intensity of its colour, as, for example, in the upper part of the painting, where the roofs and walls of several houses are depicted in green, blue, pink and yellow shades so light that they seem to fade into thin air. Another noteworthy aspect of this painting is the lyrical language employed to express its very ordinary theme.

In later years Polenov often returned to landscape, although without ever again reaching the same level of perfection. One episode connected with his work in this field is worthy of mention. In the 1880s, when he was engaged on preliminary work for his gospel paintings, he travelled in the Middle East and made many studies which were later exhibited in travelling exhibitions. This was the first time that studies were deemed worthy of being shown to the public; hitherto they had been considered merely part of the artist's studio and devoid of any intrinsic interest. The cult of the study rapidly became part of the Moscow artistic tradition, and a pupil of Polenov's, Konstantin Korovin, developed this aspect of Polenov's work with a brilliance all his own.

Polenov forms a link between the two generations of landscape painters of the 1870s and 1890s referred to at the beginning of this chapter, for he was one of the teachers of Isaac Levitan (1860–1900), the outstanding Russian landscape painter of the 1890s. Savrasov also taught Levitan, who thus enjoyed the benefit of Savrasov's lyrical insights together with Polenov's *plein air* experience. Many of Levitan's contemporaries, younger and older, such as Vrubel, Serov, Korovin, Arkhipov and Ivanov, can now be seen as figures of the new artistic epoch which flowered at the turn of the new century, whereas Levitan summed up all the traditions of the second half of the old. It is not that he was no innovator or lagged behind his colleagues, for some of his works of the 1880s were seminal to the development of early Russian Impressionism. The fact is that his work contains too many features deriving from the 1870s and 1880s *peredvizhniki*, whose paintings were basically narrative and concentrated on the visual presentation of ideas equally capable of verbal expression. Almost up to his death Levitan was working on landscapes tinged with narrative.

He was inspired in turn by various painters of the 1860s, among them Vasiliev, Kuindzhi, Savrasov, Polenov and even Shishkin, whose interests fundamentally differed from Levitan's. He experimented with most of the important themes of *peredvizhniki* landscape and added many of his own, resolutely asserting the right of the Russian countryside itself to be considered a fit subject for fine art. He completed the transition from Italy to Russia and the Russian north. He blended Savrasov's lyrical approach with Polenov's *plein air* techniques and combined the result with Kuindzhi's breadth of generalization and Shishkin's epic tendencies. All these special features of Levitan's predecessors cross-fertilized each other; the outcome was not just a repetition but an enrichment of what had gone before. He enabled landscape to express the most crucial questions of the day. His *Vladimirka* and *Above Eternal Peace* touched a raw nerve in contemporary Russian society quite as effectively as genre or history painting. His work is an intimate expression of his understanding of man's place in the universe and of the world itself. This was a quality new to landscape, even if his canvases may lack the specifically social aspects of genre painting in the 1870s and 1880s. Their philosophical elements and complex literary allusions derived from nineteenth-century realism, although Levitan's brand of realism was enriched with lyricism. The lyrical concept of landscape became dominant in the 1890s and greatly influenced other genres, spreading first from landscape into genre and thence into history and portrait painting. Its leading position in the landscape genre itself was short-lived, however, lasting only into the first decade of the twentieth century. Levitan stood at the head of the movement during most of this period.

His career developed in a rather unusual way. Phases of experimental art alternated with periods of consolidation and retreat from his latest purely pictorial achievements, in a struggle between the spontaneity of the study and the perfection of the finished work of art. Levitan constantly sought a synthesis of the two impulses. His last painting, *The Lake*, might have been its embodiment, but it remained uncompleted at the time of his death. His student works (he was theoretically a student at the Moscow Art College in the mid-1880s) were primarily studies in character. An exception is *Autumn Day: Sokolniki* (1879), which brought fame to the precocious nineteen-year-old and was purchased by Tretyakov. Its subject, a woman walking along a lane which disappears into the background, enabled him to tell a real story about man and nature in a very personal way. In general, however, he set himself, and convincingly achieved, rather narrower goals until the mid-1880s. Gradually the concept of the sketch yielded to that of the finished picture, a process evident in, for example, *The Little Bridge* and *Birch Grove* (both 1885–89).

31　**Alexei Savrasov** *The Rooks Have Arrived* 1871

32 Fyodor Vasiliev *Marshland in the Forest* 1871–73

33 Alexei Savrasov *Cart Track* 1873

34　**Ivan Shishkin** *Ship Timber* 1898

35　**Ivan Shishkin** *Midday: Countryside near Moscow* 1869　>

36 **Arkhip Kuindzhi** *Birch Grove* 1879

37 **Arkhip Kuindzhi** *After the Storm* 1879

38 Vasily Polenov *Moscow Courtyard* 1878

39 Isaac Levitan *Evening Bells* 1892

40　**Isaac Levitan** *Twilight: Haystacks* 1899

The Little Bridge is painted from close by, giving the impression that the artist has deliberately crouched down in the grass to peer at the little wooden bridge and the gully through which the stream flows. Beyond this foreground several details of the distant landscape are visible – a clearing, boards, a log-cabin. The focus of attention is the bridge itself – everything else seems to be an insignificant setting in which the main object exists. Light and air are conveyed with great naturalness; the air seems particularly transparent, almost vibrating as it wraps itself around the objects, while the earth and boards in the foreground have a somewhat bluish tinge.

Birch Grove can be thought of as an early Russian Impressionist work. Impressionistic techniques are used both in the composition and the colour scheme. Thus we see a fragment of forest interior chosen, it seems, at random. The frame cuts the trees top and bottom as they spread sideways and into the distance. The way we glimpse the trees at the edges of the painting out of the corner of the eye is typically impressionistic, as is the general lack of focus. The white trunks set against a green background create a very striking effect. (Incidentally, this 'white' consists of shades of light blue, yellow and green.) The brushwork is noticeably thick and textured.

Early signs of Russian Impressionism may also be detected in the work of Korovin and Serov who, like Levitan himself, were at that time unfamiliar with the experiments and experience of the French. Unlike Korovin, however, who continued to develop his own brand of Impressionism during the following decade, Levitan abandoned this line for a time, retreated to the narrative and literary idiom and only later returned to impressionistic *plein air* techniques. His paintings of the 1880s were the products of one of the earliest such retreats, when he took a trip to the Volga. He was fascinated by the grandeur of the region, and the image of this great Russian river became inseparable in his mind from the fate of Russia and her people.

Evening on the Volga (1886–88), *After the Rain: Plyoss* and *Evening: Golden Plyoss* (both 1889) mark the onset of this new period. For this last work he selected an elevated vantage point which excluded the foreground and displayed a broad panorama of the river, hills, distant landscape and sky. Implicit in this view is the idea of a sort of flight over the earth. This space does not totally embrace infinite distance; instead it fills in the gaps between the hilltops and the valley and then rolls over the horizon still in search of an all-consuming infinity. As it flows it becomes a sort of arena for the actions of natural powers and man-made objects. In the distance we see a typical little Volga town with its towering belfry. Somewhere over there life is going on as usual, linked with eternity by the mood the painter has imposed. Levitan's

approach here was quite strongly philosophical and continued to be so during the 1890s, in such pictures as *Quiet Cloister* (1890), *By the Whirlpool, Evening Bells* and *Vladimirka* (all 1892) and *Above Eternal Peace* (1894). Tonality is dominant in these paintings and impressionist techniques are almost entirely lacking. *Quiet Cloister* and *Evening Bells* are linked by a common theme. Their model is a combination and adaptation of a number of remarkable buildings. Comparison of these two paintings alone can tell us much about the workings of Levitan's imagination. Water surrounds the little island with its monastery – the quiet little cloister of the title – whose strange world is so remote from the concerns of ordinary men and women. Its people are absorbed in their prayers; their whole life and work is of the spirit. The imprint of this spirituality is the true mark of Levitan's landscapes.

Vladimirka is one of his best-loved works. It evoked a sense of melancholy in his contemporaries as they contemplated the track (known familiarly as the Vladimirka) along which political exiles trudged under guard to Siberia, reminding them of the absence of human rights in their society and of the tragic fate of mankind in general. The theme of the endless road, so characteristic of Russian art, here acquired yet another meaning, that of despair. There is no genre element in this work, only the faintly discernible figure of a solitary woman walking along the track, and indeed few other signs of human presence. The track itself seems to exist in a state of solitude; it is concentrated on itself and its very straightness confers on it this sense of its own value.

Above Eternal Peace is dedicated to the fate of mankind and to the idea of man's puny size in the face of eternal and majestic nature. Levitan selected an unnaturally high angle from which to paint the picture – unnatural in the sense that in this flat northern country of lakes and marshes it was probably impossible, in reality, to find such an elevated point from which to survey this small area of land with its tiny wooden church and cemetery. The idea behind the painting is as stark and simple as the 'purified' version of nature here presented. Comparison of the painting with its preparatory sketches and studies reveals this process of purification. The landscape, divided into large areas of colour separated by clear outlines, has the sort of broad symbolic character more appropriate to decorative panels than to a painting. Levitan's mode of expressing ideas of general, if rather vague, significance was as close to Symbolism as his individual artistic idiom was to Art Nouveau.

1895 marked the beginning of the last phase of his career, a phase characterized by his desire to synthesize all his previous achievements. From this time onwards he abandoned themes of hopelessness and melancholy and

39

Isaac Levitan *Birch Grove* 1885–89

expressed his newfound optimism in such works as *March, Golden Autumn* (both 1895) and *Spring Flood* and *Autumn Track* (both 1897).

March became a model for many other snowy landscapes which appeared at the turn of the century. The deliberately fragmentary quality of the composition and the spontaneity of expression give it the air of a study; unlike a study, however, it contains a strong narrative element. The apparently simple description of empty sledges awaiting the return of their riders, and the open door of a *dacha* allow us to conjure up a whole story about the family who have come to inspect their home in the country after the long winter months. There are other signs of human life, such as sleigh-tracks and a path trodden through the blue, virgin snow. This particular sunny March day has the power to evoke in us general feelings of joy and exhilaration and a sense of wonder at the natural cycle. Comparing it to *Birch Grove* we see little further progress towards Impressionism, a style which might well have sat ill with the narrative aspect essential to Levitan's brand of lyricism.

The technique of his later work is broader and the paintings themselves more decorative, attempting to combine the spontaneity of the study with the finished quality of the picturesque. In the unfinished *The Lake* (1900) – whose original title was the more poetic *Rus* – he intended to bring together several different tendencies

and themes of his art: water and reeds in the foreground, alternating strips of light and shade, high skies with scudding clouds, a tiny village in the distance and a church on the opposite shore. These motifs are contained within the vast depth and breadth of the pictorial space. He had never before achieved so all-embracing an image of homeland and water. The foreground is harmoniously united with the panoramic background. The painting's uncalculating vision of nature does not prevent Levitan from revealing a complex associative chain of thoughts and feelings typical of his 'landscape of mood'. He did not live to complete what might have become the ultimate and supreme synthesis of his art.

Levitan played a crucial role in the history of Russian painting. The majority of landscape painters in the Society of Russian Artists, an important organization during the early years of the twentieth century, were following directly in his footsteps. He also had a powerful influence on his fellow artists of the 1890s such as Svetoslavsky – a graduate of the Moscow Art College – and I.S. Ostroukhov (1858–1929), who was not only a painter but a distinguished collector, museum enthusiast and supporter and shrewd judge of art. Only one of the great landscape painters of the time, Apollinari Vasnetsov (1856–1933) – Viktor's brother – who painted with scrupulous historical realism, remained relatively unaffected by the impact of his great contemporary.

Isaac Levitan *March* 1895

Isaac Levitan *Spring Flood*
1897

Isaac Levitan *Golden Autumn* 1895

Isaac Levitan *Above Eternal Peace* 1894

Isaac Levitan *Vladimirka* 1892
Isaac Levitan *The Lake* 1899–1900

6 Sculpture and Architecture

In the second half of the nineteenth century sculpture and architecture lagged far behind painting in creative vigour. This was not as apparent to the contemporary public as it is to us today. There was much serious talk of the success of architecture, and Surikov, for example, was highly appreciative of the sculptor Antokolsky. Time, however, has put these matters into a truer perspective, so that in spite of all the efforts of some modern historians to trumpet the qualities of Russian architecture of the period it cannot even be compared with the work of the Russian classical or Art Nouveau painters.

The crisis in sculpture was evidenced not only by the absence of great names and works but by the profound changes which took place in the very structure of this branch of art. In all the styles up to and including classicism only portraiture had been represented in sculpture as strongly as in painting. Otherwise the two arts were completely different. Only rarely, for example during the Hellenic era, has sculpture begun to develop a genre or landscape tradition, and the latter only in relief, never independently. Genres in sculpture, unlike those in painting, are generally determined not by the object of depiction itself, but by the way the object is to be treated and by the task the artist has been set or has set himself. In the second half of the nineteenth century this range of genres was transformed and approached more closely that of painting. Along with portraiture, which retained its popularity, sculptors now worked in 'genre' itself and in the history genre (inspired by real episodes of Russian history as well as biblical and mythological themes). Only landscape and still-life were missing, but at the turn of the century landscape duly appeared in Russian sculpture, and still-life made its appearance a few years later. By then, however, painting's dominance over sculpture was a thing of the past.

It is interesting to compare some of the subjects, themes and characters treated by painters with those commonly found in sculpture at this time. Chizhov's *Peasant in Distress* or Posen's *Pauper* recall some of the characters of Perov and the *peredvizhniki*, the tramps, paupers and unfortunate folk who had lost all their possessions in a fire. Kamensky's *Widow with her Child* continues Fedotov's theme of the widow. Antokolsky portrayed in sculpture Ivan the Terrible, Peter the Great, Christ and Yermak. Lansere's *Knight* brings to mind one of Vasnetsov's paintings. And so it goes on.

In other ways, however, sculpture was very different from painting. It was not marked by the clear division into Academic and Realist schools so evident in painting, although a kind of semi-academic school, through which sculpture attempted to approach fresh themes, did have an important part to play. It tended more to the formal techniques of 'pure' academic art rather than to realism. An interesting example of this semi-academic art is *Boy in a Bathhouse* (1854) by the Moscow sculptor Sergei Ivanov (1828–1903). His happy choice of subject enabled him to combine an academic interest in the naked figure with his

Sergei Ivanov
Boy in a Bathhouse
1854

desire to depict realistic, everyday scenes. Although this work contains some realistic detail unworthy of its 'noble material' (i.e. marble), such as the expressive gesture of the hand stroking the body in anticipation of the scalding water, *Boy in a Bathhouse* possesses a considerable plastic integrity. Even the stream of water pouring from the bowl (a rather risky subject for sculpture!) cannot destroy this integrity.

In St Petersburg the most important genre sculptors were Fyodor Kamensky (1838–1913) and Matvei Chizhov (1838–1916). Kamensky flourished in the late 1860s and early 1870s (in 1871 he emigrated to America). The figure of a child was the central point of many of his works, such as *Boy-sculptor* (1866), *Widow with her Child* (1868) and *The First Step* (1869–72). The interest in childhood shown by Kamensky, Chizhov and many others was somewhat sentimental and clearly marked such works as genre pieces. Whereas classicism took young men for its heroes, the naturalism of the second half of the nineteenth century concentrated on the child. In *Widow* Kamensky focuses his attention on ordinary human relationships, aiming to convey real emotions by bending the mother's head downwards and giving her an expression of great concentration, thus exploiting the eternal theme of motherhood. At the same time there is a certain degree of abstraction in the sculpture, which

enables it to achieve a quality of plastic expressiveness in the figures as well as in the clothing.

In his sculptural group *The First Step* Kamensky found plastic integrity harder to achieve. The group falls into separate parts and the space between them splits the unity of the composition. The naturalistic element is quite tangible. In addition, the sculptor made use of a number of allegorical symbols which he assumed his public would understand: at the feet of the standing child, next to the kneeling mother, he placed a toy steam engine, and on the pedestal a microscope, a printing press and other symbols of technical progress. The first steps being taken by the child offer the hope of unlimited progress. We do not, however, perceive this allegory figuratively, but read it as some kind of accompanying text.

Chizhov's most remarkable work was his *Peasant in Distress* (1872). Although it is a thoroughly serious attempt to empathize with the preoccupations of simple folk, to convey their suffering and describe the hardships of peasant life, this aim was not fully realized in the sculpture. He certainly found convincing poses for the depressed peasant and the boy clinging to his father, but the group as a whole is excessively detailed and lacks unity. This is most noticeable in the marble version, made a year after the bronze original, in which the bark of the tree trunk on which the peasant sits, the beetle crawling

Fyodor Kamensky *The First Step* 1869–72

Matvei Chizhov *Peasant in Distress* 1872

along it and other details hinting at the recent fire (which is the immediate cause of the peasant's distress) seem particularly out of place.

The most prominent Russian sculptor of the second half of the nineteenth century, Mark Antokolsky (1842–1902) also began his career with genre sculpture but later dedicated himself entirely to historical characters and events. He stood apart from the other sculptors of his day, the only one possessed of the talent to match the high achievements of contemporary painters. On occasion he succeeded in overcoming the many pitfalls and contradictions of contemporary sculpture, though some of the latter are still to be found in his work. While still at the Academy Antokolsky was befriended by Repin, met Kramskoi and Stasov, who highly appreciated and supported the young sculptor, and became close to the composer Serov, thus finding himself at the very centre of the progressive intelligentsia interested in the arts. Later he was closely associated with many members of the Abramtsevo circle. His works dating from the 1860s were strongly influenced by naturalism. He began by using a kind of modelling technique to realize various contemporary and historical themes he drew from Jewish life. In *Inquisition* (1869), depicting a scene from Spanish medie-

Mark Antokolsky *Ivan the Terrible* 1875

Mark Antokolsky *Spinoza* 1882

Mark Antokolsky
Peter the Great
1872

val history, the relief seems to become transformed into a round sculpture. The group of figures is placed as if on a stage so that what we see recalls a theatrical scene.

Antokolsky's talent, however, demanded other means of expression. The 1870s marked the onset of his best period, which produced his remarkable *Ivan the Terrible* (1875) and *Peter the Great* (1872). These pieces took their place among other outstanding works of art, literature and theatre of the time and Antokolsky became famous overnight. In *Ivan the Terrible* his aim was to recreate all the complex psychology of the Tsar, at once 'martyr and tormentor', as the sculptor himself put it. Generally speaking the sculptural portrait, unlike its pictorial counterpart, does not lend itself easily to deep psychological analysis of character. This makes Antokolsky's success in penetrating the soul of his subject and understanding his spiritual conflict all the more impressive. Details of clothing, the throne, and the open book serve as a mere commentary and accompaniment to the main theme, which is conveyed primarily through the Tsar's expression and bodily movement. Antokolsky saw his artistic task as the faithful recreation of an historical personality with all his attributes. The form fulfils no particular figurative or expressive purpose, nor did the sculptor apparently attach much significance to the choice of material he used. Plaster, bronze and marble versions are identical, a fact which itself implies that the plastic potential of the portrait was not fully exploited. This weakness was not noticed by his contemporaries, who were perhaps overawed by the novelty of the work and its imposing dimensions.

In *Peter the Great* the very personality of the subject, his role in history and the fact that Antokolsky intended the statue as a monument, demanded a quite different composition and artistic idiom. The traditional type of monument required a purely heroic interpretation, especially as he was military leader, emperor, statesman and illustrious reformer. Sure enough, Antokolsky bestowed on his *Peter* all the appropriate signs of greatness. His head is raised, and crowned with a cocked hat; he stares into the distance, his face expressing energy, determination and severity; the right hand is held behind his back in order to give the impression of movement and the feet are turned outwards to avoid the appearance of an artificial pose. In spite of all these devices the figure still strikes us as rather stilted and pompous. Moreover, the bronze version, from which the sculptor attempted to remove all superfluous detail, seems insufficiently generalized in its plasticity. It was fated to remain a piece of sculpture rather than a monument.

One of Antokolsky's most successful works was his *Christ before the People* (1874), a figure of Christ standing with bound hands. This piece fits well with

Mark Antokolsky
*Christ before
the People*
1874

Evgeny Lansere *Saviour* 1886

many *peredvizhniki* paintings of the time. After his *Christ in the Wilderness* Kramskoi, for example, began a new work entitled *Rejoice, King of the Jews*, which remained unfinished. The interests of the two artists coincided remarkably. It was significant that the *peredvizhniki* themselves highly appreciated Antokolsky's work and considered it an essential element in their cycle dedicated to the figure of Christ. Antokolsky's Christ expresses neither doubt nor tragedy but faith, wisdom and a determination to fulfil his appointed role on earth.

From the mid-1870s onwards moral questions dominated Antokolsky's work. *Dying Socrates* (1876) was followed by *Spinoza* (1882) and a female *Christian Martyr* (1887). After these works he returned to themes from Russian history with *Yermak* (1888) and *Nestor the Chronicler* (1889). All these later pieces were to a greater or lesser degree inferior to the work of the early 1870s which had earned him his reputation and his place in the annals of Russian culture.

Another sculptor worthy of mention is Evgeny Lansere (1848–87), the father of two famous painters, Evgeny Lansere and Zinaida Serebryakova. He continued and developed the tradition of small sculpture, which often avoided the pitfalls and contradictions of other sculptural forms. His small bronze statuettes or groups, generally serving to decorate studies or drawing-rooms, were, by virtue of their size alone, alien to the very idea of naturalism. Lansere used themes from Russian history and the daily life of ordinary people, not only Russians but folk from the Caucasus and the Asiatic regions of the Empire, where he travelled extensively. All his work is marked by sharp observation, precise forms and a masterly treatment of movement. Remarkably, his choice of subjects led him to include some elements of landscape, enough to enable us to imagine the rest. Thus some earth, visible beneath the horses' hooves, covers a small area at the foot of the sculpture. Sometimes it is smooth, almost flat, sometimes studded with small mounds, depending on subject and composition.

While small sculpture was enjoying its modest successes monumental sculpture was in the throes of a serious crisis. As in other European countries at the time, many monuments were being erected in honour of historic personalities and events. Most of these second-rate memorials were based on designs which, at the time, won national and international competitions and prizes. M.O. Mikeshin (1835–96) was one of the most popular and successful of these artists and the recipient of many prizes. He was educated as a battle painter and his main occupation was as a draughtsman and caricaturist. He never worked as a sculptor himself but conceived and designed monuments which were later realized by a group of professional sculptors. Among such well-known monuments are *Russia's Millennium* (1862) in Novgorod and *Catherine the Great* in St Petersburg (1873). Mikeshin chose the form of a sphere or bell, included dozens of human figures – historical and otherwise – in his designs and devised complete scenes and episodes. These monuments can be studied and enjoyed from all angles but they are totally lacking in plastic expressiveness. The division of labour involved in their creation – one man designing the project while others carry it out – is revealing in itself and telling evidence of the decline and decay of the sculptural concept.

Probably the only monument worthy of unstinted praise is A.M. Opekushin's (1841–1923) memorial to Alexander Pushkin in Moscow (1880). The day of its unveiling was a national celebration marked by a famous speech by Dostoevsky. Opekushin employed no decorative elements, excessive gesticulation nor any of the other dramatic effects widely used by Russian monumental sculptors of the time, but the pose and gesture of the poet are full of expression and completely fulfil the sculptor's intention. The inclined head seems to conceal Pushkin's spiritual agitation behind a mask of reverie and contemplative melancholy. His hand, resting inside his tailcoat, somehow distances the figure from its surroundings in a pose which powerfully evokes his personal dignity. His frozen step symbolizes the fate which has brought him to a halt. All these associations are subtly and finely conveyed in this simple and modest monument to the genius of Russian literature.

Alexander Opekushin, Monument to Alexander Pushkin
(detail), Moscow, 1880

To sum up this short survey, we do not find, in Russian sculpture of the second half of the nineteenth century, a true expression of figurative or plastic values. For many years sculpture remained in a state of confusion, simply waiting and hoping for better times to come.

The situation in architecture was, if anything, even more perplexing. The principal challenge of the time – the revelation of man's complex relationship with the world – required figurative and pictorial forms and lay beyond the capabilities of architecture as an art. It was hardly surprising that many cultural luminaries of the day (N.G. Chernyshevsky, for example) did not even consider architecture to be an art at all. Architecture itself attempted to be pictorial, 'depicting' various historic styles on facades in a rather two-dimensional way, using the architectural orders as decorative and representation-al devices and enthusiastically recreating ancient forms. This figurativeness, however, did not address the most urgent contemporary concerns and therefore could not compete with the more potent figurative contribution of literature and painting. All those barriers which stood in

the way of architecture slowed down its progress and made it backward in comparison to the other arts. This was equally true of Europe as a whole. In recent years, admittedly, attempts have been made to find positive elements and pointers to the future in the architecture of this period. The term 'eclecticism' is now frequently replaced by 'historicism', and our attention is directed towards the new architectural questions which were raised at the time, even if they remained unanswered. Of course, certain successes were achieved even in the midst of the crisis, but they were mainly concerned with overcoming the past rather than with discovering the new. Building methods were revolutionized as the result of technical progress and even when mistakes were made, or the technology was insufficiently advanced, important lessons were learned for the future.

Let us begin our review with some of the new architectural genres or types of building which started to develop in the 1830s to the 1850s and became fully established in the second half of the century. Railway stations were widely built, and seen not just as a necessity of city life, but as a symbol of the prestige of a city, a capital or the state itself. This formal and stylistic approach came into some conflict with those technical problems which were presented by the new kinds of building intended to accommodate machines rather than men alone. Some balance between the formal and decorative elements and technical innovations was achieved by A.I. Krakau (1817–88) in his design for the Peterhof (now Baltiisky) (1855–57) and Warsaw (1858–62) stations in St Petersburg. He crowned the facades of these buildings with small turrets and combined Baroque and Renaissance decorative elements with huge glazed arches which separated the platforms from the rest of the station.

We are frequently aware, in the buildings of this period, of the clash between Renaissance or Baroque facades and the new constructions which were easy enough to conceal in the interior of a palace but impossible to disguise inside a station. Metal structures were already widely used, but they were generally masked by decor and could only be seen in a few types of building. One of the most 'constructivist' buildings of the second half of the century was the Sennoi (originally the Haymarket) market in St Petersburg (1883–86), designed by I.S. Kitner (1839–1929), and employing the system of the engineers Pauker and Krell. The constructional base of the market consists of metal girders placed in a row along the perimeter and closed in with glass. The utilitarian purpose of the building justified the attractive and expressive simplicity of its forms.

Similar methods of construction were successfully used in the erection of shopping arcades, although the facades were still usually clothed in various decorative styles, as for example in the case of the Upper Arcade (1894–96) in Moscow's Red Square, designed by A.N. Pomerantsev (1848–1918) and built on the site of the earlier arcade by Bove. The facade of Pomerantsev's building was decorated in the Old Russian style and intended by the architect to blend in with the walls of the Kremlin, but this application of an older style paradoxically destroyed the unity of the ensemble rather than strengthening it.

Exhibition halls were designed with a relatively greater freedom than any other types of building. They were erected in large numbers at this time because of the boom in exhibitions in Russia as well as in the rest of Europe. Two opposite tendencies dominated the architecture of such halls. Some architects took London and Paris as their models and made use of the most modern technical achievements, as, for example, in the unrealized design by G.A. Bossé (1812–92) for the permanent exhibition of the Russian Horticultural Society in St Petersburg (1860). The pavilion, of cast iron and glass, would have resembled a kind of transparent spider's web.

Alexander Pomerantsev, Shopping Arcade, Moscow, interior (now GUM), 1889–93

Vladimir Shervud/A.A. Semenov, The Historical Museum, Moscow, 1875–83

The second approach was concerned with the traditions of Old Russian architecture. Its principal practitioners were V.A. Gartman (1834–73) and I.P. Ropet (Petrov) (1844–1908). Gartman's pavilion for the military section of the Polytechnical Exhibition of 1872 was built of wood and the centre of its circular composition was crowned by a tent roof which recalled the belfries of the seventeenth century. Ropet's best-known building was his Russian Pavilion for the 1878 World Exhibition in Paris. The complex design of this wooden building was an echo of seventeenth-century Russian palaces, in particular the famous palace at Kolomenskoye. Ropet abandoned the idea of total symmetry for the facade, giving it instead a picturesque look by freely combining volumes of various sizes and heights crowned by roofs of differing shapes. He and his contemporaries found the Old Russian style most appropriate for the world exhibition, where every country had to be represented by its most typical national characteristics.

Museums, unlike exhibition pavilions, usually occupied the most important architectural sites in the city. They were generally restricted to a single style in each case, whether Old Russian, classical or renaissance. If the New Hermitage was the most representative museum built in the second third of the nineteenth century, that distinction belonged, in the 1870s and 1880s, to the

Moscow Historical Museum (1875–83), designed by V.O. Shervud and A.A. Semenov. The architects divided their tasks as follows: Shervud, the draughtsman, devised the facade while Semenov, the engineer, drew up the layout of the building itself and solved any problems of construction. This division of labour was typical of the second half of the nineteenth century. Many historians, including Zabelin, participated in the design of this building, taking as their models ancient architectural monuments, book covers and illustrations etc. Interiors were designed to accord with the material exhibited. The closeness of the museum to the Kremlin once again determined its appearance: the two architects based its exterior on traditional sixteenth- and seventeenth-century Russian architecture.

Museums were bound to retain many formal and decorative features and this was equally true of theatres, which at this time began to appear in many towns and cities. One single architect, V.A. Shreter, built theatres in Rybinsk, Tiflis, Irkutsk, Nizhny Novgorod and Kiev. A great variety of styles were to be found in theatre design as well as in houses containing apartments for rent. Such houses, very widely built at the time, were frequently designed by distinguished architects who were particularly attracted by the opportunity to apply themselves to the new task of erecting multi-storey structures. On the other hand, their architectural freedom was limited because such apartment blocks had to be built close to each other and along the line of the existing road. Perhaps as a result of this, architects concentrated on the main facades, which were usually richly decorated and highly impressive. The facade became a sort of screen whose ornate and fanciful surface bore no relationship to what was going on behind. Indeed, the difference between the facade and the reality could hardly have been greater.

A similar approach was evident in palace architecture, which was not as important as it once had been. One of the most remarkable palaces of the time was that of the Grand Duke Vladimir Alexandrovich on the Palace Embankment in St Petersburg (1867–72), designed by A.I. Rezanov (1817–88). Its facade recalls an Italian palazzo; the interiors were executed in various styles – Baroque, Rococo, Byzantine and Old Russian. The palace was a perfect illustration of one of the main principles of eclecticism in that the choice of style for each room was determined by that room's purpose.

In contrast to all the other genres, church architecture had only one style at its disposal. It was dominated by Old Russian forms and the result was pitiful indeed. A good example of this wretched state of affairs is the Church of the Resurrection in St Petersburg (1883–1907), built on the spot where Alexander II was assassinated and

Alexander Rezanov, Palace of Grand Duke Vladimir Alexandrovich, St Petersburg, 1867–72

familiarly known as the 'Church on the Blood'. It is a strange mixture of various forms borrowed from St Basil's Cathedral in Red Square, the seventeenth-century architecture of Yaroslavl and the Byzantine tradition.

It is clear from this short analysis that although various types of building favoured certain styles there was no absolute attachment of any one style to any one type, and that the description of this period as 'eclectic' is fully justified. This term signifies the freedom to choose between various styles and the opportunity to express artistic individuality, but this victory of creativity over the rigidity of the canons was only relative. Close symmetry and centricity of composition were gradually abandoned and the freedom with which artists used various styles contributed to the development of artistic intuition and spontaneity. On the other hand a new, rational and scientific approach to architecture was developing, manifested above all in the profound and scrupulous study of architectural history now embarked on by its practitioners. Their first concern was, of course, Russian architecture. Serious interest in the national heritage had been aroused as early as the 1830s; by the middle of the century it had become a mass enthusiasm which further stimulated the development of a 'Russian style'. This style gradually replaced Byzantine and came to dominate the second half of the nineteenth century, although it did not disturb the general principles of architectural eclecticism. Its adherents considered that their contribution lay in the fact that they did not blindly copy ancient monuments but only made use of decorative elements of their style. The great danger of this process, however, was that it led to the mechanical transfer of decorative elements borrowed from applied art and Old Russian architecture to the walls of totally innovative structures. This was the Achilles' heel of 'Russian style' which was unable to shake off the shackles of eclecticism.

There were, nevertheless, some serious and original talents among the devotees of 'Russian style'. One important architect in the middle years of the century was A.M. Gornostaev (1808–62) who had many followers. Later Gartman and Ropet made major contributions to the style. Gartman was particularly interested in exhibition pavilions, temporary theatres, apartment blocks and business premises, and successfully used ornamentation taken from folk art (especially embroidery) and skilfully applied it to brick decoration on walls. Two examples of such decorative finish of a facade are the printing house of A.I. Mamontov in Leontievsky Lane in Moscow and a design for a public lecture hall. These facades are graphically decorative and their flat designs, unlimited by any elements of composition, seem to strive towards the infinite. Graphics were Gartman's strong point, and he left a huge graphic legacy of drawings, designs, sketches and studies which inspired Mussorgsky to compose his famous piano cycle *Pictures from an Exhibition*. However, many of the designs which seemed so interesting and convincing on paper could never have been realized in practice.

Ropet was quite different; he was strongly inclined to stability and formality; traditional compositional forms may often be perceived behind the picturesque designs of his Old Russian facades. His smaller projects and furniture designs, however, were often full of elaborate fantasy and intricate whimsy.

In the last decade of the century 'Russian style' began to dominate city architecture. In Moscow and some other towns with extant medieval structures – such as kremlins (citadels), palaces, churches and monasteries – the main squares were now built up with large modern buildings in Old Russian style. Some examples in Moscow are the Historical and Polytechnical Museums, the Upper Shopping Arcade and the city *duma* (council); to these may be added the Assembly Hall of the Nobility (*Dvoryanskoye*

Sobraniye) in Kursk and the theatre in Samara. But the 'Russian style' could not integrate such buildings into true architectural ensembles, for it lacked the ability to differentiate between large and small, monumental and intimate. Small, over-detailed ornamentation lost its effect when viewed from a distance and did not create the necessary unity of rhythm.

Neither 'Russian style' nor the rest of Russian eclecticism was capable of meeting the ancient urban requirements of organizing a city centre and creating a unified ensemble which would define a city's image. The true role of eclecticism in urban architecture must be sought elsewhere. E.A. Borisova, an historian of nineteenth-century Russian architecture, writes: 'Eclectic architecture's task was to unite the buildings of various periods, fill in the gaps and free spaces and thus create a dynamic and constantly changing city environment.'[13] And indeed, the second half of the century confirmed a specific concept of a city whose streets are unbroken lines of houses pressed close up to one another into something like corridors. It was at this time that the principle of strict economy in the use of land evolved, so that every free space was used, even in the areas around prominent public buildings, which now lost their earlier role of providing a focus and defining particular ensembles. In these circumstances the former distinction between principal and secondary areas and buildings disappeared (although the various types of architecture within them were growing ever further apart) because a theatre or palace would be built under the same urban conditions and restrictions as, say, an apartment block. Whatever the purpose of the building it could not neutralize the unifying tendency of the eclectic style, which in its urban form was coming close to Art Nouveau.

Russian architecture of the 1880s showed other signs of the increasing trend towards Russian Art Nouveau (*Modern*). As historians of architecture now put it, pseudo-Russian was now developing into neo-Russian style. Models were changing: seventeenth-century Russian architecture gave way to the architectural styles and folk art which had flourished before the Tartar invasions. New types of buildings appeared, especially the private mansions which now began to dominate the urban scene; later they were to become the most characteristic element of architectural Art Nouveau. In other words, architecture, like other arts, was ready to produce those new creative concepts whose time had now arrived.

PART III · 1895–1917

No chronology is absolute. This is particularly true of cultural history, where different periods are separated from each other not by years but by generations. The date 1895, therefore, cannot draw a line between the old and the new with mathematical precision. Repin, as we have seen, flourished right up to the early years of the twentieth century, whereas in the 1880s Vrubel and Serov had already begun the experiments which were to revolutionize the whole of Russian painting. However, the mid-1890s did see the clear predominance of the new over the old; hence the choice of the year 1895 as a turning-point in Russian art.

The period to be considered in Part III of this book is a short one. It is marked not only by an upsurge of Russian culture but by a real explosion of new, original and intriguing ideas which expanded into fields as yet untouched by the arts. It was a time of tremendous creativity and marvellous works of art. However valuable in themselves the artistic phenomena of the nineteenth century may have been, they were nearly always afterthoughts to what had gone before in England and France. The turn of the century, however, saw the emergence of the uniquely talented Vrubel, while the 1910s gave us Malevich, Kandinsky, Filonov, Chagall and Tatlin, all of whom formed part of the avantgarde of *world* culture. Their appearance at this time was no mere coincidence. In the nineteenth century the energies of Russian art had been devoted to problems of human personality, the emancipation of the downtrodden and the struggle for justice. In a word, art was socially committed. By the turn of the century the picture had changed. As the historical process began to lift the social burden from literature and the arts they could at last indulge themselves a little. Of course, social problems were not totally forgotten and Russian culture continued to be a synthesis, as the great Russian poet Alexander Blok expressed it: 'Russia is a young country and her culture is a synthesis. The Russian artist need not and should not be a narrow specialist. The writer should not forget the painter, the architect and musician; it is even more important for the writer of prose to remember the poet, and vice versa . . . In Russia, painting, music, prose and poetry are inseparable from each other, and equally at one with philosophy, religion, public-spiritedness, even politics. Together they make up a single powerful current which bears the treasure of our national culture.'[1] Poetry, theatre and painting did become involved in ethics, religion, politics and ideas of social change, especially as some artists believed that such change could be achieved not by bitter criticism of social defects but through the cult of beauty, the elevation of the spirit and the union of all the people in aesthetic activity. This was the synthesis which defined the unique character of Russian art at the turn of the century. Malevich, Kandinsky and Filonov were not only painters but philosophers, engaged in the search for God and not afraid to prophesy the future. Again, the World of Art group's attempt to keep to 'pure art' was in vain; Dobuzhinsky, Lansere, Bilibin, Kustodiev and other members were shaken by the events of the 1905 Revolution and responded with sharp political caricatures against the Tsar and his brutal generals. Many other examples could be adduced to illustrate this synthesis, which is so characteristic of early twentieth-century Russian painting; the fact remains, nevertheless, that those social obligations which had been laid on Russian culture in the nineteenth century were removed. Henceforward social problems could be analysed in a more complex and oblique manner.

Another peculiarity of Russian culture at the turn of the century was that in the course of some twenty years it had developed to a point that had taken other countries several generations to reach. Art in Russia evolved unevenly, slowing down, leaping forward, coming to a halt and surging forward once again. Realism lasted longer in Russia than elsewhere, and as it came to an end it was challenged, almost simultaneously, by many different artistic movements and groups. Academic art, especially of the salon variety, still enjoyed great public success; the *peredvizhniki* continued their activities as energetically as before; and in the 1890s a new movement in Moscow encouraged a moderate type of Impressionism and soon established itself as the Union of Russian Painters. Meanwhile, the World of Art group was forming in St Petersburg. This society, which upheld the principles of *Modern* (Russian Art Nouveau), disintegrated for some time and then reformed. Shortly before, a new society, the Blue Rose, had sprung up, marking the second wave of Symbolism in Russian painting, and three years later, in 1910, two avantgarde groups appeared: in Moscow, the Knave of Diamonds and in St Petersburg, the Union of Youth. Two years after that the Donkey's Tail group was formed and dedicated itself to neo-primitivism in painting. In the mid-1910s there was a veritable explosion of avantgarde exhibitions, discoveries and innovative movements. Probably no other country provided so extraordinary a panorama of artistic life.

Everything that has been described above refers to painting, which may give the impression that it continued to occupy the dominant position in the arts. This, however, was not the case. Even though the principal events in the artistic world still occurred – perhaps by sheer force of habit – in the field of painting, it was no longer 'superior' to sculpture, architecture or the applied and decorative arts. The stage was set for an artistic synthesis on equal terms.

41 **Mikhail Vrubel** *Fortune Teller* 1895

42　**Mikhail Vrubel** *Lilac* 1900

43　**Mikhail Vrubel** *Portrait of Nadezhda Zabela-Vrubel, the Artist's Wife* 1898　>

44 **Mikhail Vrubel** *Tamara's Dance* Illustration to Lermontov's poem, *The Demon* 1890–91

45 **Mikhail Vrubel** *Demon Seated* 1890

46 **Valentin Serov** *October: Domotkanovo* 1895

47   **Valentin Serov** *Girl with Peaches* 1887

48　**Valentin Serov** *Portrait of Ivan Morozov* 1910

1 The Beginnings of Symbolism and Russian Art Nouveau

Mikhail Vrubel (1856–1910) drastically upset the chronology and measured development of Russian painting. He ignored the conventional path which led from Realism to Impressionism and established the *Modern* – or Russian Art Nouveau – style before Russian Impressionism had even had time to develop. Moreover, unlike most of the other painters of the day, he came not from the ranks of the *peredvizhniki* but from the Academy.

His personality was a continual source of astonishment to his contemporaries. He was exceptionally well educated, having graduated from the University with a degree in law before becoming a student at the St Petersburg Academy of Fine Arts. He was deeply interested in philosophy and particularly impressed by Kant and Schopenhauer. His behaviour was that of a true artist – neither nervous of his public nor self-abasing before authority. He modelled himself on the artists of the Renaissance, whom he saw as a free, independent, proud and enlightened breed of men. Vrubel created for himself a kind of myth by neglecting certain unwritten rules of behaviour and conducting himself like some hero of history or literature. There were echoes here, no doubt, of Romantic ideas about the artist, whose life and art should be inseparable. Contemporary Symbolist poets, such as Alexander Blok, Valery Briusov and Viacheslav Ivanov particularly admired this quality of Vrubel's. In his graveside eulogy at Vrubel's funeral Blok spoke of the painter's ability to live according to the rules of creativity and to burn ceaselessly in the fire of artistic inspiration. A new Romanticism (now termed Neo-romanticism by art-historians) was reborn with Vrubel, whose own art was a union of Neo-romanticism and Symbolism. This is why early twentieth-century poets admired him so warmly, for they saw in him a forerunner and a founding father of the whole new movement in Russian culture. For the first time in Russia a painter found himself ahead of his literary counterparts, confident of his own gifts and independent of all theories: at that time there was no coherent theory of symbolism in Russia and Vrubel had, presumably, no knowledge of the manifesto by Jean Moréas which appeared in *Le Figaro* on 18 September 1886 and which first gave general currency to the word 'Symbolism'. In spite of all this, however, he was a solitary figure for most of his creative life, for fame and followers came too late.

Vrubel's professor at the Academy was Chistyakov, from whom he learnt a disciplined method of constructing forms by means of intersecting planes, a method he took to extremes and regarded as indispensable. While still at the Academy he began to work independently in a studio which he shared with his friends and fellow students Serov and Derviz. The young painters challenged the *peredvizhniki* principles, considering that Repin and his contemporaries did not pay sufficient attention to questions of form. Before long, however, Vrubel's studies at the Academy were interrupted. Professor Prakhov, who was supervising restoration work in Kiev, arrived in St Petersburg and, on Chistyakov's advice, took Vrubel with him back to Kiev as the only person capable of recreating the iconostasis and murals of the ancient Church of St Cyril. 1884 marked the beginning of Vrubel's Kiev period, which was to last until the end of the decade. Many historians believe that these years of experiment were crucial to his development.

His work on monumental painting in Kiev was fraught with problems. The task was twofold: to recreate the portions missing from the fragments of the twelfth-century frescos which had been preserved in the ancient church, and to create a complete new mural on the theme of *The Descent of the Holy Spirit*. He was guided in this work by a specific idea, namely, that if he preserved the plane of the wall intact he would discover the secret of medieval Byzantine painting and thus find a satisfactory solution to the challenge he had been set. However, he did not allow for the fact that Byzantine painting was attempting not to overcome space but to create its own mystical and irrational image of that space. There was another contradiction contained in his work at St Cyril's: the impersonal canon of Byzantine art which served as his model was irreconcilable with the exultant individualization of particular characters upon which Vrubel was intent. His contemporaries considered that the young artist had succeeded brilliantly, but he himself was

Mikhail Vrubel *Resurrection* 1887

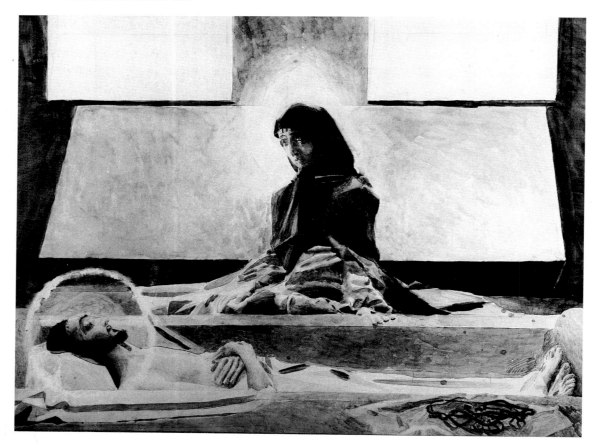

Mikhail Vrubel *The Lamentation* 1887

uneasy and his doubts persisted as he worked on the iconostasis, which he based on Italian as well as Byzantine models. (He made a special trip to Venice in order to study a tradition with which he was unfamiliar.) His iconostasis had eclectic features and was clearly not a true reflection of his artistic vision. He was only to find his own, individual vision as he worked on studies for the murals for St Vladimir's Cathedral in Kiev.

He was not, unfortunately, permitted to execute the murals themselves, as his suggestions were too unusual and shocked the organizers of the project, so it is difficult to judge whether his designs would have looked well on the cathedral walls, but in all likelihood they would have been a success. He proposed two themes, *Resurrection* and *The Lamentation* (1887) in both of which he interpreted the iconography very freely. Orthodox iconography usually substituted the Descent into Hell for the Resurrection, but the central section of Vrubel's triptych depicts Christ rising from the grave with the signs of death on his face. Vrubel was concerned not with Christ's ecstasy but with the infernal abyss and the mystery of existence beyond the grave, although he does incorporate his vision of the mystical beauty of this world: figures, objects and flowers spread around the grave all shine with a miraculous light. Vrubel's world consists of fragile, almost crystalline forms.

As well as these studies, many other works contributed to the evolution of his new approach, for example a painting entitled *Girl against background of Persian Rug*, various portrait drawings and graphic studies of flowers.[2] He preferred to paint objects with some intrinsic aesthetic value, and developed a language which placed them on the boundary between the real and the fantastic. It requires some effort to recognize his objects, for he interpreted them in many different ways and enriched them with abstract ornamentation. For the rest of his career he was to make continued use of these techniques with which he first experimented in the 1880s.

1889, the year Vrubel moved from Kiev to Moscow, marked the beginning of his mature period, which lasted until 1902 when he was struck by the mental illness which was to confine him, more or less permanently, to a clinic for the insane. The period begins with one demon, *Demon Seated* (1890), and ends with another, *Demon Cast Down* (1902). He had conceived the idea of the demon while still in Kiev and he worked on it all his life, frequently changing both concept and composition. It was to become the expression of his artistic credo and the embodiment of a symbolism related to the romanticism of the first half of the nineteenth century. It is no coincidence that his subject was derived from Lermontov's poem *Demon* – one of the most romantic works in all Russian literature.

45

Mikhail Vrubel *Self-portrait with Mother-of-Pearl Shell* 1905

Mikhail Vrubel *Girl against background of Persian Rug* 1886

Mikhail Vrubel *Demon Cast Down* 1902

Vrubel's seated demon is half-naked, his torso so powerful it seems to have been carved out of stone. He stares into the distance with an expression of mysterious melancholy. At first glance he could be taken for a cliché figure of hack symbolism, but this impression is soon dispelled. As we are first pierced by the demon's very real anguish and then moved to sympathy we begin to comprehend the infinite complexity of the total image: the demonic quality itself seems relative rather than absolute. Vrubel provides a new interpretation of a traditional character, surrounded for centuries with the halo of 'evil majesty', by adding the crucial element of suffering. Vrubel himself wrote that his demon was 'a spirit not so much evil as suffering and grieving, but still powerful . . . and noble'.[3] What identifies this painting as a work of symbolism is its many layers of meaning. Grief, protest, melancholy, foreboding, regret, remembrance, pain, restrained anger and resignation – all these are contained within the demon, but this inexhaustible work transcends them all.

Although he condemned his hero to death in *Demon Cast Down* he also endowed him with two new qualities, namely, the power of a destructive idea which will lead to his own annihilation, and his premonition of imminent universal catastrophe. In this painting the symbolism, with Vrubel's own tragic personality looming through, is clearer. Although he called the work an icon, it is actually more an expression of the self than a worship of the divine. Comparison of the two demons vividly demonstrates Vrubel's evolution over a decade as well as the unchanging qualities of his art. He was a true creator of original form. He constructed it 'from within', refusing to attempt a mere copy of reality. He did not mould or shape his form so much as carve it from the crystal-clear, stone-like material of which the demon's body, the sky, flowers and mountains consist. Hence Vrubel's acute sense that

all the elements of the universe were of one kind. A certain analogy with Cubism comes to mind here, and we should not be surprised that the parallel between Vrubel and Cubism occurred to so many art historians and painters. A prominent member of the Russian avant-garde, N. Kulbin, was the first to formulate this idea, in an article on Cubism in the 1915 anthology *Strelets*. But elements of Art Nouveau were also prominent; indeed the ornamental principle dominates *Demon Cast Down*, and the horizontal format of this large canvas seems to suggest the movement of the ornamental forms from one side of the painting to the other. Another indication of Art Nouveau is the combination of symbolic and naturalistic forms: the demon's body is broken and deformed, whereas the whole background landscape, with its mountains and sky, was painted on the basis of photographs of the Caucasian mountains and only deviates from realism in its intensive colour scheme. The stylistic parameters of the two *Demons* embrace all of Vrubel's mature art.

In the 1890s he worked in many different fields. He painted easel pictures and panels, all commissioned for private mansions, with one exception: the panels for the pavilions of the Nizhny Novgorod Exhibition of 1896. He tried his hand at pottery, sculpture and architecture; and he was active in theatre design and applied arts, including such apparent trivia as decorating balalaikas for the famous orchestra of folk instruments founded by Princess Tenisheva, a distinguished patroness of the arts. This breadth of interests was very much in the spirit of the times and reveals him as a true representative of Russian Art Nouveau.

His many panels, dating from the 1890s, were often intended for buildings designed by Shekhtel, the most brilliant architect of Russian Art Nouveau. These panels were of uneven merit but they were invariably in tune with the interiors for which they were intended, especially in the way they picked up and strengthened the rhythm of the building's design. They are the fullest expression of Vrubel's synthesizing talent.

Painting, however, remained his true calling. His best works date from the turn of the century and include *Pan* (1899), *Lilac, Swan-Princess, Towards Nightfall* (all 1900), and a number of portraits, including those of K.D. Artsibushev and S.I. Mamontov (both 1897), and of his wife, N.I. Zabela-Vrubel (1898). His early work *Fortune Teller* (1895) may be added to this list of masterpieces. They are all, in their various ways, interpreted mythologically. Features of fairy tale and opera are combined in the figure of the *Swan-Princess*, a portrait of his wife, Zabela-Vrubel, who took the part in an opera by Rimsky-Korsakov. *Pan* is a Russian treatment of one of the traditional characters of Greek mythology. *Fortune Teller*, which at first glance seems like a straightforward portrait of a real person, is actually a complex image of symbolic ideas. The canvas is covered by a kind of patina of time, almost of eternity, through which we discern the dark outlines of the thin woman with her penetrating gaze, turning over the cards. This fortune-telling theme has its own message for everyone who looks at the picture. A mythological element also finds its way into the very ordinary subject of pasturing horses for the night in *Towards Nightfall*, where the figure of a half-naked man (Pan or horse-thief?) approaching the horses is only just confined within the mysterious twilight of the landscape.

The relationship between the real and the fantastic, the natural and the symbolic, is crucial to all Vrubel's mature works. He often operated on the very edge of reality, in some paintings immersing himself in nature, in others offering the observer marvellous flights of imagination and invention. Both truth and invention serve the same purpose. In *Lilac* he drowns us in a moving sea of flowers. As so often with Vrubel, they are animistically treated: the head of a girl, an incarnation of the spirit of lilac, may be perceived among the bushes. Here he deliberately contrasts a naturalistic treatment with his own symbolic and fantastical interpretation.

This applies to his portraits as well as to his major fairy-tale and mythological paintings. Even in the portrait of Zabela-Vrubel in an Empire dress, which unusually for Vrubel has a *plein air* feel to it, the famous singer is made to resemble a kind of beautiful flower with gently drooping petals, whose rhythms are expressed in the texture and brushwork.

The portrait of S.I. Mamontov is particularly imbued with mythological significance. The subject, a close friend of Vrubel's and the patron of the Abramtsevo community of artists, literally provided the artist with a roof over his

Mikhail Vrubel *Swan-Princess* 1900

head and supported all his experimental endeavours. Mamontov, who sat for many artists, usually comes across as a calm sort of man, optimistic by nature and satisfied with the way he lives his life. Vrubel saw this great patron of the arts as a new Lorenzo the Magnificent whose character he could forge in the furnace of the passions and sufferings of contemporary life. There is more than a hint of demonism about this Mamontov, who appears as an agitated and disturbed figure consumed by the fire of some inner torment. He is depicted in a strange pose, as if paralysed for ever in an instant of interrupted movement, which conveys his dissatisfaction and unease. Space seems to press onto his figure as though nailing him to the canvas, while his surroundings are in a state of flux expressed by alternating light and shade. Mamontov himself seems paralysed by a weakness which has suddenly overcome him in spite of the gigantic strength concealed in his character and personality. The portrait is built on a number of pictorial paradoxes. Thus space is flattened, but the area of white shirt-front – the principal link in the composition – is balanced on a single point, the

42

43
41

Mikhail Vrubel *Portrait of S.I. Mamontov* 1897

Mikhail Vrubel *Portrait of V.N. Briusov* 1906

apex of a triangle; the figure's movement is static, yet those objects static by nature are moving. Vrubel's creative vision of his subject offers us, characteristically, much more than just a portrait.

Vrubel was ill for most of the last ten years of his life, able to leave his mental hospital more and more rarely, and for shorter periods. After *Demon Cast Down* he never again used brush or oils and worked only in graphics. His earlier ideas about the great questions of life underwent drastic change. Whereas he had previously insisted that beauty was the true new religion, now the mistakes of his youth began to torment him he sought repentance and regretted his wasted years. The Demon was replaced by the Prophet, a theme which appeared in his work from the end of the 1890s until the end of his career. He continued to work as he grew weaker and his last creative period, which was to last until 1906, was rich in artistic achievement. His drawings from life, which make up the greater part of his graphic legacy, depicted patients, medical orderlies, doctors and everyday objects. While particularly concerned with the structure of form, they are also profoundly spiritual. A masterpiece from this period is his charcoal portrait of the renowned poet and leader of the Symbolist movement, Valery Briusov, who visited Vrubel in hospital. (The drawing was commissioned by the literary magazine *The Golden Fleece*.) We find the poet against a background of semi-ornamental forms, his arms folded against his chest, his head slightly raised, a restrained glint in his eye. He personifies the poet as prophet, an early nineteenth-century concept which was still current but gradually losing its force.

A cycle of graphic self-portraits, comparable to those of Dürer or Van Gogh, also date from these last years. The Vrubel of these drawings questions us with his piercing gaze. These drawings marvellously combine a three-dimensional form with the ornamental structure of the total picture.

Vrubel brought Russian art into the twentieth century, and his work embodies all the various problems of the era. One aspect of that work, the existential nature of creativity, i.e. not the making of art but life in, or through, art, would be taken up by writers and artists of succeeding generations. Another concerns his contribution to the creation and establishment of new styles and movements – specifically Russian Art Nouveau (*Modern*) and Symbolism. Some of his work foreshadows Expressionism. This synthesis of ideas, so characteristic of Russian culture, was epitomized in the work of Alexander Ivanov and, after Vrubel, by certain artists of the Russian avantgarde. Vrubel made the transition from the old era to the new rapidly and decisively; and, having discovered his path into the future, he was never to deviate from it.

2 *From Impressionism to Russian Art Nouveau*

Another artist who helped to take Russian painting into the twentieth century was Valentin Serov (1865–1911). He was a friend of Vrubel's but a very different personality. He considered his art as an elevated craft. His artistry was superb, his drawing clear and precise, he combined colours in exquisite harmony. His work reflects his own state of mind, its anxiety and pain, and he pursued psychological truth and objectivity in his portraits. His authority was immense in artistic circles and the public believed that his work was the effortless product of a free and spontaneous gift; only a posthumous exhibition, which included a large number of his studies, revealed his extraordinary struggle to overcome the obstacles which lay behind this apparent facility. Then followed talk of the tragedy of his career and an appreciation of the marvellous consistency with which his genius had bridged the gap between the nineteenth and twentieth centuries. Serov, whose work can serve as an illustration of the general development of Russian art at the turn of the century, attracted a great number of followers and students, who took guidance and inspiration from their teacher and went their separate ways. He was one of the most significant figures in Russian painting, but as a great reformer, unlike Vrubel, who was a great revolutionary.

Serov's father was a well-known composer who died when Valentin was still a baby, but the family were passionate art lovers and he grew up in cultured and creative surroundings. Repin gave him lessons in Paris and later Moscow, thus passing on his craft in the tradition of the Italian Renaissance. At the age of fifteen he was sent, at Repin's recommendation, to study under Professor Chistyakov; he spent five years at the St Petersburg Academy, where he became friends with Vrubel, but he finally dropped out without actually graduating and threw himself into a period of intensive artistic activity. At the age of twenty-two or twenty-three he produced two masterpieces of Russian painting, *Girl with Peaches* (1887) and *Girl in Sunlight* (1888). These works, which Serov himself counted among his best, did not appear out of thin air. He did numerous preliminary studies and went abroad to acquaint himself with the old masters, who deeply impressed him. He also fell in love with the woman who was to become his wife. Above all, he formulated his own artistic credo, in which he rejected the 'critical' approach and vowed to paint only what appealed to his sense of beauty. Although he spent a great deal of time on each of the 'Girls' the task was made less arduous by the fact that his sitters were drawn from his circle of friends and relations. The *Girl with Peaches* was Mamontov's twelve-year-old daughter, who sat for Serov at her father's estate in Abramtsevo, while his cousin Masha Simonovich was the *Girl in Sunlight*. He did not call these works by the girls' names because they were not portraits; their essential elements were landscape and interiors. Imagine a different situation or background and

Valentin Serov *Girl in Sunlight* 1888

Valentin Serov *Portrait of Francesco Tamanio* 1891–93

Valentin Serov *Portrait of Mika Morozov* 1901

you would have another painting. Both works are strongly impressionistic – each little bit of reality contains within itself something to admire, an excuse to indulge in beauty and delight the eye. *Girl with Peaches* has something in common with Repin's *They Did Not Expect Him* – both are *plein air* works – but there is one major difference between them. Repin uses *plein air* to stage his drama as convincingly as possible, whereas for Serov it is

purely an occasion to explore the beauty of changing colours. Beauty reigns supreme; henceforward, one of the principal aims of his painting would be to seek out the beauty inherent in all aspects of life, however ordinary they might appear.

Serov was at this time unfamiliar with French Impressionism; his favourite French painter was Bastien Lepage. Russian painting was itself exploring new frontiers and Serov's version of Impressionism was of a different kind. In *Girl with Peaches* the texture varies a great deal, sometimes as smooth as porcelain, sometimes rendered much more freely, but it lacks the unity of texture to be found in the Monet or Pissarro of the 1870s. The composition of his paintings is still very traditional. At the centre of the canvas, behind the casual arrangement of the table and the fragmentary way the objects are depicted (simply as they have fallen into the painter's line of sight), the figure of the girl is still safely contained within an unwavering outline.

Serov's early, impressionistic period did not last long. In the 1890s his style and technique began to change. It gradually lost clarity while occasionally reverting to the past, then acquired the 'smudged' look associated with northern Impressionism. Finally the old style disappeared altogether.

New challenges beckoned. The born portraitist emerged to reveal his special insights into human character and behaviour. His creative method became more calculated and economical; rather than allowing himself to be carried away by every spontaneous impulse, he concentrated on the specific task in hand, namely the methodical building up of the required image. He viewed people more subtly and became fascinated by their artistic and creative potential, as can be seen from his choice of models. In the early 1890s portraits appeared of the painters Konstantin Korovin, Levitan and Repin, of the writer Leskov and of the actors Mazzini, Tamanio and D'Andrade.

Most of the artistes painted by Serov were Italian singers who had been engaged by Mamontov for his private opera company. World-renowned, confident of their celebrity, they appear in these portraits inseparable from their stage roles, even though Serov never painted them on stage. They command our attention and respond to us with their customary gestures and expressions which create a kind of mask revealing rather than concealing the essence of their personalities. One of the most successful portraits is that of *Tamanio* (1891–93). In this traditional bust, viewed by the painter slightly from below, the head is raised so that a large part of the canvas is occupied by the singer's powerful throat, the symbol of that remarkable voice. The singer's genius finds corroboration in the 'Venetian' – warm red-brown – colours. In the 1890s, portraits of the *Tamanio* type sometimes tended towards the monumental form, but only reached it a decade later, by which time Serov's portraits too had undergone drastic change.

Portraiture showed two different tendencies at the turn of the century. The first, more formal approach, was represented by commissioned portraits. Serov, by then very fashionable, was besieged by such requests, which he accepted even though he found the sitters' personalities trivial and uninspiring. These formal portraits typically depict a bored society lady seated on a divan in her boudoir with a lapdog on her knee, or an imposing gentleman by, or astride, a fine horse. One such, of the Grand Duke Paul Alexandrovich (1897), won the Grand Prix at the World Exhibition in Paris in 1900. The second, more intimate and lyrical approach, was centred on women and children. Among the best examples of this kind are Serov's portraits of Lukomskaya (1900, watercolour), Mika Morozov (1901) and *Children* (1891). These subjects are still unsullied by life and able to share their hopes and fears with us in a simple, open way.

There is some similarity between these portraits and a series of paintings by Serov on peasant themes, at which he worked mainly in the 1890s. The same blend of genre and landscape was being developed by the so-called 'young *peredvizhniki*' at the time. They are very simple pictures, based on themes rather than subjects. One excellent example is *October: Domotkanovo* (1895). There is no beauty about the greyish landscape. The crude log-cabins, little sheds, unprepossessing horses grazing on the autumn stubble, the boy-herdsman whittling a stick, all present a picture of ingenuous and poetic simplicity. This is not, however, the poetry of Levitan, which was usually inspired by beautiful landscape. In *October* genre and landscape are combined rather as they were in Polenov's *Moscow Courtyard*. Serov was only one of Polenov's followers, who also included Arkhipov, Stepanov, S. Ivanov and other graduates of the Moscow Art College. As a landscape painter Serov was very much in tune with the Moscow tradition; as a portraitist and history painter, however, he was totally individual.

The spirit of the times put an end to this lyrical period in Serov's career. The mid-1900s were years of social upheaval, when he gradually but consistently abandoned his earlier approach, namely the simple, even neutral reflection of various aspects of reality. Russian Art Nouveau, which now began to appear ever more strongly in Serov's work, required a more engaged attitude to reality. History, myth, allusion and metaphor became the ingredients of his new artistic programme, rather than the mere reproduction of some aspect of life which had happened to catch his eye. The last picture in the peasant

46

Valentin Serov *Portrait of the Grand Duke Paul Alexandrovich* 1897

series, *Foals Drinking* (1904), is remarkable for its romantic elation and the elements of a new style. For example, the figures, horses and sheds are clearly silhouetted against a background of sunset sky in order to heighten the expressive power of the painting by means of its linear rhythms.

In his later life Serov concentrated mainly on portraits. The last ten years of his career produced some of his best, including those of M.A. Morozova (1902), A.M. Gorky (1905), M.N. Ermolova (1905), G.L. Girshman (1907), Ida Rubinstein (1910) and Princess Orlova (1911). The portraits of Gorky and Ermolova indicate the changes taking place in formal portraits as artists, writers and other members of the artistic intelligentsia replaced aristocrats such as the Grand Duke Paul Alexandrovich and Princess Yussupova.

Serov's new choice of subject and new style of painting is revealed most clearly in *Ermolova*, in which he proclaims a kind of heroic artistry. The great tragedienne appears as a tribune. Her pose and expression are like a message or appeal addressed to the people, and the portrait as a whole is a summation of all her roles and dramatic pathos. This new type of portrait, which to some extent recalls those of the early 1890s, required a new form. There is no element of accident in the positioning of her figure and its relationship to the field of the canvas. Her body, silhouetted against the plane of the wall, is an

area of dark blue. The contour of her figure, made up of curved and expressive lines, is neatly integrated into the system of verticals and horizontals. A sense of space is conveyed by the presence of the mirror. Serov combines the plane with the volume freely but in strict accordance with his new style. The head is carefully modelled: as in a mask, its volume is drawn towards the surface. The form appears to be empty. The frozen set of her face recalls a monument.

In his last portraits Serov exaggerated various characteristics of his models. He frequently spoke of this process when responding to the criticism that he had made his sitters into caricatures. Some art historians (A. Efros, for one) drew attention to the way Serov likened human figures and faces to those of animals. Whatever the rights and wrongs of this argument there is no doubt that Serov's approach to portraiture was very individual and creative.

One of his most remarkable late works is the portrait of Ida Rubinstein, the famous dancer particularly renowned for her interpretations of Oriental roles, whom he painted in Paris. She is seated naked on drapery against a grey background. There are only three colours in this tempera painting, which might be more accurately termed a coloured drawing. The decision to show her naked was itself risky, but her very nature excluded a naturalistic interpretation. Serov wished to depict her transformed by her role. He singled out the essential

(*opposite above*) **Valentin Serov** *Portrait of Princess Orlova* 1911

(*left*) **Valentin Serov** *Portrait of Ida Rubinstein* 1910

(*right*) **Valentin Serov** *Portrait of M.N. Ermolova* 1905

Valentin Serov *Odysseus and Nausicaa* 1910

Valentin Serov *The Rape of Europa* 1910

element of his model – the extravagance of her manner and her tragic fragility. She is like a beautiful butterfly pinned to the canvas. Her angular figure seems delicate and incorporeal. Serov expresses this duality in a linear composition whose extremes are tremendous tension and total relaxation. His line, laden with metaphor, is one of the finest examples of Russian Art Nouveau.

At the turn of the century Serov joined the movement initiated by the World of Art group and turned to historical themes. He did a number of small tempera paintings for a lavishly illustrated edition of *Emperors Hunting: Peter the Great Hunting with Hounds* (1900), *Peter II and Elisaveta Petrovna Leaving for the Hunt* and *Catherine the Great Leaving for the Falcon Hunt* (both 1902). The World of Art approach is dominant here,

especially in the choice of subject – not the critical moments of history or its social implications but the spirit, style and beauty of the times. Unlike Benois or Lansere, however, Serov did aim for a convincing effect. In *Peter II*, for example, the horses race towards us at such speed that we are almost part of the movement. History here is presented as real rather than, as with World of Art, invented.

He continued to work on history painting throughout the mid-1900s. In 1907 he did a small tempera painting of Peter the Great depicting the reforming emperor with his entourage on Vasily Island in St Petersburg, at a time when the island was still in the process of being built up. It stands open to the Baltic winds and freezing clouds. Peter is majestic, formidable; he bestrides the land and confronts the elements like a giant. We perceive the emperor and his entourage, painted in profile, as a solemn, even monumental procession.

The figure of Peter the Great continued to attract Serov for the rest of his life, but in his last years he concentrated more on Greek mythology than Russian history. He was fascinated by two subjects in particular: *Odysseus and Nausicaa* and *The Rape of Europa*. In 1910 he painted a number of versions of both subjects. His interest in ancient Greece was fired by a journey to that country with Bakst in 1907. He was struck by its living antiquity and its unique blend of myth and reality, a combination which was to become a special feature of his interpretation of ancient myth. The theme of the procession reappears in *Odysseus and Nausicaa*. Nausicaa in a chariot drawn by an ass, her servants, and a little further on, Odysseus in borrowed robes, all take part in this joyful and festive progress. The scene, which might almost have been taken from an antique relief, harmoniously augments the airy seascape, high skies and white-tipped waves. Living experience is more closely united with past styles in Serov's work than in that of any other World of Art painter; it is this union which makes the landscape and figures of *Odysseus* so marvellously natural.

In the *Rape of Europa* everything looks simultaneously real and fantastical. The stagy mock bull, his huge body ploughing between two gigantic waves, glances back at his bride-victim with an all too convincing eye. Europa is as plausible as an antique maiden as she is a contemporary model. Serov needed to peel away many layers of classicism before reaching the archaic essence which enabled him to convey an authentic picture of antiquity. He penetrated to the very sources of myth and comprehended it without creating a myth himself, as Vrubel did and Petrov-Vodkin (Serov's pupil) would. But when he died he was, surely, on the threshold of new discoveries, for he could never be satisfied with what he had already achieved.

3   The Moscow Painters

A third seminal artist of the time was Konstantin Korovin (1861–1939). He was an impulsive but subtle painter who reacted instantaneously to the events around him. He mastered Impressionism early and remained an Impressionist all his life, becoming particularly prominent in the 1880s.

Korovin was very representative of the Moscow tradition. He was a fellow student of Levitan's at the Moscow Art College (though his own work was closer to Polenov's than to Savrasov's), where he was occupied with *plein air* painting and the then fashionable genre of the study. His impressionistic *Chorus-girl* (1883) was ahead of its time and not understood by his contemporaries. His whole approach to painting is illustrated by this subtly nuanced painting built on gradations of shade, colour reflexes and an expressive, open texture. The chorus-girl herself is not particularly interesting psychologically or in appearance. Korovin was not much concerned with the realistic features or the surfaces of objects – these features become textural devices on the surface of the canvas – having rid himself of every vestige of the naturalistic thinking which had, to a greater or lesser degree, dominated late nineteenth-century painting.

After *Chorus girl*, the first Russian Impressionist work, Korovin consolidated his position for the next ten years. Returning home after extensive travel abroad in the late 1880s he turned to new themes, for example *By the Balcony* (1886), in which he temporarily abandoned Impressionism and explored the beautiful range of colours dominated by black. However, national, and particularly northern Russian, themes remained his chief interest, which was further stimulated by a trip to Murmansk with Serov in the early 1890s. He brought back a great number of studies for subsequent paintings, including the well-known *Winter* (1894), which is reminiscent of Levitan's *March*. A horse-drawn sledge waits outside a log cabin; there is no one about. Colourful washing hangs from the fence. The colours, dominated by greys and silvers, are rather dull. Korovin was fascinated by the subtle juxtaposition of colours and created wonderfully harmonious combinations. Unlike Levitan's picture, *Winter* concentrates not on narrative but on impression and gradations of colour.

Konstantin Korovin *Fish, Wine and Fruit* 1916

Konstantin Korovin *Paris at Night, Boulevard des Italiens* 1908

Konstantin Korovin *The Spaniards Lenora and Ampara* 1886

Decorative experiment began to dominate Korovin's work from the mid-1890s on. In the 1880s his decorative ideas were far from impressionistic, as may be seen from a Vasnetsov-like painting entitled *Northern Idyll* (1886), but works from the 1890s, such as *Paper Lanterns* (1898) and *In Summer* (1895) reveal a fresh impressionistic tendency. They were followed by his Parisian landscapes, executed in a broad, decorative and impressionistic manner, and by some freely picturesque, study-like work. Korovin was a master of the study form and could draw inspiration from any theme, but he was particularly attracted to Russian nature and to village life, with its sheds, fences, clearings and edges of forests, clumps of trees and log houses. The studies were done quickly, usually at a single session. Their strong point is not a complex interpretation of colour or texture but the precision of Korovin's brush, his convincing combinations of tone and his generally superb artistry. The cult of the study had a considerable influence on Korovin's painting and on Russian Impressionism as a whole.

The two special features of Korovin's Impressionism – its decorative and study-like character – are best illustrated by his Paris landscapes dating from 1900. Their subjects are similar to those of French Impressionists between the 1870s and the 1890s (streets viewed from above or from a balcony, crossroads, boulevards and squares crowded with people), but the differences between Korovin and Claude Monet are striking. Of course, Monet was the originator, Korovin only the follower, but there was nothing remarkable in this, for Russia's artistic development had lagged behind France's by a decade or two throughout the nineteenth century. Again, Monet's technical skill was unrivalled. But the real divergence was in their respective approaches to painting. Korovin's Parisian landscapes are evening or night scenes, for example *Paris at Night, Boulevard des Italiens* (1908) and *Paris, Boulevard des Capucines* (1906). The city is flooded with lights; street scenes are brought to life with a fast, broad brush and impulsive, even crude brushwork. Not surprisingly, there is a theatrical air about them, for Korovin was a famous theatre designer, particularly well known for his opera sets. More than any of his contemporaries he epitomized the obsession with theatre in Russian art at the turn of the century. All this – decorativism, theatricality, animation, spectacle – gave Korovin's Impressionism its particular character.

These qualities continued to influence his work for many years. In the 1910s he worked mainly in the Crimea on sunlit southern landscapes and discovered still-life. Still-life in Impressionism is by no means rare (and quite common in French painting) but Korovin's brand was part of the new trend found among the young painters of the Blue Rose and Knave of Diamonds groups. Korovin, of course, interpreted still-life impressionistically; he treated space as though it were part of a landscape and his objects dissolved into the aerial environment instead of dominating it. In some of his still-lifes and landscapes of the 1910s decorativism is taken to extremes, which may be explained by the fact that many of his pupils – Saryan, for one – who had also pursued the path of decorativism, were now mature painters in their own right. Korovin himself remained within the limits of Impressionism.

Korovin's work was central to the Moscow tradition, and a perfect example of the Moscow painters' desire to achieve spontaneity in their reflection of life and of the beauty and poetry of simple phenomena. Among them were the so-called 'young *peredvizhniki*' – Abram Arkhipov (1862–1930), A.S. Stepanov (1858–1923), Sergei Ivanov (1864–1910) and Sergei Korovin (1858–1908, Konstantin's elder brother). Arkhipov and Stepanov were particularly acclaimed for the lyrical quality of their work. Other painters, as well as the public, especially

Abram Arkhipov *Laundresses* Late 1890s

50   liked Arkhipov's *On the River Oka* (1890), which was a good illustration of the 'eventless' genre. And indeed nothing actually happens in the picture. A ferryman's boat, seen from the stern, carries a group of peasants with their backs to us, deep in thought during these few minutes of involuntary rest. It is not their inner lives which interest Arkhipov, but the simple beauty of Russian nature, sunlight (conveyed by *plein air* techniques) and the union of man and the universe. It was an approach typical of Arkhipov as well as many other painters at the turn of the century. S. Ivanov was another remarkable Moscow artist of the time who 'dissolved' genre into landscape, but his pictures are concerned with some of the burning and tragic issues of the day, such as the Revolution of 1905 and the earlier armed uprisings in towns and villages; and the refugees, driven from their homes, who died in their hundreds or were forced to return in despair. The feeling of desperation is particularly striking in Ivanov's *On the Road: Death of a Refugee*.

  The work of another Moscow artist, L.O. Pasternak (1862–1945, the father of Boris), is a kind of equivalent in graphics to *plein air* and even Impressionist painting. He did mainly pastel drawings of individuals and groups, immersing them in a kind of haze to convey the surrounding aerial milieu. These portraits are remarkable for their serious and meditative tone. He was also famous for his book illustrations, particularly those for the first, magazine edition of Leo Tolstoy's *Resurrection*. He was sent the portions of manuscript to be illustrated direct from the writer's desk.

  Another member of the 'young *peredvizhniki*' was Andrei Ryabushkin (1861–1904), who studied first at the Moscow Art College and later at the St Petersburg Academy. He began working in genre, but then decided that village life could not provide him with suitable material for the poetic interpretation of reality he sought. He gradually worked out his own approach to history, which in some ways resembled the World of Art method. In Ryabushkin's paintings, as in Benois's and Lansere's, nothing really happens. Ryabushkin selected scenes from everyday life but, unlike the World of Art group, preferred the old Rus of the Slavophiles to the more modern, westernized Russia. At first he experimented with themes from the era of Peter the Great, but eventually settled on the seventeenth century, the most decorative in Russian history. His predilection was for the traditional Russia of the time, with its beautiful rituals, majestic processions and pious religious festivals, and he dedicated the last ten years of his life to such subjects. He continued to work in oils, against the general trend of Russian painting (including the World of Art), which gradually switched to tempera, then gouache and finally watercolour. As far as style was concerned, however, Ryabushkin, in his progression from naturalism and *plein air* to Russian Art Nouveau (*Modern*), fitted in well with the developments of the time.

Sergei Ivanov *On the Road: Death of a Refugee* 1889

Among his best works dealing with the seventeenth century are *Seventeenth-century Moscow Street* (1895), *Seventeenth-century Russian Women in Church* (1899) and *Seventeenth-century Wedding Procession in Moscow* (1901). *Moscow Street* poeticizes an ordinary street scene: a muddy track, wooden fences and a little church, shining white. Mass is over, and people dressed in their Sunday best are picking their way home along a shaky planked walkway thrown over the mud. There are echoes here of Shwartz and Surikov, who also admired the beauty of the Old Russian way of life with its traditional clothing, objects and architecture.

53

The theme of *Russian Women* brings real seventeenth-century people together with Old Russian iconography. Ryabushkin did much copying of icons and frescos (in Rostov and Yaroslavl, for instance) and this painting shows how much he had been influenced by the art of Old Russia. He was probably the first modern Russian painter to follow the traditions of Old Russian art so meticulously. For Vasnetsov, the academic tradition had been the most important source of inspiration, while for Vrubel it had been Byzantine art as a whole (of which Old Russian art was only a part). Ryabushkin took as his model Old Russian art of the period when it had been liberated from Byzantine influences.

Wedding Procession, which expresses Ryabushkin's vision of seventeenth-century Russia with particular clarity, well illustrates his search for a true style of his own. He emphasizes the pictorial plane by the movement – parallel to that plane – of the splendid procession of horses, riders, carriages and people in festive dress hurrying behind. Ryabushkin uses a harmonious colour range of red, yellow and dark blue to achieve a striking decorative effect. Linear rhythm is important – the figures' outlines are cleanly and lithely drawn.

One other feature of Ryabushkin's style which differentiates him from his Moscow fellow artists was his use of iconographic techniques; thus he often repeated his figures, transferring them from one painting to another and preserving their postures, gestures etc.

Ryabushkin was among those painters at the end of the nineteenth century who set out to define and describe the features which made Russia unique. Vasnetsov was the first; he was followed by members of the Abramtsevo circle who formed a vast collection of folk artefacts. Ryabushkin also joined this movement, which was later continued by M.V. Nesterov and by some of the World of Art group. All the various artistic groups joined in this project, which was profoundly important – indeed essential – to Russian culture at the turn of the century.

Mikhail Nesterov (1862–1942) contributed to this search in his own way. He was also a graduate of the Moscow Art College, where he was a particular admirer of Perov, who was one of his teachers. He was a highly individual artist. In the mid-1880s he rejected traditional genre and history painting and found his own style, which is well illustrated by two early masterpieces: *The Hermit* (1889) and *The Vision of St Bartholomew* (1890). These, together with some portraits of the 1930s, are among his very best works. *The Hermit* is a poetic description of the quiet life of a recluse, an old man who has retired from the hustle and bustle of the world. The idea of monastic life was growing in popularity at the time; in addition, Nesterov was particularly concerned with the concept of man's unity with nature. The figure of the hermit is placed in the square of the canvas so that its outline is linked with the plane of the water and the shoreline. There is something incorporeal about this figure, which strikes us as just another element of this transparent landscape. *St Bartholomew* relates an episode from the childhood of the great Saint Sergii Radonezhsky, in which the boy awakens to faith and wisdom. He stands before an old man who has appeared to him; in the background is a frozen landscape filled with light. Nesterov dedicated many portraits to Sergii in the next ten years, but most of his pre-revolutionary paintings are concerned with nameless characters – hermits, monks and nuns or suffering young women. From the 1890s onwards he painted church murals – at first together with Vasnetsov in Kiev, and later on his own in various places. They show his ever-growing inclination to *Modern*, or Russian Art Nouveau. When he tried easel painting he was not successful, as in his *Holy Rus* (1905) which shows Christ walking towards some ordinary Russian folk who have come to greet him. This large canvas, which Tolstoy described as a 'requiem for Orthodoxy', is dripping with a quite operatic artificiality. After the Revolution he continued his career – though his style changed a great deal – with some considerable success.

By the end of the nineteenth century a number of Moscow painters had evolved a more or less common method and style, a development which led inevitably to the formation of a group. At the start of the 1890s the young Muscovites were not full members of the Society for Travelling Art Exhibitions (*peredvizhniki*) – they could exhibit but did not have the right to vote. Having attempted, unsuccessfully, to gain full rights in the Society, they began to look for an alternative and eventually formed the Union of Russian Painters in 1903. A year later it merged with the older World of Art group of St Petersburg, but the union was short-lived because of irreconcilable differences between the two sides. The Muscovites were, to a greater or lesser degree, dominated by Impressionism, whereas the World of Art group were already moving towards *Modern*. The two groups split in 1910 exhibiting under their original names.

Most of the artists discussed in this chapter joined the Union of Russian Painters, which was later enlarged by members of the new generation. The majority were landscape painters, followers of Levitan and Korovin. Their vision of nature was based on a moderate Impressionism; they often preferred the study form. This was the style typical of the Union, though some of its members did not even graduate to Impressionism and continued to work in the post-*peredvizhniki plein air* manner.

Igor Grabar (1874–1960) was a special kind of Impressionist, close both to the Union of Russian Painters and to the World of Art group. He studied Impressionism in Munich, at the Azbé school, and was for some time assistant to the *maître*. On his return to Russia in the mid-1900s, he painted a number of successful landscapes and still-lifes. Among the best are *February Azure* (1904), *March Snow* (1904), *Chrysanthemums* (1905) and *Uncleared Table* (1907). He applied the new technique of Impressionism – even Neo-impressionism – to traditional Russian themes. This is particularly evident in *February Azure*, where the influence of Savrasov and Levitan may be discerned. Grabar uses strokes of pure, unmixed colour which blend together to create the overall tone, and the rough surface of the canvas seems to vibrate in an attempt to convey nature's own tremors. The theme of *March Snow* is much simpler. Snow lies everywhere, with a whole range of colours reflected in its surface. A woman carrying buckets, walking across the snow, has almost reached the edge of the painting; it is this which gives the composition the character of a study.

Grabar's still-lifes have some of the qualities of landscape. This is especially true of *Uncleared Table*, where the still-life is placed outside the house rather than within. Although it is undoubtedly a still-life, a certain constructivist element may be detected. Thus the objects are carefully laid out in their separate planes so that the foreground, parallel to the surface of the picture, is emphasized by the cloth hanging down from the table, and the articles on the table are deliberately arranged by the painter. Grabar had begun to understand the need for a corrective to the pure Impressionist method, but he never put this understanding fully into practice because he gave up painting and dedicated himself wholly to art criticism and history. (It was around this time that he conceived the idea of his major work, *A History of Russian Art*.)

The work of Filipp Malyavin (1869–1940) is a peculiar synthesis of Impressionism and Expressionism. He became a painter almost by accident. When he was still a   49

(left, above) **Igor Grabar** *February Azure* 1904

(left, below) **Igor Grabar** *Uncleared Table* 1907

Filipp Malyavin *Whirlwind* 1906

child he was sent to train as an icon-painter at the monastery of Afon, where he remained for many years. The sculptor Beklemishev met him at the monastery and, struck by his talent, brought him back to Russia. Malyavin became a student of Repin's at the St Petersburg Academy, where he painted a series of portraits which impressed young and old alike with their originality. Portraits of peasants appeared next, followed by a large painting entitled *Laughter*, which was highly praised when shown at an international exhibition. *Three Peasant Women* and *Peasant Woman in Yellow* appeared in 1902, and *Peasant Girl* in 1903, but the major work of his career was undoubtedly *Whirlwind*, which appeared in 1906. He created an image of elemental impulse, an explosion of fervour and joy. Peasant women, dancing or frozen for a moment in mid-movement in a sudden rush of wind, symbolize the idea of wild revelry and the sudden release of pure instinct. The whirlwind of red dresses and skirts is depicted by a riot of colour which covers the huge canvas in a free, seemingly uncontrolled sweep. Malyavin's contemporaries saw this picture as a symbol of the elemental force of the peasantry which exploded at the time of the Revolution.

Both Grabar and Malyavin made an important contribution to the understanding of the national character, as did other members of the Union of Russian Painters. Many of them found it most clearly expressed in the Russian national heritage, the beauty of Old Russian

art and the traditional way of life. Konstantin Yuon (1875–1958) was a pupil of Serov at the Moscow Art College. After a period of experiment, during which he was drawn in turn to the World of Art group and the Blue Rose, he eventually settled on themes and a style of his own at the beginning of the century. He was particularly fascinated by ancient Russian towns such as Rostov, Yglich and Sergiev Possad, with their monastery walls, kremlins, cathedrals and markets on the town squares, filled with sledges in winter and carts in summer. He perceived an authentic beauty and poetic charm in the pristine and stable life of the Russian provinces.

Yuon was by no means unique. Other members of the Union also turned to these themes and to landscapes reflecting the tranquil life of old Russian estates and country houses. They were also attracted to the interiors of these houses and lovingly reproduced the antique objets d'art, the rays of light pouring through windows and the peaceful atmosphere they found there. For pure landscapes they relied on typical seasonal scenes. Wintry, snowy landscapes, previously quite rare in spite of the rich possibilities of the Russian winters, suddenly appeared in abundance. The output of the Union's members became intimate and small-scale. It was content to occupy its anachronistic little niche in the broad panorama of Russian art and gradually fade into the background, quite irrelevant to the new movements making up the Russian avantgarde.

(*opposite, above*) **Konstantin Yuon** *Towards the Trinity* 1903

(*opposite, below*) **Andrei Ryabushkin** *Seventeenth-century Russian Women in Church* 1899

(*right*) **Mikhail Nesterov** *The Hermit* 1889

(*below*) **Mikhail Nesterov** *The Vision of St Bartholomew* 1890

4 The 'World of Art' Group

The 'World of Art' group (*Mir iskusstva*) was formed by a group of St Petersburg intellectuals in 1898 and continued to exist, with some interruptions, until 1924, although its heyday lasted only into the first decade of the new century. After the process of formation had been completed the group began to publish their journal (which ran for six years) and to organize exhibitions. In 1906, as has already been mentioned, World of Art merged with the Muscovite Union of Russian Painters, only to reappear in 1910 under its original name.

The members had broad and varied cultural interests and ambitions. They were concerned with literature (with a particular penchant for illustration), music and theatre (both design and directing), but painting was their main *raison d'être*. They were cultural dilettantes in all these spheres, even in painting, where they cultivated a kind of gifted amateurism. This was partly because not all of them had a formal artistic education, but also because dilettantism was their formula for creative freedom and escape from the shackles of academe. Apart from their professional training they drew on their general familiarity with the arts, their wide knowledge of styles and periods and their ability to exploit the most varied cultural traditions. They inclined strongly towards the past – naturally enough, for the informal circle which preceded the World of Art was made up of people whose fathers and grandfathers had been among the leaders of contemporary Russian culture. For example, Benois's father was a famous Russian architect, Somov's was a distinguished art historian as well as the curator of the Hermitage collection, and the father of Lansere and Serebryakova was the late nineteenth-century sculptor discussed in an earlier chapter.

The founders of the World of Art included A.N. Benois, L.S. Bakst, E.E. Lansere, K.A. Somov, S.P. Diaghilev and men of letters such as D.V. Filosofov and V.F. Nuvel, who made significant contributions to the Society's magazine. Later they were joined by A.P. Ostroumova-Lebedeva, M.V. Dobuzhinsky, A.Ya. Golovin, I.Ya. Bilibin and N.K. Roerich. The second phase (after 1910) is additionally associated with such names as B.M. Kustodiev, Z.E. Serebryakova, K.F. Bogaevsky, A.E. Yakovlev, V.I. Shukhaev and the graphic artists S.V. Chekhonin, D.I. Mitrokhin and G.I. Narbut. For a short time some religious philosophers and writers also participated in the group and edited the literary section of the magazine. They included D.S. Merezhkovsky, N. Minsky, V.V. Rozanov and Lev Shestov, who all left the magazine in the early 1900s following disagreements with the painters and later formed their own journal, *The New Way*.

The members of the group expressed their artistic credo in articles and books. One such article, 'Complex Questions' by Sergei Diaghilev, was published in the first two issues of the magazine *World of Art*. Its main concern was artistic individualism and the primacy of the subjective. Without such individualism, according to Diaghilev, true art was impossible. The second question dealt with in the article had to do with the primacy of beauty as the only basis for art. These ideas, of course, offended the established nineteenth-century Russian egalitarian approach to aesthetics and particularly the views of N. Chernyshevsky, which had dominated the thinking of writers and painters for many decades.

Another fundamental work which contributed to the formulation of the World of Art philosophy was Alexandre Benois's *History of Nineteenth-Century Painting: Russian Art*, originally intended as a supplement to a book by Muter on nineteenth-century art and later published separately (in 1901). Benois gave a rather critical account of the *peredvizhniki*. He did not deny Repin's or Perov's talents but suggested that they were distorted by the social and political problems which had preoccupied the two painters and distracted them from purely artistic concerns. This book is still pertinent today. Benois provided a subtle, accurate and profound analysis which clearly revealed that his sympathies lay with the early nineteenth-century painters such as Venetsianov, Kiprensky, Alexander Ivanov and Fedotov.

Benois also made a vital contribution to the re-evaluation of Russian classical and Baroque architecture of the eighteenth and early nineteenth centuries, particularly in his enthusiastic celebrations of St Petersburg and its surrounding palaces and parks. His opinions began to

Alexandre Benois *The King's Promenade* 1906

change, however, and by the end of the 1900s he was criticizing individualism, demanding the establishment of state art, and proposing a more influential role for the St Petersburg Academy. These views were closer to those of the later World of Art painters with their inclination to Neo-classicism.

The World of Art group revived interest in foreign art of the past and present. They sang the praises of classical and early nineteenth-century romantic art as well as contemporary English and German painting and graphics. They underestimated Impressionism, however, and were rather intimidated by all aspects of the avantgarde. Their tastes in contemporary graphics were reflected in the appearance and layout of their magazine, a typical Art Nouveau journal which was greatly influenced by English and German magazines. More evidence that World of Art belonged to *Modern* was provided by the opening of an exhibition of 'Contemporary Art' in St Petersburg in 1903 which recalled the Parisian Art Nouveau salons. Interiors, jewellery and

objects of decorative art were on display and all could be bought or ordered, but the Russian public were not yet ready for the style and no orders were forthcoming.

The group's chief characteristic was a dreamily romantic taste, lightly spiced with irony, for days gone by. They were not interested in the social conflicts, historic deeds or dramatic turning points of the past. They sought, instead, the beauty and spirit of past styles and preferred to depict light-hearted and amusing episodes, both real and invented. They admired and idealized a world long since vanished; at the same time they gently mocked that world – and themselves as backward-looking observers. Their ironic philosophy was inspired by Hoffman, the famous German romantic writer. In their attempt to revive Romanticism they eschewed the support of the Russian romantic tradition, which struck them as too simplistic (and which had, in any case, ceased to exist by the middle of the nineteenth century), turning instead to various other periods. Benois favoured Louis XIV's Versailles and the Russia of the eighteenth century;

Evgeny Lansere *The Empress Elizaveta Petrovna at Tsarskoye Selo* 1905

Alexandre Benois *The Marquise Bathing* 1906

Lansere inclined to the era of Peter the Great, Somov to the eighteenth and early nineteenth centuries; Bakst was fascinated by antiquity, Bilibin by ancient Rus. However, Bilibin also borrowed features of eighteenth- and nineteenth-century Japanese engraving, Benois was influenced by Menzel, and Bakst was drawn to Gogol's Russia. And of course, all these borrowings rested on a base of *Modern*, which gave these seemingly disparate tendencies a common direction.

Apart from Diaghilev, who was the practical organizer of the group's activities, the dominant personality was that of Alexandre Benois (1870–1960). He studied law at St Petersburg University but his interests were universal; he was a painter, illustrator, theatre designer

and director, choreographer, critic and historian of art, traveller and finally littérateur and memoirist. He achieved some distinction in all these fields. A very cultured man, with a broad knowledge of literature, philosophy and history, he had a tremendous influence on his colleagues, who were particularly infected by his obsession with the past.

His first large series, *The Last Promenades of Louis XIV*, summed up all his basic artistic creed. He exaggerated perspective, selected elevated angles and frequently bordered his compositions with 'coulisses', or side-scenes. Later, stylized forms predominated at the expense of naturalistic elements, but the main principle of *Modern* – the combination of naturalistic and symbolic – remained unchanged.

His major work in the field of painting is the Versailles series, which included *The King's Promenade*, *The Marquise Bathing*, *The Chinese Pavilion: Jealous Man* and *Italian Comedy* (all 1906, in gouache, on paper or cardboard). They are a product of his mature style. Their technique is consistently graphic, combined with a moderate amount of decorativism and neo-classical elements of composition. Benois's historical scenes resemble theatrical performances transferred to canvas or paper. He liked painting real theatrical performances too, either from the auditorium or from backstage. Many of his themes – promenades and processions, for example – derived from seventeenth- and eighteenth-century European painting. In *The King's Promenade* a ceremonial procession of pairs of cavaliers and their ladies pass slowly before us. The putti on the fountain reflected in the water seem to ape them, thus making the interplay of outlines more complex. Reflection in water was a theme much favoured by the World of Art for its ephemeral and phantasmal effect. One nuance of the irony which dominates the picture is this motif of wavering between the real and the illusory. Benois's affection for the Louis XIV style and the playful splendour of the park of Versailles somehow increases this sense of irony.

Between 1900 and 1920 Benois did brilliant work as a book illustrator and theatre designer. In 1903 he began several series of drawings illustrating Pushkin's *Bronze Horseman* (published separately in 1922 and 1923). They reveal Benois's marvellous understanding of Pushkin's great poem and the era in which it is set.

Benois's theatre designs display an equally profound familiarity with various artistic styles. Scenery and costume reflect the styles both of the time when the play or opera was written and of the era in which it was set. His designs for Pushkin's *Feast during the Plague* (1914) are full of dramatic tension. The drawings (1912) for the ballet *Festivities*, set to music by Debussy, are of a

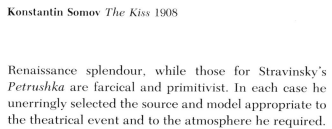

Konstantin Somov *The Kiss* 1908

Renaissance splendour, while those for Stravinsky's
57 *Petrushka* are farcical and primitivist. In each case he
unerringly selected the source and model appropriate to
the theatrical event and to the atmosphere he required.

Evgeny Lansere (1877–1946), like his friend and
colleague Benois, had a broad range of artistic interests.
He did easel and monumental paintings, book and
magazine illustration, theatre design and political caricature. Where Benois used irony, Lansere was openly
satirical. His well-known picture *Empress Elisaveta
Petrovna at Tsarskoye Selo* is imbued with the usual
World of Art admiration for baroque architecture and the
ceremony of court life, but the Empress's figure, face and
character (and those of her entourage) are a deliberately
ambiguous blend of the amusing and the grotesque.

Konstantin Somov (1869–1939) was an important
member of the group whose work combined seriousness
and irony in a very individual way. For example, his
enthusiasm for Beardsley went hand in hand with a
passion for the old masters, particularly Vermeer. His
style was free and elegant but his pictures were carefully
finished. He liked erotic themes. Behind the elegance was
a potent brew of the frightening and the funny which was
popular in Europe, especially Germany.

Somov studied for nearly ten years at the Academy,
where he worked in Repin's studio. His works dating
from the 1890s are picturesque and freely impressionistic,
but at the turn of the century his style changed as he
turned to themes from 'invented history' (inspired by
contemporary events) and nostalgic dreams of childhood.
His *Lady in Blue* (1897–1900) was an important stepping-
stone to this mature work. He clothed his model (actually

(*top*) **Konstantin Somov** *Lady in Blue* 1897–1900

(*above*) **Konstantin Somov** *Portrait of the Poet Alexander
Blok* 1907

the artist Martinova) according to the fashion of the 1840s, placed her in an eighteenth-century park landscape and added a hint of the 'gallant' genre. In spite of this blend of different eras he created a picture of a suffering individual who had resigned herself to her fate; and indeed, Martinova died shortly afterwards.

Most of his later work (apart from portraits) depicted episodes from the past invented by himself and based on the 'gallant' genre. A billet-doux being passed to the object of a lover's passionate dreams, scenes of rendezvous, groups of ladies with their cavaliers (always including a 'gooseberry'), lovers kissing while being gently mocked by secret onlookers – such are Somov's favourite themes. They take place against a background of ancient parks, arbours, belvederes and the like. His ephemeral world is sometimes illuminated by fireworks or an elaborate rainbow which pick out the ladies and gentlemen hiding in the bushes. Somov applies his ironic touch to his characters, to himself and to us; he seems to catch us out admiring these slightly vulgar banalities and fashionable trumperies whose grace and elegance we cannot deny.

Somov did not abandon oil painting, as most of the group did, although he also produced many watercolours. All his work is meticulously finished – he would spend days at a time stylizing the detail of a small section of canvas. The degree of stylization depended on the genre; it was more intensive in 'gallant' scenes but relatively insignificant in portrait.

These last ranged from grand portraits of society beauties, immaculately executed but slightly cold in atmosphere, to intimate pictures of friends. Best known are his graphic portraits of contemporary painters and writers in pencil, brush and gouache. Among his masterpieces of this type is his portrait of the great Russian poet Alexander Blok (1907), which was received by his contemporaries with mixed feelings. Some pointed out that it was only a partial picture of Blok and that Somov had omitted many features which expressed Blok's true nature. Nowadays we see this work more as a portrait of the era than of Blok alone. His rigid face and fixed gaze are a kind of mask, concealing any movement of his skin, eyes or lips, but signifying his personal unhappiness as well as his extreme individualism, self-disgust and secret

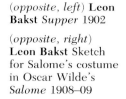

(*opposite, left*) **Leon Bakst** *Supper* 1902

(*opposite, right*) **Leon Bakst** Sketch for Salome's costume in Oscar Wilde's *Salome* 1908–09

(*right*) **Leon Bakst** *Terror Antiquus* 1908

demonic qualities. Blok himself wrote that Somov's portrait drawings would 'describe our era as truly and fully as Holbein's drawings evoke the court of Henry VIII and Latour's pastels the days of Madame de Pompadour'.[4]

Somov's popularity in the West was equalled by that of Leon Bakst (1866–1924). His best work was in theatre design and costume studies mainly done for Diaghilev's company in the 1900s and 1910s. He was also known for his easel paintings, book illustrations and interior designs. He was passionately interested in antiquity, especially ancient Greece. His most important easel painting is *Terror Antiquus* which appeared in 1908. It portrays the destruction of some ancient civilization. Earth disappears under water and ancient temples collapse, all behind an Aphrodite staring at us with her stiff archaic smile. The illusion of a theatrical performance is heightened by the distance from which the catastrophe appears to be painted.

Bakst was always attracted to the theatre and found his true vocation designing productions on Oriental and ancient Greek themes: *Salome* (1908–09), *Cleopatra*

(1909), *Shéhérezade* (1910), *Narcissus* (1911) and *L'Après-midi d'un faune* (1912). He brilliantly combined intensity of colour with grace and elegance of line, in particular in his costume designs, which can be seen as independent, finished polychrome graphics. Bakst's world is one of curved, taut lines, complex foreshortening of figures and explosions of pure reds, dark blues and greens. His decorative style became fashionable, widespread and, later, the vehicle for the transition from Art Nouveau to Art Deco in the decorative arts. Towards the end of his life his contemporaries wittily dubbed him 'the first tailor of Europe'.

Another prominent member of the group was Anna Ostroumova-Lebedeva (1871–1955), who devoted herself exclusively to graphics – mainly wood engraving and watercolours. She began her studies at the St Petersburg Academy with Repin and the engraver Mate, and completed them in Paris under Whistler. Together with other European artists she contributed to the revival of polychrome wood engraving. Her main genre was cityscape. She celebrated St Petersburg and its magnificent bridges and embankments, the Kazan cathedral, the

58, 56

Admiralty and the Stock Exchange. Her economical and classic style was expressed in clear perspectives, large areas of wall, columns, floodlit squares and deep shadows – all arranged simply, clearly and imbued with her love and admiration of the city.

Mstislav Dobuzhinsky (1875–1957) also devoted himself to St Petersburg, but to its contemporary life. He loved the city but condemned it too, seeing in it a source of evil and an element alien to man. Dobuzhinsky's city – and particularly St Petersburg – resembled the city as seen by the Symbolist poets. Indeed, he took as the title of one of his works the first line of Blok's short poem 'Night, street, lantern, chemist'. Two of his paintings are based on historical themes, *Province in the 1830s* and *Peter the Great in Holland*. They differ little from the paintings of Lansere and Benois, but on the whole he was not attracted to their nostalgic fantasies, stylization and cult of historical epochs. He was too greatly concerned by the despair inherent in contemporary city life and by the indestructible evil of a new civilization which confined man to a cage.

One of his most impressive works is *Man in Glasses* (1905–06), a portrait of the well-known literary critic and poet K. Erberg (Syunnerberg). He stands in front of a window, his back to the light pouring through the window and flowing around his figure and head to highlight his cheekbones and the upper part of his head. His sensitive face and nervous hands vividly express a man in a state of tension and acute conflict with the world outside the window, a panorama of waste land, high blocks of flats and eyeless slabs of wall – a kind of big city backwater.

Dobuzhinsky's small canvas *The Hairdresser's Window* (1906) reveals another difference between him and the rest of the World of Art group. The subject of this eventless scene is the figure of a passer-by walking away from the window in the lamplight. Its impact is due to a wordless psychological insight expressed not in the stranger's face (for it is hidden), nor in his bent figure, but in the general atmosphere of brooding tragedy, anguish and despair. This disjointed drawing may strike us as a forerunner of Expressionism, but the daubed faces on the hairdresser's signboard are more akin to what was later termed Neoprimitivism.

Dobuzhinsky visited and drew a great number of different cities, such as his native Vilna (now Vilnius – his father was Lithuanian), St Petersburg, Munich, where he studied, London, Amsterdam, Naples, Haarlem, Paris, Chernigov and Voronezh. He chose backyards, little lanes, depots, wharves, old houses next to overcrowded blocks of flats, ignoring all that was elegant, formal or pleasing to the eye, as if he could find nothing to admire in the cities of his day. Only in his late series of illustrations for Dostoevsky's *White Nights* (1922) did his St Peters-

burg appear, if not majestic then at least imposing, and occasionally illuminated by hope and inspiration.

Among those who, like Dobuzhinsky, joined the World of Art before its merger with the Union of Russian Painters were Golovin, Bilibin and Roerich. Alexander Golovin (1863–1930) painted monumental murals and striking decorative portraits (often using an actor on stage as his model). He was also an interior designer, but his finest achievements were in theatre design, a field he discovered at the turn of the century when already in his forties. Unlike Benois, whose designs took account of the author's style and era, Golovin devised his own style with the aim of creating the greatest possible effect. Thus his designs for Ostrovsky's *Thunderstorm* (1916) resembled his sets for Gluck's *Orpheus and Eurydice* (1911) and Lermontov's *Masquerade* (1916–17). These productions, so very different from each other in content, were very similar stylistically, and typical of early twentieth-century theatre design. Golovin's style was extremely decorative. His complex compositions consisted of lines, figures and areas of colour projected, so to speak, onto the stage.

Ivan Bilibin (1876–1942) worked in the sphere of graphics and book illustration. He came to *Modern* via the same route as Vasnetsov, Polenov and Malyutin. His basic sources were Russian fairy tales, which he interpreted in a very individual manner combining exquisite professionalism and graphic skill with the traditions of popular art, especially *lubki*, the cheap popular prints discussed in earlier chapters. Ornamental forms are dominant in his precise graphic style. The illustration of fairy tales and legends provided him with endless possibilities for stylization, fantastic transformations of reality and the exploitation of all the rich potential of the printing press.

S. Chekhonin, G. Narbut and D. Mitrokhin were younger members of the World of Art group who followed in Bilibin's footsteps and made their own contributions to the field of book illustration. They were not merely illustrators, like Benois, Lansere and Bilibin, but total book designers. Their graphic idiom was more economical, even austere, and less colourful than their predecessors.

Whereas the younger graphic designers of the World of Art made up a distinct subgroup with a common style, the painters were a very diverse set of individuals. Roerich, Kustodiev and Serebryakova were the most remarkable representatives of the World of Art after 1910. Nikolai Roerich (1874–1947) joined the World of Art before the merger with the Moscow Union but it was not until its later years that he played an important role in the Society and even became its leader. He studied at the Academy under Kuindzhi but did not become a

Anna Ostroumova-Lebedeva
*Petersburg, View of the Neva through
Columns of the Stock Exchange* 1908

Mstislav Dobuzhinsky *Man in Glasses*
1905–06

Alexander Golovin *Terrible Playing* 1917

Boris Kustodiev *Merchants' Wives* 1912

Nikolai Roerich *Guests from across the Seas* 1901

professional landscape painter. His favourite subject was ancient history, particularly pre-Christian Rus, a mysterious era of impenetrable secrets. Like his characters, the ancient Slavs, he deified nature, ascribing to it both will and intelligence. He made more use of the symbolic idiom than other members of the group, as for instance in *Heavenly Battle* (1912), where the heavens stand for the dramatic collision of opposing forces. In his figure compositions, instead of focusing on individual characters he preferred to depict human masses taking part in battles or rituals. With time his pictures became increasingly 'Old Russian' and his faces more iconic, inspired by ancient church frescos and totally excluding the academic elements still perceptible in Vasnetsov and Nesterov. His work took on a mystical character as he discovered a passionate interest in the philosophy and timeless enigma of the Orient. This period is unfortunately not within the ambit of our study, although it undoubtedly springs from the early years of the century.

Boris Kustodiev (1878–1927) also turned for inspiration to the national heritage. Opposed to the Western tastes and inclination of some of his colleagues and not in the least nostalgic for a Russia that was gone for ever, he was completely absorbed by contemporary provincial and village life. His world of village fairs, markets and religious festivals with their mellow chimes eclipsed Vasnetsov's and Polenov's folkloric and Ryabushkin's historical worlds. Kustodiev continued the tradition which studied and celebrated the uniqueness of Russian life, but his work is crowded with the characters of his day, the peasants and town dwellers – craftsmen, merchants, dealers, shopkeepers, cabmen, carriers, cooks and labourers – who were creating a new kind of folklore. Like many of his colleagues in the group, he was not averse to irony. He had great affection for his characters, and even idolized them a little, without, however, concealing the gently mocking smile they provoked in him. His idealized world of petty bourgeois Russia is a vivid and convincing one.

Kustodiev began his career in Repin's studio, where a natural and impressionistic style was encouraged, but in the late 1900s he went beyond Impressionism and began to develop his own version of Art Nouveau in which the figures are clearly outlined and the heads are rendered sculpturally, while clothing and other objects are made up of bright, unshaded areas of local colour. Colour is concentrated on the surface of the seemingly hollow volumes to create a kind of mask of colour. His individual style is well illustrated by such paintings as *The Fair* (two versions, 1906 and 1908), *Merchants' Wives* (1912), *The Beauty* (1915), *Moscow Inn* (1916) and *Shrovetide* (two versions, 1916).

Kustodiev made use of his easel-painting experience

Zinaida Serebryakova *In Front of the Mirror* (self-portrait) 1909

in his theatre designs and book illustrations. His designs for *The Flea*, Zamyatin's adaptation of Leskov's famous story *The Lefthander*, are inventive and amusing. Ostrovsky was another playwright whose plays he designed. The mixture of everyday literature, drama and popular humour practised by Ostrovsky and Leskov was very much to his taste.

Zinaida Serebryakova (1884–1967) was a prominent member of the younger World of Art generation. Her originality of style was noticed as soon as she began to exhibit. It is a simple and clear vision of the world, tinged with classicism and the influence of early nineteenth-century Russian painting. Her taste is reflected in her chosen genres – portraits set in interiors, and peasant genre scenes. There was no irony in her interpretation of contemporary life, whose peaceful customary flow she preferred to poeticize.

Russian avantgarde painting was already far advanced when she was in her prime. It is interesting to observe how the World of Art group, which had begun its existence with an outspoken protest against everything that had preceded it, came to an end with sublime and poetic painters like Serebryakova, who seemed removed from the tensions and troubles of their day. She herself stood to one side of the general trend towards the avantgarde, as if personifying the fate of the World of Art Society, which now found itself being pushed aside by other groups and movements.

54, 55

61

5   The 'Blue Rose' Group

A number of pre-avantgarde exhibitions were staged after 1905, including the 'Link', 'Wreath', 'Triangle' and 'Blue Rose'; only the last-named led to the formation of a group of painters, all second generation Symbolists. They were greatly influenced by Borisov-Musatov, the founder of their movement, who sadly died too early to see the birth of the new group.

Viktor Borisov-Musatov (1870–1905) was a contemporary of the older World of Art painters, with whom he shared a contemplative observation of the past, a dreamlike sense of fantasy and a general involvement in the Russian Art Nouveau. His admirers often compared him with the World of Art, and Andrei Bely, for example, wrote verses inspired by themes of both Somov and Borisov-Musatov, but the latter's talents were only appreciated by the group shortly before his death. He was, in fact, very different from this fashionable group and not particularly interested in being accepted by them. There was no hint of irony or theatricality in him, nor the desire to substitute a mask for the human face. Moreover, his painting remained untouched by graphic techniques, although he worked intensively in both fields.

His student days were spent searching for the right school. He tried the Moscow Art College, then the St Petersburg Academy (where he studied under Chistyakov). He moved to Paris in the hope of joining the studio of Puvis de Chavannes, but the old *maître* had by then stopped accepting new students, so Borisov-Musatov had to be content with Cormon; even so, Borisov-Musatov was strongly influenced by Puvis de Chavannes all his life. He returned to Russia in 1898. Quite early on in his career he discovered a taste for French art, unlike the World of Art group, who were more inclined towards Germany. At the beginning of the 1890s he adopted an Impressionist style; some of his paintings from these years recall works by Vuillard, Bonnard and other Nabi artists (although, since this period predated his stay in Paris, he could not have seen such pictures in Russia at the time). Later, the parallel with the Nabi group grew stronger, particularly with Denis.

Borisov-Musatov's Impressionist period continued until the end of the 1890s, when a new style began to show through. For his *Self-portrait with the Artist's Sister* (1898) he chose a two-figure composition in which the brother and sister, unconnected by any action or event, are nevertheless bound together by invisible ties. 59

The portrait was a stepping stone to his mature period and to such paintings as *Gobelins* (1901) and *The Reservoir* (1902). Nothing happens in these two pictures. Each portrays two women, seen at a moment of rest; their poses are unexplained but their souls are in tune with each other and with the surrounding landscape – an ancient park, a reservoir, a building lit up by a ray of sun like a flash of memory. There is another intangible element we can only sense between the lines, not so much in the figures, objects or landscape as in the colourful and spacious atmosphere, which is rich in metaphorical meaning. It is this intangibility which permits us to call Borisov-Musatov's Symbolism pictorial, for the literary element is reduced to a minimum. Since the painting is not an Impressionist or Realist window onto the world, the composition is of a new type (new compared with his Impressionist works), dictated by the painting's symbolic character and constructed according to its own inner laws, laws which guarantee its integrity and organic quality. Borisov-Musatov looks at the scene of *The Reservoir* from several points of view: from one he observes the reservoir itself, from another the figure of the seated girl, from a third the figure of the standing girl. We see not the reality of space but its reflection, if to some extent metaphorically. Dabs of blue, green, white and lilac are distributed over the surface of the canvas without the domination of any one colour. Line is harmoniously integrated with colour in a balanced relationship in spite of the sharpness of the outlines. 60

The picture deviates in some ways from Art Nouveau, whose laws it to some extent infringes. It contains an element of rationalism which is used to convey something understated and intangible and to express the hidden essence of the event. The unconscious is expressed by means of conscious composition, a method employed by Borisov-Musatov in several other paintings.

49　**Filipp Malyavin** *Peasant Women* 1904

50 Abram Arkhipov *On the River Oka* 1890

51 Konstantin Korovin *Winter* 1894

52 Konstantin Korovin *Portrait of a Chorus-girl* 1883

53 **Andrei Ryabushkin** *Seventeenth-century Wedding Procession in Moscow* 1901

54 **Boris Kustodiev** *The Fair* 1906

55 **Boris Kustodiev** *Merchant's Wife* 1915 >

56 **Leon Bakst** *Two Boeotian Girls*, costume designs for Nikolai Cherepnin's ballet, *Narcisse* 1911

58 **Leon Bakst** *The Red Sultana* 1910 >

57 **Alexandre Benois** Sketch for stage design for Stravinsky's *Petrushka* 1911

59   Viktor Borisov-Musatov *Self-portrait with the Artist's Sister* 1898

60   Viktor Borisov-Musatov *The Reservoir* 1902

Viktor Borisov-Musatov *Gobelins* 1901

Viktor Borisov-Musatov *Requiem* 1905

In *Ghosts* (1903) the figures are even more incorporeal and resemble shadows in fog. His earlier Constructivism (almost absent in *Ghosts*) reappears in *Necklace of Emeralds* (1903–04) and *Requiem* (1905). These two scenes are like processions, each with its own meaning. In the former we see a group of young women, whose glittering beauty and rhythmical movement evoke a string of precious stones, in the latter a solemn scene of mourning.

In his later years Borisov-Musatov painted many panels commissioned for specific interiors. Shortly before his death he completed a series of watercolour studies for the murals of a private house, consisting of four horizontal compositions illustrating the seasons. These studies well illustrate his inclination to synthesis and synaesthetics. Borisov-Musatov's later works are particularly musical in quality: he 'leads' the melody through the composition, paying particular attention to rhythmical movements, i.e. the gaps (analogous to caesuras or musical pauses) between the figures and objects, and to the smoothness and softness of the melodic line ('a musical cantilena'). This association with music links him closely with the Nabis. His late pastel drawings, *Hazelnut Bush* and *Autumn Song* (both 1905), with their exquisite gradations of colour, are particularly melodious. Their compositions hint at a return to classical principles in their use of centricity, coulisses and harmonious balance. This reference to classicism was common to many European artists, particularly the Nabis, whom Borisov-Musatov and his pupils much resembled. Almost the only difference between them, in fact, is that the Nabis were at the end of their cycle of development and Borisov-Musatov was just embarking on his.

Other painters beside the Blue Rose group were influenced by Borisov-Musatov, who helped to set the future course of twentieth-century Russian painting. The explanation for this is partly geographical, for he was born and lived in Saratov, a small provincial town on the Lower Volga, and the painters P. Kuznetsov, P. Utkin, M. Saryan, K. Petrov-Vodkin, and the sculptor A. Matveev, also came from Saratov or nearby towns in southern Russia. In their young days they were all in touch with Borisov-Musatov and came under his influence, and an exhibition with the name 'Scarlet Rose', a forerunner of the Blue Rose group, was held in Saratov in 1904. Among the exhibitors were Vrubel, Borisov-Musatov himself and a number of younger painters who later formed the nucleus of the Blue Rose. These younger artists deliberately adhered to the Russian Symbolist tradition and invited a number of Moscow painters (including N. Sapunov, S. Sudeikin and N. Krymov) to join their 1907 Blue Rose exhibition, in which altogether sixteen artists took part. The group remained intact until 1910, showing their work at exhibitions organized by the art and literature journal *The Golden Fleece*, which was published between 1906 and 1909 by N. Ryabushinsky, a painter himself as well as a fabulously rich patron of the arts. Towards the end of the journal's existence two other painters joined the group; they were Larionov and Goncharova, later to be leading members of the Knave of Diamonds. The Golden Fleece group continued the tradition of the World of Art by inviting foreign artists to join their exhibitions.

Pavel Kuznetsov (1878–1968) was probably the most talented of Borisov-Musatov's followers. He moved from Saratov to Moscow, where he studied at the Art College under Serov and Korovin, whose style he adopted at the time. By the mid-1900s he had abandoned Impressionism and was developing an approach of his own. His aim was to 'deconcretize' thoughts and feelings, to give abstract expression to ideas of universal significance and to achieve a kind of syncretism of thought and emotions in which those ideas would be dominant. He was not concerned with specific phenomena of real life; he was a seeker, and a dreamer of unknown dreams. In *Blue Fountain* (1905–06), where various melancholy characters are gathered round the streaming waters of the fountain, the objects and figures lack clear outlines, so that they seem weightless and incorporeal. Kuznetsov remained faithful to his brand of Symbolism, which was the fullest expression of the essence of the Blue Rose movement, until around 1910, when he felt that he had exhausted its potential. He ceased to be a theorist of Symbolism while continuing to practise it in a modified form.

This new period in his career saw the appearance of his finest and best-known paintings, which were based on trans-Volga and Central Asian themes. He was stimulated to discover the Orient by Gauguin, whose retrospective exhibition he admired in Paris in 1906. Unlike Gauguin, however, Kuznetsov was not in search of the exotic – he had been familiar with the world of the nomadic tribes beyond the Volga since his childhood in Saratov, where the steppes come down to the very banks of the great river. These paintings were the expression of those vague yearnings of his earlier days. He was not interested in ethnographic exactitude or the daily life of the peoples he depicted. He was drawn to the spirit of the Orient, which he felt still preserved certain fundamental principles of humanity which had disappeared in the West. He transformed reality by a process of generalization before committing it to his canvas, where he created a whole world (based, as he believed, on natural and primeval laws of existence) out of his Oriental impressions and experiences. A second transformation, on the canvas itself, was realized through harmonies of colour and composition, together with iconographic canons of his own devising.

63

Kuznetsov's 'double transformation' approach excluded the element of coincidence from his choice of objects and their interpretation. In such paintings as *Evening on the Steppe* and *Mirage on the Steppe* (both 1912) the rhythms in the bowed heads and twisted figures unite the characters with a landscape almost devoid of sudden rhythmical contrasts. Similarly, the uniformity of colour in the human and animal figures, the earth and sky, trees and grass – the whole colour harmony of Kuznetsov's world – expresses the homogeneity of all its elements. This harmony is realized in purified form in Kuznetsov's works and thus refers not only to the specific event depicted but to the world in general, which is to be found (in his Oriental paintings) not in the wide horizons or distant views which link the event to the infinite, but in the characters, each of whom comprises a world in himself.

From the mid-1910s he worked in two new genres, still-life and portrait, which required some specific definition of time and place. He did define them but continued to preserve the idea of universality as far as possible. His still-lifes reveal, in addition to the familiar harmonious interpretation of reality, a marvellous vitality in the objects. Typical objects of his still-lifes include sharply-drawn begonia leaves radiating strength, the shiny surfaces of colourful trays and gleaming facets of crystal and glass. The compositions – unlike those of the steppe landscapes – are vertical and usually finished at the top with a dab of intensive colour or a rhythmical stroke. Here, unlike in his other genres, it is the objects themselves which seem to organize space.

Oriental themes continued to preoccupy Kuznetsov throughout the 1910s. His subtle, delicate interpretations, with just a hint of Primitivism, are full of 'realistic symbolism'. Then times changed, and Kuznetsov with them, but his later career, in the 1920s and after, is unfortunately outside the scope of this book.

P.S. Utkin, a colleague of Kuznetsov's, developed along similar lines and shared his symbolist approach. Two others were the brothers N.D. and V.D. Milioti, who practised their own version of symbolism. They too chose themes of fantasy, but were closer to Vrubel than to Borisov-Musatov. In their reinterpretation of Impressionism light acquired a mystical rather than a realistic quality, as if it had detached itself from the objects to assume the form of vortices.

Martiros Saryan (1880–1972) also developed similarly to Kuznetsov, though entirely independently of him. Of Armenian extraction, he was born in Rostov-on-Don and moved to Moscow at the end of the nineteenth century to become a student at the Art College. He began his career as a Realist and then turned for a while to Impressionism. In the mid-1910s he exhibited (with Blue Rose) a series of

Pavel Kuznetsov *Evening on the Steppe* 1912

Pavel Kuznetsov *Sleeping in the Sheepfold* 1912

paintings on themes of Oriental fantasy in traditional Eastern ornamental style. He gradually outgrew this over-elaborate ornamentalism as he began to use long parallel brushstrokes, feathery, light and rapid, sometimes grouped in the shape of a fan. The contrast between the sleepy themes and energetic rhythms of his paintings contains the seed of the synthesis between the general and the particular which Saryan was to achieve in his best works of the 1910s.

They were inspired by his travels in the East – in Turkey, Egypt and Persia. In paintings such as *Constantinople Street: Midday* (1910), *Date Palm: Egypt, Night*

Landscape: Egypt and *Woman Walking* (all 1911) he created laconic but resonant images reminiscent of the couplets and quatrains of Eastern poetry. It was at this time that he formed his own individual style, combining intensity of expression, majestic monumentalism and colourful decorativism with a subtle and lyrical perception of nature. The paintings of Henri Matisse had an important influence on the formation of this new style.

Constantinople Street: Midday, in only two colours, orange and dark blue, gives the impression of direct contact with reality. Frozen in lifeless immobility, the short dark blue shadows of the houses might have been cut with a knife. The figures are pinned to the ground by the relentless midday sun. The angle from which the scene is viewed – from above – adds to the realism. But the symmetry of the composition, an almost heraldic arrangement of right and left, top and bottom, seems to interfere with the actual existence of the people and objects. Transfixed for ever, they turn into symbols of the East itself.

In *Date Palm* Saryan conveyed the unique rhythms of life in the mysterious land of the pyramids. In a still-life entitled *Egyptian Masks* (1912) he scrutinized these faces, which come alive in his hands. Each acquires its own life history and character, and their souls seem to live on in the Egyptian women he met on the streets and immortalized on canvas. He divined aspects of the present in what was ancient and poeticized the great traditions of the Eastern peoples.

Sapunov and Sudeikin, like other members of the Blue Rose, reached their prime in the mid-1910s. After the Blue Rose ceased to exhibit they showed their works successfully with the World of Art group. Both artists were closely associated with experimental theatre design, in which they occasionally collaborated.

Nikolai Sapunov (1880–1912) studied at the Moscow Art College and began to exhibit with the *peredvizhniki* around 1900. His highly individual paintings on musical and theatrical themes, such as *Nocturne, Masquerade* and *Ballet*, began to appear in the mid-1900s. His main genre was to be paintings inspired by theatrical productions he himself had designed. They were full of symbolic significance, particularly *Dance of Death*, after the play by Wedekind (1907), and *Mystical Meeting*, after Blok's lyrical drama *Balaganchik* (1909). *Balaganchik* received its premiere in 1906 and became a seminal event in theatrical life, the product of the talents of four outstand-

Martiros Saryan *Portrait of Ivan Shchukin* 1911

Martiros Saryan *Constantinople Street: Midday* 1910

ing artists: the brilliant Blok, the remarkable experimental director Meyerhold, the composer and poet M. Kuzmin (who wrote the music) and Sapunov, who designed the scenery and costumes. The ghostly atmosphere of the play, its puppet-like acting and grotesque subtext were effectively transformed by Sapunov into a painting whose symbolic character is emphasized by his depiction of a scene within a scene.

Sapunov's use of irony increased with time. Even his luxurious still-lifes are shot through with irony; admiration and mockery force the objective world to lead a double life on the borders of the real and the imaginary. His Primitivism was also emerging at this time. In fact, a World of Art theatricality, his own picturesque leanings and elements of Primitivism, particularly in some versions of *Carousel* and *Tea-drinking*, were always present in his work. In a 1912 version of *Tea-drinking*, for example, frightening faces stare out at us like fantastic monsters; we can hardly make them out through their blurred contours and smudged colours. This Primitivist tendency was unfortunately interrupted by his untimely death (by drowning in the Gulf of Finland). Painters, poets, musicians, critics, actors and all who knew him mourned an original and talented man who turned his own life into a work of art.

Sergei Sudeikin (1882–1946), who was at one time very close to Sapunov, was something of an artistic mischief maker. His trademark was an acute sense of the grotesque spiced with eroticism and a lighthearted buffoonery. He was influenced by Somov and other World of Art admirers of the eighteenth-century French 'gallant' genre (and Watteau in particular) who exploited the paradoxical combination of the absurd and the picturesque. *Poet of the North* is an ironic depiction of a poet of Pushkin's day, posing in fashionable early nineteenth-century dress against a snow-bound Russian village landscape. The irony is underlined by the muse who hovers above his head. This mockery concealed the bitter truth that poetic freedom had never existed in Russia, and perhaps never could.

Sudeikin was a painter of curiosities. He would place a beautiful woman in a tree, holding a harp or lyre like a mythological heroine; or send lovers sailing on some strange reservoir adorned with fountains, waterfalls and ancient statues; or mock the eternal theme of motherhood by showing an older lady, dressed to kill, with a lover half her age reaching for her breast like a baby.

65

Nikolai Sapunov *Still-life with Vases and Flowers* 1910

Nikolai Sapunov *The Green Bull Hotel* 1910

Sergei Sudeikin *Still-life with a China Statuette* 1909–11

Nikolai Krymov *Windy Day* 1908

Nikolai Krymov *Yellow Barn* 1909

Sudeikin's imagination was inexhaustible but his grotesqueries, always containing a hint of aesthetic delicacy, never turned into open Primitivism.

Nikolai Krymov (1854–1958) was a more consistent practitioner of Primitivism. Whereas Sapunov and Sudeikin inclined to the World of Art, Krymov tended towards the Union of Russian Painters and specialized in studies from life. He too experimented with various styles. Within the space of ten years or so he used the 'Gobelins' technique (i.e. a large canvas painted in a gently decorative manner), then tried Primitivism and later, just before the Revolution, was much taken with the classical approach to landscape.

His Primitivist period was perhaps the most fruitful of his long career. Some outstanding examples are *Windy Day* (1908), *Yellow Barn* (1909) and *Cloud* (1910). They draw on primitive and folk art (*lubki*, toys, traditional gingerbread boards and moulds etc) to create a fresh and striking effect, an approach later (particularly in the 1910s) developed by Larionov, Goncharova and other painters of the Knave of Diamonds group.

Georgi Yakulov (1884–1928), while not a formal member of the Blue Rose, shared their approach and particularly an interest in Primitivism. He did not take part in the original Blue Rose exhibition but was invited to join their retrospective exhibition in the 1920s in recognition of their common interests. Unlike most of the Blue Rose artists he was rather inclined to theorize, and formulated a theory of 'multicoloured suns' which resembles Delaunay's 'simultaneity'. He also enjoyed designing interiors of cafés, clubs and settings for parties. After the Revolution he became a noted theatre designer. Yakulov, an Armenian, always tried to combine Oriental and European approaches to painting, and incorporated Chinese and Japanese pictorial and graphic techniques into his own, very individual style.

Kuzma Petrov-Vodkin (1878–1939) cut an independent figure in early twentieth-century Russian art. As a friend of Kuznetsov and Utkin, he might well have joined the Blue Rose if he had been in Russia in 1907 – but he was abroad at the time. On his return to Russia in 1910 he formally joined the World of Art, although he was never intimately involved with the group.

Petrov-Vodkin was born in Khvalinsk, a little provincial town in the south of Russia where he became acquainted with the craft of icon painting. Later his studies took him to St Petersburg and Moscow, where he studied under Serov. He undertook a long journey through Europe and also visited Africa. During these years he was influenced by Puvis de Chavannes, the Nabis, Zodler and the German Symbolists, until in the early 1910s he formed his own style, based on a blend of contemporary Symbolism, Old Russian art, and to a lesser extent the traditions of the Italian Renaissance, Alexander Ivanov and others.

His 1911 painting, *Boys Playing*, portrays the unaccountable cruelty as well as the defencelessness of childhood. He achieved a stark effect by using pure colours and removing the 'accidental' effects of sunlight and impressionistic elements. His most mature painting is *Red Horse Swimming* (1912), which contains many layers of symbolic meaning. It represents the past awakening to the future and the presentiment of that future; the traditional, Old Russian theme of the horse as the hero's faithful friend; and a newly-created myth which persuades us of the reality of the 'red horse'. Petrov-Vodkin here demonstrates his way of thinking through general concepts and categories which cannot be fully decoded or expressed in terms of everyday reality. His pictorial idiom is also far removed from everyday reality, and the colour scheme is based on an unfamiliar harmony of very dissimilar colour qualities.

Kuzma Petrov-Vodkin *Red Horse Swimming* 1912

Kuzma Petrov-Vodkin *Mother* 1913

Kuzma Petrov-Vodkin *Girls on the Volga* 1915

Red Horse Swimming was followed by such master-pieces as *Mother* (1913), *Girls on the Volga* (1915), *Morning: Women Bathing* and *Midday* (both 1917), all echoes of Old Russian painting. In *Girls on the Volga* the spiritual communication between the two central figures is of a quality of which only such biblical characters as Mary and Elisabeth are capable. *Morning* might be Petrov-Vodkin's version of the theme of the 'Presentation of the Blessed Virgin'. In *Midday*, as in a hagiological icon, we see a full sequence of episodes from the character's life, from birth to burial. Petrov-Vodkin also worked in the field of straightforward religious art, painting modern icons, frescos and murals and creating mosaics for churches.

Shortly before the 1917 Revolution he turned to still-life, through which he sought to comprehend the essence of objects and the philosophy of space and mass. As he himself put it, he realized that 'a simple apple lying on the table contained all the secrets of the universe'. His still-lifes illustrate his general Symbolist orientation, but it is a Symbolism of a particular, rather medieval kind. Using a traditional Russian idiom he created a mythology of the modern world described in metaphorical images. He yearned for the purification and renewal of man. These ideas led Petrov-Vodkin to the monumental art of 'large form'. This monumentalism is to be found even in his small still-lifes, in that his objects are ideal, pure and beautiful in their perfection. The idea that each object and component of the picture is valuable in its own right determines the character of the colour scheme, in which the accords are sometimes complex and the contrasts insoluble. He often isolates his colours, as if to emphasize the great value of each fragment of the world. His art is the high point of Russian Symbolism, which originated with Vrubel, continued through Borisov-Musatov and the Blue Rose and culminated in Petrov-Vodkin.

69

6 The 'Knave of Diamonds', the 'Donkey's Tail' and Neoprimitivism

The year 1910 was a turning point in the development of Russian culture. It is generally considered to mark the end of the Symbolist period in poetry, and a number of important events made it a significant year for the arts. The World of Art group was revived, the Golden Fleece staged its last exhibition, the Knave of Diamonds its first, and the Union of Youth was formed in St Petersburg.

The Knave of Diamonds was a more formal association of artists than the Blue Rose. Its first exhibition in 1910 was followed by the official establishment of the group in 1911. It exhibited regularly between 1910 and 1916, then broke up, reappeared after the Revolution and continued its existence for some time under various different names. Following in the World of Art tradition the Knaves invited foreign artists to exhibit, including Matisse, Picasso, Braque, Derain, Van Dongen, Delaunay, Léger, Heckel, Marc, Muenter, Kirchner and Macke. Artists of the Russian avantgarde of the 1910s, such as Malevich, Kandinsky, Chagall, Popova, Udaltsova and Burliuk, also exhibited their works with the Knave of Diamonds, which gave them the opportunity to show the results of their latest artistic experiments. Larionov and Goncharova also joined the group but left it in 1912 to organize a new society called the Donkey's Tail. The nucleus of the Knave of Diamonds consisted of Konchalovsky, Mashkov, Lentulov, Falk, Kuprin and Rozhdestvensky, who were all close friends as well as colleagues.

A few words about the artistic credo of the Knave of Diamonds are in order here. One central element was the negativist position, i.e. the wholesale rejection of all their predecessors and contemporaries – Academists, *peredvizhniki*, Symbolists and World of Art members. The rejection took the form of deliberately provocative works and outspoken mockery of philistine tastes and ideals and all that was old and outmoded. Members of the Knave of Diamonds loved teasing the public – and very effective they were, too. But their negativism went hand in hand with the creation of new art and traditions. They found their inspiration in national folk and primitive art; the term 'primitive' embraced provincial photography, tradesmen's signboards, *lubki* (popular prints) and toys. They were particularly interested in the folklore of the cities, and there was more than a hint of burlesque and the fairground about their first exhibition.[5]

Apart from national sources they were also influenced by German Expressionism and above all by French painting of the turn of the century. Many of the Knaves went to France to study, while others got to know the latest French innovations through works in the private collections of connoisseurs such as Shchukin and Morozov. They were attracted by Cézanne, Matisse and the early Cubists, under whose influence they rediscovered the mass, colour and three-dimensional form of objects and achieved a new synthesis of colour and form. Hence their interest in still-life, which now acquired a greater importance in Russian art than ever before. Landscape and portrait became so much closer to still-life that some critics actually discern a still-life approach to all genres. Divisions between genres began to disappear and no one genre was more important than another. These artists held that each object could express some truth about the world and should be respected not only for its inherent significance but for its plastic qualities.

Pyotr Konchalovsky (1876–1956) was one of the most esteemed leaders of the group. Painting was his lifelong passion. When he was asked what was the most important thing about painting, he replied: 'Painting!' He enjoyed the simple routine of mixing paint and applying it with thick brushstrokes as much as the creative and interpretive aspects of his art. This love of his craft was shared by all his fellow artists in the Knave of Diamonds. Konchalovsky was a little older than the rest of the group. He studied at the St Petersburg Academy of Fine Arts, but was unhappy there and went to France to continue his training. His return to Russia was marked by a fascination with Primitivism, particularly well illustrated in a series of pictures painted during a trip to Spain with his father-in-law, the famous Surikov, in 1910. In *Bullfight* the expressive movements and colours which make up the toy-like figures of the bull and the torero convince us of the danger and bloodiness of this exciting but lethal game. In the same year he painted his famous, highly decorative and unmistakable portrait of the artist Yakulov, depicted as an exotic *flâneur*, dandy and eccentric. Yakulov poses, fashionably dressed, with his collection of

(*left*) **Pyotr Konchalovsky** *Agave* 1916
Ilya Mashkov *Fruit on a Dish. Blue Plums* 1910

swords and pistols in the background. Konchalovsky often entered into a kind of competition with his model, not simply transforming it but directly exploiting its presence on the canvas. Thus in his still-life *Dry Paints* (1913) a bottle label is glued to the canvas; far from destroying the pictorial convention, the label becomes an integral part of the total work of art.

Konchalovsky's wildness of temperament moderated in the mid-1910s as reason began to tame his natural vitality. This change is demonstrated in his still-life *Agave* (1916). The central section is made up, as in his earlier work, of intensely expressive and decorative reds, greens and yellows, but they weaken as they move towards the sides. Those objects spread out on the plane of the painting are balanced by others which are foreshortened towards the background.

62 Ilya Mashkov (1881–1944) was even wilder and more shocking than his friend and colleague Konchalovsky, and deliberately created a world of hyperbole about himself and his art. The fruit on his canvases are sometimes twice life size, the glowing colours of his plums, apples and strawberries are highly exaggerated. His ideas continually evoke fecundity. His preferred genres were still-life, nudes and portraits.

Mashkov studied at the Moscow Art College under Serov, whom he irritated by giving his models green armpits. Even before graduating, he opened his own private art school to prepare budding painters for their entrance examinations. He discovered a style of his own in the late 1900s, when he became one of the founder-members of the Knave of Diamonds. His still-life *Fruit on a Dish. Blue Plums* (1910), a typical product of this period, reveals the unmistakable influence of signboards on his

style. There is a noticeable Primitivism about the painting: objects are exaggerated in size, surrounded by dark outlines and placed on the table with deliberate symmetry to create a circle with a big splash of orange at the centre. Mashkov's aesthetic criteria are deliberately degraded in this painting, but a striking, explosively joyful (yet ironic) and truly artistic image emerges from this highly individual version of Primitivism.

Irony is even more evident in Mashkov's portraits. At the first Knave of Diamonds exhibition he showed a large double portrait of Konchalovsky and himself, dressed as athletes with weights at their feet but standing by a piano, violin in hand. The typical Knave of Diamonds boldness is all too obviously expressed in the mighty figures, huge biceps and heavily muscled legs of these two 'weight-lifters and wrestlers'.

Mashkov often gave traditional portrait forms a grotesque interpretation, as for example in the portrait of himself as a boatman (1911). Russian avantgarde painters often depicted themselves in other guises than that of artists: Tatlin, for example, showed himself as a sailor, Konchalovsky as a hunter, Larionov and Shevchenko as soldiers, Lentulov as a kind of fairground touter. Mashkov's self-portrait evokes a provincial photograph; the misshapen head looks as though it has been inserted into a specially cut-out hole in a fantastically decorated back-drop composed of sea, a ship and a sailing-boat. The static quality of the figure is emphasized, as though it is not sure how to move and can only be put into motion by some mechanical means.

Aristarkh Lentulov (1882–1943) was the boldest experimenter and artistic revolutionary of his circle. He studied for long periods under various teachers with

Ilya Mashkov *Self-portrait* 1911

Aristarkh Lentulov *Peal of Bells: Bell Tower of Ivan the Great* 1915

whom he had little in common. He became close to other avantgarde artists he met at the 'Wreath', 'Link' and 'Contemporary Movements' exhibitions in Moscow, St Petersburg and Kiev. By the time he took part in the first Knave of Diamonds exhibition he had already developed an individual style, though it was to change in the future. He progressed from decorative Expressionism to Cubism, encouraged by his stay in Paris in 1911–12 and his studies with Metzinger and Le Fauconnier at the La Palette Academy. Paris also stimulated his interest in abstract art. In his 1913 landscapes *Asters* and *Samovar*, painted in Kislovodsk (Caucasus), buildings and mountains turn into oblongs and squares, while household objects, flowers and petals, although still easily recognizable, resemble circles and semicircles. His major works of the 1910s dealt with the theme of the city in general and Russian architecture in particular, among them his well-known panels *Moscow* and *St Basil's Cathedral* (both 1913), *Nizhny Novgorod, Peal of Bells: Bell Tower of Ivan the Great, Firmament* (all 1915), *At Iverskaya* (1916) and *Tverskoi Boulevard* (1917). The motif of each is one or more monuments of Old Russian architecture. *Moscow*, for example, contains several: the Red (= beautiful) Gates, St Basil's and the bell tower of Ivan the Great. On the panel they are arranged according to the artist's will rather than as they really are, in order to achieve a greater decorative effect. Lentulov's Moscow is full of beautiful buildings, old and new, enlivened by a festive and exultant atmosphere. The complex Cubist forms of the composition jostle each other to create the

impression of movement and the hum of city life. Incidentally, Lentulov's musical gifts and consequent interest in sound eventually led to his experiments in colour-music after the Revolution.

Most of Lentulov's works of the 1910s are noticeably two-dimensional. His interest in the decorative element led him to concentrate on the plane of the canvas. In 1915 he formulated a method of his own, which he named 'Ornéism', and gave a warning that he would 'punish' any untalented imitators. Ornéism really amounted to decorating the surface of the canvas by glueing bits of various materials to it.

At the end of the 1910s his Ornéism gave way to a more 'constructive' style, when his continuing interest in architectural landscape developed into 'Cézannism'. In a series of pictures painted in 1917 at New Jerusalem (near Moscow) he used only paint and brush and achieved his three-dimensional effects by arranging architectural objects at an angle to the plane. The year of the Revolution caught him at a moment of change, on the threshold of new discoveries.

Robert Falk (1886–1958) occupied a special place among the Knave of Diamonds group. He progressed from the 'Moscow Impressionism' which he imbibed at the Art College to the 'Cézannism-Cubism' of the Knave of Diamonds. At first, like other members of the group, he aimed for decorative expressiveness, making use of planes of colour, sharpening rhythms, distorting objects and figures to transform reality into an imaginary world of his own.

Gradually his style changed and became more philosophical and contemplative. His portrait of the Crimean Tartar poet Midkhad Refatov (1915) illustrates his concept of restrained lyrical Cubism, behind which the true meanings of the forms are concealed. We sense the motif of descending rhythms. The downward movement of the trees and cubic forms of the Crimean houses suggests a kind of unstoppable flow of forms down the figure of the poet, particularly in the folds in his sleeves and the corners of his waistcoat. This flow comes to a stop in the hand which rests on his knee. Refatov's sad, wise eyes accompany the flow, unable to staunch it; his head, too, seems engaged in a vain attempt to counteract the flow. All this makes us the more aware of the weariness of the poet and of the world he inhabits.

Falk possessed the secret of animating matter. His 'plastic and pictorial psychological insight' is applied to man, objects and nature, above all in his still-lifes and landscapes. In the still-lifes, much depends on how the objects are arranged. The space around them either isolates them, or else unites them in a complex whole. In his landscapes, every brushstroke and movement of the forms is put to the service of the theme. In *Crimea:*

(*left*) **Robert Falk** *Crimea: Lombardy Poplar* 1915

(*right*) **Robert Falk** *Portrait of Midkhad Refatov* 1915

(*below*) **Robert Falk** *Landscape with a Sail* 1912

Lombardy Poplar (1915) the expressive power of the image is based on a strong contrast between the mighty tree with its thick crown, and the fine crystalline forms and gentle colours of the background with its alternating reds, pinks and greys of the roofs and walls.

Falk also used the technique of intensifying certain features of the scene depicted. His landscape *Sun. Crimea. Goats* is vibrant and glowing; the southern heat and the brilliance of the Crimean sun are conveyed by the intensity of colour. Calculation and temperament combine to celebrate the union of mind and emotion. Falk used texture differently from his fellow painters. Whereas Lentulov, for example, applied not only paint but various foreign objects, Falk used only mixtures of colour which became more complex as time went on, so that in his later work he applied many layers of paint to the canvas in order to augment the expressive effect. Falk continued to develop after the 1910s; indeed he was probably the only member of the Knave of Diamonds whose work not only did not suffer in quality but actually improved after the Revolution.

Alexander Kuprin (1880–1960) combined a lyrical talent – which he shared with Falk – with a penchant for experiment. He used a limited number of themes and subjects but constantly looked for new ways to depict them. He usually painted landscapes (mainly Crimean) and still-lifes with crockery or artificial flowers. His experimental work explored three problems in particular: how to unite space with the pictorial plane; destroying illusory three-dimensionality; and merging colour with form. The rhythms of his still-lifes are less broad and energetic and more restrained than, for example, Mashkov's.

Vasily Rozhdestvensky (1884–1963) was as restrained as Kuprin. He was at his best in paintings where the object had a particularly delicate texture and complex structure (for example, still-lifes with cut glass).

However great the differences between Konchalovsky and Mashkov, Lentulov and Kuprin, Rozhdestvensky and Falk, they were all part of the same movement. There were other painters, who, while not formal members of the Knave of Diamonds, nevertheless shared many of its concerns. These included N.I. Altman (we may recall his brilliant portrait of Anna Akhmatova); D.P. Shterenberg, who painted elegant and economical still-lifes based on combinations of simple lines and

68

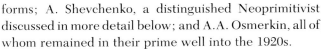

forms; A. Shevchenko, a distinguished Neoprimitivist discussed in more detail below; and A.A. Osmerkin, all of whom remained in their prime well into the 1920s.

Although Mikhail Larionov and Natalia Goncharova were among the founders of the Knave of Diamonds they were not truly typical of its mainstream; they were leaders and creators by nature, and too individual to brook competition. This was particularly true of Larionov, an energetic organizer as well as an outstandingly gifted painter who aspired to the leadership of Russian avantgarde painting. He staged four exhibitions, namely the 'Knave of Diamonds' (of which he considered himself the driving force), the 'Donkey's Tail' (1912), 'Target' (1913) and finally '4' (1914), whose title is self-explanatory. Larionov and Goncharova were far more than organizers, however; their crucial contribution to Russian art was the essential role they played in the establishment of Neoprimitivism, of which they were the earliest and principal practitioners.

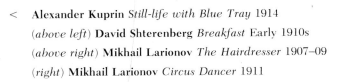

<   **Alexander Kuprin** *Still-life with Blue Tray* 1914
(*above left*) **David Shterenberg** *Breakfast* Early 1910s
(*above right*) **Mikhail Larionov** *The Hairdresser* 1907–09
(*right*) **Mikhail Larionov** *Circus Dancer* 1911

Russian Neoprimitivism was rooted in national traditions but greatly influenced by early twentieth-century French painters (particularly the Fauves) and by German Expressionism (the Brücke and Blaue Reiter groups). Chronologically, Russian Neoprimitivism coincided with German Expressionism: born in 1906–07, it was at its height between 1910 and 1913 but later occupied a less important place in the avantgarde movement.

In the Donkey's Tail and the Target manifestos, as well as in a speech by S. Bobrov at the second Congress of Russian Painters and various articles and interviews, the Neoprimitivists proclaimed their determination to follow in the national artistic traditions. They considered the East to be the cradle of all the artistic values which were later adopted by the West. The term 'East' embraced a very broad spectrum, including, for example, the whole of the Russian empire. It was this bias towards the national which led to Larionov's and Goncharova's break with the Knave of Diamonds. It had become too slavishly devoted, in their opinion, to French painting. It should be noted, however, that Larionov never renounced the influences of French painting in his own work, and to that extent his complaints were unfair. All the same, the factor which differentiated *Russian* Neoprimitivism from German Expressionism and from the French Symbolists, Cubists and Fauves was its overwhelming emphasis on the national artistic heritage. The Germans and French divided their loyalty between their national, primitive and exotic traditions.

Another characteristic of the Russian Neoprimitives was their incidental continuation of the traditions of nineteenth-century Russian art, especially its detailed treatment of themes and its fascination with real, everyday life. Larionov, Goncharova, Chagall, Shevchenko and Malevich all made extensive use of genre themes during their Primitivist periods. Perhaps the most important distinguishing feature of Russian Neoprimitivism was the fact that it constituted an independent movement, whereas in other countries the style was just a part of Expressionism, Cubism or Fauvism.

We have already mentioned that the Neoprimitive tendencies present in the World of Art and Blue Rose groups were continued by the Knave of Diamonds (particularly in its earlier days). They reached their culmination in the Donkey's Tail, in which Neoprimitivism itself achieved an independent existence.

Mikhail Larionov (1881–1964), the undoubted leader and progenitor of Neoprimitivism, occupied a unique place among his colleagues in the avantgarde thanks to his exceptional talents, which combined the explosive energy of the experimenter with an acute and instinctive understanding of pictorial harmony. His early period, coinciding with his studies at the Moscow Art College,

was brilliantly Impressionistic. His favourite themes included secluded corners of gardens, bushes and trees depicted in various light conditions and times of day. His attention to fine gradations of colour demanded a particularly careful treatment of the surface of the canvas, a technique which was to remain with him for the rest of his career. It is discernible even in his later Primitivist paintings, however crude they may appear at first glance.

Larionov began his Neoprimitive period with the provincial scenes so familiar to him from childhood. (He was born in a small town in southern Russia.) These early works are primarily descriptive, featuring various aspects of provincial street life and typical provincial characters such as would-be dandies waiting for their girlfriends, waiters, and girls selling cold drinks. These were followed by the 'Hairdresser' series, one of the most original examples of Russian Neoprimitive fantasy, which revealed Larionov's powers of observation and his deep insight into the ways of his fellow men.

Officer at the Hairdresser's (1909) is a masterpiece. It is a kind of imitation of a provincial signboard in which both characters behave as prescribed by their public and professional status. The client, with his hand resting on his sword and his chest puffed out, admires himself in the mirror. The barber, displaying the tools of his trade – huge scissors, hand-towel and comb – bows in the customary way as he attends to his duties. There is a deliberate use of elements of folk art, seen particularly in Larionov's emphasis on the typical and in the affectionate game he plays with his characters, depersonalizing them to the point where any of us – including the painter – may imagine himself in their place.

Larionov continued this tendency to identify himself with his depersonalized characters in his next major work, the 'Soldier' series. These paintings recall his army days and his familiarity with the soldier's life. Masterpieces such as *Soldiers* (c. 1910), *Soldier on Horseback, Seated Soldier, Morning in the Barracks* (all 1910) and *Soldier Resting* (1911) illustrate his fondly ironical treatment of his characters.

The *Soldier on Horseback* is so toy-like he is unable to move, and Larionov deliberately placed a large tree stump under the front legs of the shying horse to prevent the horse going forward. The tension in the soldier's eyes, hands and figure, the horse's almost human expression of meekness, even the motif of arrested movement are all borrowed from the craft of carved wooden toys. *Soldier Resting* is a marvellously precise description of a conscript almost at the end of his term of service; his behaviour is best illustrated by a well-known Russian saying which might be rendered as 'Sleep, soldier – you'll soon be back in civvy street'.

72

61 **Zinaida Serebryakova** *Bath House* 1912

62 Ilya Mashkov
*Portrait of a Boy in
an Embroidered Shirt* 1909

63 Pavel Kuznetsov
Still-life with Tapestry
1913

64   **Pyotr Konchalovsky** *Portrait of G. Yakulov* 1910

65 **Nikolai Sapunov** *Tea-drinking* 1912

66 **Robert Falk** *Portrait of an Unknown Man* 1915–17

67 **Aristarkh Lentulov** *Tverskoi Boulevard* 1917

68　**Nathan Altman** *Portrait of Anna Akhmatova* 1914

69 Kuzma Petrov-Vodkin *Morning: Women Bathing* 1917

The pictorial idiom became even simpler during Larionov's last Neoprimitivist phase, as for example in his many versions of 'Venus' and 'Seasons' (1912). In the 'Seasons' series, large canvases are divided into separate areas devoted to the picture, the text and the symbolic signs. At first glance they seem crude and amateurish, but closer examination reveals a pictorial boldness and sureness of aim as unmistakable as it is difficult to put into words. The brushstrokes of his earlier painting are replaced by large patches of colour, which retain the complex fluctuations of tone to be found even in his earliest, Impressionist work.

Larionov increasingly resorted to popular folk themes to shock the public. His 'soldier' style gave way to a kind of graffiti manner, sometimes including four-letter words, in which the sublime and the degraded were given equal treatment. He also turned to abstract painting and devised his own method which he called *Luchism*, from the Russian word *luch*, meaning 'ray', and usually translated as Rayonism. In 1913 he published his manifesto, also entitled *Luchism*, although he probably began to experiment with the technique two years earlier. According to this theory, Rayonist painting was based on the recreation of spatial forms obtained as a result of 'the crossing of reflected rays from various objects'. There were, therefore, two versions of Rayonism, one realist, the other abstract. They were not dissimilar, but the essential condition of the first, namely the recognizability of the object undergoing Rayonist treatment, was absent in the second. In both cases, however, the power of Rayonist paintings derives from their harmonious combination of lines with dabs of colour and from the expressiveness of the texture. For this reason it is sometimes said that Larionov's Rayonism is an echo of Impressionism.

The Rayonist *Cockerel* (1912) was shown under the title *Cock and Hen* (dated '1911') at the Donkey's Tail exhibition. With a little guesswork both the object and the event can be recognized. (Requiring the observer to guess was not an original ploy; Vrubel and other predecessors of Larionov had done the same.) Larionov's picture speaks to us at both the objective and the abstract level. The noisy flapping of the cockerel's wings, and its claws dug into the hen with her head bowed, are clear and vivid signposts to the meaning of the painting. By concentrating red in the lower left corner, where the cockerel's comb glows bright, Larionov creates an energetic surge of 'rays' which ascend towards the upper frame and then turn down again. This whole rhythmical movement both symbolizes the event and is pictorially and plastically expressive in its own right. It is a perfect example of colour harmonization. The deepest shade of red gradually weakens as it moves, at first mixed with yellow

(though remaining dominant), then acquiring some white, and later brown and green. The mixtures become progressively more complex; at the lower right, where the rays descend, they are pink, a cold shade which has the effect of calming and slowing down movement. But this border dividing 'energy' from 'rest' and 'beginning' from 'end' in the lower part of the canvas is flexible and easily crossed. The whole surface of the picture has a wonderful integrity, reminiscent of the traditional classical painting Larionov studied early in his career. He was to continue the search for pictorial harmony in his later career.

Larionov's influence on other painters was immense, though hardly greater than that of his wife and colleague Natalia Goncharova (1881–1962). She did adopt her husband's Rayonism, but also had stylistic inclinations of her own – Futurism, for example – which she did not share with him.

Goncharova's artistic development was similar to Larionov's. In her early period, however, which extended into the mid-1900s, when she was working mainly in pastels, she was closer to the Nabis than to the Impressionists. This was followed by a Primitivist period, which yielded to Rayonism and Futurism in 1912–13. Her Primitivism was of a very individual kind. Her favourite themes included peasants at work and biblical scenes; thus she added icons to the usual sources – *lubki*, toys, signboards etc – of Neoprimitivist inspiration. The presence of biblical themes and her tense, broken painting technique places her closer than Larionov to German Expressionism. She was attracted to austere images redolent of a dimly remembered past. She painted still-lifes using Scythian women as models, and the clumsy gestures and petrified frenzy of her peasants, for all their modern dress, evoke their ancient archetypes. All these features of her art link her with Russian Futurist poetry, and particularly to Khlebnikov.

Goncharova's tetraptych *Evangelists* (1910) is the finest of her biblical paintings. It consists of four standing figures, each occupying its own section of canvas. For all the clumsiness of their big hands and feet, their striking concentration and grim severity recall the prophets of fifteenth- and sixteenth-century Russian icons as well as Dürer's *Apostles*. Another example of her creative use of the religious theme is her lithographic cycle entitled *Mystical Images of War*, interpreted as a contemporary Apocalypse. It is full of a dramatic tension born of her prophetic vision of the future.

Her favourite peasant themes included potato gathering and fruit picking, linen washing and brushwood collecting, mowers going off to work and peasant women dancing the *khorovod* (a traditional Slavonic round dance). The actions depicted are always simple and

70

Mikhail Larionov *Cockerel* 1912

Natalia Goncharova *Aeroplane above a Train* 1913

straightforward, without conflict or violence, but they possess a certain dramatic quality, resulting, perhaps, from Goncharova's distinctive treatment of her characters' heads and figures. Her peasant women have the air of stone idols, their movements fixed at some moment in time and petrified for ever. The most ordinary events seem momentarily transformed into sacred rituals to be conducted with reverence and an atmosphere of spirituality.

Goncharova's style is more decorative than Larionov's. She revels in the sonorities of colour and strengthens her contours with thick dark lines. Her compositions often breach true spatial perspective, with background figures placed high in the picture (rather than in the distance), which also increases decorativeness. This heightened expressiveness does not, however, disturb the harmony of colour and composition, which are always handled with care and tact.

In the early 1910s Goncharova, like Larionov and many others, devoted herself largely to lithographic book illustration of works by Khlebnikov, Kruchenykh and Bobrov, and, together with some of her colleagues, created a new type of book, handwritten and illustrated on lithographic stone. Although this collaborative work brought painters and Futurist poets together it did little to

Natalia Goncharova *Evangelists* (Tetraptych) 1910

Natalia Goncharova *Round Dance* 1910

David Burliuk *Portrait of the Futurist and Singer Warrior Vasily Kamensky* 1916

Alexander Shevchenko *Musicians* 1913

spread Futurism into painting as a whole; Goncharova herself, however, was greatly influenced by these writers. 1913 saw the appearance of her Futurist works, *Factory, Cyclist, Station* and *Aeroplane above a Train*, all reminiscent of certain Italian painters of the time, but Goncharova, unlike some of her contemporaries, never made a cult of modern technology.

In the mid-1910s she conceived a passion for the theatre. She became a great innovator in the field of theatrical design, though unfortunately not in Russia. In 1914 Larionov was shell-shocked at the front and demobilized. The couple went abroad and eventually settled down permanently in Paris for the last phase of their artistic careers.

David Burliuk (1882–1967) was one of those Neo-primitives who never exhibited with the Donkey's Tail or Target and had little in common with Larionov. He was, however, one of the founders of the Knave of Diamonds and a very active participant in the avantgarde movement both as painter and poet. His work combined the most modern techniques of contemporary and Western European art with a traditional, impressionistic vision of nature, but Neoprimitivism remained its most prominent feature. While his distinctive habit of distorting figures and objects is not always convincing or justified, we cannot deny the richness of an imagination which filled his canvases with extraordinary scenes and wonderful detail.

Of all the artists exhibiting with the Donkey's Tail and Target Alexander Shevchenko (1883–1948) was the most productive in the years before the Revolution. He studied in Moscow and Paris, where he became familiar with the latest artistic techniques and joined forces with the Moscow Neoprimitive community. His preferred themes were soldiers, wandering musicians, caretakers and circus riders as well as artists and poets. His work varies from the thoroughgoing Primitive to carefully organized paintings in the style of Gleizes and Metzinger. They include *Portrait of a Poet* and the almost square canvas *Musicians* (both 1913). Still-life was another of his favourite genres. Shevchenko could have moved just as easily among the artists of the Knave of Diamonds, although in some of his work he made use of Rayonism and moved very close to abstraction.

Other members of the Donkey's Tail were A. Fonvizin, who began his career in the Blue Rose, continued it in the Knave of Diamonds and eventually joined Larionov; M.V. Le Dantiu (a champion of the Georgian painter Pirosmanashvili); and V. Chekrigin and S. Romanovich, both in their prime during the 1920s, when many former members of the Donkey's Tail established a new society by the name of Makovets, which retained certain intangible resemblances to Larionov.

7   The Avantgarde

Russian avantgarde painting began with the Knave of Diamonds, Goncharova and particularly Larionov, a true avantgarde artist and brilliant organizer, always in search of new ideas, who gathered around him such great artists as Tatlin and Malevich. Goncharova and Larionov also forged links with the Blaue Reiter group in Munich and the Union of Youth in St Petersburg. Also at this time, David Burliuk was actively involved in an attempt to draw avantgarde poets and painters closer together.

The avantgarde movement of the early 1910s is known by the name 'Cubo-Futurism'. This term was used for a short time in France but, in spite of its imprecision, had a longer currency in Russia. This imprecision is due partly to the fact that Cubism and Futurism were to some extent antagonistic, and partly because Futurism never really took root in Russia. Nevertheless, the term 'Cubo-Futurism' was very convenient, since it embraced Futurist poets as well as Cubist painters. The Cubo-Futurist group also included painters who did not practise Cubism and were closer to Expressionism.

The general picture, therefore, is rather confused; to clarify it we must examine the main tendencies and internal movements within the avantgarde. One was connected with the Expressionistic approach, the other with Cubo-Constructivism. The former was more fragmented and its chief representatives, Marc Chagall, Pavel Filonov and Vasily Kandinsky, actually had little in common. The latter was somewhat more united, and its main driving forces, Kazimir Malevich and Vladimir Tatlin, gathered a close group of followers around them. It should be noted, however, that the artists themselves denied any such affiliations; Chagall and Filonov, for example, insisted that they had no connection with Expressionism. The art historian is, of course, entitled to disagree with his subject, but in this case it must be conceded that the truth lies mainly with the painters. Both Chagall and Filonov were, indeed, unique artists unlike any of the Expressionists, even though they were undoubtedly influenced by Expressionism as a whole.

Marc Chagall (1887–1985), although the youngest of the group of avantgarde painters of the 1910s, was the most traditional, and avoided the provocative acts and manifestos associated with the avantgarde. He was born near Vitebsk within the Pale of Settlement (the area to which Jews were confined in Tsarist Russia) where he grew up in a traditional religious family. There was nothing in his early life to indicate his future fame, but his life took a dramatic turn, and within two or three years, thanks to his irrepressible talent and general good fortune, he found himself among the most brilliant artists and sophisticated art lovers of his day. In Vitebsk he studied under the Byelorussian painter I. Pen, but he took the first step into his new life when he moved to St Petersburg and the private studio organized by E. Zvantseva, where his teachers were Bakst and Dobuzhinsky. He soon moved again, this time to Paris (in 1910), where he was befriended by Guillaume Apollinaire. The change from his native backwater to two world capitals was a kind of miracle, but Chagall, with his ability to harmonize near and far, small and great, accepted it as natural. From the very beginning he devoted his art to the eternal themes of birth, death, love, joy, good and evil. He easily transferred to the great metropolis all the oddities of life and traditions of a religious Jewish family in Vitebsk. They were the source of his inspiration.

His career may be divided into several periods. The first lasted until the early 1910s, when he moved to Paris. His interior scenes dating from this time are very expressive; chairs are misshapen, figures at the table are frozen into absurd and twisted poses; tension seems poised to explode into catastrophe. His second period is marked by a new maturity and calm. His images are based on a complex amalgam of visionary fantasies, personal and folk memories, Jewish ritual and folklore, sublime dreams, a naive perception of the world and childlike anxieties and forebodings. These ingredients combined with Chagall's marvellous artistry to produce a universe of his own.

One illustration of this mature period is *I and the Village* (1911). Its spontaneous and expressionistic view of the world is blended with elements of Cubism; this internal contradiction itself increases the very absurdity on which Chagall's world is based. In addition, the fragmentation of time indicates the influence of

Marc Chagall *Promenade* 1917–18

Marc Chagall *Over the Town* 1914–18   >

Futurism. These components – Cubism, Expressionism and Futurism – acquire new meanings in this painting, primarily because his world exists in a kind of new dimension, like all the pictures Chagall painted in Paris between 1910 and 1914, and later in Russia. Some of the best are *Blue Lovers* (1914), *Green Lovers* (after 1914), *Over the Town* (1914–18), *Window in a Dacha* (1915), *Self-portrait with Muse* (1917–18) and *Promenade* (1917–18).

74

Chagall's unbridled imagination is no artificial device intended to shock. The behaviour of the flying lovers does not strike us as miraculous; all such activity is justified by his peculiar 'mythology of the everyday'. Chagall is uniquely able to interweave memories and dreams, preserving their every detail, however minute and intimate, and uniting them with the vast and eternal. His characters, their actions and the objects surrounding them, exist in their own separate scales of time and space. The inner meanings and symbolism of the various episodes and scenes are juxtaposed and compared, and the observer uses the process of association to understand them and the painter's intentions in juxtaposing them as he does. Thus Chagall's work cannot be described as fairy-tale, genre or Neoprimitivism, which all have a complete narrative structure. It contains some elements of Neoprimitivism, although Chagall never borrowed directly from folk art (like Larionov and Goncharova) and cannot be considered a typical Neoprimitive.

Chagall's 'symbolism of the everyday' determined the character of his compositions and use of colour. The position of each figure, detail and episode is individually dictated by its own symbolic significance as well as by the structure of the whole work. *Promenade*, for example, depicts the fantastic flight of Bella (Chagall's wife) in a wide open sky which seems specially intended for flying; but she is linked with the earth by the hand and figure of Chagall himself. The main compositional lines and areas of colour correspond with each other, the corners are strong and the diagonal movements are in balance, but this harmony appears mobile, fragile and unstable, like the flight itself and the characters' facial expressions, which are at once joyful and anxious. The intensified lilac, red and green emphasize a surrealistic aspect, but the balance of colour renders the unnatural natural; this transformation is at the heart of the meaning behind the painting.

The mid-1910s were of particular significance for Chagall in shaping his future career, method and style.

He returned from Paris to Vitebsk and his family – the original sources of his inspiration. Here he gathered the material which was to provide him with ideas, forms and detail for the rest of his life. Sometimes he put fantasy to one side and depicted simply what he saw. Even so, his objects were transformed; Chagall was able to penetrate their concealed inner meaning, and his agitated, trembling soul radiantly illuminated everything within them that was significant to mankind. *The Clocks, Hens* and *Soldiers* all date from this period. In his later years he revived these themes and interpreted them surrealistically, preserving these impressions of his youth to the end of his very long life.

Chagall's experience highlights one of the features common to all Russian avantgarde painters, namely their transformation of the impressions awakened in them by reality. Chagall never abandoned the narrative element, and it played an important role in the careers of all of them.

Pavel Filonov (1883–1941) stood near the mighty stream of European Expressionism but retained a very individual style. He was a child of his time, no less than Chagall. He lost his parents at a very early age; from his childhood on he struggled with poverty and was obliged to earn his own living. At the turn of the century he moved from Moscow to St Petersburg, where he became a pupil at the private studio of L.E. Dmitriev Kavkasky, and later at the Academy of Fine Arts, from which he was soon expelled for rebelling against the Academy's rigid rules. These years formed him as an artist. In 1911 he joined the Union of Youth and three years later published his artistic manifesto entitled *'Finished Pictures', the Intimate Studio of Painters and Draughtsmen.*

The most productive years of Filonov's pre-revolutionary career were between 1912 and 1915, after which he was called to military service and spent several years fighting on the Romanian front. This period saw the appearance of some of his best early work, for example *West and East* and *East and West* (both 1912–13), *Feast of Kings* (1913), *Man and Woman, Shrovetide Carnival* (both 1913–14), *Dairymaids, Peasant Family* (both 1914) and *Victor of the City* (1914–15). Filonov's creative approach, first expressed in his manifesto, was later developed in his theory of 'analytic art', according to which the artist should devote all his own inner tension and skill to every tiny section of the canvas, beginning with a profound pictorial analysis of the particular, then combine all the individual elements into the general, and

76

Pavel Filonov *Dairymaids* 1914

eventually take the whole to the 'finished stage'. Filonov used this term to replace what he considered the outmoded concept of the creative process.

Filonov was a unique phenomenon in Russian art. Unlike Malevich or Tatlin, for example, he had no collaborators during the period when he was developing his artistic method. On the other hand, he did draw on the traditions of Bosch and Breughel, and in the 1920s and 1930s influenced many of the pupils who surrounded him. It was inevitable that someone like Filonov would appear on the horizon of Russian art in the 1910s; his art linked him with those crucial events in national life – wars and revolutions – which so drastically transformed the fate of Russia. These dramatic historical changes gave contemporary artists the feeling that they were part of a global process in the development of mankind and inspired them to look into the future while casting an analytical eye over the past. Thus Filonov's approach is Futuristic (though closer to literary than to pictorial Futurism) and at the same time inseparable from all the Russian culture of the past.

Filonov developed out of Symbolism. Symbolism never relies on external appearances but seeks the meaning of things in their depths, beyond some barrier separating essence from appearance. Similarly, Filonov's images are never born at the point of contact, literal or figurative, with the surfaces of the objects, etc, which they represent. From the literal point of view, he shows the bones and muscles of his figures as if skinning them, creating a kind of 'écorché' effect, wrenches away the plaster from house walls to reveal the bare stone, and pulls the bark from trees. From the figurative point of view, the paintings' symbolic language, realized in metaphor, symbol and sign, reveals a greater historical perspective than that of the Symbolists of the turn of the

century. His fish always signify Christ, his trees are the tree of life, his boats are Noah's Ark, his men and women are the naked Adam and Eve standing before the world and all history, past and future. However specific Filonov's intention may be, his images contain many layers of meaning, which demand an equally rich and generous variety of response.

The same may be said of the *Modern*, or Russian Art Nouveau, style, which saw the meaning of existence in life's elemental manifestations, in the thirst for self-renewal and the expression of the instinct for life. All this applies to Filonov, although on the surface his painting hardly reminds us of *Modern*. It is especially true of his symbioses – those animal-like people, and that animal world where animals are like people; and of a kind of common level of existence, created by Filonov, inhabited by every living thing, where faces are petrified and stones are brought to life, where the world consists of live, primeval particles and matter is made up of pulsating molecules with a living, sculptural form. Filonov's working method itself reveals his predilection for a peculiar kind of spontaneous movement of forms. Sometimes, beginning a painting from one or other edge, he enlivens his forms, so to speak, with his own creative charge; then they seem to grow, develop and renew themselves according to their own, rather than the artist's will. The downright, 'biological' nature of his art overwhelms even the vitalism of Art Nouveau and Expressionism, especially in the miraculous way his paintings convince us of the reality of such growth. This objectivity, which differentiates Filonov from most of his contemporaries, is in distinct contrast to both the refined subjectivism of Art Nouveau and the tragic character of Expressionism.

Another aspect of Filonov's originality is his interpretation of time. Whereas avantgarde painters arrest time by creating the effect of a state of inaction or pause in the way they depict their characters, in Expressionism time may be described as 'open', emphasized and concentrated in an impulse. Filonov's time is epic and mythologized. It seems to freeze after a man and a woman are paralysed in inhuman poses; or after water, stopped in mid-movement, is turned to the ice binding the 'ship of life' sailing into the 'blossoming of the world'; or after the dagger, poised above the victim, has fixed the eternal moment between life and death for ever. The relative nature of time, the violation of concrete time and trespass beyond its limits – these are all characteristic of Filonov's work. But there is yet another aspect. A kind of general conception of time arises from our observation of Filonov's pictures. It is not an historical (there are no traces of specific eras in his work) but a super-historical time, which unites the remote past with the present and future. Medieval theologians might well have described it as

Pavel Filonov *Shrovetide Carnival* 1913–14

'apocalyptic' time or the time after the Last Judgment. A twentieth-century philosopher or physicist would call it the fourth dimension. Minkovsky, Khonton and Uspensky – noted scholars of our day – insist on the oneness of the past, present and future. They claim that everything is contained within the universe, for which past and present do not exist and which is itself the eternal present. Filonov's time, too, is beyond absolute points of measurement, for his universe exists in a special dimension of its own.

Vasily Kandinsky (1866–1944) was the only painter of the Russian avantgarde whom we may, with complete confidence, class as an Expressionist. He cannot, in fact, be described simply as a Russian painter, because he spent only the very early part of his career and, later, about ten years from the mid-1910s, in Russia itself. Chagall's Russian period, of course, was also short, but Kandinsky's roots make him as much a German as a Russian painter. Scholars detect the influence of Goethe's

theory of colours, Schelling's philosophy, Worringer's art criticism and Stefan George's poetry in Kandinsky's theory and practice. Early on in his career, at the turn of the century, he was influenced by the Azbé school (which preserved a large measure of Academism and a hint of Impressionism), by the Munich Jugendstil and Symbolism (particularly the architect Endel and two painters, Stuck and Holzel) and by the Old German Primitives. His Russian sources of inspiration included religious *lubki*, various forms of folk art (he was interested in ethnography), Russian Symbolists, Borisov-Musatov and the World of Art painters – Somov, Dobuzhinsky and especially Bilibin, with his Old Russian themes. Kandinsky's *plein air* studies dating from the 1900s remind us of the restrained Impressionism of the Union of Russian Painters. To this list may be added European Art Nouveau and the French Fauves.

By about 1910 Kandinsky had matured as an artist and had developed theoretical views. He formulated his guiding principles in a book entitled *On the Spiritual in*

Vasily Kandinsky *The Lake* 1910

Art, written in 1910, quoted by Kulbin at the Second Congress of Russian Painters at the end of 1911 and published in full in 1912. He also published two articles at around this time, namely 'Content and Form' (in the catalogue to the second exhibition of the Izdebsky Salon) and 'On the Problem of Form' (in the almanac of the Blaue Reiter). Unlike most Russian avantgarde artists, who used their manifestos to expound futuristic ideas deliberately intended to shock, Kandinsky expressed his theories in traditional scientific form. In spite of his very intuitive approach to painting, theory was inseparable from practice in his work; in combination they created new artistic principles and opened up unlimited horizons.

Kandinsky's most important and challenging task was to find new forms in which to express the spiritual element. These forms must be freed from all material trappings, which he identified with the representational world of objects. This could only be achieved by bold exploration of a new dimension. For some time he interpreted reality abstractly and 'encoded' his objects into a non-objective language while leaving a bridge between the objective and abstract worlds. It was not that he lacked the daring to abandon material representation, nor that he wished to offer the observer some help in decoding the puzzle. It had nothing to do with the observer and everything with the evolution of Kandinsky's own understanding of art. He needed the abstract world to seem just as natural and organic to him as the world of objects had been hitherto. The former links between real objects had to be replaced with new relationships between pure expressions of emotion and of spiritual ideas, expressions based on the possibilities

provided by abstract forms, lines and colours. In this situation the laws of artistic creation (which are in any case different from the general laws of nature) found their ultimate expression. Whereas this difference was hardly noticeable in representational art, it became absolute in abstract art. The essence of Kandinsky's artistic evolution is to be found in this movement towards the absolute.

At first he sought a balance (between the real and the abstract) in which the inherent laws of the artistic image could be realized, a balance he did not fully achieve. Then, distancing himself from the outer appearance of objects, he kept control over the new-found unity of real and abstract by preserving some traces of that outer appearance. Only after this did he finally abandon every trace of objective reality. This process (uneven, hesitant, and often more of a tendency than a *fait accompli*) was possible because art, whether abstract or otherwise, is subject to certain general laws. For Kandinsky a work of art, like the universe, was born of an act of creation, catastrophe and miracle, and although he saw the aims of art and nature as opposed, these general laws of creation were common to both.

Kandinsky's career took a crucial turn in the late 1900s when he painted the Murnau landscapes which first revealed his desire to unleash the non-figurative potential of painting. The outlines of his roofs and towers, trees and hills, could not contain the unbroken flow of colour boldly sweeping over every 'objective' obstacle. Relationships between zones of colour sprang up almost without reference to their 'objective' purpose. Areas of colour became the most important elements of the colour composition; later they were to play a crucial role in Kandinsky's opposition to the 'geometrical' tendency in abstract painting.

Round about 1910 he painted a number of works which may be described as semi-abstract. *The Lake*, for example, contains both abstract and objective elements. We can make out the boat, the rowers, their oars and the church's silhouette easily enough. As for the rest of the composition, it is up to us to guess its meaning. Thus, we may take the blue stripes for water; other stripes, at the upper part of the painting, may signify sky. Alternatively, we may divorce these areas of colour from any particular natural phenomenon. Colour itself becomes independent. At the centre of the painting Kandinsky creates a kind of explosion which charges the whole canvas with energy. The white boats, gliding above the black abyss, seem to be illuminated by the light emanating from this explosion. The water appears as fathomless space while the sky, with its gleaming patches of light, resembles water. The act of perception, like the act of creation, is linked, for Kandinsky, with the ability to pick out and

Vasily Kandinsky *Composition No. 7* 1913

recognize the object, and then to re-immerse it into non-existence.

Although 1910 also saw the appearance of his first abstract watercolour, many of his 'Improvisations' and 'Compositions' (1910–12 and later) preserve links with the world of real objects. Recognizable details are usually distributed all over the canvas, revealing many layers of meaning which awaken various associations. As modern studies have shown,[6] many of these associations are derived from apocalyptic motifs – trumpets, collapsing towers, galloping horses and city silhouettes. Even those paintings which the observer might consider totally abstract contain a mild representational subtext. Nevertheless, the main content is expressed by purely pictorial techniques of colour and composition, namely the particular potentials offered by patches of pure or mixed colour and lines. Some of the best examples of this new method are his large canvases *Composition No. 6* and *Composition No. 7* (both 1913). They are almost the same size but differ in their content and manner of realization. Each is a 'composition' in the full meaning of the word – i.e. a form actively desired, even dreamed of, by Kandinsky. At long last he won the struggle for this

form by avoiding flat ornamentalism in this abstract work, by unfolding the dramatic pictorial and plastic situation *in space* and, finally, by achieving absolute integrity and completeness in the artistic image. Both *Compositions*, with their atmosphere of extreme tension, resemble a kind of catastrophe, explosion or flood. Lines, and patches of colour, act in them like living creatures. The fact that they are abstract formulas rather than real people, animals or objects, only increases the expressive power of the events and gives them a universal quality. The tragedy unfolding within the time frame of each of these two paintings contains within itself catharsis, the harmonious resolution of a seemingly insoluble contradiction. In building his compositions Kandinsky does not invent new forms, only rearranges, corrects and controls all that appears in his imagination. His new method is characterized by this combination of the conscious and the spontaneous, as is well shown by his graphic, watercolour and oil studies for *Composition No. 7*.

Although Kandinsky's creative potential weakened somewhat after his return to Russia during World War I he continued to develop this method, always attempting to give more specific definition to the emotions expressed.

Kazimir Malevich *Vanity Case* 1911

79 *Clarity, Overcast* and *Twilight* (all 1917) – such titles themselves expressed the themes of many of his paintings. The October Revolution caught Kandinsky at the close of the most productive period in his career. After 1917 he played an active part in the organization and establishment of Soviet culture.

Kandinsky was the prophet of a new creative principle. He claimed that the most important element of art was its spiritual content, which should be expressed by a combination of abstract forms. He drew attention to the question of 'What?' rather than 'How?', a question which

went far beyond problems of art. This prophetic element, which was characteristic of all the Russian avantgarde, is also to be found in Filonov (as we saw earlier) and in Malevich, who discovered his own way of expressing prophetic ideas.

Kazimir Malevich (1878–1935) was one of the greatest figures of the world avantgarde movement. His achievements are inseparable from his individual creative potential and from the general development of the Russian national artistic tradition. His formal education was not extensive: he never attended the St Petersburg Academy and left the Moscow Art College without graduating. He spent most of his student years, between 1905 and 1910, in the private studio of F. Rerberg, where he finally outgrew his teacher and fellow students. In his autobiography Malevich described what it was he was searching for in those early years. He spoke of his Neoprimitive studies of peasants (his earliest works), of naturalism in the spirit of Shishkin and Repin, and of Impressionism. His first portraits known to us recall the *peredvizhniki*. As with the majority of Russian avantgarde artists, his impressionistic period, around 1905–10, was crucial to his later development. This was in contrast to most of the Western European avantgarde, for whom Art Nouveau was the seminal experience. Malevich only touched on Art Nouveau, for example in *The Wedding* (*c.* 1903), whereas he reinterpreted Impressionism in an interesting and individual way. In his landscape studies of this period he put much effort into creating a restrained dynamic on the pictorial surface; the compositions tend to stability in spite of their fragmented nature; patches of colour are particularly active; objects are thickly outlined, and thus 'fastened' to the plane. These impressionistic studies strike us as rather static; indeed, there is a kind of clumsiness about them which is in itself meaningful.

Towards the end of the 1910s Malevich was experimenting with various tendencies of contemporary art and beginning to form a style of his own. His *Bathers* of 1908 combines Impressionism with Blue Rose Symbolism, while his self-portraits of the period reveal features of Fauvism and Expressionism. He became close to Goncharova and Larionov and took part in the first exhibitions of the Knave of Diamonds and the Donkey's Tail, adapting Neoprimitivism to his own needs but not remaining for long within the ambit of those who were setting the tone of the Russian avantgarde.

Peasants were the main theme of his Neoprimitive period (between 1909 and 1912). His characters, particularly in the early series, are very similar to those of Goncharova – gloomy peasants at work in the fields and in church, frozen in awkward poses – but their constrained

Kazimir Malevich *Haymaking* 1911

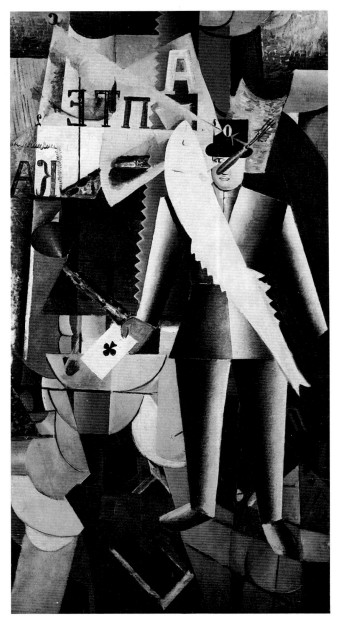

Kazimir Malevich *Aviator* 1914

Among his Cubist paintings of the early 1910s are *Vanity Case, Through Station: Kuntsevo,* and the portrait of Kliun (all 1911). Some paintings from his peasant series may also be described as Cubist. All are very close to the work of Braque, Picasso and other Parisian artists of the time. Although 1911 and 1912 saw the appearance of some of his best paintings of peasants he was already searching for fresh themes. In 1912 he painted the well-known *Knife Grinder,* an attempt to combine his own method with Futuristic techniques. In the same year he exhibited several works (at the Union of Youth) which were described as '*Zaumny* (or unintelligible) Realism'. He termed his next style, dating from 1914, 'Cubo-futuristic Realism'. His use of such terms is significant in itself. Malevich's development as a painter, like that of other avantgarde artists, progressed hand in hand with his theoretical formulations. His interest in transrationalism, for example, was an important part of his campaign against practicality and common sense and in favour of freedom of artistic expression. But for his period of transrationalism – however short – Malevich would not have made the transition to Suprematism, which he considered to be the highest expression of the artist's will.

It is now generally accepted that the 'invention' of Suprematism was preceded by Matiushin's production of the opera *Victory over the Sun* with words by Kruchenykh (and a prologue by Khlebnikov) and stage design and costumes by Malevich. The costume designs contained the seeds of many Suprematist compositions. We do not know exactly when *Black Square* was painted, but it made its appearance at the '0.10' exhibition in 1915, along with other of his Suprematist paintings. Presumably several of these works were painted some time before the exhibition, so the date of the *Black Square* itself is not necessarily 1915. Malevich himself dated both versions '1913' (one at the Tretyakov Gallery in Moscow, the other in the Russian Museum in Leningrad), but this date cannot be accepted unconditionally.

Black Square and the series of Suprematist paintings which followed it were Malevich's leap into abstraction. In his own mind they represented a transition to a totally new way of understanding the world. He rejected the outer appearance of things and overcame the condition of earthly existence so as to be able to operate solely with spiritual categories and escape the limits of gravitation.[7] As he wrote: 'The keys of Suprematism lead me to the discovery of something as yet uncomprehended. My new method does not belong to the earth alone. The earth is abandoned like a house eaten by woodworm. And indeed, there is in man's consciousness a yearning for space and a desire to "break away from the earthly globe"'.[8] This transition was not merely an artistic phenomenon; it was an expression of the general

inner strength, tense almost to breaking-point, is much more striking than in Goncharova. Malevich's figures are heavier and more static, and he constructs his compositions from voluminous, almost ideal forms, as buildings are constructed of stone. (He frequently used square canvases in order to increase the static element.) He depicted the Russian village, with its traditional way of life, as petrified, crude but mighty. His peasant 'Heads' evoke memories of Novgorodian frescos and ancient icons. This approach led inevitably to Suprematism, though by way of several other movements in contemporary art.

Kazimir Malevich *Black Square* 1914–15

Kazimir Malevich *Dynamic Suprematism/Supremus No. 57 c.* 1916

tendency to synthesis which had become a tradition in Russian culture and which united art, literature, philosophy, religion, politics and other forms of intellectual endeavour. *Black Square* was not just a challenge thrown to a public which had lost all interest in artistic innovation, but a kind of search for God and a hazardous step towards a situation which faces man with Nothing and Everything. The bewitching effect of *Black Square* derives from its ability to concentrate the infinity of the cosmos within itself, and to transform itself into other universal formulas of the world; to absorb the 'All' in the universe by concentrating this 'All' in both an absolutely impersonal geometrical form and an impenetrable black surface. With this 'manifesto-painting' Malevich summed up the whole rich period of Symbolist thinking in European culture. In this one work he moved from symbol to sign, which thereafter acquired an independent existence.

81   Malevich's other Suprematist paintings, following *Black Square*, were particularly successful in developing the idea of overcoming gravity. They express movement of form, but no longer obey the logic of gravitational laws; they have abandoned the concepts of 'above' and 'below' and convey the idea of independently valid forms, not representational but primary, floating freely in space. Though Suprematist paintings tended towards the iconic, Malevich insisted that they must be different from icons. For him, a Suprematist work depicts nothing and nobody,

whereas the icon always represents the divine presence in our visible world.

The importance Malevich ascribed to his Suprematist pictures earned him the position of explorer, prophet and messiah. 'Kazimir the Great' accepted and indeed emphasized this role, and considered himself, if not a 'representative of the Earth' like Khlebnikov, then at least 'the President of space'. Malevich shared this messianic spirit and refusal to compromise, sometimes known as maximalism, with other major figures of early twentieth-century Russian culture. It was an attitude which reflected both their excitement at the changes which were felt to be imminent just before the 1917 Revolutions and a general yearning for universal renewal. Malevich's straightforward habit of absorbing, and then vaulting over, the discoveries of his predecessors was typical of the Russian avantgarde, which was, perhaps, cruder and coarser, but at the same time more uncompromising than its French and German counterparts.

A similar revolutionary boldness marks the work of Vladimir Tatlin (1885–1953), although his artistic explorations culminated in a movement very different from Suprematism, namely Constructivism. Tatlin's best-known works are his counter-reliefs and his project for the tower commemorating the Third International. He began his career, like Larionov and Malevich, as an Impressionist. *Carnation* (1908), his first known painting from this period, summed up his experiences as a student at the Penza Art School. The next stage in his development towards the avantgarde was Neoprimitivism. He joined Larionov's circle, where he studied and assimilated Cézannism and Old Russian art. Like other Neoprimitivists he soon found a satisfying range of themes, among them sailors, fishermen and fishmongers – everything, in fact, to do with the sea. (He had gone to sea as a ship's boy and later became a sailor, and his pictures reflect these early experiences just as Larionov's recalled his army days.) As early as 1910 Constructivist features began to show through the conventional Neoprimitivist techniques in Tatlin's work. He tended to give his figures harsh and exaggerated poses; their outlines are stretched and the figures as a whole are as tense as springs. He attempted to treat these outlines as parts of a large circle or oval; sometimes, in order to preserve such forms, he destroyed his figures' natural contours by dividing them into separate parts. He was fascinated by the constructivist possibilities of the human body, and his still-lifes from this period reveal his interest in the pictorial concentration and internal structure of Cézanne and his school. These various tendencies in Tatlin's work resulted in the development of 'pictorial constructivism', illustrated by 73 paintings such as *Sailor* and *Fishmonger* (both 1911).

In *Sailor*, a self-portrait, Tatlin is both innovator and traditionalist. It recalls the hagiological composition of some Russian icons in the way the small-scale versions (presumably) of the main character are placed on either side of the central figure. Also worthy of note is the way in which a circle (made up by the smaller figures, the sailor's cap and his collar) is inserted into the square format of the canvas; this tendency to geometrical harmony is reminiscent of two traditional iconographic compositions, *The All-powerful Saviour* and *Christ in Glory*. It would, of course, be a mistake to imagine that Tatlin mechanically transferred iconic techniques to his own work; what is reflected here is a general experience of Old Russian artistic concepts. Unlike Larionov, Goncharova and Lentulov, Tatlin chose as his model not the primitive but the classical version of the Russian icon tradition, from which the idea of uniting the square with the circle derives. There is also an element of the classical formal portrait in *Sailor*, particularly in the decisive turn of his head, and in the suggestion of a battle scene conveyed by the smaller figures, the cannon in the right upper corner and the general tension of the contours outlining all the figures, which has the effect of fixing their poses and arresting time. The momentary becomes continuous as the artist, by depicting the culminating moment of a particular passage of time, liberates the sailor from the power of time.

Tatlin's finest achievement is his series of 'Female 71 models', on which he worked for several years. It was completed by two pictures dating from 1913, one in the Tretyakov Gallery, the other in the Russian Museum. In the course of the series he gradually eliminated the 'everyday' content and the realistic aspects of his model, generalizing her more and more and eventually creating a living organism as a perfect mechanism for expressing the most important laws of life. His Tretyakov *Model* is traditionally compared with a Russian icon because of its impersonality and the general plan of its composition, but the similarity is only partial. Tatlin did not wish to create an image of spirituality realized in physical form; at the same time he adapted the traditional 'nude' genre by excluding the element of admiration for the naked female body. This admiration is absent not because he wished to spiritualize the human body but because he concentrated entirely on an analysis of bodily structure. It is no coincidence that among Tatlin's paintings exhibited at the time were two entitled *Composition on a Naked Figure* and *Analysis of a Composition*. (A watercolour sketch of the latter, which perhaps depicts a Madonna and Child, survives.) These works bring his pre-revolutionary painting to a close; thereafter, he addressed himself to fresh challenges, including the creation of a new kind of 'painting-relief'.

Tatlin's first counter-relief was probably devised under the influence of Picasso, although the object (a bottle) was depicted by a cut-out section rather than a three-dimensional form. Soon, however, he abandoned representationalism entirely, and concentrated on 'constructions' comprised of various materials, which he juxtaposed with the purpose of exploring their special qualities and potentials. He sometimes applied paint to his metal or wood surfaces, not for the sake of colour itself but in order to achieve a particular textural effect. These works were not intended to represent objects or emotions; their significance lay in their very existence – they were, simply, manifestations of reality. Since they were also objects of no conceivable practical use they remained firmly in the realm of aesthetics. Tatlin emerged from what may be considered the aesthetic stage of Constructivism to devote himself to creating useful objects which achieved aesthetic perfection because their form was totally appropriate to their function.

His rejection of representationalism and consequent move to abstract art (if his painting-reliefs may be so described) was very different from the equally innovative approaches of Malevich and Kandinsky. Kandinsky extolled the spiritual, and Malevich, who introduced the idea of the cosmos into painting, saw abstraction as a means to explore new ideas and comprehend universal categories. For Tatlin, on the other hand, materials were important in their own right; his later career, indeed, was devoted to practical design.

70 Natalia Goncharova *Collecting Fruit* Late 1900s

73 **Vladimir Tatlin** *Sailor* 1911

<   **71 Vladimir Tatlin** *Female Model* 1910/14

<   **72 Mikhail Larionov** *Soldier Resting* 1911

74 Marc Chagall
Window in a Dacha
1915

75 Marc Chagall
The Red Jew
1915

76 Pavel Filonov >
Peasant Family
1914

77 Liubov Popova
Painterly Architectonics
1916

78 Olga Rozanova
Suprematism 1916

79 Vasily Kandinsky >
Twilight 1917

80 Ivan Kliun
Suprematism 1915

81 Kazimir Malevich
Suprematism 1916

Although, as we have seen, Russian avantgarde art could boast many outstanding practitioners, at the end of the 1910s not all of them had much immediate impact on the process of artistic change. Filonov and Chagall, for example, remained somewhat detached from, and exercised little influence on their contemporaries, although they represent an essential and indispensable aspect of Russian painting. Kandinsky's impact was considerable but limited by the fact that Munich was the main focus of his work and organizational activity. The influence of Larionov and Goncharova was restricted principally to the late 1900s and early 1910s. Malevich and Tatlin were the main authorities of the mid-1910s, and all later developments bear their imprint to some extent. Udaltsova and Popova were linked with Tatlin, who also influenced Alexandra Exter, although these three women artists joined Malevich after his proclamation of Suprematism in 1915. Among the many other followers of the new prophet were Rozanova, Puni, Kliun, Menkov and Morgunov.

Ivan Kliun (Kliunkov–1878–1942) was the same age as Malevich, and the two became friends when they were fellow students at Rerberg's studio. His early years were influenced by Symbolism, which he abandoned to follow other admirers of Malevich along the well-trodden path from Cubism to Suprematism. Kliun produced two kinds of Cubist work, namely pure painting and painting reliefs. Dispensing with Cubism, he then took a great deal from Malevich's Suprematist style, although his own was less abstract and contained more specific detail and, later, more colour. He became an editor of the unpublished journal *Supremus*, together with other members of Malevich's circle, notably Ivan Puni (1894–1956), whose career was somewhat unusual. He studied at the Julien Academy in Paris and developed a style which may be tentatively described as a fusion of Fauvism and Cubism. He became close to the Russian avantgarde artists, particularly Malevich, through the Union of Youth. Like Tatlin and Kliun, he used the painting-relief technique, although he added individual features untypical of the Russian avantgarde. In *White Sphere* (1915), for example, he concentrated principally on a three-dimensional form actually existing in reality.

In the mid-1910s Malevich's circle was joined by one of the most talented Russian women painters, Olga Rozanova (1886–1918). She started her career in the St Petersburg Union of Youth, through which she also published several theoretical works. Later she progressed decisively to Futurism. Several of her works dating from 1913/14 (some of which were exhibited in Italian Futurist exhibitions) were executed in an impulsive, Futurist manner; they are very expressive, deconstructive and full of inner tension. From 1912 onwards

Ivan Kliun *Ozonator* 1914

she devoted much time to futuristic books, illustrating poems by Kruchenykh and Khlebnikov, and later completed a coloured lithographic cycle entitled *War*, all of which led inevitably to abstract painting. Like many others she followed Malevich into Suprematism, but also tried other abstract techniques, based on the effect of rays of light and colour, and on a harmonious combination of seemingly transparent patches of colour. Her life was cut tragically short before she could develop her rich talents to the full.

Another Russian avantgarde painter was Nadezhda Udaltsova (1886–1961); she was born in the same year as Rozanova but her life turned out very differently. She studied under Metzinger, Le Fauconnier and Segonzac in Paris, where she absorbed the lessons of Cubism (which she later successfully applied in Russia). By the mid-1910s she had developed a very individual version of the style. As a rule her pictures were of considerable size and had about them an air of 'domestic iconography'. For example, in *At the Piano* (1914), *The Kitchen* and *The Restaurant* (both 1915) parts of the objects comprise the material for the construction of the pictorial forms and are freely distributed about the surface of the canvas. The transition from this kind of Cubism to Suprematism was easy enough and occurred when Udaltsova became familiar with Malevich's Suprematist works.

Vladimir Tatlin *Board No. 1* 1916

Nadezhda Udaltsova *Cubist Composition: Blue Jug* 1915

Alexandra Exter *The Town c.* 1915

Ivan Puni *White Sphere* 1915

Olga Rozanova *Abstract Composition with Yellow and Violet* 1910/19

Liubov Popova (1889–1924) studied with Udaltsova in Paris. She was associated with Tatlin, whose Constructivism she later added to her Parisian training. She progressed via Cubism to abstract art under the influence of Malevich; from the end of 1915 she was a true abstractionist and described her works as 'painterly architectonics'. They were intended to bring out the architectonic elements present in pictorial material. She sought out and created correspondences with various forms of a particular colour, and juxtaposed geometric forms, paying special attention to their physical stability as well as to the harmony and integrity of the whole picture.

However individual Popova may seem, her style places her somewhere between Malevich and Tatlin. Together with Vesnin, Rodchenko, Stepanova and Exter she took part in the 1921 Constructivist exhibition entitled '5 × 5 = 25', but later abandoned easel painting to work in a textile factory designing cotton prints.

Varvara Stepanova and Alexander Rodchenko are outside the scope of this book, for they had not become fully-formed artists by the time of the Revolution, but Alexandra Exter (1882–1949), who also worked with Constructivists in the 1920s, had an interesting body of work behind her by 1917. She went to Paris in 1908 and thus discovered the new trends in French painting earlier than many of her compatriots. Thereafter she became a conduit for French influence on Russian art. She took part in a wide range of exhibitions, including 'The Link', 'The Wreath', 'The Union of Youth', 'The Knave of Diamonds', 'Tramway V', the Izdebsky Salon, the 'Salon des Indépendants' in Paris and the Futurist exhibition in Rome. She mastered and adapted Fauvism, Cubism and Abstraction, to all of which she added her own exquisite artistry. All this led to a brilliant career as a stage designer after the Revolution.

The Russian avantgarde included an enormous number of artists; we have concentrated only on its most prominent and talented representatives.

8 Sculpture and Architecture

At the turn of the century Russian sculpture and architecture finally emerged from their mid-nineteenth-century crisis. Painting no longer dominated the arts. Sculpture was closer than architecture to the processes taking place in painting and, as a result, responded to them earlier, stimulated by the spread of Impressionism at the end of the century.

Compared to painting, sculpture was slow in its acceptance of Impressionist techniques, which Pavel Trubetskoi (1866–1938) was the first Russian sculptor to use. Trubetskoi spent his youth in Italy and returned to Russia at the very end of the century with a good working knowledge of Italian sculpture. His first successful works back home were portraits and small statues. In his portraits of I. Levitan and M. Tenisheva (both 1899) and his small equestrian portrait of Leo Tolstoy (*Leo Tolstoy on Horseback*, 1900) he displays a remarkable psychological insight into his sitters as well as an ability to select their most characteristic pose, express their individual body-language and convey apparently insignificant details convincingly. His technique itself contributed to this lifelike quality. He worked in clay and plasticine in order to cast them later in bronze or plaster. His way of bringing the material to life was to work it briskly with a pallet knife, creating a chiaroscuro effect from the resulting uneven surface. The sculptural volume, now animated and 'breathing', interacted with the surrounding space, and this animation was then passed on to the images themselves, catching them, as it seems, at a specific moment of their existence.

Although Trubetskoi worked mainly in small-scale and intimate forms, he did not confine himself totally to the genre. He began his career in Italy designing monuments to various personalities, and at the turn of the century accepted a commission for a monument to Alexander III in St Petersburg (1909). He worked long on this project and made a large number of models before he found the perfect solution. Placed at the centre of Znamenskaya (now Insurrection) Square opposite the railway station, on a simple pedestal, the monument created quite a sensation although, or perhaps because, it did not resemble traditional equestrian monuments, with their riders in heroic poses seated on prancing steeds. Alexander's horse, its head bent stubbornly down, refuses to go forward, and its rider is depicted as a huge hulk weighing down the horse's back. Horse and rider together make up a frozen, immobile pyramid. The Emperor is presented as an obtuse, heartless and loud-mouthed soldier smugly towering above the ordinary folk gathered on the Square. Trubetskoi did not, of course, intend to caricature the Russian Tsar (who was not known for his intellect or compassion), for caricature is incompatible with the monumental form, but he skilfully introduced elements of the grotesque into the figure. His contemporaries were understandably surprised that erection of the monument was permitted, and ironically dubbed it 'the scarecrow'. Indeed, but for the support of the Dowager Empress, who insisted that the statue faithfully resembled her late husband, the work would not have gained the necessary approval of various committees and would never have seen the light of day. What makes this memorial so successful, and earns it a unique place in world sculpture, is Trubetskoi's success in transferring the psychological insight and subtlety of characterization he applied in his small-scale sculptures to the monumental form.

Trubetskoi's work teaches us that we should not unconditionally impose the stylistic divisions of turn of the century painting on its sculptural contemporary. For all his inclination to Impressionism with its insight, mobility and free treatment of surfaces, his work is also related to the *Modern* style, especially in its flowing forms, contoured lines and combination of the symbolic and the natural. This betwixt and between style characterizes the work of another prominent sculptor of the day, Anna Golubkina (1864–1927), many of whose pieces had a profoundly symbolic content.

Golubkina studied first at the Moscow Art College, later attended the Academy of Fine Arts, continued her training at the studio of Colarossi in Paris and concluded it at the very end of the century with Rodin. Her life and personality were marked by an elevated sense of morality and honesty, qualities she also tried to express in her art. She was moved by the fate of the downtrodden whose

Pavel Trubetskoi, Monument to Alexander III, St Petersburg, 1909

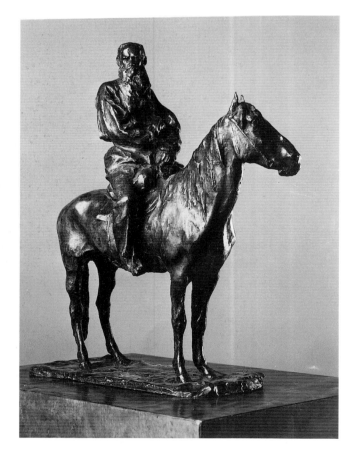

Pavel Trubetskoi *Leo Tolstoy on Horseback* 1900

faces bore the mark of inner collapse, and excited by those who were awakening to the new possibilities of life and glimpsing the light of hope after many centuries of oppression. Russia, above all other countries, with her eternal contradictions and complex contrasts, was bound eventually to produce a talent such as Golubkina's. As the poet and critic Maximilian Voloshin put it: 'As an artist whose work is an inextinguishably burning conscience, Golubkina is an exclusively Russian, and profoundly national, phenomenon.'[9]

One of her favourite themes was a man or woman awakening to consciousness. *Worker* (1900), *Man Striding* (1903), *Soldier* (1907), *Slave* (1908) and *Seated Man* (1912) are profound symbolic studies dealing with suffering, the first occurrence of a thought, or victory, inspired by a still undefined stirring of the soul, over physical inertia. Golubkina's portraits are also imbued with her humanity. She was a profound, sensitive and wise portraitist with the ability to reveal both the soul of man and those elemental forces within him which unite that soul with the soul of nature, the earth and the cosmos.

Nevertheless, Golubkina did not allow the universal and ageless relevance of her characters to obscure their individual and unique features. Her subjects stand at a crossroads of the universal and the particular. The marble portrait of L.I. Sidorova (1906) presents an image of nobility and grace. The portrait, in wood, of the philosopher V. F. Ern (1914) forges a link between the frozen, Buddha-like mask of his face, immersed in profound self-contemplation, with the lively look in his almost squinting eyes and the lifelike skin of his face and neck. The portrait of Andrei Bely (plaster, 1907), imprisoned within a mysterious world of his own, is an evocative image of a typical Symbolist poet. In each of these portraits the material – marble, plaster or wood – is in organic harmony with the artistic concept, the idea and the sitter. Golubkina had a very fine feeling for her materials, and displayed extraordinary skills in modelling, hewing and carving; towards the end of her life she even produced some small cameos. All her work bears witness to her remarkable artistry. However, it is not in this that Golubkina's uniqueness resides, but in her spiritual grace and the demands she made of herself and her art, in which harmony between the material and the spiritual is triumphantly achieved.

Nikolai Andreev (1873–1932) worked in the same genres as Golubkina and Trubetskoi, i.e. portraits and small statues (for the latter his preferred medium was ceramic). He carved the relief for the Hotel Metropol in Moscow (as Golubkina did for the Moscow Arts Theatre) and, like Trubetskoi, designed a famous monument – to Nikolai Gogol in Moscow (1909). Andreev's portraits reveal an impressionistic insight into the personalities of

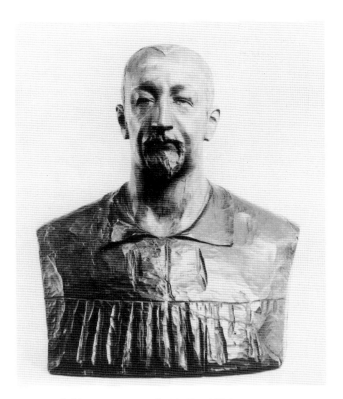

Anna Golubkina *Portrait of V.F. Ern* 1914

Anna Golubkina
Seated Man
1912

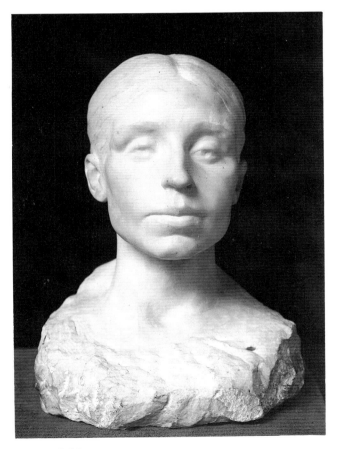

Anna Golubkina *Maria* 1906

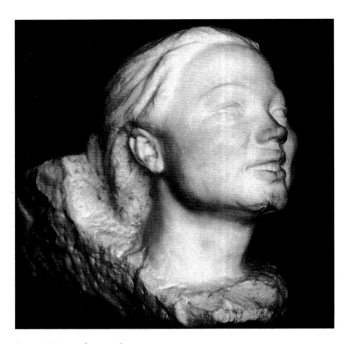

Sergei Konenkov *Nike* 1906

his sitters, usually portrayed in their most characteristic pose. His small-scale work, rather Art Nouveau in style, relies on techniques of stylization and a free use of colour and ornamentation. The monument to Gogol is his most significant pre-revolutionary work. Like Trubetskoi, Andreev dispensed with the dramatic pose traditional for such monuments, creating instead a convincing image of this master of psychological insight and the grotesque. Gogol's whole figure is muffled in his cloak; only his head and right hand are free of this monkish garment. Far from laughing at the picture of life going on around him, Gogol is depressed by its joylessness. He is a pessimist, and his whole aspect is dominated by a sense of despair. The power of this monument is due to the contrast between the broadly drawn, generalized lines of the cloak and the freely worked detail of the hand and the head, which is rich in psychological expression. A second contrast is between the figure itself and the planes of the base, smooth but for the relief depicting characters from Gogol's works which girdles it. In this work Andreev reveals himself as less of an innovator than Trubetskoi; nevertheless his *Gogol* is indubitably a work of the twentieth century, and one which could only have been created after the appearance of Rodin's statue of Balzac.

Whereas Golubkina and Andreev were influenced by Rodin, Sergei Konenkov (1874–1971) was attracted by Michelangelo, antiquity and Russian folk sculpture in wood. In fact his work is a melange of several interests and traditions. He began his career at the very end of the

nineteenth century with *peredvizhniki*-like pieces, but his style and tastes soon changed: his diploma-work, *Samson Breaking his Bonds* (1902, it has not survived), marked his break with the 'genre' interpretation of reality, aiming for accuracy and verisimilitude, which was now replaced by a myth-making element to which Konenkov remained faithful for the rest of his career. Impressions from life merged in his mind with various ideal images taken from the Golden Age of antiquity. For his *Nike*, a marble head dating from 1906, he took as his model (or rather, as his imaginary model) a Russian girl whose movement expresses the life instinct and a longing for happiness – and then named her after the Greek goddess of Victory. Konenkov's *Nike* is no triumphant heroine but a symbol of purity of emotion, a kind of prevision of the true antiquity with which he himself became directly familiar when he visited Greece in 1912.

Even before this trip – but after the appearance of *Nike* – Konenkov was leaning more and more towards antiquity, whose works he studied in museums and books. *Young Boy, Kneeling Woman* (both 1907) and *Horus* (1909) are landmarks in the understanding of the essence of antiquity. Their significance lies not in some imitation of antiquity, but in Konenkov's understanding of that marvellous perfection of soul and body which is to be found in antique sculpture, and in the desire to combine this elevated canon with specific features picked out from reality. The same vitality marks the marble torsos Konenkov carved while still under the spell of what he had seen in Greece. Although at first glance they may recall fragments of Greek statues which had lain hidden beneath the soil for many centuries, they are not simply the fruit of classical influence but the result of a profound and passionate study of life. This is particularly well illustrated in his marble *Torso* dating from 1913, in which the warmth and beauty of the young body is conveyed with tenderness and delicacy. The torso is not dominated by strict rules of classical beauty; it moves us because it seems to depict a real person. A melodious, unbroken line makes up the contour of the figure, whose decorative grace is skilfully combined with a rich voluminousness of form.

From the early 1910s the theme of the female nude became prominent in his work, at first in marble but later more often in wood. His wood sculptures include *Winged Female* (1913), *Girl* (1914), *Female Model, Kneeling* and *Wounded Female* (all 1916). Analysis of these works illustrates a gradual weakening of his interest in antiquity. As he moved away from Neo-classicism he came closer to Art Nouveau, as is shown by, among other things, his growing preference for wood.

It must be stressed, however, that Konenkov's interest in wood began earlier – in the late 1900s. For him, wood

Sergei Konenkov *Sleep* 1913

Sergei Konenkov *Starichok-Polevichok* 1910

was inseparable from folk art, with which he had been familiar from childhood. (He was born and brought up in a little village not far from the ancient city of Smolensk, surrounded by the world of Old Russian folk fantasy – fairy tale, myth and legend.) He felt that wood was the most suitable material for his own ideas, for it seemed to be kith and kin with those creatures of the forest which inhabited his imagination and with his recreations of fantastical characters from Russian fairy tale. He devised an individual approach based closely on the techniques and traditions of folk art. *Lesovik* (a spirit of the forest, 1909), *Stribog* (the god of the winds, 1910), *Starichok-Polevichok* (a spirit of the fields, 1910) and many others are very far from lifelike – fantastic creatures with incredibly elongated fingers and toes, flat bodies, horns and mysteriously flickering eyes charmingly fashioned from little stones. Nevertheless, these fantasies possess some uncannily realistic traits. What a sly smile plays on the lips of the Starichok-Polevichok, and how convincingly Stribog looks at us! One of the most remarkable works in this series is a sculptural group entitled *Paupers* (1917). The two old down-and-outs are a symbol of old peasant Russia with all its suffering, misfortune, poverty and deprivation, beneath which, however, fury and power lie waiting for their hour to strike. Here real features are merged with fantasy born of dozens of folk songs and legends expressing the people's faith in eventual happiness as well as the bitter plaint of the wretched of the earth who have never known joy.

Alexander Matveev *Youth* 1911

If we compare *Paupers* or *Stribog* with Konenkov's antique torsos of this period it is hard to credit that they are the work of the same artist. One feature, however, is common to all his work – a mythological approach which opened his way to the world of antiquity, related his *Samson* to Michelangelo's giant, and provided him with a medium for his folklore fantasies.

The last great Russian sculptor to appear at the turn of the century was Alexander Matveev (1878–1960). He spent his student years at the Moscow Art College, where he was greatly influenced by Trubetskoi. His artistic maturity was rapid; one of his first works, a portrait of V.E. Borisov-Musatov (1900), revealed not only that he possessed a sharp eye and strong arm but also that he had found his ideal, one imbued with the classical spirit, and was searching for plastic harmony. This search soon drove him to change his style in an attempt to reject certain features of Impressionism, to acquire a new

generalizing technique and to make the transfer from soft to hard materials. He found a style of his own in the latter half of the 1900s, when he was working on a series of statues to decorate the Zhukovsky Park in the Crimea. Simultaneously he was working on smaller sculptures which complemented the ideas behind the park statues. They were generally single-figure, or at most two-figure compositions, often nudes, including women, youths and boys, asleep or falling asleep, sunk in meditation, in a state of relaxation or else waking up. These various states determined not only the figures' movements but the treatment of the sculptural surface.

A good example is *Awakening Boy* (1907, plaster), which was exhibited at a Blue Rose exhibition, executed in marble and placed in the Zhukovsky Park. The boy's arms and bent torso express the drama of his inner struggle with torpidity, the difficulty of awakening and the unavoidable, ceaseless fight against sluggish flesh.

Youth, a marble statue dating from 1911, offers a different view and treatment of a young man. The struggle seems to be over; harmony informs the soft curve of his torso, the hands clasped over his head and the general proportions of this still growing body. In this, as in many other statues, Matveev reveals his fascination with the architecture of the human figure. He does not surrender to the lure of smooth surfaces which beautify the body with an outward gloss. Seeking neither decorative effect nor an obvious correspondence of contours, he constructs the figure like a kind of architectural organism, paying due attention to the logical integration of individual elements and the inherent integrity of forms. This overall harmony of the parts is inseparable from the significance and spiritual perfection of man himself.

Among Matveev's masterpieces is the funerary memorial (1910–12) to his older friend and fellow townsman from Saratov, Viktor Borisov-Musatov. The monument was erected in Tarusa near Moscow. Executed in granite, it again shows the figure of a boy, this time sunk in a dream, as if chained to the stone pedestal. The theme of luminous calm is in accord with the substance and meaning of the monument and also with the general character of Borisov-Musatov's work. We must not forget that Matveev, like Kuznetsov and Utkin, continued the Borisov-Musatov tradition, though in his own genre. Matveev's work is part of the second wave of Symbolism which occurred in the mid-1900s, but unlike his two colleagues he based himself on classical models, i.e. the sculpture of Greek antiquity and the Italian Renaissance. He sought ways and means of blending the classical tradition with the innovations introduced by Symbolism, just as Borisov-Musatov, the French artist Maurice Denis and other painters of the turn of the century had done. When comparing Matveev with

French artists it is, of course, impossible to ignore Maillol. However different Matveev's soft and lyrical style may be from that of the great French sculptor, the parallel between them of itself reserves a place for the Russian in the annals of world sculpture.

We have omitted from our study many sculptors who began their careers before the Revolution but whose main achievements properly belong in the Soviet era, and whose early works do not drastically change the overall picture described above. In attempting to define the general development of Russian sculpture we should stress the lack of clear divisions in style. Thus, Impressionism blended into Art Nouveau, from which, in turn, sprang a tendency to Neo-classicism. Individual sculptors did not necessarily remain true to one or other particular style, but happily combined various techniques in order to achieve their desired effects.

As for architecture, the situation was similarly involved, but the range of styles available was rather different. We cannot speak of Impressionism in Russian architecture; on the other hand, the so-called Neo-Russian style became almost as important as *Modern* and Neo-classicism.

Modern was the dominant tendency in the period under review. It began to develop in the 1890s and achieved some considerable success in the first decade of the century. The architect who most influenced Russian – and particularly Muscovite – *Modern* was Fyodor Shekhtel (1859–1926). The early part of his career was largely spent designing private residences for rich Moscow merchants in a Neo-gothic style he later abandoned. At the turn of the century he created a perfect example of an Art Nouveau mansion (1900) for S.P. Ryabushinsky. The genre of the modest-sized private residence, set in its own grounds, permitted architects to create free compositions and arrange volumes in a picturesque way. Art historians usually say that the structure of forms in a *Modern* building progresses from the inside outwards, an approach consistently applied throughout the Ryabushinsky house. Each of the large volumes of the general composition is realized on the outside and freely arranged in a picturesque way. Horizontal divisions, marked by the window casings, the upper parts of the porches and the roof cornices, occur at various levels. The shapes of the windows vary from floor to floor and from facade to facade, each of which is different from the others. Just as the outside volumes are in harmony with each other, so too the inner space flows easily from one room to another. Vertical lines play an important role in the interior, whose principal element we may take to be the main staircase, starting in the spacious hall and leading upstairs. Its wave-like lines set the tone for all the rooms of the

Fyodor Shekhtel, Ryabushinsky House, Moscow, main staircase, 1900

Fyodor Shekhtel, Ryabushinsky House, Moscow, 1900

mansion. The Ryabushinsky house, like some others by
Shekhtel (for example the Derozhinskaya mansion, also
in Moscow, built in 1901), together with private houses by
contemporary Moscow architects such as L. Kekushev
and W. Walcott, achieve the same high standard as the
best Brussels mansions of V. Horta, P. Hankar and other
Art Nouveau architects.

Shekhtel also worked in other architectural genres
and was brilliantly productive in the 1900s. In 1901 he
designed the Russian pavilions for the international
exhibition in Glasgow; in 1902 he rebuilt the Moscow
Arts Theatre; in 1902–04 he designed the Yaroslavl
railway station in Moscow; and in 1903 his design for the
Ryabushinsky Bank launched 'rationalistic *Modern*', as it
was called. All these works reveal his passion for
experiment. The Glasgow Russian pavilions are an
illustration of Neo-Russian's enrichment of Art Nouveau.
Neo-Russian was a new variation on the 'pseudo-Russian'
style widespread in the second half of the nineteenth
century. The new version was initiated by V. Vasnetsov in
the late 1880s. The painter Korovin was the first to use it
for pavilion architecture, when he designed pavilions for
the Nizhny Novgorod and Paris exhibitions in 1896 and
1900 respectively. They were built of wood, a traditional
Russian material, and thus contributed to the development of traditional national forms.

The leaders of Neo-Russian style were determined to
abandon the mechanistic use of traditional decor as
practised by Ropet, Gartman and others in the second
half of the nineteenth century. Using techniques of
pictorial composition characteristic of ancient Russian
architecture, they recreated many essential elements of
the latter and were inevitably drawn towards *Modern*,
which was largely based on concepts of Russian medieval
architecture. The Russian pavilions in Glasgow incorporated elaborately decorated tents, onion-domes, bell-
towers and sloping roofs. All these elements of Russian
wooden architecture coexist on equal terms with elements of *Modern*. The latter prevailed as Shekhtel began
to use stone rather than wood and to design urban and
public buildings instead of pavilions. The Yaroslavl
station repeats some aspects of the Glasgow pavilions,
namely the principles of picturesqueness, free asymmetry and lively balance. All the same, the design is free
of superfluous components and every element of the
building is an integral part of the composition. The overall
silhouette of the station is stepped; sharp angles and
rounded forms are combined in the ensemble. *Modern*
came to dominate and finally assimilate the Neo-Russian
style, as is illustrated by the work of Shekhtel and other
architects at the beginning of the century.

Shekhtel himself moved on from the mature stage of
Modern, and was the first to lead it to its final phase,

Lev Kekushev, Isakov House, Moscow, 1906

namely the 'rationalistic' period. Having completed the
Ryabushinsky Bank he designed the *Utro Rossii* (Morning
of Russia) printing house in 1907 and the Moscow
Merchants' Society building in 1909. These buildings
displayed new features, namely the absence of decorative elements, a preference for straight lines, large right-
angled windows and clear correlations between verticals
and horizontals. These features of late *Modern* would be
further developed into Constructivism in the 1920s.

Moscow *Modern* is inseparable from the blocks of
apartments which sprang up in large numbers along the
main streets of the city. A typical example is the Isakov
house on Prechistenka Street, designed by L. Kekushev in
1906. Like most of these blocks it is multi-storey (in this
case with five floors) and its main facade runs along the
street. The window embrasures on the various levels are
very similar in shape and size. The symmetry of the
facade is disturbed only by a small displacement to the left
of the arch leading into the courtyard. The facade is so
designed as to give the impression that the wall is alive
and breathing. Thus, it projects in the shape of oriel
windows at the sides, recedes towards its central balco-

Fyodor Shekhtel,
Yaroslavl Station,
Moscow, 1902–04

Fyodor Shekhtel,
Moscow Merchants'
Society Building,
1909–11

William Walcott, Metropol Hotel, Moscow, 1898–1903

nies, is covered in some places with a decorative pattern
and in others left quite bare.

The main facade of the Metropol Hotel in Moscow
(1898–1903), designed by William Walcott, is based on
the same principle. In fact there are three facades, as the
hotel occupies a whole block and overlooks two squares
and a broad thoroughfare. The building is crowned by a
wave-shaped line of towers and other superstructures
rising from the roof. The interior and exterior of the hotel
are decorated with sculptures and paintings. Majolica
friezes realized by Golovin from drawings by Vrubel and
himself, sculptural reliefs, wall and ceiling paintings and
stained glass – all these make up a grandiose ensemble
typifying the mature phase of Moscow *Modern*.

The Petersburg version of *Modern* evolved simultaneously with Moscow *Modern*, but with certain differences due to its well-established classical appearance.
Whereas the Moscow version of the new style adapted
Neo-Russian forms, Petersburg *Modern* did the same
with classical forms, which generally remained subordinate. Petersburg *Modern* is perfectly illustrated by the
work of Frederik Lidval, and in particular by his Azov-
Don Bank (1907–10). A four-columned portico, a triangular pediment cut through by an arch, garlands and
meander, or fret, friezes – all these elements make up the
plane of the facade, which is decorated in a kind of
Empire style. The stepped (but unrounded) projections
and recesses of the walls and various decorative elements
arranged on different levels are authentically *Modern*.

The *Modern* classicism epitomized in this building
was widespread in St Petersburg, but in some cases the
accent was on classicism, particularly in the work of Ivan
Fomin (1872–1936), who was, however, by no means
opposed to *Modern*. One early work strongly dominated
by *Modern* was his design for the furniture and interior
decor of the 1902 Moscow exhibition entitled 'Architecture and Industrial Design of the New Style'. However, as
various branches of art began to rediscover a growing
interest in the classical heritage – classicism, Renaissance
and Antiquity – classical tendencies also came to the fore
in Fomin's work. The early 1910s saw the construction of
two private residences in St Petersburg which probably
represent the highest point in the revival of classical
architecture, namely the Polovtsev mansion (1911–13)
and the Abamelek-Lazarev house (1912–14). The Polovtsev mansion was designed as an aristocrat's private house
in the spirit of late eighteenth and early nineteenth-
century Moscow classicism. The centre of the composition is marked by a columned portico of typical Moscow
construction (as in Bove's Gagarina house). The main
facade and the two wings projecting toward the front
create a *cour d'honneur*. The arrangement along the
main axis of an oval hall (under a cupola), a gallery and a
winter garden, strongly recalls Neoclassical St Petersburg palace architecture. But Fomin was not mechanisti-
cally dragging compositional techniques from the past
and imposing them on the present. He deliberately
changed the classical design by increasing the number of

Frederik Lidval, Azov-Don Bank, St Petersburg, 1907–10

columns on the main facade (while preserving their regularity) and making the forest of columns in the central section more dense. They may be seen as an element of grotesque; it certainly indicates that this building is the work of an architect of a new era, one not afraid to emphasize detail or exploit the old style as basic material to achieve a more powerful effect. This approach was very characteristic of Fomin. In his drawings of old and new buildings of classical Moscow, for example, he distorted – albeit subtly – various details of their construction: he exaggerated the entasis of columns (their slight convex curve), transforming them almost into barrels, flattened and purified smooth surfaces and increased contrasts of form. Again, there is a strong element of geometrism in his designs for buildings destined for new areas of St Petersburg.

Architectural Neo-classicism took various forms. The early 1910s saw a fashion for decorating multi-storey *Modern* apartment blocks with Empire ornamentation such as pediments, decorative garlands etc. In St Petersburg such blocks often boasted columns up to four or five storeys in height. In Moscow, A. Tamanyan designed a block (of which the upper floors were reserved for the owner, Prince Shcherbatov) in classical style, with a *cour d'honneur* and wings; however, he increased the height of the building and in this way deviated from the pure classical model. Ivan Zholtovsky (1867–1959), a connoisseur and historian of antique and Renaissance architecture, built the Tarasov residence in Moscow (1912) in the

Ivan Fomin, Polovtsev Mansion, St Petersburg, 1911–13

Alexei Shchusev, Kazan Station, Moscow, 1913–26

continued to design facades, including one which was incorporated in the Tretyakov Gallery building. S. Malyutin continued in Vasnetsov's tradition, at first at Princess Tenisheva's estate of Talashkino, where he designed many projects, including the Talashkino church. Later, in collaboration with N. Zhukov, he built the Pertsov house in Moscow (1907), a fantastic building with high, pointed roofs, painted pediments, sharply angled lintels and other ornamentation.

The most prominent representative of the Neo-Russian tendency in *Modern* was Alexei Shchusev (1873–1949), a professional architect who was much occupied with church design. His primary source of inspiration was the Novgorod or Pskov Old Russian church with one cupola, of the type common before the Tartar yoke descended on Russia. The best example of Shchusev's ecclesiastical style is the church built for the Martha and Mary convent in Moscow between 1908 and 1912. It is a monolithic construction with all its elements – *trapeznaya* (refectory), *pritvor* (foyer), apses and the main part of the church – arranged close together. The walls are smooth, and its rounded forms – the apses, drum and dome – curve along flowing and supple lines, so that the whole building is reminiscent of a sculpture. The picturesque mobility, asymmetry and organic integrity of the forms all seem to be borrowed from ancient architecture, but in fact they are the main features of *Modern*.

Shchusev was very well aware that different architectural genres were subject to different laws and that each required its own points of reference. In his design for the Kazan railway station in Moscow (1913–26) he abandoned the pre-Tartar Russian church style as a model in favour of seventeenth-century palace architecture, which likewise harmonized well with *Modern*, and borrowed elements of decor and ornaments from late seventeenth-century Russian architecture, the so-called Naryshkin Baroque. Shchusev imposed his own will on all these models with a harmonious linear arrangement of various right-angled volumes all bound together by a row of window embrasures. He also prepared the eye for the rise of the central tower (copied from a medieval tower in the city of Kazan) by creating a number of levels leading towards it.

The general picture of Russian architecture during the first two decades of the twentieth century creates an impression of comfortable unity in spite of the presence of various movements within the one dominant style, but cataclysmic changes awaited it in the 1920s, and only the 'rationalistic' version of *Modern* would play some part in the shaping of the approaching Constructivist style. Herein lies a crucial distinction between architecture and painting, for the latter continued, in the 1920s, to develop the new trends and discoveries of the 1910s.

style of an Italian palazzo. This was probably the most extreme departure from *Modern* in favour of Neo-classical (in this case Renaissance) forms in early twentieth-century Russian architecture.

Far from disappearing after its merger with *Modern*, Neo-Russian found a legitimate position within the new style. Interestingly enough, it was painters who continued to play a leading role in its development. V. Vasnetsov, who had launched the Neo-Russian movement in the 1880s with the church at Abramtsevo,

Afterword

It is difficult to draw conclusions from all that we have described in this book. Our story did not begin with the origins of Russian culture, nor has it ended with the present day. It is impossible to make a judgment about the contribution of Russian art to world culture without taking into consideration Russian icon-painting or the best of the Russian avantgarde of the 1920s. All the same, we can make some general observations about the special features of Russian art, even if our analysis covers only a limited period.

Russian art developed spasmodically, occasionally slowing down and then boldly leaping forward, but without ever losing sight of certain constant ideals. Historians of Russian literature, in attempting to define its special nature, point to its anthropocentrism, that is its total concentration on man.[10] Regarding man as of paramount importance, the great figures of Russian culture valued moral ideas above all else. Even during those periods when writers and artists strove to put themselves above and beyond questions of good and evil they were unable to ignore certain moral obligations which had become an essential part of the national cultural tradition. Art in Russia acquired a peculiar significance of its own by becoming the focus of the nation's social conscience, remaining in close contact with many different aspects of human activity and always preserving its integrity and indivisibility.

Another special characteristic of Russian art (and one always emphasized by Russian thinkers like Belinsky, Herzen, Dostoevsky and Blok) is its receptiveness, in other words its ability to adopt and adapt the achievements of other national schools. This ability was strengthened by those drastic changes which have occurred throughout the history of Russia, for example at such times as the introduction of Christianity, the reforms of Peter the Great and the revolutions of the early twentieth century. Russia always contrived to assimilate new ideas without ever becoming their slave. This is not to imply that the path of Russian art was totally different from those of England, France or Germany. Russia's social development and art went through approximately the same stages as their Western European counterparts, but each of its artistic movements had a character of its own which was dependent on the background against which it developed as well as on certain undying national traditions.

Russian art never reached a stage at which it could be considered fully established. It was always on the move, as though fearful of becoming too defined or turned into a formula. 'Look around you!', exclaimed P. Ya. Chaadaev. 'Everything seems to be on the move. We are all like wanderers.'[11] This state of flux, which destined Russian culture to experience one shock after another, was present even during those frequent periods in Russian history during which the nation appeared to be stagnating. It was, indeed, at just such times that the agitation became ever more intense, more prophetic of the explosion to come, and that culture entered into a particularly dramatic relationship with the State, one which amounted to a kind of perpetual opposition. All the efforts of the champions of 'art for art's sake' to neutralize this relationship were in vain.

Many of these special features of Russian culture found full expression in the art of the nineteenth and early twentieth centuries.

Notes

PART I

1 D.E. Arkin deals interestingly with this question in his study of the Admiralty. See D. Arkin, *Obrazi arkhitekturi*. Moscow 1941, pp. 219–272.
2 See D.E. Arkin, 'Skulptura Admiralteistva', in D.E. Arkin, *Obrazi skulpturi*. Moscow 1961, pp. 98–118.
3 See 'Semiotika goroda i gorodskoi kulturi. Petersburg.' *Uchenie zapiski Tartuskogo gosudarstvennogo universiteta.* Issue 664. Trudi po znakovim sistemam. XVIII. Tartu 1984.
4 Compare: Werner Hofman, *Das irdische Paradies*. Munich 1974. Chapter: 'Die irdische Hölle.'
5 D.E. Arkin, *Obrazi skulpturi*. Moscow 1961, p. 111.
6 See V.S. Turchin, *Orest Adamovich Kiprensky*. Moscow 1975.
7 See N.N. Kovalenskaya, *Istoria russkogo iskusstva pervoi polovini XIX veka*. Moscow 1951, p. 150.
8 See M.M. Allenov, *Aleksandr Andreevich Ivanov*. Moscow 1980, p. 91.

PART II

1 See L. Nochlin, *Realism*. Harmondsworth 1971.
2 A.I. Herzen, *Sobraniye sochinenii v tritsati tomakh*, Vol. 14. Moscow 1958, p. 157.
3 ibid, Vol. 7. Moscow 1956, p. 198.
4 G.D. Gachev, *Obraz v russkoi khudozhestvennoi kulture*. Moscow 1981, p. 59.
5 *L.N. Tolstoi v vospominanyakh sovremennikov*, Vol. 2. Moscow 1955, p. 18.
6 Quoted from book by A.A. Fedorov-Davydov, *V.G. Perov*. Moscow 1934, p. 88.
7 *Kramskoi ob iskusstve*. Moscow 1960, p. 53.
8 I.N. Kramskoi, *Pisma*. Leningrad–Moscow 1937, Vol. I, p. 222.
9 A. Benois, *Istoria zhivopisi v XIX veke. Russkaya zhivopis*. St Petersburg 1901, p. 175.

10 G. Ge, 'Vospominaniye o khudozhnike N.N. Ge, kak materyal dlya yego biografii.' – *Artist*, No. 44, p. 135.
11 *Perepiska I.N. Kramskogo*. 2. Perepiska s khudozhnikami. Moscow 1954, p. 414.
12 *Perepiska, I.N. Kramskogo*. 2, Moscow 1954, pp. 48–9.
13 E.A. Borisova, *Russkaya arkhitektura vtoroi polovini XIX veka*. Moscow 1979, p. 164.

PART III

1 A.A. Blok, *Sobraniye sochinenii v 8-mi tomakh*. Vol. 6, Moscow-Leningrad 1962, pp. 175–6.
2 See M.M. Allenov, *Etyudi tsvetov Vrubelya (1886–1887)*. Sovetskoye iskusstvoznaniye '77/2. Moscow 1978, pp. 191–209.
3 Vrubel, *Perepiska. Vospominaniya o khudozhnike*. Leningrad 1976, p. 118.
4 A. Benois, 'Khudozhestvenniye pisma. Pervaya vystavka *Mir iskusstva*' – in the newpaper *Rech*, 7 January 1911.
5 This question is dealt with in detail by G.G. Pospelov in several books and articles. See G.G. Pospelov, *Karo-Bube. Aus der Geschichte der Moskauer Malerei zu Beginn des 20. Jahrhunderts*. Dresden 1985.
6 See for example Rose-Carol Washton-Long, 'Kandinsky's Abstract Style: The Veiling of Apocalyptic Folk Imagery' – *Art Journal*, Vol. XXXIV, Spring 1975, pp. 217–28.
7 See introduction by E.F. Kovtun to K.S. Malevich, *Pisma k M.V. Matyushiny* – Yezhegodnik rukopisnogo otdela Pushkinskogo doma na 1974 god. Leningrad 1976, pp. 177–95.
8 ibid, p. 192.
9 M. Voloshin, 'A.S. Golubkina' – *Apollon*, 1911, No. 6, p. 12.
10 See N. Ya. Berkovsky, *O mirovom znachenii russkoi literaturi*. Leningrad 1975.
11 *Sochineniya i pisma P. Ya Chaadaeva v 2-x tomakh*, Vol. 2, Moscow 1914, p. 109.

Select Bibliography

ANDERSEN, T., *Malevich*, Amsterdam, 1970
——, *Moderne Russisk Kunst 1910–1930*, Copenhagen, 1967 (in Danish)
The Avant-Garde in Russia, 1910–1930: New Perspectives, S. Barron and M. Tuchman (eds.), exh. cat., Los Angeles County Museum of Art, 1980
BENOIS, A., *The Russian School of Painting*, trans. A. Yarmolinsky, New York, 1916; London, 1919
——, *Memoirs*, 2 vols., London, 1960 and 1964
BIRD, A., *A History of Russian Painting*, Oxford, 1987
BOWLT, J.E., 'The Chronology of Larionov's Early Work', *Burlington Magazine*, vol. 114, Oct. 1972, pp. 719–20 (Correspondence)
——, 'Two Russian Maecenases. Savva Mamontov and Princess Tenisheva', *Apollo*, vol. XCVIII, no. 142 (n.s.), Dec. 1973, pp. 444–53
——, 'Neo-primitivism and Russian Painting', *Burlington Magazine*, vol. 116, 1974, pp. 133–40
——, 'The Blue Rose: Russian Symbolism in Art', *Burlington Magazine*, vol. 118, Aug. 1976, pp. 566–74
——, *Russian Art of the Avant-Garde: Theory and Criticism, 1902–1934*, New York, 1976 (revised edn. London and New York, 1988)
—— with R.-C. Washton-Long, *The Life of Vasilii Kandinsky in Russian Art: A Study of 'On the Spiritual in Art'*, Newtonville, 1980
——, *The Silver Age: Russian Art of the Early Twentieth Century and the 'World of Art' Group*, Newtonville, 1982 (2nd revised edn.)
Chagall, S. Compton, exh. cat., Royal Academy of Arts, London, 1985
CHAMOT, M., *Gontcharova*, Paris, 1972
——, *Russian Painting and Sculpture*, London, 1969
DECTER, J., *Nicholas Roerich*, London and New York, 1989
DOUGLAS, C., 'Malevich's Painting – Some Problems of Chronology', *Soviet Union*, vol. 5, pt. 2, 1978, pp. 301–26
——, *Swans of Other Worlds: Kazimir Malevich and the Origins of Abstraction in Russia*, Ann Arbor, 1980
ELLIOTT, D., *New Worlds – Russian Art and Society 1900–1937*, London and New York, 1986
FIALA, V., *Russian Painting of the Nineteenth and Twentieth Centuries*, Prague, 1955
GEORGE, W., *Larionov*, Paris, 1966
GRAY, C., *The Russian Experiment in Art 1863–1922*, revised and updated by Marian Burleigh-Motley, London and New York, 1986
HAMILTON, G. Heard, *The Art and Architecture of Russia*, Harmondsworth and Baltimore, 1954 (integrated edn. 1983)
An Introduction to Russian Art and Architecture, R. Auty and D. Obolensky (eds.), *Companion to Russian Studies*, vol. 3, Cambridge, 1980

ISDEBSKY-PRITCHARD, A., *The Art of Mikhail Vrubel (1856–1910)*, Ann Arbor, 1982
KAMENSKY, A., *Chagall – The Russian Years, 1907–1922*, London and New York, 1989
KANDINSKY, V., *Complete Writings on Art*, K. Lindsay and P. Vergo (eds.), 2 vols., Boston, 1982
KAPLANOVA, S., *Vrubel*, Leningrad, 1975
KEAN, B.W., *All the Empty Palaces: The Merchant Patrons of Modern Art in Pre-Revolutionary Russia*, New York, 1983
KEMENOV, V., *Vasily Surikov*, Leningrad, 1979
KENNEDY, J., *The 'Mir iskusstva' Group and Russian Art*, New York, 1977
KHAN-MAGOMEDOV, S.O., *Pioneers of Soviet Architecture*, London, 1987
KOROTKINA, L., *Nikolay Roerich*, Leningrad, 1976
Larionov and Goncharova, M. Chamot and C. Gray, exh. cat., Arts Council, London, 1961
LEBEDEV, A., *The Itinerants*, Leningrad, 1974
LODDER, C., *Russian Constructivism*, New Haven and London, 1983
K.S. Malevich: Essays on Art 1915–1933, T. Andersen (ed.), 2 vols., Copenhagen, 1971
K.S. Malevich: The World as Non-Objectivity (Unpublished Writings 1922–1925), T. Andersen (ed.), vol. 3, Copenhagen, 1976
K.S. Malevich: The Artist, Infinity, Suprematism (Unpublished Writings 1913–1933), T. Andersen (ed.), vol. 4, Copenhagen, 1978
MARKOV, V., *Russian Futurism: A History*, Berkeley, 1968
MEYER, F., *Marc Chagall*, New York, 1963
MILNER, J., *Vladimir Tatlin and the Russian Avant-Garde*, New Haven and London, 1983
NAKOV, A., *L'Avant-Garde Russe*, Paris, 1984
Paris-Moscou, 1900–1930, exh. cat., Centre National d'Art et de Culture Georges Pompidou, Paris, 1979 (2nd revised edn.)
La Peinture russe à l'époque romantique, exh. cat., Grand Palais, Paris, 1976
POSPELOW, G.G., *Moderne Russische Malerei: Die Künstlergruppe Karo-Bube*, Dresden, 1985
ROETHEL, H., and J. Benjamin, *Kandinsky. Catalogue raisonné of the Oil Paintings*, 2 vols., London, 1982 and 1984
RUSAKOVA, A., *Borisov-Musatov*, Leningrad, 1975
——, *V. Kuznetsov*, Leningrad, 1977
Russian and Soviet Paintings 1900–1930: Selection from the State Tretyakov Gallery, Moscow, and the State Russian Museum, Leningrad, exh. cat., Hirshhorn Museum and Sculpture Garden, Washington, D.C., 1988
Russian Avant-Garde Art: The George Costakis Collection, A. Zander Rudenstine (ed.), New York, 1981
Russian Futurism, E. Proffer and C. Proffer (eds.), Ann Arbor, 1980

Russian Women Artists of the Avant-garde 1910–1930, exh. cat., Galerie Gmurzynska, Cologne, 1979

SARABIANOV, D., *Russian Masters of the Early Twentieth Century (New Trends)*, Leningrad, 1973

——, *Valentin Serov*, New York, 1982

SHANINA, N., *Victor Vasnetsov*, Leningrad, 1979

The Spiritual in Art: Abstract Painting 1890–1985, exh. cat., Los Angeles County Museum of Art, 1986, pp. 165–183 and 361–365

STARR, S. Frederick, *Melnikov: Solo Architect in a Mass Society*, Princeton, 1978

VALKENIER, E., *Russian Realist Art, the State and Society; the Peredvizhniki and their Tradition*, Ann Arbor, 1977

Venetsianov and his School, G. Smirnov, Leningrad, 1973

YABLONSKAYA, M.N., *Women Artists of Russia's New Age 1900–1935*, London and New York, 1990

ZHADOVA, L., *Malevich: Suprematism and Revolution in Russian Art, 1910–1930*, London, 1982

——, *Tatlin*, Budapest, 1984, London and New York, 1989

In Russian

DIMITRIEVA, N., *Vrubel*, Leningrad, 1984

EFROS, A., *Two Centuries of Russian Art*, Moscow, 1969

The Golden Fleece, Moscow, 1906–09 (1910)

KAMENSKY, A.M., *Saryan*, Moscow, 1968

LAPSHINA, N., *Mir Iskusstva* (World of Art), Moscow, 1977

Mir Iskusstva, St Petersburg, 1898–1904

Moscow–Paris 1900–1930, Pushkin Museum of Fine Arts, Moscow, 1981

RUSAKOVA, A., *Russian Genre Painting in the Nineteenth and the Early Twentieth Centuries*, Moscow, 1964

RUSAKOV, Yu., *Petrov-Vodkin*, Leningrad, 1975

——, *Russian Painters of the Early Twentieth Century*, Leningrad, 1973

SARABIANOV, D.V., *Pavel Kuznetsov*, Moscow, 1975

——, *Late 1900s and Early 1910s – Essays*, Moscow, 1971

Tretyakov Gallery: The Drawings and Watercolours of I.E. Repin, V.I. Surikov, V.M. Vasnetsov, Moscow, 1952

List of Illustrations

Index